PUBLICATIONS
OF THE
ARMY RECORDS SOCIETY
VOL. 10

LORD CHELMSFORD'S ZULULAND CAMPAIGN 1878–1879

The Army Records Society was founded in 1984 in order to publish original records describing the development, organisation, administration and activities of the British Army from early times.

Any person wishing to become a Member of the Society is requested to apply to the Hon. Secretary, c/o the National Army Museum, Royal Hospital Road, London, SW3 4HT. The annual subscription entitles the Member to receive a copy of each volume issued by the Society in that year, and to purchase back volumes at reduced prices. Current subscription details, whether for individuals living within the British Isles, for individuals living overseas, or for institutuons, will be furnished on request.

Standing, left to right: Major M.W.E. Gossett, 54th Regt.; Lieutenant A. Berkeley Milne, R.N. Sitting, left to right: Commander H.J.F. Campbell, R.N.; Lieutenant-General Lord Chelmsford; Lieutenant-Colonel J.N. Crealock, 95th Regt.

LORD CHELMSFORD'S ZULULAND CAMPAIGN 1878–1879

Edited by

JOHN P.C. LABAND

Published by
ALAN SUTTON PUBLISHING LTD
for the
ARMY RECORDS SOCIETY
1994

First Published in the United Kingdom in 1994
Alan Sutton Publishing Ltd · Phoenix Mill · Far Thrupp · Stroud
Gloucestershire

First published in the United States of America in 1994
Alan Sutton Publishing Inc · 83 Washington Street · Dover NH 03820

British Library Cataloguing in Publication Data

A catalogue record for this book is available from the British Library

ISBN 0 7509 0665 0

Library of Congress Cataloging in Publication Data applied for

Typeset in Ehrhardt
Typesetting and origination by
Alan Sutton Publishing Limited.
Printed in Great Britain by
The Bath Press, Avon.

Contents

Maps

Editorial Acknowledgements

I gratefully acknowledge the generosity of the following in enabling me to consult and, where requested, to reproduce archives in their possession and/or copyright: the Killie Campbell Africana Library, Durban; the Natal Archives Depot, Pietermaritzburg; the National Army Museum, Chelsea; and the Public Record Office, Kew.

The assistance many people have given me in the preparation of this volume has been considerable and has taken various forms; I wish, however, to thank in particular those mentioned below.

Dr Ian Beckett, Honorary Secretary of the Army Records Society, first raised this project with me, arranged the despatch of microfilms of requested documents from the National Army Museum and the Public Record Office, and generally gave me every assistance over the years in bringing this book to fruition. Mr Peter Simkins of the Imperial War Museum stood in on occasion for Dr Beckett and also willingly helped me with research and production problems. Miss Jenny Duggan of the Killie Campbell Africana Library and Mrs Judith Hawley of the Natal Archives Depot greatly eased my access to the documents in their care. Mrs Thuli Radebe of the Main Campus Library, University of Natal, Pietermaritzburg, came to my aid in mastering the microfilm-reader. She also provided the information I requested when I began editing the documents. So too did Mrs Barbara Worby of the South African National Museum of Military History, Johannesburg, Dr Peter Boyden of the National Army Museum, Ms Liza Verity of the Maritime Information Centre, National Maritime Museum, Greenwich, and Mr Meurig Jones of the Anglo-Boer War Memorials Project. I could not have proceeded without their full and generous assistance. Ms Helena Margeot and Mr Raymond Poonsamy of the Cartographic Unit in the Department of Geography, University of Natal, Pietermaritzburg, once more provided me with maps of the highest quality. My colleague in the Department of Historical Studies, Professor John Wright, and Mr Adrian Koopman, Head of the Department of Zulu, University of Natal, Pietermaritzburg, ensured that I correctly identified Zulu place-names and people mentioned in the documents and spelled them in conformity with modern practice. Special thanks are due to Dr Jeff Mathews of the Natal Education Department, my colleague, Professor Paul Thompson, Mr David Rattray of Fugitives' Drift Lodge and Mr Ian Knight for their readiness to share their great knowledge of the Anglo-Zulu War and to discuss the campaign with me.

I received a grant from the University of Natal's Research Fund for the purchase of microfilms from the National Army Museum and the Public Record Office, and further grants from the University's Publications Committee to cover the cost of generating the maps and preparing the index. I was also afforded help from the Research Incentive Fund administered by the Department of Historical Studies. The Army Records Society paid out of its funds for some research assistance. I am most grateful for all this open-handed financial aid, for I should hardly have found it possible to have proceeded without it.

Assistance of a different, but absolutely essential, kind has been lent by my wife, Fenella. Her understanding and encouragement while I was once again locked in close combat with a recalcitrant manuscript has been an unfailing source of support.

John P.C. Laband
Department of Historical Studies
University of Natal, Pietermaritzburg

Note on Editorial Method

Thousands of documents relating to Lord Chelmsford's conduct of the Zululand campaign are preserved in repositories both in the United Kingdom and in South Africa. If published, they would fill multiple volumes. For a single volume such as this, it has inevitably been necessary to make a most rigorous selection according to two principles.

The first is that only documents emanating from Chelmsford himself should be included. This decision could be regarded as rendering the collection inherently lopsided, and it was with initial misgiving that the sheaves of correspondence Chelmsford received during the course of the campaign from his military associates, political masters and civilian antagonists were excluded. Yet the advantage of such a course is to concentrate attention on Chelmsford's own plans and decisions, and to point up his responses to the multifarious problems which confronted him. His performance as a commander consequently comes into sharper focus, making it more susceptible to critical scrutiny.

The second principle of selection, namely, that documents should not automatically be excluded because they have appeared in print elsewhere, might seem paradoxical considering the number of unpublished documents eliminated from inclusion in terms of the first principle, explained above. Yet this decision was made unavoidable by the existence in particular of two relatively available published sources which reproduce numbers of Chelmsford's letters and despatches: the *British Parliamentary Papers* and Gerald French, *Lord Chelmsford and the Zulu War*. Thus, of the 116 documents selected for this present collection, thirteen have already been printed in full in the *BPP*, five in French, and one in both; while extracts from one are to be found in the *BPP*, from eleven in French and from five in both. Clearly, excuse is hardly necessary for printing the complete texts of the seventeen extracts appearing in the *BPP* or in French, though there might be some doubt concerning the nineteen complete documents already reproduced. Yet the latter are inescapably all key documents, which is why they were previously selected for inclusion in the *BPP* and in French. To have excluded them from this volume, simply on the grounds that they can be found elsewhere, would have produced deleterious effects. Their absence would not only have created uncomfortable gaps in the coherent narrative, but also have distorted the self-portrait of Chelmsford as military commander, which it was the editor's intention to build up through the chronologically arranged presentation of significant documents written or dicated by the General.

It has been the practice to reproduce the documents in full, except for opening and closing familiarities and for some references to cross-correspondence and enclosures. The omission of such references is indicated by dots. In a very few cases entirely extraneous comment on affairs elsewhere in southern Africa has been excluded and is similarly denoted.

Grammar, spelling, capitalization and punctuation have not been altered, though obviously missing words have been supplied between square brackets. Illegible words have also been noted in the text between square brackets. Attention is drawn to the Glossary and to the Gazetteer, which follow the Notes. There Chelmsford's inconsistent spelling is correlated with modern practice. The names on the maps correspond to the modern form.

Where individuals have been repeatedly named in the text, biographical information is to be found in Biographical Notes. Short biographical details of those mentioned only in passing are supplied in the Notes.

The title or rank accorded the correspondents at the top of each document and in the Notes are those borne at the time of writing. It should be noted that a British officer could hold higher rank in the army than in his regiment. Such brevet (or army) rank was usually awarded for distinguished service in the field or for long service. Command, promotion, duties and pay in the regiment were determined by regimental rank; while duties outside the regiment as well as army promotion were governed by brevet rank. An officer might also hold superior local rank, which was conferred for the duration of a specific campaign. Officers of the colonial forces serving in Zululand with regular officers ranked as juniors of their respective ranks.

The source of each document is given at the end, as well as the reference to the *BPP* or French, should it have been previously printed there. Where only extracts have been reproduced in these works, the omitted words are clearly indicated in the complete text.

The abbreviations used for the sources are as follows:

BPP	*British Parliamentary Papers*
CP	Chelmsford Papers, National Army Museum, London
GH	Government House, Natal, papers in Natal Archives Depot, Pietermaritzburg
PP	Pearson Papers, National Army Museum, London
TS	Sir Theophilus Shepstone Papers, Natal Archives Depot, Pietermaritzburg
WC	Sir Evelyn Wood Collection, Natal Archives Depot, Pietermaritzburg
WO	War Office, papers in Public Record Office, London
WP	Sir Evelyn Wood Papers, Killie Campbell Africana Library, Durban

Abbreviations

AAG	Assistant Adjutant-General
ADC	aide-de-camp
AQMG	Assistant Quartermaster-General
DAG	Deputy Adjutant-General
DAQMG	Deputy Assistant Quartermaster-General
DCG	Deputy Commissary-General
DQMG	Deputy Quartermaster-General
LI	Light Infantry
NCO	non-commissioned officer
NNC	Natal Native Contingent
QMG	Quartermaster-General
RA	Royal Artillery
RE	Royal Engineers
RN	Royal Navy

Introduction

The battle of Isandlwana cost Lieutenant-General Lord Chelmsford his reputation. It was bad enough that the Zulu army out-manoeuvred him into dividing his forces and, in his absence, overran his camp on 22 January 1879 and killed 1,357 of the 1,768 British officers and men left to defend it.[1] Worse, this debacle dislocated his strategy for the invasion of Zululand, threw him onto the defensive, and exposed the British colonies of Natal and the Transvaal to Zulu counter-thrusts. Yet, worst of all, Isandlwana transformed what had been planned as a short, sharp strike to destroy the military power of the Zulu kingdom into an unacceptably protracted and expensive campaign.

For it took over eight months from the moment when Chelmsford first invaded Zululand on 11 January 1879 finally to break Zulu resistance and pacify the country; and when the last British detachments eventually marched away at the end of September 1879, it was more than two months since Chelmsford himself had laid down his command to General Sir Garnet Wolseley and returned to England. To defeat the relatively unsophisticated Zulu army which, when fully mobilized, could put no more than 29,000 men into the field,[2] it became necessary to build up a force of nearly 17,000 troops, some 7,000 of whom were black,[3] and to raise over 8,000 black levies to defend the borders of Natal.[4] To transport and supply these forces, an establishment was required which eventually numbered 748 horses, 4,635 mules, 27,125 oxen, 641 horse and mule carriages, 1,770 ox wagons, 796 ox carts, and 4,080 drivers and leaders.[5] The financial cost of this unsatisfactory campaign was put at £5,230,328, considerably more than the British government was any longer prepared to countenance for a colonial campaign.[6] Even more unacceptable were the casualties sustained, especially since battlefield fatalities in colonial wars were not expected to exceed deaths from disease and accidents.[7] But in Zululand, according to official returns, 76 officers and 1,007 NCOs and men were killed in action (of whom 241 were white colonial volunteers), and 37 officers and 206 NCOs and men were wounded. Over 600 black auxiliaries, for whom no complete returns were kept, also died in service of the British. In comparison, only 17 officers

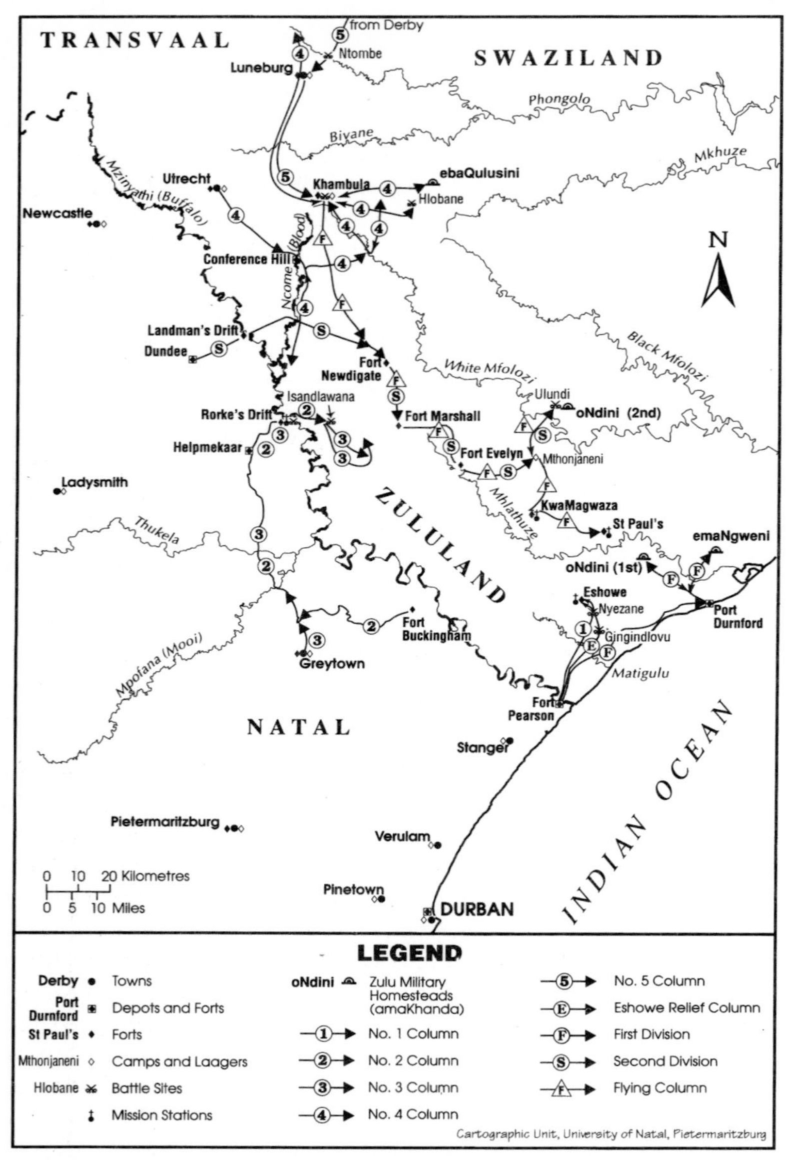

British military operations in Zululand, January to July 1879.

and 330 men died of disease, and 99 officers and 1,286 NCOs and men were invalided.[8]

The tide of criticism of Chelmsford's conduct of the Zululand campaign, to which the Isandlwana disaster first gave rise, was swelled by his inability to bring the war to a swift conclusion. Uncomplimentary voices were raised in the British and colonial press,[9] war correspondents were contemptuously critical,[10] Chelmsford's own staff discreetly questioned his generalship,[11] both Houses of Parliament repeatedly debated the matter,[12] and even his patron, the Commander-in-Chief of the Army, H.R.H. the Duke of Cambridge, found grounds for disquiet.[13] Yet Chelmsford's supersession in May 1879 by the nakedly ambitious Wolseley brought him a degree of sympathy. The satisfaction was consequently not Chelmsford's alone when he defeated the Zulu army decisively at Ulundi on 4 July 1879, just before Wolseley could personally take up his command. And though Chelmford's handling of the aftermath of the battle was again a matter for controversy, his victory allowed him to resign his command with honour and reputation at least partially restored. Thereafter, he maintained a dignified reticence in the face of his critics, publicly answering them only in a number of speeches, such as in Cape Town on his way home,[14] and in the House of Lords the following year.[15] Meanwhile, some of those who had served with him in Zululand, most notably Lieutenant-Colonel Arthur Harness, RA, who felt loyalty and genuine affection for Chelmsford,[16] rallied to his defence in print.[17]

Inevitably, public interest in Chelmsford's controversial leadership during the Anglo-Zulu War soon waned, but historians have periodically revived the question. In 1936 W.H. Clements roundly condemned Chelmsford's generalship in *The Glamour and Tragedy of the Zulu War*,[18] uncritically basing most of his charges on the often ill-informed and prejudiced commentary of contemporary journalists. Major the Hon. Gerald French was stung by what he considered this malicious repetition of 'worthless tittle-tattle'[19] into writing a partisan refutation,[20] published in 1939 as *Lord Chelmsford and the Zulu War*. This, the only published biography of Lord Chelmsford, is indeed marred by what Donald Morris called its 'continual air of righteous indignation and triumphant vindication'.[21] But in writing it, French enjoyed a special advantage denied Clements and all other previous commentators on the Anglo-Zulu War. He was given access to Chelmsford's military correspondence, a mass of private, semi-official and official papers concerning the Zululand campaign, from which he quoted extensively to support his arguments. These papers had been carefully classified and authoritatively annotated in 1906 by General M.W.E. Gossett, who had been on Chelmsford's staff throughout 1878–9.

Gossett's purpose in 1906 had been the same as French's was to be in 1939. As he wrote to Chelmsford's widow on the completion of his task of sorting the papers:

> . . . I need not say that it has been a pleasure, though a painful one, to read the records of that time, but the perusal of them has still further raised Ld Chelmsford in my estimation – His foresight, his consideration for everyone under his command & his zeal for the public service and the brave front he opposed to calumny & misrepresentation all shew what a great & good man he was – I hope some day when the principal actors in these days are gone that justice will be done to his memory – [22]

Sir Reginald Coupland tempered French's exculpatory work in 1948 with *Zulu Battle Piece: Isandhlwana*.[23] His was the more objective approach of a professional historian, and he attempted to place the major charges levelled against Chelmsford into proper perspective. However, he made little attempt at deeper research into Chelmsford's role. This superficiality was to mark the spate of books published on the Anglo-Zulu War during the 1960s and 1970s, the most deservedly influential of which has been Donald Morris's *Washing of the Spears*.[24] But in Morris as in the others, the non-interpretative concentration on details of specific battles and skirmishes failed to illuminate any further Chelmsford's overall conduct of the campaign. This inadequate level of analysis called for fresh attempts at interpretation, and these were made possible through the emergence of vital new evidence.

In 1973 Adrian Preston brought out his edition of Wolseley's Journal of 1879–80, which was full of the General's perceptive, if waspishly uncharitable, comments on Chelmsford's conduct of the war.[25] Of yet greater significance was the publication in 1984 of the Alison Collection, edited by Sonia Clarke, in *Zululand at War 1879*. The ninety letters of the collection, now in the Brenthurst Library, Johannesburg, were addressed to Major-General Sir Archibald Alison (the DQMG for Intelligence at the War Office) by various officers in the field with Chelmsford, many of them Staff College graduates. Alison had solicited these letters as a means of gaining confidential information on the conduct of the war for the Intelligence Branch. The opinions expressed in these semi-official, semi-private letters on various aspects of Chelmsford's generalship were of such a controversial and sensitive nature that they had been kept confidential. Their accessibility, taken in conjunction with Chelmsford's military correspondence (now housed as the Chelmsford Papers in the National Army Museum, London), as well as with other smaller collections open to scrutiny, notably the Pearson Papers also in the National Army Museum, the Wood Papers in the Killie Africana Library, Durban, and the Wood Collection in the Natal Archive Depot, Pietermaritzburg, has made an informed reassessment of Chelmsford's conduct of the Zululand campaign both possible and necessary.

The most recent and comprehensive study of Chelmsford's generalship in southern Africa, and one which made full use of the available sources, is Jeffrey Mathews's doctoral dissertation of 1986.[26] Mathews's conclusion is that Chelmsford's earlier critics, although they lacked sufficient detailed information to support their arguments, were nevertheless largely correct in their condemnation of his generalship.[27]

When himself analysing Chelmsford's poor performance as a commander, Mathews identifies two related factors: firstly, leadership inadequacies consequent on Chelmsford's career as a typical product of the conservative military establishment; and secondly, structural and administrative deficiencies in the army he commanded. Mathews shows how these weaknesses led in turn to problematical relations with the local colonial authorities upon whose assistance he depended for supplies, auxiliaries and intelligence, and culminated in poor strategic decisions in the field.

Frederic Augustus Thesiger was born on 31 May 1827, and succeeded his father on 5 October 1878 as the second Baron Chelmsford. His grandfather, John Andrew Thesiger of Dresden (b. 1722), was a Saxon gentleman who migrated to England and became secretary to an influential statesman, the second Marquess of Rockingham. His father, Frederic (1794–1878), pursued a distinguished career at the bar and in the House of Commons in the Tory interest. In 1844 he became Solicitor-General and was knighted, and in 1858 was constituted Lord High Chancellor of England and raised to the peerage as the first Baron Chelmsford. In 1822 he married Anna Maria Tinling and had four sons and three daughters, of whom Frederic Augustus was the eldest.[28]

Chelmsford (as it remains convenient to address him), was educated at Eton, and entered his military career in 1844 when he was commissioned by purchase as second-lieutenant in the Rifle Brigade. The following year he purchased an exchange to the Grenadier Guards as ensign and lieutenant, and proved an able and diligent officer. He was promoted lieutenant and captain in 1850, and went to Ireland in 1852 as ADC, first to the lord-lieutenant, and from 1853 to the commander of the forces there. On 31 May 1855 he joined his battalion in the Crimea.[29]

Chelmsford's successful service during the Crimean campaign opened the door to swift promotion and recognition in his profession. Twenty-five years later, when it was becoming painfully apparent to him that his performance during the Anglo-Zulu War had terminated his active military career, he petitioned the Duke of Cambridge for any available military appointment appropriate to his rank as major-general. His preference was for India, where he had spent sixteen years and acquired, in his opinion, a special understanding of its military requirements.[30] It was in India too that he had married on 1 January 1867. Adria Fanny (d. 1926) was the eldest daughter of Major-General John Heath of the Bombay Army. They had four surviving sons who pursued careers in the army, law and diplomatic service. The eldest, Frederick John Napier, who was to succeed his father as the third Baron Chelmsford in 1905, later consummated his family's Indian connection by becoming Viceroy of India, 1916–21, and in 1921 was created first Viscount Chelmsford.[31]

Chelmsford, when making his plea for military employment in January 1881, enclosed a statement of his service between 1855 and 1880. Since this document discloses better than any biographical summary Chelmsford's own estimation of his career, it is reproduced in its entirety below:

Statement of Foreign, Staff and active service of Major General Lord Chelmsford GCB –

1855 Crimea – mentioned in despatches – Brevet Majority –
1856 Deputy Asst Quartermaster General at Head Quarters – Crimea –

1858 Embarked for India as Lieut Col of 95th Regiment –
1859 Indian Mutiny campaign in Central India – Mentioned in despatches –

1861 Deputy Adjutant General British Forces – Bombay
1863 Presidency – Passed interpreters examination in Hindustani

1863 On amalgamation of British and Indian armies, offered post of Deputy Adjutant General – preferred however command of 95th Regiment –

1868 Specially selected by Sir Robert, now Lord Napier of Magdala, for post of
Deputy Adjutant General Abyssinian Field Force.

1868 Abyssinian campaign –
Mentioned in despatches –
Companion of the Bath –
ADC to the Queen –

1868 Name submitted to Government of India by Sir William Mansfield, with that of two others (Sir Donald Stewart and Sir Peter Lumsden) as eligible in every respect for post of Quartermaster General in India then vacant –

1869 Adjutant General in India
1874

1874 Specially selected by Lord Napier of Magdala for the command of a camp of exercise in India –

Received thanks of Government of India for the manner in which I exercised that command.

1874 Left India –

Received letters from Government of India and Commander in Chief expressing their sense of the ability and success with which I had performed the important and responsible duties devolving on me as Adjutant General in India –

1874 Selected to command a brigade at the manoeuvres in the neighbourhood of Aldershot –

1874 Colonel on the Staff in command of camp at Shornecliffe
1876

1876 Received reward for meritorious service.

1877 Offered post of Deputy Adjutant General, Horse Guards –
Asked permission to decline it being anxious for a command in India –

1877 Brigadier General commanding 1st Infantry Brigade
1878 Aldershot

1878 Specially selected to command H Ms Forces in South Africa –

Finished Gaika war in three months –
Received thanks of both houses of the Cape Government Legislature
Knight Companion of the Bath –

1879 Finished Zulu war in six months.
Grand Cross of the Bath –

1880 Offered command of Western District –
Asked permission to decline it on account of limited private income, and also being anxious for an Indian command –

Total Service		=	36 years
Foreign service –	India	=	16 years
	Other	=	4 years
Total Foreign service			20 years –

Military honours & rewards received –

Brevet Majority – 1855
Companion of the Bath } – 1868.
ADC to the Queen }
Reward for meritorious service – 1876
Knight Commander of the Bath – 1878
Grand Cross of the Bath – 1879.

Staff appointments held

Dep. Asst Q.M. General Crimea – 1855–6.
Dep Adj-General British Forces – 1861–63.
Dep Adj Genl. Abyssinian F. Force – 1868 –
Adjutant General in India – 1869–74
Colonel on the Staff – 1874–76
Brigadier General – 1877–78.
Lieut General commding in S. Africa – 1878–79 –

Chelmsford
MG –

50 Stanhope Gardens
1 January 1881 – [32]

As this record shows, Chelmsford in 1879 had enjoyed a varied and successful career, though one with a prosaic emphasis on the staff and administrative duties in which he excelled,[33] rather than on practical experience in commanding an army in the field. In this, as in other ways, Chelmsford was typical of many senior officers of the late Victorian army, and was, with them, a product of the privileged, conservative military establishment of the day.

Senior officers such as Chelmsford had gained their commissions before the abolition of the purchase system in 1871, which they had exploited to further their careers.[34] Purchase was an expensive business, and Chelmsford was later to lament the sacrifice of the large sum invested.[35] Yet it was necessary. There were few acceptable career opportunities open to the sons of gentlemen. One was a military career, and it could confirm social status and recognition for relative newcomers such as the Thesiger family, because it had become a traditional and highly regarded career for sons of landed families. Indeed, the ambitious Thesigers had rapidly established a family tradition in the armed services. Of Chelmsford's two uncles, Sir Frederic had been a captain in the Royal Navy and George a major in the army; while his brother Charles was to retire a lieutenant-general.[36]

The social exclusivity and homogeneity of the officer corps was preserved through substantial recruiting from public schools and the necessary possession of private means. A public school education, with its emphasis on order, authority, discipline and loyalty, was supposed to inculcate qualities necessary in an officer. In particular, the training of body and spirit through the cult of team games was intended to develop health, strength, coordination and quickness of eye, as well as moral virtues like self-discipline and team spirit. And indeed, officers from the public schools tended to cleave to an honorific and gentlemanly code of values, and indulged their passion for sports, especially field sports. Chelmsford, who was educated at Eton, was no exception. He was noted for his unfailingly gentlemanly, courteous and modest behaviour, which he combined with a considerate yet firm manner to his subordinates. He remained fond of sport and outdoor pursuits, and always displayed considerable physical energy. Although naturally tending to be somewhat introspective and withdrawn, he was able to adopt a genial manner in the company of others. He was a keen participant in the amateur theatricals so popular at the time, and gained a reputation as a good public speaker. As with many another talented officer, he did not hide his musical abilities and was an accomplished clarinet-player.[37]

Like many officers from public schools, Chelmsford associated the ingrained concept of a gentleman with Christian virtues: unselfishness, thoughtfulness and a sense of noblesse oblige. In the context of changing attitudes in late Victorian society in general, and of the army in particular, this entailed a more conspicuous recognition of an officer's paternalistic responsibilities towards other ranks and a concern about their conditions. Chelmsford consequently set an example, not only of the calm resolve under fire traditionally expected of an officer (he exposed himself fearlessly during the battles of Gingindlovu and Ulundi), but of moderation and frugality. As a teetotaller, he attempted to stamp out drunkenness in his command and, in order to combat idleness among young officers, he induced them to study further. Although capable of sharp, stinging rebukes, he disliked hurting people and would write kind, personal notes to officers who had received official censure. Those under his command always appreciated his essential decency and high character, which made him genuinely popular among them and earned their loyalty.[38] Such qualities, when translated into the field, predisposed him to fight as chivalrously and as humanely as possible.[39]

Yet, although in the pattern of the successful officer of the time, Chelmsford suffered certain weaknesses. Sufficient means posed a problem. A substantial private income was essential to supplement army pay (particularly when based at home in Britain) in order to support heavy expenses for uniforms, mess bills, entertainment, sport, horses, and the constant moves of army life. However, these unavoidable expenses required of an officer could be more cheaply sustained in India, the colonies and on campaign. For a man of his class, Chelmsford possessed only a limited private income and, after twenty years on foreign service, he found it impossible in 1880 to contemplate the expensive demands of a home command.[40]

Lack of means might have proved a source of concern and the occasional obstacle to a successful career, but there were other aspects to Chelmsford which brought his fitness for command into question. Contemporaries commented that he was unable to delegate successfully. Consequently, he spent time and energy on tasks his subordinates should have undertaken and lost sight of the greater picture. His diffident manner discouraged discussion with his staff, but he was too willing to allow his habitually swift decisions to be swayed by contrary advice. The result was frequent vacillation. Crucially, he championed stereotyped military tactics, maintaining while still in India that little change was needed to the well-tried formulae, and in South Africa initially refusing to adapt European strategy to colonial conditions.[41]

Both Mathews and Clarke have attempted to sum up Chelmsford's attributes as a commander. They agree that he was an industrious, conscientious, reliable and brave officer. But he was also a prosaic product of the system within which he had built his career, and both charge that he was lacking somewhat in flair, intuition, breadth of vision and military acumen, which put him out of his depth in a campaign on the scale and complexity of the Anglo-Zulu War.[42] A pen-portrait of Chelmsford on campaign in Zululand poignantly reveals both his air of command, and his underlying sense of inadequacy in the face of a situation chronically beyond his control:

> From under a rather low white helmet his anxious face peered out; a nose long and thin, and, if anything, hooked; the principal feature black bushy eyebrows, from under which his dark eyes seem to move restlessly, ever on the watch for something sudden, coming. A pleasant manner; sharp, rather jerky sentences; and a general air of watchfulness pervading all his actions.[43]

However, as Mathews suggests, Chelmsford's difficulties as a commander in Zululand must be analysed not only in terms of his training and character, but also in the context of the inadequacies of the army he had at his disposal.

Between 1815 and 1914 the British army fought a European opponent only once: the Russians in the Crimea. Outside Europe it barely ever stopped fighting, and waged more overseas campaigns than any other power besides France.[44] Such colonial campaigns, not against regular troops trained in the European fashion, but against irregulars generally inferior in armaments, organization and discipline, though exhibiting varied and unpredictable military styles, were a highly specialized form of combat, requiring considerable adaptability in both strategy and tactics. Thus the emphasis remained on individual flair among officers and disciplined solidarity among the men, rather than on the technical knowledge and complex managerial skills necessary to cope with the problems of mass organization and movement that characterized warfare between great industrialized powers.[45]

British regulars were the main striking-force in any of the minor imperial expeditions undertaken by Britain during the nineteenth century. Regularly paid, trained in the complex manipulation of modern weapons, strongly cohesive in battle and sustained by a comparatively reliable administrative and logistical infrastructure, they were the product of eighteenth century European culture and the key to imperial expansion overseas.[46] Their numbers, however, were limited, for the professional Victorian army was small, and its manpower and capabilities were constantly overstretched by a multiplicity of commitments, both routine and emergency, across the globe. The defence of the British Empire was, however, the Victorian army's primary responsibility and the determinant of its character and institutions.[47]

The forces of conservatism were deeply entrenched in an authoritarian and self-contained institution like the British Army.[48] No tropical uniform was issued to the British soldier, with the exception of those stationed in India, and war was still a matter of the scarlet tunic. The only concession to the African sun was the foreign service helmet, first issued in 1877.[49] Nevertheless, the demands of imperial defence encouraged some reforms,[50] such as those carried out under Edward Cardwell, Secretary of State for War (1868–74).

The Cardwell reforms, although essentially conservative and limited, effected organizational changes which were to be of great significance to the army's ability to wage colonial campaigns. For the sake of economy and efficiency, Cardwell reduced Britain's military presence overseas by completing the withdrawal of troops from settlement colonies, and by scaling down garrisons elsewhere (except in India). He hoped thereby to establish a better balance between home and imperial defence. The introduction of short service in 1870, whereby recruits spent six years in the regular army and six in the reserve, was designed to create a large reservoir of trained reservists, reduce unhealthy service abroad, and save money. In 1872 Cardwell created brigade districts in Britain with two linked battalions to be attached to each depot. The battalions would alternate in recruiting at home and serving abroad, so ensuring (it was intended) that the Empire be guarded only by seasoned troops. In 1871 the purchase of commissions was abolished to encourage the development of a professional officer corps.[51]

This system, although admirably suited on paper to an empire with scattered and diverse military requirements, did not work in practice. The reserve was only to be called out in the event of a national emergency, which meant that minor colonial campaigns could only be provided for by calling upon regular and reserve units for volunteers, and by reducing standing garrisons – thus breaching the principle of regimental *esprit de corps*. Moreover, as colonial commitments increased, a growing number of home-based and imperfectly trained battalions found themselves serving abroad. Thus, in 1879, 82 battalions were abroad, and only 59 at home depots. In order to maintain establishments and meet the larger turnover of men caused by short-term enlistment, the army had to lower physical standards.[52] Furthermore, as experienced soldiers now left the ranks earlier, the proportion of young men rose to such an extent that the efficiency of regiments for active service was undermined. Nor had the abolition of purchase changed the nature of the officer corps, and most were still conservative and stereotyped in their approach,[53] as was Chelmsford himself.

In this, they took their lead from the Field Marshal Commanding-in-Chief, the Duke of Cambridge, who held office at the pleasure of the crown. Although he greatly resented the interference of civilians in military affairs, the Duke had conceded that the supreme control of the army rested with the Secretary of State for War. Nevertheless, with the Queen his cousin's support, he maintained his grip on matters of command, discipline, appointments and promotions. He thus remained an immensely powerful figure in the army, and his opposition to many of Cardwell's policies, particularly on matters such as linked battalions, short service and the abolition of purchase, was only too evident and encouraged some officers to believe that the reforms of 1870–2 could be reversed.[54]

Chelmsford, as an Indian officer and therefore a believer in the merits of long-term recruitment that led to stable and experienced garrisons, naturally agreed with the Duke in finding the short service system both unreliable and unworkable.[55] But until it could be changed he had to operate within it, and to his chagrin he found increasingly towards the end of the Zululand campaign that many of the regular troops available to him suffered from handicaps of youth and inexperience, and proved militarily unsatisfactory [80].[56]

Yet untried or not, British regulars serving in Zululand were too valuable and scarce to be dispersed on garrison and convoy duty, and had to be augmented by black levies raised in the Natal Native Reserves and put under white officers. The Natal Native Contingent, as this force was known, was poorly armed and trained and, despite early hopes, proved of doubtful morale and effectiveness [17, 30, 33, 53, 55, 84]. A far better fighting force, but underestimated by the British regulars with their inflated professional self-esteem and metropolitan contempt for all things colonial, was the colonial irregular horse [18, 33].[57] Mounted troops retained an importance in colonial war long after it had been lost in European. They were essential for reconnaissance and raiding purposes, and vital in pursuit of a broken enemy. The absence of sufficient horsemen (there was no regular cavalry available to Chelmsford until the latter stages of the campaign) was perhaps the single greatest defect in his army, especially when their intelligence gathering function is properly stressed. Lack of accurate maps in particular forced field commanders such as Chelmsford to rely upon reconnaissance patrols to provide information about the terrain to be traversed, and to locate military objectives.[58]

Yet the professional accumulation and analysis of intelligence was not adequately addressed in the late Victorian army. This was the result of a combination of factors. One was the pervasive but amateurish gentleman-ideal among officers; and the other was the positive hostility of the Duke of Cambridge to a General Staff on the Prussian model and to the professional military colleges that would make staffing it feasible. Thus the Staff College at Camberley, established in 1858 with the purpose of turning out officers better prepared than previously for strategic intelligence as well as other staff duties, was allowed to languish. The reputation of the College only really began to rise when Sir Garnet Wolseley favoured its graduates in his staff appointments to the various field forces he commanded. By assembling his 'ring' from officers chosen for their distinguished war service or promise, rather than for their seniority in the service, Wolseley alienated the Duke and those officers who deplored reform and advanced military ideas.[59]

Thus Chelmsford, who was of the Duke's party, did not follow Wolseley's lead in selecting a talented staff as vital to the success of the

Zululand campaign. Instead, he was content to recruit it from among those officers who had served him at Aldershot.[60] Major J.N. Crealock accompanied him as his military secretary,[61] and Chelmsford did not appoint a chief-of-staff, for it seems he had confidence in his own organizational abilities and was reluctant to delegate. As operations became more complex, however, Chelmsford's poorly structured staff organization and lack of trained staff officers became increasingly apparent. Additional numbers were eventually sent out from England, but they arrived too late to make a significant impact on the campaign.[62]

In these circumstances, it is hardly surprising that field intelligence under Chelmsford during the Anglo-Zulu War was minimal. He had no intelligence officer on his staff in January 1879, for he saw no need for such an appointment [25]. It was only after the Isandlwana disaster, for which lack of proper intelligence was partly responsible, that in May he appointed a Natal civilian with a knowledge of the country, the Hon. W. Drummond, to take charge of an Intelligence Department in his Headquarters Staff in the field. Even then, lack of sufficient properly trained or appointed intelligence officers made the processing of intelligence inadequate, for this specialized work had to be carried out by regular staff officers as a normal part of their other, multifarious duties. Not until Wolseley took command did field intelligence become properly formalized under a staff officer who was a graduate of the Staff College.[63]

Chelmsford did grasp that it is necessary for a commander to study in advance the military methods of the enemy so as best to understand how to overcome him. What he did not appreciate nearly so well was that prior estimates of his fighting qualities might be confounded in practice.[64] Thus, while he had booklets prepared for his officers supplying detailed information on the Zulu military system and instructions on how British troops should be managed in the field,[65] it was nevertheless clear that he and his staff wholly underrated the enemy.[66] Their basic ethnocentrism played its habitually seductive part in leading them to undervalue the military prowess of 'savages',[67] but in this case over-confidence derived directly from the recent Ninth Frontier War of 1877–8 in the eastern Cape. Experiences there, where the Ngqika-Gcaleka Xhosa had habitually melted away to evade pitched battle,[68] misled them into presuming that the Zulu would be an only slightly superior adversary, and it was on this mistaken premise that from mid-1878 Chelmsford began to devise his strategy for crushing the Zulu [1, 2]. Yet a strategy based on an under-estimation of the enemy is fraught with danger.

The High Commissioner of South Africa, Sir Bartle Frere, was the driving force behind the impending war. His mission in southern Africa was to create a confederation of the British colonies in the interests of imperial security and economy.[69] An obstacle was the existence of various neighbouring black polities whose independence was construed as a potential threat, none more so than that of the militarily powerful Zulu kingdom. Thus, for Frere to achieve his political objectives, it was necessary first to neutralize Zulu military might which he, misled by Chelmsford's recent success in the Ninth Frontier War, fondly imagined could be achieved at the price of a minor campaign. Chelmsford was again to be his instrument in this, and he gave him all the assistance he could in securing him the cooperation of the colonial authorities [3].

Naturally, Chelmsford preferred to fight on Zulu, rather than British soil. An offensive into Zululand would, however, leave the borders of the British colonies of Natal and the Transvaal vulnerable to the Zulu raids white settlers so dreaded, especially since they anticipated that the colonial blacks might rise up in support.[70] Potential Zulu raids were a far greater threat in the broken terrain of the Natal frontier than in the open country of the Transvaal, where they could be more easily detected and countered. But Chelmsford noted with alarm that the Natal authorities' contingency plans in the event of a Zulu raid stopped with the advice to settlers that they should take refuge in the various government laagers, which were mainly situated in the small and widely scattered towns [4].

Accordingly, on 10 September he persuaded the Natal government to take more appropriate measures. However, since the garrisons of Imperial troops along the army's line of communications into Zululand would be very small [36], and because the numbers of available colonial volunteers would be minimal, there would be enough armed men to hold only the fortified posts. To dissuade the Zulu from raiding the countryside in between, it was necessary to raise a large field-force of black levies in the border Colonial Defensive Districts (proclaimed on 26 November 1878 for the more effective organization of Natal's defence), and this the Natal government authorized on 20 December 1878. Unlike the Natal Native Contingent, which had been recruited as Imperial troops and were intended for service in Zululand, the border levies were Natal's responsibility. They were only to be activated in the event of a Zulu raid. Besides these part-time levies, the Natal government also provided for small standing reserves of Border Guards at strategic points, as well as Border Police along the river frontiers [9, 10, 17, 18, 33]. On

11 January, when poised to invade Zululand, Chelmsford placed the entire crucial border region under military control.[71]

Despite these arrangements border defences remained weak [9], and this consideration helped determine the timing of Chelmsford's offensive. The rivers along Natal's frontiers with Zululand were usually unfordable from January to March, except at a limited number of drifts which could be effectively guarded. Chelmsford confidently expected the campaign to be over before the rivers had subsided, and until then they should form an effective line of defence against Zulu raids.[72] The timing of Chelmsford's campaign was also affected by the condition of the countryside after the late spring rains and the consequently delayed harvest. For while the Zulu would still be short of food in January, which would adversely affect their capacity to wage a campaign, the grazing, upon which the British draft-animals subsisted, was plentiful. Soon, though, the grass would be higher and so afford the Zulu even better cover; while later still, in the winter months, grazing would give out and be dry enough to be burned by the Zulu. January 1879, then, was the optimum moment to launch the invasion of Zululand.[73]

These military considerations determined that Frere's ultimatum be delivered to the representatives of the Zulu king on 11 December 1878. Its terms were such that Cetshwayo was highly unlikely to accept them, except in the unrealistic eventuality that he would submit without a fight to the dismantling of the Zulu military system and to the concomitant social disruption and political subordination of his kingdom [21]. He was given thirty days in which to respond, meaning in effect that the invasion for which Chelmsford was preparing could commence on the ideal date of 11 January 1879.[74]

Success in a vigorous, offensive campaign such as Chelmsford intended to conduct depended upon firm logistics. Indeed, the role of the modern commander was not primarily that of heroic leader in battle, but rather of military manager, whose prime task was to put his men into the field and keep them supplied.[75] Good logistics involved not only the prior accumulation of necessary supplies and ammunition, but also the organization of sufficient transport.[76] In this sense, the Anglo-Zulu War exemplified one of the basic features of colonial warfare: it was a campaign against distance and natural obstacles as much as against hostile man, and one in which problems of supply were at the root of most of the difficulties encountered and, indeed, governed its whole course.[77] Since most supplies could not be obtained from the theatre of war, they had to be carried, turning the army into an escort for its food and requiring the establishment of garrisoned depots along its line of advance.[78]

It is hardly surprising, then, that Chelmsford's greatest difficulty and concern in the months before his invasion of Zululand should have revolved around collecting and organizing sufficient supplies and transport. The ox-drawn wagons, which he preferred as being the most suitable form of transport considering local circumstances,[79] had to be hired at exorbitant rates from the colonists. If he had succeeded in establishing better relations with the Natal government, its full co-operation would have eased the transport problem. But the civil authorities quickly took umbrage at the military's high-handed style, especially since they were wary of war with Zululand and the additional risk and expense that would involve.[80] Meanwhile, the Commissariat and Transport Department (created in the course of the army reforms of 1875) showed itself to be inefficient and unable to adapt to South African conditions. Its inexperience in purchasing methods and in animal husbandry, for example, helped drive up the cost of transport animals. Chelmsford, while painfully aware of the Department's weaknesses, proved incapable of restructuring it, and in the end left it to its own inadequate devices [82]. Perhaps, if he had attached more importance to the selection of better trained staff officers effectively to augment the over-stretched officers in the Department, many of the organizational problems would have been overcome.[81] As it was, Chelmsford succeeded only with great difficulty and expense in assembling the draught animals and vehicles necessary to supply his invading army [13–15, 18, 27, 36]. Yet essential as they were, they limited his strategic options.

An army's movement is based on the speed of its slowest component. Wagons, even when drawn over favourable terrain by animals in peak condition, could hardly travel further than eleven miles a day. Their pace would be even slower across the enormous distances and broken countryside of the Zulu theatre of war. Moreover, they required all-round protection on the march, and the larger the convoy the slower it moved.[82] Colonists, especially the Boers, advised Chelmsford to form defensive wagon-laagers when he halted in Zulu territory. But until the dreadful lesson of Isandlwana was administered, he was reluctant to laager because it was such a time-consuming procedure and his progress was already so slow.[83]

In planning his strategy, therefore, Chelmsford was faced with certain constraints. When he advanced into Zululand he would leave his own frontiers inadequately protected; while his dependence on slow-moving and vulnerable supply-trains would limit both his manoeuvrability and the size of the columns they were to support.[84]

Chelmsford's solution to these problems was to send in five relatively small columns (later reduced effectively to three) to converge on an appropriate point: oNdini, King Cetshwayo's chief residence. This deployment of several columns echoed his original strategy in the Ninth Frontier War. Yet there it had proved unsuccessful against a mobile foe. He had consequently been constrained to take the advice urged on him by the Cape colonists, abandon his conventional offensives, and create eleven military districts in which mounted forces were stationed.[85] Nevertheless, he was undeterred by his setbacks in the Cape, for the strategy of converging columns still seemed appropriate for Zululand.

Conventional military wisdom has it that a division of forces is bad strategy. Yet in the small colonial wars waged by the British Army in the nineteenth century, such a division had come to be considered excusable because of the usual problems of supply and mobility, and because a separate number of invading forces might have the advantage of seeming more formidable to a relatively unsophisticated enemy than a single larger one.[86] Besides, Chelmsford hoped to move with greater speed with smaller columns, and to have more forage at the disposal of each. Moreover, the presence of a number of supporting columns would engross more of the enemy's territory, reduce the chance of their being outflanked, and discourage Zulu counter-thrusts against the British frontiers. With the matter of Zulu raids particularly in mind, Chelmsford selected invasion routes in sectors considered vulnerable to Zulu attack. The advance across the lower Thukela by No. 1 Column, under Colonel Pearson, would protect the coastal plain; that across Rorke's Drift by No. 3 Column, under Colonel Glyn, central Natal; and that across the Blood (Ncome) River by No. 4 Column, under Colonel Wood, the Transvaal. Moreover, by invading at three points, he hoped to force Cetshwayo to keep his *amabutho* fully mobilized in order to face the diverse threat, and so to present him with supply problems as great as his own [5, 16, 116].[87]

To improve the defence of the Natal middle border and to strengthen No. 3 Column, which he decided to accompany, Chelmsford broke up No. 2 Column, under Colonel Durnford, which he had originally intended should advance across the Thukela at Middle Drift. Part remained on garrison duty above Middle Drift, and the rest moved up to support No. 3 Column [43]. He also decided to keep No. 5 Column, under Colonel Rowlands, in a defensive role. This was the consequence of Rowlands's unsuccessful operations during September–October 1878 against Sekhukhune's Pedi in the north-eastern Transvaal, which had left the region unpacified. Chelmsford ordered that Rowlands should therefore remain in garrison on the Phongolo River frontier to protect the Transvaal from the Pedi, and to cover No. 4 Column's northern flank from both the Zulu and the equivocal Swazi. This open frontier of the Phongolo region, where Zulu, Swazi, Boers and German settlers contended for supremacy, was the most volatile of Zululand's borders, and during the final tense months of 1878 Wood had to over-stretch the resources of No. 4 Column to secure it [7, 8, 11].[88] That is why Chelmsford hoped an alliance with the Swazi would relieve some pressure, though they proved too canny to commit themselves until certain of the outcome of the war [17, 19, 20, 24].

Chelmsford's initial strategy of converging columns required considerable coordination. But, because of deficient staff work, maps were unreliable, while insufficient cavalry meant inadequate reconnaissance. Consequently, he had no accurate conception of the terrain over which his columns were to advance [102]. In such circumstances, it was unlikely that several forces converging on a distant point such as oNdini, and beset by decided logistical problems, would arrive simultaneously, or even be in a position to provide much mutual support [17,19]. With memories doubtless alive of the difficulties he had experienced during the Ninth Frontier War in coordinating the movements of the various columns,[89] it is no wonder that, as the day of invasion approached, Chelmsford became ever more concerned to ensure that his various commanders liaise closely, improve their logistical arrangements and coordinate their operations [13, 23, 24, 26–8, 30–2, 34–6]. But the practical difficulties of doing so soon asserted themselves, and on the eve of invasion Chelmsford found it problematical enough even to arrange a rendezvous with Wood [32, 33, 35].

Once he actually began the invasion of Zululand on 11 January 1879, experienced the difficult broken terrain for himself, and discovered the rain-sodden ground to be holding up his advance even more than he had anticipated, Chelmsford was forced to modify his original plans. Looking to the long term, he came to the conclusion that the only way to secure Natal from future Zulu attack would be to maintain control of both sides of the river frontier; while to break Zulu power finally, the country should be 'parcelled out into small divisions under small chiefs' [48].[90] This solution precisely prefigured the settlement Sir Garnet Wolseley was to impose on Zululand in September 1879. More immediately, Chelmsford abandoned his hopes for a rapid, coordinated advance. He decided instead that the toiling columns should halt inside Zululand and send out mobile flying columns to drive the Zulu away from the Transvaal and Natal borders. These flying columns would occupy and devastate a large part of Zululand, and constantly threaten those districts remaining under the king's control. The general advance would be resumed only once conditions had improved sufficiently [44].[91]

The question of widespread devastation was a problematical one. The British officially had no quarrel with the Zulu nation, only with its king,[92] and Chelmsford initially forbade excesses against the civilian population [29]. After Isandlwana the distinction between the king and his 'savage' subjects would no longer be observed, and the complete destruction sanctioned of the enemy's means of subsistence along the British line of march. This naturally included the *amakhanda*, which were the centres of the king's authority, the rallying-points for the *amabutho* and the depots for Zulu supplies. That is why their systematic destruction, culminating in that of oNdini, would ensure the reduction of the king's capacity to resist and fatally damage his ability to exercise authority.[93] Unfortunately for the Zulu, destruction of ordinary *imizi* and their grain stores, as well as the capture of livestock, was also considered efficacious in ending resistance among a people whose very livelihood was threatened. Mounted troops were essential for this raiding activity, and consequently another reason for Chelmsford's wide dispersal of the invading columns was to maximise the impact of the limited numbers of horsemen at his disposal.[94] For he well understood that one of the most effectual ways of defeating a people such as the Zulu was 'through the stomach'.[95]

Chelmsford calculated that, by pushing the increasingly hungry and shelterless Zulu up to the north-eastern corner of Zululand, he might provoke Cetshwayo's dissatisfied subjects into deposing him and surrendering.[96] He was heartened by intelligence of existing dissensions within the Zulu kingdom, and hoped to exploit these by encouraging disaffected chiefs and their adherents to defect.[97] He therefore instructed his commanders and border officials to pursue negotiations with Zulu notables (as he himself did), and laid down guidelines for the accommodation of Zulu refugees in Natal [12, 22, 24, 39, 48].

Any possible unravelling of the Zulu kingdom depended, however, on successful military operations in the first instance. What was to be avoided, if at all possible, was protracted and desultory warfare, for it favoured the more mobile Zulu fighting on home ground. That is why, despite the far-flung dispositions of his columns and his willingness methodically to drive Cetshwayo into a corner, Chelmsford preferred to conclude the campaign swiftly with a decisive battle.[98]

The experience of small wars proved beyond doubt that those which were the most decisive were marked by pitched battles. All the advantages lay with properly trained troops, and a severe general engagement was calculated to bring home to the enemy the superiority of even heavily outnumbered regulars. The object, then, was to bring the enemy to battle. This was especially important when, as in the case of Zululand, the war was undertaken to overthrow a militarily powerful state, whose army was its most potent manifestation. Victory in the field was thus necessary to assert ascendancy. Happily, when fighting a people with strong military traditions, there was a much greater chance of their being willing to risk all in battle.[99] Chelmsford's operational gambit of dividing the army into several columns must consequently also be seen as a means of enticing the Zulu into attacking one or more of them [16].[100] Only when they were committed to battle would the Zulu discover that the numerical inferiority of the apparently weak columns would be more than compensated for by superior firepower and tactics.

A disciplined British force, once it was properly positioned and handled so as to give maximum effect to the destructive weight of fire of modern breach-loading, rapid-firing rifles, Gatling-guns and artillery, was normally invulnerable against the poorly armed mass attacks of warriors such as the Zulu.[101] The most effective way of concentrating fire and stemming the enemy's rush was to place troops in prepared all-round defensive positions, such as fieldworks (whether of earth or stone), or wagon-laagers.[102] It was to be repeatedly proven that the Zulu were helpless against even elementarily fortified posts or hastily arranged march-laagers. Consequently, in the wake of Isandlwana – which demonstrated conclusively that a massed charge could break through a loose skirmishing line no matter how superior its armament – it became the dominant British concern to entice the Zulu into destroying themselves against the invader's prepared positions.

The defensive was the essence of the Zulu King's military strategy in 1879, and conformed with his political programme of presenting himself as the pacific victim of an unwarranted attack, prepared only to fight in self-defence within the borders of his own country.[103] He knew well that the British had the resources overseas to reinforce their army in southern Africa until it was ultimately successful. The campaign had therefore to be swift and limited, and the hope was that, if the Zulu armies were able through victory in pitched battle to menace the borders of Natal, the

British would be pressured into concluding a peace favourable to the Zulu before reinforcements could arrive.[104] Zulu tacticians were very conscious, too, of the dangers involved in trying to storm prepared positions such as forts or laagers. They knew their greatest chance of success lay in forcing the British to give battle in the open field, where they ought to overwhelm their enemy with their superior numbers deployed for the traditional frontal mass-attack.[105] That they should ever have succeeded in catching the British in the open, was a consequence of the way in which Chelmsford and his staff persisted (until taught otherwise) in underrating the Zulu.

Zulu intelligence identified Glyn's No. 3 Column as the main British force since it was stronger than the two other columns invading their country, and because Chelmsford was accompanying it.[106] Cetshwayo consequently directed his main army against it, and despatched a smaller force to the coast to impede the advance of Pearson's No. 1 Column. Local irregulars were left to confront Wood's No. 4 Column in the north-west.

Chelmsford's force (he had effectively assumed command of No. 3 Column) scored an easy success in a skirmish at Sokhexe on 12 January 1879, but the difficult, muddy terrain held up the advance [37–42, 44–6]. On 20 January a camp was set up at Isandlwana mountain and left unentrenched (despite the warnings of the local settlers) because it was only intended as a temporary staging-post. The following day Chelmsford sent out a strong reconnaissance in the direction of the Qudeni forest on his eastern flank [47, 48]. It met some resistance, and early on the morning of 22 January Chelmsford set out from camp to reinforce it. Since over half of No. 3 Column was now committed in the Qudeni area, he ordered up Durnford with part of No. 2 Column [43] to reinforce the camp. However, because Chelmsford had not the slightest apprehension that the Zulu might attack the camp during his absence, he neglected to leave specific orders for its defence. To his great subsequent relief, Major C.F. Clery, Glyn's staff officer, on his own initiative instructed Lieutenant-Colonel Pulleine, the senior officer in camp until Durnford's arrival, to act strictly on the defensive.

It seems clear that the commanders of the advancing Zulu army deliberately manoeuvred Chelmsford into the fatal division of his forces. For while the Zulu army advanced undetected on Isandlwana, small detached forces skirmished brilliantly, leading Chelmsford ever further away from his threatened camp and its depleted garrison. Meanwhile, Durnford, who had arrived in camp, upset the defensive arrangements by advancing to prevent Chelmsford from being attacked in the rear (as he supposed) by the small decoy Zulu forces he observed, and by requiring Pulleine to move up in his support if required. Durnford's patrols unexpectedly encountered the main Zulu army and provoked it into a somewhat disorganized and premature advance. The British forces tried to fall back on the camp and consolidate, but the rapidly deploying Zulu succeeded in outflanking their firing-line and entered the camp from the rear. The battle ended in desperate hand-to-hand fighting in the camp and along the 'fugitives' trail' to Natal, along which a few of the British managed to escape. The Zulu reserve, which had not been engaged, continued into Natal and proceeded to raid the valley of the Buffalo (Mzinyathi) River. While doing so, they came across the hastily fortified British depot at Rorke's Drift, which its greatly outnumbered garrison successfully defended in a desperate struggle which lasted well into the night.

Chelmsford, meanwhile, had been inexcusably out of communication for much of the day as he scouted ahead with a small party, adhering to his own precept that a commander 'must ride about and see the country himself' [20]. It was not until the late afternoon that he finally credited reports, which at first he and his staff found inconceivable, that his camp was actually under attack. He then acted decisively to recapture it, and the Zulu withdrew with their plunder as he advanced in battle order on Isandlwana. After an appalling night spent among the dead in the looted camp, Chelmsford retired with the demoralized remnant of his force into Natal [49].

The defeat at Isandlwana shattered Chelmsford's invasion plans [53].[107] The heavy loss of life, weapons, ammunition and transport meant that he could make no further advance until his forces had regrouped and been reinforced, and fresh transport assembled. Until then, he would have to stand on the defensive. Meanwhile, Pearson's column, which had fought through a Zulu ambush at the Nyezane River on 22 January, was effectively blockaded by Zulu forces at Eshowe where it had decided to hold fast to divert Zulu attention from Natal [54, 55]; while Wood's force, which had been enjoying considerable success in its sector [44–6], withdrew to a strongly-defended position at Khambula. Natal was thrown into a panic at the prospect of a Zulu invasion. The settlers resorted to their laagers, threw up improvised defences, or trekked away to safety [50, 59]. Only the glorious defence of Rorke's Drift provided some morale-building compensation [58]. What was clear, though, was that the battle of Isandlwana had changed the nature of the campaign. Compromises and negotiated settlements were no longer possible. The British, if they were to maintain their prestige and hegemony in southern

Africa, had now to prosecute the war until the Zulu were utterly defeated in battle and their kingdom overthrown.

The Isandlwana campaign severely affected Chelmsford's health and morale, and for a time he seemed on the verge of a breakdown [60]. During this crisis, he turned particularly to Wood at Khambula to retrieve the situation [51, 52, 55]. And Wood, thanks to the number of experienced mounted men at his disposal, retained the ascendancy in the north-west with some successful raids [51, 57, 59, 61–3, 65]. Pearson, on the other hand, for lack of initiative and mounted men, failed to mount punitive raids from Eshowe, and effectively settled down to be relieved [57, 61–3, 65].

Meanwhile, back in Natal, Chelmsford set about rallying the colony's defences, preparing for a new offensive, and containing the damage to his reputation [63–5]. His first act after Isandlwana was to convene a Court of Enquiry [50]. Its instruction was to enquire very specifically into the loss of the camp, rather than into the surrounding circumstances. It is clear that Chelmsford had no intention that it should probe too deeply into his responsibility for the disaster. Much of the evidence heard was not recorded. The Court found that most of the blame for the disaster should be attributed to the imprudent actions of Durnford (who had been conveniently killed); and to the poor performance of the Natal Native Contingent (equally conveniently neither white nor regular infantry) [56]. The honour of both Chelmsford and the British army was thus secured, and this version of events passed into the official account.[108]

However, criticism in Natal of Chelmsford's conduct of the war was not stilled, especially since the threat of invasion hung over the colony. In England, the news of Isandlwana was received with consternation and angry questioning, but the authorities acted positively to send out the reinforcements Chelmsford requested. Their rapid arrival in Durban in growing and reassuring numbers did much to calm the colonists. Soon enough were concentrated and sufficient transport assembled (despite difficulties) to make possible the early relief of Eshowe [68–71]. This had become a necessary preliminary to a second major thrust into Zululand, for the garrison was running out of supplies and suffering increasingly from sickness [69].

Indeed, the time seemed ripe to renew the offensive. The Zulu were discouraged by the heavy casualties they had already suffered, even in victory. In the north-west, where Wood's raiding activity continued so effectively to demoralize the inhabitants, there were some significant defections to the British side, with the prospect of more to follow [69]. The Zulu leadership were consternated and in March sent out peace feelers. But Chelmsford, encouraged by his burgeoning strength, refused to consider any overtures which did not accept the terms of the British ultimatum of 11 December 1878 [66, 69].

On 28 March Chelmsford led the Eshowe Relief Column across the Thukela River into Zululand.[109] He was determined to rectify the deficiencies which had led to the Isandlwana disaster. This time he organized effective forward reconnaissance and followed regular laagering procedures. He also marched closer to the coast than had Pearson in order to keep to more open terrain and avoid ambush [70–73]. On 1 April he laagered near the kwaGingindlovu *ikhanda* within sight of Eshowe. The reinforced Zulu forces investing Eshowe attacked him there in his all-round defensive position at dawn the following day. Despite the unsteadiness of the many inexperienced recruits with the Relief Column, the Zulu attack stalled before the impenetrable wall of fire, and this time found no flank to turn. A sortie by the mounted men turned the Zulu retreat into a rout. The defeated Zulu dispersed, and the following day Chelmsford advanced to relieve Eshowe. He decided to evacuate the garrison and abandon Fort Eshowe, for he considered the coastal route he had followed more suitable for the future operations he had in mind [74, 75].

Meanwhile, the real turning-point of the war had just occurred at Khambula where, on 29 March in the most hard-fought battle of the campaign, Wood routed the veterans of Isandlwana sent against his camp [77].[110] The unpalatable lesson absorbed by the Zulu, which the battle of Gingindlovu four days later confirmed, was that it was hopeless to attack fortified positions, and that they could not hope to prevail unless they again caught the British in the open field. Since Cetshwayo realized this to be unlikely, he began to concentrate on achieving a negotiated peace. But Chelmsford, buoyed up by the realization that after the overwhelming victories at Khambula and Gingindlovu his forces had entirely regained the initiative, was determined to pursue the war to its conclusion.

For this purpose, it was necessary to devise a new invasion strategy.[111] More than enough troops (and a superfluity of special service officers anxious for action) had arrived in Natal to resume the march on oNdini. However, their very numbers meant increased strain on the Commissariat and Transport Department and highlighted its deficiencies, for additional transport had to be organized, supplies collected and depots established [79, 80, 82, 83, 85]. Chelmsford seemed embarrassed by the large numbers of troops at his disposal and uncertain how best to use them. On one thing, though, he was determined: this time he would exercise extreme caution to avoid a repetition of the Isandlwana debacle. Henceforth, his conduct of the campaign would be determined by that uninspiring proverb which became his motto: 'slow and steady wins the race' [90].

In the event, he decided he would employ two widely spaced columns. His senior officers had advocated a single column as placing less strain on the Commissariat and Transport Department, but Chelmsford insisted that the deployment of two would screen both the Transvaal and Natal from a Zulu counter-blow [75, 81]. He arranged that the 1st Division, under the command of Major-General Crealock, would advance along the coast from Fort Pearson [76]; while the 2nd Division, under Major-General Newdigate, would concentrate at Dundee [79]. In its advance it would cooperate with Wood's force, to be renamed the Flying Column, trusting the Transvaal border to the protection of its garrisons [80, 81].

Chelmsford chose Dundee as the 2nd Division's chief depot over Helpmekaar, which had served as such during the first invasion, for a number of reasons. The roads were better by way of Ladysmith than by Greytown and were less exposed to the Zulu border; and Dundee was nearer the Orange Free State whence considerable supplies were being obtained [116]. Yet the most powerful consideration was the unspoken one: no one wished to follow the road sign-posted by Isandlwana and its still unburied British dead. Instead, the 2nd Division would advance by a longer and unfamiliar route which would require considerable and time-consuming reconnaissance.

During May, the 2nd Division began to mass at Landman's Drift in advance of Dundee, and frequent sorties ensured that the country to Chelmsford's front and immediate right was clear of Zulu forces. One reconnaissance in force advanced to Isandlwana and on 21 May commenced the burial of the dead, thus stilling considerable criticism in Natal and England, and quietening Chelmsford's own conscience [70, 71, 88–91].[112] Meanwhile, to draw Zulu forces further away to the east who might later fall on his right flank or Natal, Chelmsford required raids to be mounted across the Thukela from Natal.

These raids were the last in a series Chelmsford had first ordered to divert the Zulu from his advance during the relief of Eshowe, and they became a crucial factor in his supersession in May by Sir Garnet Wolseley.[113] As a proponent of the 'active defence', Chelmsford believed that it was necessary to maintain the strategic initiative. Thus, in order to put the troops positioned along the border to positive use and to improve their morale, he encouraged trans-border raids. However, Bulwer and the Natal authorities feared that a damaging cycle of raid and counter-raid would be set up. They disputed the wisdom of the 'active defence' and forbade the use of Natal troops in such operations, despite Chelmsford's indignant claims as overall commander to have the final say in their training and deployment. Nor were Bulwer's apprehensions ungrounded, for the destructive Zulu counter-raid of 25 June at Middle Drift would expose the weakness of Natal's border defences and prove Chelmsford's policy of raiding to be as self-defeating as Bulwer had predicted. Chelmsford, meanwhile, had reversed his earlier opinion and decided that black levies were, after all, good only for the 'passive defence' of the border. Yet the bitterness of the dispute caused a sharp deterioration in relations between Chelmsford and Bulwer, and both subjected the authorities in England to a barrage of mutually recriminatory despatches [66, 67, 69, 70, 75, 78, 84, 100].

This shrill contest between the military and civil authorities in Natal was the last straw for the British government. They already perceived Chelmsford to be demoralized, vacillating and uncertain of his strategy, and despaired of his ability to bring the increasingly expensive war to a speedy conclusion. Chelmsford had survived as commander thanks to the influence of the Horse Guards, but now even the Duke of Cambridge began to question his conduct of the campaign [102]. The Cabinet's solution was to create a single, unified command in southern Africa, which would subordinate both Bulwer and Chelmsford and sideline Frere. Their choice for the position, much deprecated by the Duke of Cambridge's circle, fell on the dynamic and reformist General Sir Garnet Wolseley. Chelmsford learned on 16 June of Wolseley's appointment, but was not apprised of the details until 5 July. In fact, it was not until 9 July that he received formal notice of his supersession. Until then, he continued to act as if he were still Officer Commanding in South Africa, though knowledge that Wolseley was on the way spurred him to bring the war to a decisive conclusion before his arrival should rob him of the credit.[114]

At home in England, Chelmsford's wife naturally knew of his true situation, and her anguished feelings spilled over in a letter to Wood, who had been her husband's greatest prop over the preceding months:

> . . . I knew you would feel for my husband. He certainly has been most cruelly abused, & I am sure you will feel still more for him

> now, when you hear he is superseded by Sir Garnet & thrown over by the Govt. without a word of thanks for all his hard work . . . [I]t is quite insulting to a man who has worked & slaved under intolerable difficulties as my husband has done, & thwarted at every turn by a petty jealous man like Sir Henry Bulwer. *He* certainly deserves to be superseded. Sir Garnet & his partisans have been moving heaven & earth to go out to the Cape, & have succeeded. I only pray the war may course to an end before he arrives to reap another man's harvest – but I fear it is impossible, tied & bound as my husband is by his transport difficulties. Sir Garnet will of course proclaim "martial law" & bring difficulties to an end. Then they will cry "What a clever General is Sir Garnet". Forgive this very bitter letter.[115]

Meanwhile, mounted reconnaissances undertaken during May from Landman's Drift had established that the shortest route for the 2nd Division to follow to oNdini was across the Blood River below Koppie Alleen [91–5, 102]. This necessitated establishing a new depot there to replace the forward base Chelmsford had already created to the north at Conference Hill. This change did nothing to enhance his already tarnished reputation as a strategist. But at last, on 31 May, the 2nd Division began its advance into Zululand to effect its junction with the Flying Column. Their march on oNdini was laboured, and Chelmsford was criticised by those serving under him for having become as 'over-cautious as he was before over-rash'.[116] The columns would move only once cavalry had reconnoitred the route ahead to ensure that there were no Zulu concentrations capable of threatening them while extended on the march; and wherever they camped for the night they undertook the laborious and time-consuming procedure of forming laager. Moreover, Chelmsford periodically halted to build fortified depots along his line of communications, and convoys had to be escorted back and forth to fill them with supplies [91, 95, 96, 104, 107].

Misfortunes and vexations continued to dog Chelmsford's progress. The death on patrol on 1 June of the Prince Imperial of France, an observer on Chelmsford's staff, caused more consternation in Britain than the battle of Isandlwana itself, and further damaged Chelmsford in the public eye [75, 97].[117] He chafed at the unwelcome presence of war correspondents, whose continuous criticisms he considered ill-informed when not plainly malicious [77, 102].[118] Matters were not made easier on account of his growing dispute with the efficient Major-General Clifford, whom the Duke of Cambridge had specifically selected as Inspector-General of the Lines of Communication.[119] Clifford resented that his command stopped at the Zulu border, and he consistently misrepresented Chelmsford's actions to the authorities in England, causing the maligned general much indignation [77, 79, 91, 110]. Nor did the over-methodical Crealock's painfully slow advance with the 1st Division help Chelmsford's cause. Rather, it bore out the criticisms of those who opposed the independent operations of a second column. Chelmsford saw the task of the 1st Division to force Cetshwayo to divide his forces in defence of the coastal region, but Crealock's lack of progress meant the Zulu were able to ignore his presence and to concentrate their forces to meet Chelmsford's advance [79, 88, 105, 108].

Yet, for his part, Cetshwayo was uncertain how best to prosecute the war. He was beset by increasing defections along the British line of advance and despaired of fighting off the invaders, but his *amabutho* were unwilling to give up before a further fight. So he compromised. He entered into intensified negotiations with the British, but assured his warriors that he would fight the invaders should they come on as far as the Mahlabathini plain.[120]

As Cetshwayo feared, Chelmsford proved unwilling to negotiate seriously. He demanded crushing and impossible terms, thus ensuring that Zulu resistance would continue until he had achieved the crushing victory in the field he so desired [89, 98, 101, 103, 105, 106, 109]. This was consummated on 4 July at the battle of Ulundi.[121] The British fought in an infantry square, a formation which gave all-round defence and produced concentrated fire. In that sense it was not unlike a laager, but with the additional moral force of not being an entrenched position. So when the Zulu broke before the square and fled from a devastating cavalry counter-attack, they knew that they had been defeated in the open field and that further resistance was pointless [111]. The Zulu army consequently dispersed. King Cetshwayo himself fled to the north, for with his army defeated, his *amakhanda* burned and his chiefs submitting to the invaders, he knew his power to be irrevocably broken.

Chelmsford was criticised for withdrawing to his base at Mthonjaneni immediately after the battle instead of advancing to consolidate his victory. His decision was doubtless influenced by his shortage of supplies and the need to get his men under better cover in the inclement winter weather, as well as by his knowledge that organized resistance by the Zulu army was no longer likely. But also playing their part were resentment at Wolseley's peremptory orders and a desire, now that he was no longer commander-in-chief, to leave South Africa immediately [108, 112–15]. Chelmsford consequently resigned his command, and sailed for England after rapturous receptions in Durban and Cape Town by the colonists, for whom the battle of Ulundi had erased his earlier blunders.[122]

Wolseley, who was only too pleased to see the back of Chelmsford,[123] wrote him in slyly ambiguous, though superficially complimentary terms. He assured him that after Ulundi he could return home 'with the halo of success' around him, confident that 'all the authorities at the Horse Guards & War Office' would receive him 'with the utmost cordiality', though, as he could not refrain from reminding Chelmsford, some outside the Duke's circle 'may not approve' of the way the war had been conducted.[124] Indeed, as Wolseley anticipated, Chelmsford's reception was not unmixed in an England where only recently they had been singing in the music halls:

Tho' Lord Chelmsford no doubt is a brave and honest man,
And Sir Bartle Frere too I daresay,
They've not led our soldiers to victory yet
But Sir Garnet will show them the way.[125]

Lord Beaconsfield, the prime minister, refused to receive the general whose campaign had brought discredit upon his ministry. Chelmsford heard the voices of his detractors everywhere, even among his peers in the House of Lords.[126] Yet there were those who applauded his final victory in Zululand, none more steadfastly than Queen Victoria herself. She was appalled that he should be victimised by the press and politicians and be turned into a stick with which to beat the government and the conservative military establishment of her cousin, the Duke of Cambridge. And though she could not ensure that he would again be offered an active command, she conspicuously favoured him with honours and her attention.[127]

Immediately on his return he was commanded to visit the Queen at Balmoral, and received the GCB. In April 1882 he was promoted to the permanent rank of lieutenant-general. When it seemed that compulsory retirement was imminent, the Queen used her influence to have him appointed Lieutenant of the Tower, a position he held from June 1884 to March 1889. He became a full general in December 1888, and was finally placed on the retired list only in June 1893. In 1887 he accepted the honourary colonelcy of the 4th Middlesex (West London) Rifle Corps; in

1898 he was appointed Colonel of the Sherwood Foresters (Derbyshire Regiment), and was transferred to the 2nd Life Guards in 1900. The Queen also appointed him Gold Stick at court. King Edward VII, on his accession, retained Chelmsford as Gold Stick, and made him GCVO in 1902. Chelmsford died on 9 April 1905 at the United Service Club following a sudden seizure while playing billiards, and was buried at Brompton Cemetery in a grave next to his father's.[128]

His later tranquil years, gilded with honours, were still occasionally troubled by unresolved resonances from the Zululand campaign. The most persistent concerned the posthumous reputation of Colonel Durnford. Chelmsford, on his return from South Africa, had responded to some of the attacks made on his generalship by placing the blame for Isandlwana on Durnford's impulsive disregard of orders. This defence provoked a determined campaign from Durnford's brother Edward and from Frances Colenso (who had been romantically attached to Durnford) to clear his name, and pass the responsibility back to Chelmsford. Their crusade took the form of letters to the newspapers, a pamphlet and two books,[129] and culminated in 1886 at a court of inquiry in Natal. The court exonerated Captain T. Shepstone from Frances Colenso's bizarre charge that he had removed papers from Durnford's body and suppressed them to protect Chelmsford's reputation.[130] This episode caused Chelmsford much vexation and embarrassment, since it raked up issues he doubtless would have preferred to have let lie.[131]

For even if, as Gerald French would have it, Chelmsford faced all criticism with forbearance and dignity, 'strong in the knowledge he was right',[132] he must surely, in his heart of hearts, have reviewed his conduct of the Zululand campaign with considerable discontent. It was all very well to continue polishing a systematic, but ultimately unpublished, refutation of the criticisms levelled against him [116].[133] Yet whatever private satisfaction this exercise might have provided him, it did nothing to rehabilitate his crippled reputation. Certainly, historians of today, even when willing to judge Chelmsford in the context of a conservative and deficient military establishment, find much in his generalship to criticise, and little to commend.

I
The First Invasion

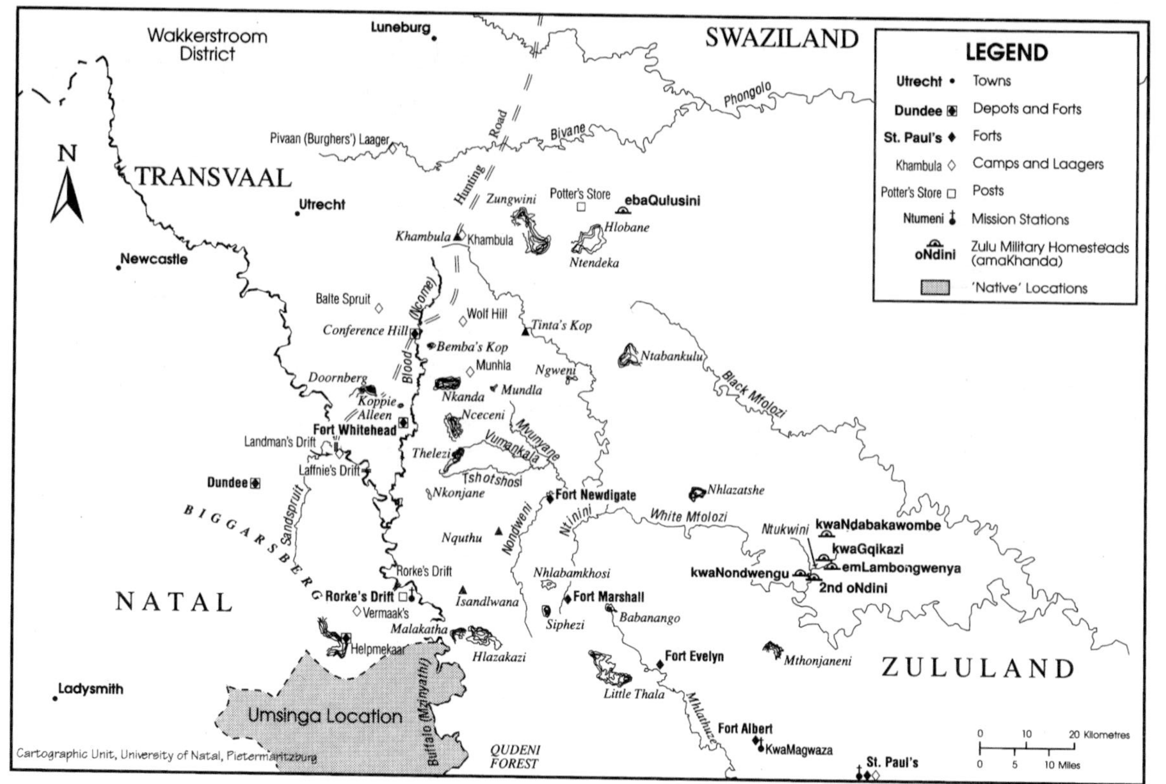

The northern theatre of military operations, showing the places mentioned by Lord Chelmsford.

Chapter 1
Planning the Campaign

1

Lieutenant-General the Hon. F.A. Thesiger to Sir Theophilus Shepstone

[Holograph] Cape Town
8 July 1878

. . . I shall hope to get away from Cape Town before very long.[1] – I am very anxious to see Natal and the Transvaal, and to gather from my own observation what the state of affairs military is in those parts –

The Zulu have been very kind to us in abstaining from any hostile movements during the time that we were so busily engaged in this colony – If they will only wait until next month I shall hope to have the troops somewhat better prepared than they are at present –[2]

The state of uncertainty however as to whether it is to be peace or war is very much against us –

Zulus are ready; we are not, and cannot be so, until I have permission to raise the requisite numbers of volunteers & native levies – This cannot of course be done until a final decision has been come to regarding the boundary question – We are now awaiting the arrival of the report of the Boundary Commissioners, when I hope some day light may be thrown upon what is now apparently rather foggy –[3]

TS 31

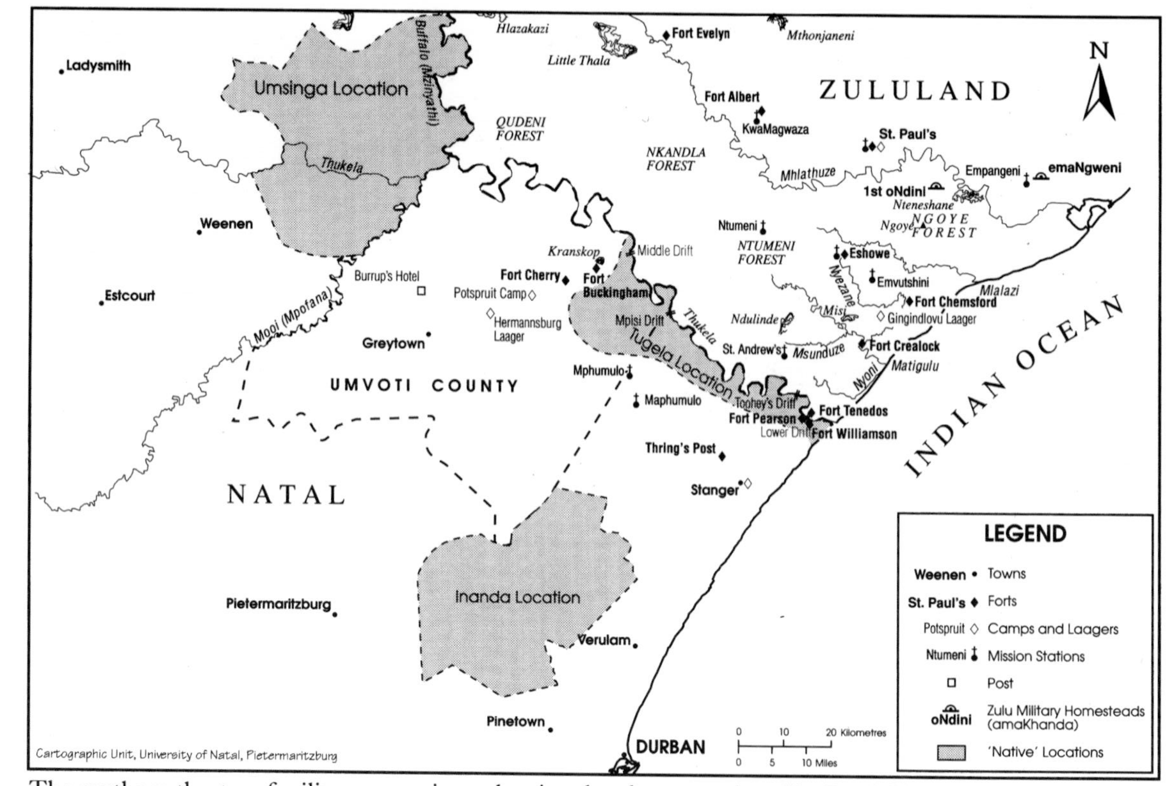

The southern theatre of military operations, showing the places mentioned by Lord Chelmsford.

2

Lieutenant-General the Hon. F.A. Thesiger to Sir Theophilus Shepstone

[Holograph]

Government House
Cape Town
21 July 1878

. . . If we are to have a fight with the Zulus, I am anxious that our arrangement should be as complete as it is possible to make them – Half measures do not answer with natives – They must be thoroughly crushed to make them believe in our superiority; and if I am called upon to conduct operations against them, I shall strive to be in a position to show them how hopelessly inferior they are to us in fighting power, altho' numerically stronger –

{I leave for Natal in the "Active"[4] on Thursday morning next (25th) –}

TS 31 [Printed in French, *Lord Chelmsford*, p. 42 with the words between {} omitted.]

3

Lieutenant-General the Hon. F.A. Thesiger to Sir Theophilus Shepstone

[Holograph]

Pieter Maritzburg
16 August 1878

. . . I am in hopes of seeing Sir Bartle Frere up here before very long. His presence will do more to expedite the settlement of the pending questions than any amount of writing – I am endeavouring to convince the people of this colony that their interests in respect to the Zulu difficulty are identical with those of the Transvaal and I hope they will soon realize it – I am off in a week's time to the St Johns river to superintend the disembarkation of the detachment which is to garrison our new acquisition . . .[5]

TS 32

4

Memorandum by Lieutenant-General the Hon. F.A. Thesiger to Sir Henry Bulwer

24 August 1878

[Signed MS copy with holograph additions]

Invasion of Zululand; or Defence of the Natal and Transvaal Colony from Invasion by the Zulus.

There are five main lines of advance from Natal and Transvaal into Zululand.

1. Durban – Tugela Mouth.
2. Fort Buckingham[6] – Middledrift.
3. Ladismith – Rorkes Drift.
4. Utrecht – Blood River.
5. Derby – Pongolo River.

These lines are equally adapted for attack or defence, and in the event of either contingency, a Column would have to be placed on each, thoroughly complete in every particular.

The base of the 1st Column would be Durban –
That of the 2nd Greytown
That of the 3rd Ladismith
That of the 4th Utrecht – and
That of the 5th either Derby or some place on the Pongolo River –

Commissariat, Medical and Transport arrangements would be required for each line.

Each Column should be, as far as possible uniform in its composition, & strong enough to take care of itself without assistance from any Column on its right or left –

The composition of the Columns will be as follows:
British Infantry
Royal Artillery
Mounted Volunteers[7]
Native Levies, both mounted & dismounted.
N.B. No 1 Column will have the assistance of some blue jackets and Marines –

Special arrangements should be made for keeping up

communication between the Column and its base of operations by telegraph, runner or mounted natives – as also between the several Columns –

A good supply of Entrenching and other tools should be furnished to each Column; and immediate steps should be taken to improve the approaches to drifts, and to other difficult parts of the road by working parties of Europeans and natives.

On the breaking out of hostilities such portions of the several Columns as are immediately available should be at once dispatched to the border stations, and at first a purely defensive line of action will be necessary –

To enable this to be done however, and to ensure the formation of several Columns in the quickest possible time, it is absolutely necessary that immediate steps should be taken to ascertain the military resources of the two Colonies of Natal and Transvaal as regards Europeans and natives; to organize these resources in the most efficient manner possible with due regard to their officering & arming; and to set forth on paper, (so that the information may be spread broadcast through the Colony), the rendezvous point of the several corps; the Column to which they would be attached; and the names of the officers to whom they would have to look to orders – &c, &c. –

If this plan be adopted, and the Commissariat, Medical & transport arrangements be provided for in anticipation, the Imperial and Colonial forces will be in a position to take the field at the shortest possible notice.

The Colonial European forces of Natal, should be prepared to garrison P.Maritzburg & Durban, and thus set free all the British troops that would otherwise be employed on that duty.

This work can be done by the dismounted portion of the Volunteers.

The mounted portion should be formed into two or more Regiments of 200 men; each under the command of a competent officer; and should be told off in equal proportions to the three Columns at Tugela Mouth, Middledrift, and Rorke's Drift.

The Police[8] might form one regiment and be also told off to one of the above named Columns – If it were preferred, Police and

Volunteers might be mixed up, by Regiments being composed of certain proportions of each force –

The Native Contingent furnished by Natal Colony[9] should be divided into three commands and be placed under competent officers, selected as soon as possible from the Imperial and Colonial list –

Every available native should be enrolled, so as to avoid any possibility of anxiety within the Colony as regards the loyalty of the native population –

If all the young blood amongst the Natal Zulus is separated into three distinct Corps and mixed up with the European portion of our army, any danger of their rising against us, which by some is considered not only possible but probable, would be at once removed –

Reckoning the available resources of the Colony in this respect at about 15000 men, each Column would have about 5000 natives attached to it –

The mounted Volunteers of Natal, as at present enrolled, number only 406 or two Regiments and the Natal Mounted Police number 157 or barely one Regiment – The dismounted Volunteers number 282 –

These numbers cannot of course represent the available strength of the Colony, and I have every reason to believe that at least two more regiments, or 400 men, could be raised for actual service in the field –

This fact however should be at once tested and not left in doubt, to be solved when the necessity for these services is great –

I would recommend therefore that some Imperial or Colonial officers be empowered to feel the pulse as it were, of the Colony, and to call upon those who would be willing to enroll for active service, on the same conditions as the Frontier Light horse[10] or Natal Volunteers, to send in their names and addresses to him – none but those who can ride & shoot being eligible – Officers might then be selected and preparations made for horses, arms, equipment, &c. – The Corps would be a paper one until called out for service in the Field –

The present requirements for the Colonial forces, therefore, are as follows:

Police & Volunteers to be formed into regiments and told off to their respective columns –

Non enrolled Volunteers to be formed into Regiments (on paper) in anticipation of their services being required –

Native Zulus to be formed into three distinct Corps, and the requisite European officers to be at once nominated –

Arms, ammunition and accoutrements for the volunteers & Native levies to be obtained and placed in store at suitable centres – Camp equipage, entrenching tools, cooking pots, and uniforms to be also provided –

CP 10/5

5

Lieutenant-General the Hon. F.A. Thesiger to Colonel F.A. Stanley

[Signed MS copy] P. Maritzburg, Natal
14 September 1878

Memo:-
In the event of an invasion of Zululand being decided upon I am of opinion that it will be necessary to operate on the five following lines, viz:-

1. Durban, Fort Williamson[11] on Tugela R.
2. P.Maritzburg, Grey Town & Middle drift on Tugela R.
3. Ladismith, Rorkes drift on Buffalo R.
4. Newcastle, Utrecht, Blood river
5. Middleburg, Derby, Pongolo river

Each of the columns on these five lines ought to have a complete battalion of eight companies of British Infantry = 5 Battalions.

At the principal base of operations P.Maritzburg there should be a reserve of one battalion, plus one depôt company.

At the intermediate bases of Durban and Fort Williamson – Grey Town and Middle drift on Tugela river – Ladismith and Rorke's drift – Newcastle, Utrecht and Blood river – Middleburg, Derby & Pongolo river, it will be necessary to leave a company for protection of stores, and of our lines of communication. For this duty therefore 12 companies will be required.

With each column there should be a detachment of Royal Engineers. Two complete companies, or 240 men, will not be in the least too large a reinforcement, as there will necessarily be a very large amount of engineering work to be done with each of the five columns.

It is most important that Companies should not be denuded of their Officers by their being taken away for Staff employ. It is absolutely certain that the number of Zulus opposed to us will be at least in the proportion of ten to one of our total regular force; and if a concentrated attack were made upon one of the columns before it had effected a junction with any of the others, this proportion might possibly rise to 30 or 40 to 1. The personal influence of Company Officers would, under such circumstances, be very valuable.

I shall therefore require a considerable addition to the Special Service Officers already in south Africa, who are now all usefully employed as shewn below *

A Staff Officer will be required for each of the five columns, and at the several intermediated bases.

Officers will be wanted for the command of Volunteer Corps which must be raised; and at least three Officers per column will be required to work and superintend the column transport:-

Capt Barton	– 2nd in command F.L. Horse[12]
Capt Woodgate[13]	– Staff Officer, Utrecht
Capt Brunker[14]	– Staff Officer do
	Administrator Griqualand W.
Bt Major Buller	– Commt. F.L. Horse
Capt Harvey[15]	– Staff Officer Transvaal

* Bt Major Russell – In command of 2nd Squadron of Mounted Infantry

Bt Col E Wood	– Commt Utrecht
Major Clery	– Special service in Transvaal
Bt Col. Rowlands	– Commt Troops Transvaal
Bt Col. Jarvis[16]	– Employed under Cape Colony.

---

5 Columns =	40 Companies
P.Maritzburg =	9 – do –
Durban & Ft. Williamson =	2 – do –
Grey Town & Middle drift =	2 – do –
Ladismith & Rorke's drift =	2 – do –
Newcastle, Utrecht & Blood R =	3 – do –
Middleburg, Derby & Pongolo R =	3 – do –
Pretoria =	3 – do –
Lydenburg =	2 – do –
	66

= 8 battalions & 2 cos.

Troops available

Transvaal 13th & 80th =	2 Battalions
Natal 1/13th–1/24th–2/24th & 90th =	4 – do –

Required

Royal Engineers =	2 Complete Companies

Available

Field Officers	Captains	Subalterns	Non-Commissioned Officers and Men
2	0	2	19

WO 32/7702 [Printed in *BPP* (C. 2234), enc. in no. 4.]

6

Lieutenant-General the Hon. F.A. Thesiger to Colonel F.A. Stanley

[MS copy] Maritzburg
28 September 1878

Memorandum:-
The demand which I have considered it my duty to make upon England for additional Troops,[17] after a careful consideration of the present military requirements of the Colonies of Natal and Transvaal, necessarily requires that I should set down in writing my reasons for demanding such an increase to the force at present under my command. –

I shall endeavour therefore to set forth as shortly, but as clearly as possible, my views of the military situation, with special reference to the Zulu border running along the Tugela, Buffalo, Blood, and Pongolo rivers.

An invasion of Natal by the Zulus must I consider be looked upon as more imminent now than it has been for many years. – So long as Natal and the Transvaal had separate interests the policy of the Chief of the Zulus was to play off the former against the latter as the Dutch were essentially encroaching neighbours, whilst the English in Natal had no desire to push their border towards Zululand – Hence the constant appeals made to the Natal Government by Cetewayo against the South African republic; and the general good behaviour of the Zulus towards the English.

With the annexation of the Transvaal[18] this state of things virtually came to an end, although Cetewayo himself has apparently been slow to recognize it.

Imperial interests are now equally at stake in the two Colonies – These are now geographically and politically bound together, and an invasion of one, must in the interests of both, be severely resented by the other.

When the full fact of this mutual interest is clearly recognized by Cetewayo, it will surely occur to him that he will be best able to injure us and benefit his own troops by an invasion of the well populated Natal border in preference to that of the scantily inhabited Transvaal.

Dingan's successful raid into Natal, in the year 1837, is, no doubt, looked back to with pride by many an old Zulu warrior; whilst in Natal but few colonists are, I expect, well acquainted with the occurrence which gave Weenen its melancholy name.[19]

The possibility of resisting a sudden raid into Natal by the present machinery for defence appears to me to be almost hopeless; and I am afraid that this fact must be well known to the Zulus.

The danger which threatens Natal appears to me, therefore, very great; and will be increased should it be decided to take a firm stand against the claims and encroachments lately made by Cetewayo.[20]

The Natal border line of defence may be conveniently mapped out into three Zones, – Lower, Middle, and Upper. The first contains the main road from Durban to Tugela mouth; The second that from Pietermaritzburg viâ Greytown to the middle Tugela; And the third that from Ladysmith to Rorkes drift on the Buffalo river. The upper Buffalo river border can only be approached through the Utrecht district, and will therefore be considered with that of the Transvaal. The border front from the Tugela mouth to Rorke's drift may be set down roughly as 100 miles; and the depth of each defensive zone as about 60 miles.

A very fair road runs along the border at a distance from the river boundary varying from two to twenty miles.

To protect such an extended front from an inroad of Zulus (who might without difficulty send at any moment 10,000 men for the purpose, and support the attack with an additional 10,000), it is absolutely necessary that the three lines already mentioned should be watched and guarded by an adequate force.

The most advanced line must be guarded by the Natal Natives who are located along the river banks, as there is no one else to do it.[21]

The second line or [sic] support, should be the mounted police, who are now about 200 strong – They should continually patrol the frontier road from Tugela mouth to Rorkes drift.

The third line, or reserve, should be British Infantry stationed at or near the towns of Durban, Greytown, and Ladysmith.

2,000 natives, 200 mounted Europeans and one battalion of Infantry and 2 guns, does not appear to me one man too many for the protection of each zone, although it would not be necessary to keep the whole force of natives and mounted men continually under arms provided a sufficient number were always on outpost duty or patrolling, and the remainder ready to assemble at short notice.

The total force required therefore is 6,000 natives, 600 mounted men, 6 guns, and three battalions of British Infantry.

In order to be able to strengthen any portion of this line of defence, should the whole force of Zulus be thrown upon it, there should be a battalion of British Infantry, 2 guns, and some mounted Infantry ready for the purpose at Pietermaritzburg.

With regard to the first line of defence the natives are liable to be called out for military service by command of the Lieut. Governor; and they are so far organised that under the orders of the Resident Magistrate they can be made to assemble under their own chiefs at certain fixed places of rendezvous.

They have not as yet however been divided and subdivided into units which represent our battalions, our companies and sections, nor have they had as yet European Commanders told off to them.

This force therefore, if called out, would be difficult to manage; and would not feel as much confidence in its own efficiency, as if it were organized on a system nearer approaching to that of our own Army, – what I should like to see carried out is as follows:-

Every tenth fighting native to have a gun and to be made a section leader of nine men. – *

Ten sections to make up a Company to be commanded by a European. –

Ten Companies to be considered a battalion, and to be commanded by a selected European, either Military or Civil, the former for choice. –

* The natives other than the section leaders being armed with assegai and shield.

The 100 rifles required for each battalion to be kept in some central place when the Companies are not called out. –

A certain amount of practice ammunition should be given for the use of the section leaders, who should be encouraged to make themselves effective shots.

With similar organization the duty of patrolling and outposts could be efficiently carried out, and the whole force put into the field at very short notice.

The first line of defence has thus been provided for.

The second line, or supports, has now to be considered. –

The position of this line is in my opinion clearly marked out by the frontier road extending from Tugela mouth to Rorkes drift.

The mounted police should be placed on this line and made to patrol it; they are at present too far back. The mounted Volunteers should be told off to reinforce this line if required.

The presence of mounted men so far to the front will give confidence both to the natives in front, and to the Colonists in rear, of them.

The British Infantry would remain at Durban, Greytown, and Ladysmith until required; but if thought advisable could push forward two Companies about half way to the supporting line.

The above rough sketch of a defensive scheme for Natal shows in my opinion the minimum of precaution which should be taken – so long as there is such a threatening force so near to its borders.

I cannot however conceal from myself that security from invasion depends almost entirely upon the forbearance of Cetewayo.

Unless the Natal natives can be not only depended upon to fight for us, but organized in such a manner as to be immediately available in our hour of need, I do not see in what manner I can reckon upon them as part of my fighting force.

There remains then but a few mounted police and Volunteers to represent the effective Colonial force.

I have at the present moment in Natal Colony but 15 Companies of British Infantry, say two battalions – but five out of this number are destined for Utrecht where they are really urgently required, as at the present moment should an invasion of

Zulus be made between the Buffalo and Pongolo rivers, there are but three Companies of British Infantry and 2 guns to meet it.

Along the border of the Blood river there are no friendly natives; there are no mounted police or volunteers; and although the Utrecht district is not as tempting, as regards plunder to be acquired, as the Natal Colony, still it can be made the door of entrance into Natal, and it also represents part of the disputed boundary territory, and as such might present inducements for invasion.

5 Companies of 90th Lt Infantry and 2 guns are now waiting at Pietermaritzburg until transport can be provided to send them to Utrecht. On their arrival that district will have 8 Companies (or one battalion), with 4 guns, for its protection. – This force can scarcely be considered sufficient to protect so extended a border as that from the junction of the Blood and Buffalo rivers to the Pongolo river a distance of at least 20 miles.

Owing to the disturbances in the N.E. portion of the Transvaal, the total force of that Colony, both Imperial and Colonial, is employed upwards of 150 miles away from the Zulu border;[22] and the S.E. portion of the Transvaal is thus without any protection from invasion.

The Amaswazi tribe on the northern border of Zululand would undoubtedly defend their own country; but although hereditary enemies of the Zulus, they could not be depended upon to assist us, unless backed up by a considerable European force.

I consider therefore that for the defence of that portion of the Transvaal border, one battalion of British Infantry should be stationed at or near Luneberg on the Pongolo river.[23]

For defensive purposes alone, therefore, Natal and Transvaal Colonies require three battalions of Infantry in addition to what they have already got.

The 1–24th Regiment from the Cape Colony may I believe be relied upon as available, but the remaining two must be sent from England.

WO 32/7699 [Printed in *BPP* (C. 2234), enc. 1 in no. 9]

7

Lieutenant-General the Hon. F.A. Thesiger to Colonel H.E. Wood

[Holograph] P. Maritzburg
1 October 1878

Sir B. Frere is very anxious to give some encouragement to the German settlers at Luneberg, who have sent him a petition pointing out the precarious position in which they are placed – I have told him that at present it will be quite out of the question to send them any troops, and that I doubt much whether, when the whole of the 90th L.I. are concentrated at Utrecht, it would be prudent to weaken that garrison – Eventually I intend that Rowlands force should come down that way, but that is in the dim future and he must finish off Sekukuni first – In the mean time what had best be done? I should be very sorry to hear of these settlers trekking away from Luneberg, but if the state of affairs gets worse, which I expect it will, we can hardly reckon upon their remaining unless they are supported in some kind of ways. Could you manage to raise a volunteer force in the neighbourhood which could be stationed at Luneberg for the present – How are the Germans off for arms and ammunition?

Is Luneberg a defensible place?, and has anything been done to improve its capabilities?[24]

I should feel much obliged if you would give the subject your attention, and let me know what you think could be done – would it be any good getting Schermbrucker over to take charge of the station, and of any volunteers that might be raised?

I was very sorry to hear of the death of your horse – What a country it is!

Try and find out what place will be the best for horses during the time for horsesickness. Standerton is too far away and in the wrong direction. –[25]

Do what you can to find out how many Boers in your neighbourhood would come out for an invasion of Zululand – I have an idea that I shall send Carrington eventually to command them – They will make good Cossacks, and as such be useful –

Is Utrecht capable of Defence in the event of a rush of Zulus being made upon it?[26] It will be well to be prepared for such a contingency as they are beginning to be somewhat suspicious of our intentions –

In all matters connected with volunteers you must work through the civil authorities of Transvaal.

WP 26/2

8

Lieutenant-General Lord Chelmsford to Sir Theophilus Shepstone

[Unsigned holograph] Pieter Maritzburg
21 October 1878

. . . I send you a memorandum regarding the redistribution of the British Troops serving under Colonel Rowlands' command – I have talked the matter over with Sir Bartle Frere and he quite agrees with me that it would be a mistake to hold onto an untenable position, and that it will be far better to accept the inevitable, and to give up any further active operations against Sekukuni, until the season becomes favourable for man and beast –

Colonel Rowlands should endeavour to fix upon healthy positions, on the two roads with Sekukuni's country which are divided by the Lulu mountains, from which a fresh advance could be made when the time arrives – Three companies of the 80th Regiment on each of these roads ought to be quite sufficient to show that we have no intention of permanently abandoning our attack upon Sekukuni – We shall have now eight months to settle the Zulu question, and by that time we ought to be free to secure sufficient force against Sekukuni, which will enable us to act with effect upon both sides of the Lulu mountains, and thus effectively undeceive him as to the impregnability of his position –

The sooner we get the 13th Regt near Swaziland the better. Cetewayo has been evidently pushing forward Umbelini in order to see what notice we shall take of it, and he will no doubt whilst secretly applauding the raid, deny his responsibility for it to us – [27]

Five companies of the 90th L.I. and 2 guns are now on their way to Utrecht – I shall feel happier when they get there, as Colonel Wood's present numbers are quite inadequate for looking after Luneberg as well as Utrecht –

I am very glad to hear that you are, at some time or other, to meet Sir Bartle Frere and Sir Henry Bulwer at Utrecht – It will save a good deal of time and a great deal of paper; but how a line of action is to be decided upon which will meet the discordant views of Natal and Transvaal, and at the same time satisfy Imperial interests, I am at a loss to understand. – The Gordian knot must be cut if no one can untie it!

TS 33

9

Memorandum by Lieutenant-General Lord Chelmsford

[MS copy] 23 October 1878

Memorandum on the military requirements of the Natal Colony with regard to its N Eastern Border should offensive or defensive measures against Zululand be considered necessary.

I have just returned from a tour of inspection of the N. Eastern border of Natal from above Rorke's drift to Tugela mouth.[28]

I rode viâ Greytown to Helmakaar and from there to the Eastern slopes of the Biggarsberg range overlooking the valley of the Buffalo.

Retracing my steps to Burrup's hotel, 9 miles from Greytown, I then struck across country to Kranz Kop and from there by the so called military road to the Lower Tugela drift. –

The direct road to Utrecht viâ Greytown is in very fair order, but requires working parties at once on the portions of it between the Mooi and Tugela rivers which is the only heavy gradient along the whole road.

The ponts at the Mooi and Tugela rivers are in very bad repair and ought to be at once replaced by new ones of greater carrying capacity. – An additional pont at each river should be provided so as to avoid delay should the one get injured and so &c [sic] to facilitate the crossing of wagons &c, when both are in good working order.

I should wish to make use of the district road to Utrecht in preference to the one viâ Estcourt and Ladysmith as being much shorter, and more convenient from a military point of view. –

Greytown would thus become the principal supply depôt, and could, if necessary, feed the three columns watching respectively Rorke's drift, Middledrift and Lower drift.

Looking to the season of the year in which active operations may have to be carried on, and to the possibility of heavy rains producing serious sickness in the low lying land both amongst men and beasts it seemed to me most desirable to select camping grounds in elevated positions, where the troops could be assembled and where they could remain either for defensive purposes, or until everything was ready for an advance.

Such positions I have found on the Biggarsberg near Helpmekaar; on the high ground near Kranz Kop; and in the military road near Thring's Store about 26 miles from the Tugela mouth.

The two first-named camps would guard effectually Rorke's drift and Middledrift, and a detachment might be pushed forward from Thring's Store Camp to watch the Lower Tugela drift.

It would I believe be impossible to find three healthier spots in the whole colony.

There are at present two wagon roads from Helpmekaar to Rorke's drift – A good one which makes a wide detour and may be considered as two days march distant: and a bad one which takes a direct line and could be easily accomplished in one day.

This second road should be at once improved to the fullest extent possible, as its importance both for offence and defence would be very great, unless a more convenient road into the Buffalo valley could be made at a point about six miles from Helpmekaar, where the features of ground appeared to me to offer great facilities – If this new road could be opened out, the distance to Rorkes drift would be still more decreased. –

After an inspection of the ground on both sides of the Tugela river as seen from Kranz Kop, I have come to the conclusion that it would be unadvisable to send a British regiment into Zululand by this route – The valley is very deep and must be extremely hot; and the country is so rugged and broken on the Zulu side as would entail very great physical exertion, which, combined with the heat, would inevitably knock off young soldiers – The difficulties of transport and hospital arrangements would also be very great.

I propose therefore to send in a well organized native column by this route, which should be well supplied with European leaders.

From Kranz Kop I took the road which passes by the Norwegian and American mission stations[29] to the Lower Tugela drift .

This road was in very fair order. It is an important one as regards the defence of the Colony from a Zulu raid, as it afforded good internal communication and is situated at a convenient distance from the border.

The position of Fort Williamson near the Lower Tugela drift is very faulty, and I do not recommend its occupation. There is a site close to Smith's Hotel overlooking the drift and the Zulu border, which is far superior in a military point of view: and whenever the time arrives for placing troops close to the Zulu country I should certainly prefer to occupy it.[30] – Additional ponts and boats will be required at this drift if an invasion of Zululand be decided upon.

The result of my inspection has been to convince me that Natal possesses a most defensible border against an attack from the Zulus, if only it be properly occupied.

The natives in the Umsinga and Tugela locations have not however, as far as I am aware, been instructed as to how they are to act in the event of a raid being made; nor are there at present any Colonial forces patrolling the border road running from Rorkes drift to Lower Tugela drift.

I have gathered from numerous sources that the Natal border natives are well disposed towards the Government, and quite ready to fight for it if required. They are puzzled however to understand why they are not told what they are expected to do, and many say openly that they feel sure the English do not trust them.

CP 10/13

10

Lieutenant-General Lord Chelmsford to Sir Bartle Frere

[Holograph (signed as Thesiger)] P. Maritzburg
26 October 1878

Border Police

Memorandum

In the event of hostilities occurring with the Zulus, it will be very desirable that every precaution should be taken to prevent, as far as possible, information being conveyed by the movement of our troops to the enemy.

This will not be an easy matter, but I consider that the experiment should be made –

It occurs to me that if a paid border police were organized, and placed under specially selected European officers, told off to fixed districts, much might be done –

Orders should be issued prohibiting natives belonging to this colony from crossing to the opposite side of the border river under any pretense whatever; and all natives coming across from Zululand into Natal, should as a matter of course be made prisoners.

This rule would not in any way prevent the employment of spies, as they might be directed to give themselves up, on their return, at one of the police stations, from which they should of course be forwarded to the European Superintendent –

In addition to the Border Police, there might also I think be extra police maintained for the inspection of native kraals on or near the Border; so as to prevent the harbouring of natives not belonging to Natal –

Special assistant magistrates should I think be employed on duty in the several native locations, so that any meetings for an improper purpose might be prevented, or at all events brought to notice; and that the pulse of the natives in Natal may be felt daily.

I merely submit this paper as a very rough outline of what appears me desirible [sic].[31]

CP 10/17

11

Lieutenant-General Lord Chelmsford to Colonel H.E. Wood

[Holograph (signed as Thesiger)] Pieter Maritzburgh
26 October 1878

. . . My view of your action,[32] as seen from a distance, was, that you had rather imitated the Irishman who, finding his sheet too short, cut off a piece from the bottom and sewed it on to the top – In order to strengthen Luneberg you weakened Utrecht and Newcastle – Charity begins at home, and I cannot but think that the two last named places deserved your first consideration – It was unfortunate also your being obliged to take away the garrison of Newcastle, as altho' I quite admit that the station is of very little use to you as Commandant of Utrecht, still it is one of halting places and depôts for troops on the move to Pretoria – The action of Mr Engelbrecht in refusing to sell you mealies at a remunerative rate after the arrival of the garrison rather confirms me in the belief that the good people of Luneberg have an eye to business – Whilst on our last trip we met five waggons one march from Greytown en route to this place that had just left Luneberg – The Germans with these waggons had left their wives and families at Luneberg altho they had signed a petition to Sir B. Frere pointing out the danger of their position! They are now on their way back with waggons, stored no doubt with articles that they will sell at a very good profit to our soldiers –

As I have no intention to leave a permanent garrison of your regiments at Luneberg when the time comes for an advance, I have telegraphed to Schermbrucker about himself and his Germans – [33] I want the 90th L.I. to be all together as one complete battalion. Will not be one man too many when we enter Zululand –

I would not trust too implicitly to Mr Rudolph to let it be known that you rely on his opinion –

The Swazis, I hear, have no faith in him, because he originally belonged to the South African Republic, and was employed then in a manner which they considered detrimental to their interests – He is also one of Sir Theophilus Shepstone's own men and I fancy of his school – [34] He will therefore, if that is so, do his best to prevent you dealing direct with the natives, and he will most assuredly turn your flank, if he sees an opportunity – I may be doing an injustice to a very estimable man, but I give you my opinion for what it is worth –

WP 26/6

12

Memorandum by Lieutenant-General Lord Chelmsford

[Holograph (signed as Thesiger)] P. Maritzburg 30 October 1878

Memorandum

In the event of an advance being made into Zululand it is I consider very probable that a large number of Cetewayo's subjects may wish to avoid fighting, and may desire to come across our Border for protection –

Every reliable account from that country shows conclusively that Cetewayo is most unpopular, and those who are best informed regarding the state of feelings in Zululand are of the opinion that an internal revolution is not only possible but probable – [35]

It would seem well therefore to be prepared for a considerable exodus of Zulus from either their own country into British territory, or into that of friendly natives on the North, South and West and to lay down beforehand instructions as to their disposal –

Even supposing that I am too sanguine regarding the numbers that will desert Cetewayo, it is certain that singly, or in small parties, refugees will come across and will have to be provided for, as it would clearly be undesirable to allow them to remain near the border line –

I would venture to recommend then that clear instructions be laid down for those officers who may be in command on the border; or for the magistrates and Police officers who may be in the Border Districts of Natal and the Transvaal as to the manner in which refugees are to be disposed of – and the locality to which they are to be sent –

It would also seem advisable to arrange beforehand the machinery by which these refugees will be housed and fed –

As also it is quite possible that Oham and his following may decide to escape from Zululand into the Swazi country, some communication should be made to the king of that country on the subject; and it would be well if some Border Agent were appointed in anticipation of such an eventuality so as to prevent the possibility of misunderstanding occurring between the Swazis and Oham's people –

As it is quite possible that refugees may even now be coming across the Natal border to escape from conscription and from the troubles which seem to be imminent, I would strongly recommend that all such be at once disarmed and forwarded to some part of this colony far away from the border where they should be fed and cared for –

I would also recommend that immediately war is proclaimed against Cetewayo, those now living under his rule should be informed that any desiring to escape from his tyranny will be allowed to take refuge in British territory and, after being disarmed, will be fed and cared for, until peace is again established –

A confidential message might be sent to John Dunn in this sense at once, as he could be very useful in getting it made known when, (as I conclude he will) he comes across to our side on the breaking out of hostilities –

Our border agent with the Swazis could also communicate with

Oham (supposing that he also comes across) and make use of him also to spread the intelligence on his side of Zululand –

I may mention that I have already received information that refugees have come across the Tugela within the last few days, and, if this be true, it would seem well at once to consider the question as to how they should be disposed of –

CP 13/1

13

Memorandum by Lieutenant-General Lord Chelmsford

[MS copy (signed as Thesiger)] 5 November 1878

Memorandum

With reference to a previous memorandum of mine regarding postal arrangements for the several columns which may be organized either for the defence of Natal, or for an advance into Zululand, I would suggest that lateral communication should, if possible, be established between Rorke's Drift, Middledrift, and the Lower Tugela drift.

This lateral communication might, I think, be established by utilising the border police posts, which have already, I understand, been organized along the Buffalo & Tugela rivers.

In order to test the practicality of this proposition, I would suggest that the border Agents, Mr Fynney and Mr Fynn, should be instructed to send a written message one to the other, through Middledrift, the date and hour of departure and receipt being carefully noted at the three points.

Full particulars regarding the experiment should then be sent to Pietermaritzburg for our information, with any suggestions that might occur to Mr Fynney or Mr Fynn for establishing regular communication along that border line.

CP 10/30

14

Lieutenant-General Lord Chelmsford to Colonel H.E. Wood

[Holograph (unsigned)]

PMBurg
7 November 1878

Many thanks for your kind letter dated 3d inst – My fathers death has been a great blow to me.[36] Up to the last his constitution was so vigorous that I had every reason to hope that I might have found him alive and well on my return from this country –

. . . Our Transport Department here has entirely broken down – I am endeavouring to place it on a more satisfactory footing by introducing combatant officers and I have my eye on Clery to be Director of Transport in your part of the country. The Commissariat, Strickland excepted, are rabid, but I do not care for that – We shall break down utterly under present arrangements –

Since finishing this letter I have made up my mind to carry out my views regarding transport as contained in the memorandum which Crealock is sending you – Kindly send it on to Clery, and help him to start the system The details will of course have to be clearly laid down – I only send you the outline –

WP 26/11

15

Memorandum by Lieutenant-General Lord Chelmsford for District Commissary-General E. Strickland

n.d. [?7 November 1878][37]

[Holograph rough notes and augmented MS copy (unsigned)]

1. The Transport Department will be divided into two distinct branches

Administrative
Executive

2. The Officers and personnel told off for duty in the first branch will have no executive duties to perform, but the Executive must of course, to a certain extent, perform some administrative work.

3. The Administrative Department will be entirely under the Commissary General and will, in fact, be his Transport Staff for purely office work.

4. Three Directors of Transport will be appointed for the three Divisions named on the accompanying paper.

5. They will receive their orders direct from the Lieut. General Commanding, through the Commissary General alone, or, in his absence through one of the Head Quarter Staff.

6. No orders will be issued direct to any of the Officers or subordinates of these Directors except under very special circumstances – a copy of such orders must always be sent to the Director for his information, and to the D.C.General for the information of the Lieut. General Commanding.

7. The Transport depôts will be entirely under the command of the Directors of Transport.

8. The Head Commissariat Officer of Districts will keep the director of Transport fully informed as to his requirements, and when such requirements cannot be met at once, a report will be made to Head Quarters both by Commissariat Officer and by Director of Transport.

9. The present Transport Staff will be at once told off, either for administrative or executive duties, and no changes will be made in the distribution when once determined upon, without the direct sanction of the Lieut. General Commanding.

10. Unless the District Commissary General is prepared with a scheme which, on consideration, may be considered superior to the one now roughly sketched out, I consider that this one should

at once be accepted, and every effort made by his Department to cause it to work smoothly.

11. I will at once, as a temporary measure, sanction the appointment of officers of the regular forces to the several posts; until the fifteen Officers for Transport duty, that I have applied for, be sent out.

12. The Directors of Transport will be authorized under the orders of the Lieut. General Commanding to make, when required, purchases of Transport within their District. The purchase of Transport outside these Districts will be made under special arrangements of the District Commissary General.

CP 5/20 [Printed in *BPP* (C. 2234), enc. 2 in no. 19.]

16

Lieutenant-General Lord Chelmsford to Colonel H.E. Wood

[Holograph (signed as Thesiger)]

PMBurg
13 November 1878.

Should I receive orders to enter Zululand my first step would be to order your force, and that at Helpmekaar (when it gets there), to enter Zululand first beyond the borders, form advanced depôts in the most advantageous position procurable, and throw up entrenchments for its protection –

It is quite possible that the Zulus would come down and attack us, and we should therefore have to be ready for such a contingency –

I should of course wish you to have all the companies of the 90th Lt Infantry at your disposal, and I shall hope to be able to arrange so that they shall all be with you – You will have 4 guns; and most probably the Mounted Infantry under Major Russell.

What you want sadly however are natives, and unless Hamo

joins you with his fighting men, I do not quite see where they are to come from –

The Lower Tugela & Rorkes drift columns[38] will each have 2000 natives and I should much like you to have the same, but I could not get them for you out of this colony without an immense deal of correspondence and of pressure on the part of the High Commissioner, which I am anxious, if possible, to avoid –

I hope you will try therefore to raise your own native force. I shall also send Colonel Pearson's column across the Tugela, as they can make themselves quite secure under the protection of the 12 lb Armstrongs, which will be in position as soon as the Naval Brigade reach Fort Pearson – Three columns placed at the points mentioned, must force Cetywayo to keep his regiments mobilized, and he will find great difficulty in feeding them – It will take some little time to fill up our advanced depôts properly, but we shall be masters of the situation and can afford to take our time –

Rowlands column[39] will I expect have to come to Luneberg, viâ Derby, and then, if necessary, can move to the East along the left bank of the Pongolo. On a map[40] drawn by Drummond he shews a road leading due South from Derby to the upper part of the Umkumyana River where it hits off the Jagpad or Hunting Road – At the point where the river and the two roads meet he says there is plenty of water and plenty of wood – By the scale it ought to be about 12 miles from where the Hunting road crosses the Pongolo R – This place, if it answers the description of Drummond's map, would be an admirable position for the 1/13th Regiment to hold preparatory to advancing, but how could supplies be got to it? On comparing Drummond's map with the latest Zululand one just sent to you,[41] it seems to me that the spot I allude to must be near that called "White Koppie" on the latters one – Any information about the road I allude to and the particular point will be thankfully received [.] Clery might get it for me – Strickland is working out my transport scheme, and I shall hope to be able to send you an account of it soon . . .

WP 26/12

17
Lieutenant-General Lord Chelmsford to Colonel H.E. Wood

[Holograph] PMBurg
23 November 1878

. . . You have authority to raise as many Dutchmen as you can turn out when you think it necessary – I am not raising any in this colony as I do not think it worth while – I can get quite as good men from the old colony[42] and at much more moderate terms –

Politically it may be a good move for you to gather some Dutchmen under your wings – as to what pay they should get I am puzzled – Durnford says that he can raise plenty in Natal at 15/- a day the man bringing his own horse and weapon – You might take that as a guide, but from what you say of Mr Potters turning up his nose at such remuneration I am afraid the amount will not bribe them – [43]

I am in hopes of getting sufficient recruits from the Old Colony to raise Buller's corps to 300 strong. If to that number I can add 100 mounted natives, will you not have enough? With two British regiments, 6 guns and Bullers lot – I should be sorry for the Zulu army if they attacked you –

The Natal Government will certainly not give their consent to your enlisting at Ladismith. I have had a good deal of trouble in getting the required number for this portion of the command – and any addition to the number already sanctioned will certainly be met with opposition – I am not giving all the natives guns – only to those who know something about how to use one – as scouts they will do quite as well with assegai & shield, and in pursuit or in charging better – We shall have to put the redcoats forward to bear the first brunt, and then I think the natives will go in – I am inclined to think that the first experience of the power of the Martini Henrys will be such a surprise to the Zulus that they will not be formidable after the first effort – I have ordered some guns and ammunition to be sent to you when it arrives from Cape Town – Things move slowly in this country. Potter senior's account of the road from Derby due South differs altogether from Potter junior. The former describes it as fairly easy – Perhaps this was because it leads towards his own abandoned store !!

Macleod's account of his interview with the Swazis shews at all events that they spoke out their opinion honestly – I am inclined to gather from it that we shall get assistance from them but not perhaps at first –

Oham must be told that "he is either for us or against us" and that if he remains passively in his kraal whilst we are advancing he must not be surprised if we take him for an enemy – I have no intention of recognizing neutrals inside the Zulu border –

I will take care that we have the power to get rid of incompetent commanders sharp –

I do not quite understand what you mean by "martial law"? Is it the old Dutch Commando law? Our martial law, if proclaimed, would not assist you in getting natives –

Major Hopton[44] is hard at work trying to get order out of chaos in the Transport department here – how is yours working?

My letter to Lt W E Gilbert which passed through your hands will have shown you that I am anxious to bring the 1/13th down near Luneberg.

I am afraid fuel will be a difficulty to us during our advance into Zululand – It seems very scarce along the Zulu-Utrecht border – Colonel Glyn & Degacher will be at Helpmekaar, with Russell and Barrow and Lonsdale. You will find Mr Hughes Commissariat[45] who has been ordered to Utrecht, a good man I think – He has worked very well in the Transvaal under difficult circumstances –

I wish I could see my way to Utrecht; but alas! I am tied by the leg here until I have got all my native contingent mobilized.

I am not in any way uneasy about you – Your sheet will soon be long enough to prevent your cutting any portion off the bottom to sew on to the top!!!

Sir Bartle Frere has just come in to read me a letter he has written to Sir Theophilus Shepstone about your desire to have Martial Law proclaimed – and he has been asked to communicate with you on the subject – Kindly get Rudolph to send you any information he can give you regarding what I assume is an old

Dutch law and rest assured that whatever can be done in this matter shall be done –

Organize your native levy in any way that you think will attract – They shall be called Wood's Irregulars, in contradistinction to our native Battalions[46] which are intended to be very regular! But if you get martial law you will be able to organize, will you not? in any manner that you chose – I have had to fight Durnford in his efforts to get something different for his portion of the contingent to what was laid down and have steadily refused.[47] So do not alter organization unless you find it absolutely necessary as it will lead to discontent here –

Sir Bartle Frere wishes you to tell Captain Macleod that "his proceedings are entirely approved".[48]

WC II/2/2

18

Lieutenant-General Lord Chelmsford to Colonel F.A. Stanley

[Signed MS copy] Pietermaritzburg
Natal
25 November 1878

Since the date of my last dispatch, nothing has been reported from Zululand to call for remark.

Messengers were dispatched about the 17th Instant, by H.E. the High Commissioner to the Zulu King, directing him to call his great council together to receive certain communications which would be ready for delivery to his messengers about the 7th December, in the neighbourhood of the Lower Tugela Drift.

This refers to the award of the High Commissioner as final Referee on the Arbitration Commission on the disputed Boundary – followed by certain demands, considered necessary by His Excellency on behalf of the Imperial Government in connection with certain outrages committed lately on our Border by those for whose good behaviour the Zulu King is responsible.

Guarantees for the future and reparation for the past are demanded, – the main point being the present disbanding of his army, its future organization, and the reception of a British resident.

There is no doubt in my mind but that the guarantees demanded are absolutely necessary for the future peace of South Africa. As to whether they will be accepted or not, is a question which I do not venture to offer an opinion, but in the event of their non-acceptance, an advance into Zululand will be absolutely necessary.

The Zulu army is at present under arms,[49] and their outposts and our own are within easy rifle shot every night in the Lower Tugela.

From the Utrecht district Colonel Wood reports signs of restlessness, but I do not anticipate any overt act of hostility at present in that direction.

The 1/13th Light Infantry are now at Derby, and will shortly move to the neighbourhood of Lüneberg – The Frontier Light Horse is between the latter place and Utrecht, recruiting after their late severe work, and great loss in horses. – [50] The 1st Squadron Imperial Mounted Infantry under Major Russell is concentrating for a like purpose at Standerton.

The 5 companies of the 1/24th will arrive here in a few days from K.W.Town[51] on their way to Helpmakaar in the neighbourhood of Rorke's Drift –

The Natal Mounted Volunteers are to be called out at once, and within 10 days from now the whole European force, Imperial and Colonial, available for operations in Zululand, should such be found necessary will be concentrated at the posts already decided upon, whence an advance can be made.

As to my power, however, of moving these forces within any specified time from now, I am not at present assured. The difficulty lies in the Commissariat and Transport arrangements necessary to enable the troops to advance, and live in an enemy's country, which is destitute of any supplies beyond cattle. On this subject, however, I have the honor of addressing you by the mail in a separate letter.

The European cadres for the Natal Native Contingent (which will number 7,000 natives) are arriving, and will be in their districts within a week's time, but delay will arise in mobilizing them, owing to my demands on the Surveyor General of the

Ordnance[52] for Camp equipment not having been met. It is impossible at this time of the year to encamp a force without shelter of some kind.

The information from the Amaswazi forwarded by the Commissioner, Captain McLeod is not, I consider, of altogether an unsatisfactory nature, inasmuch that though they decline to join us until they see that we are more than a match for the Zulus, yet there is every reason to believe that after the first success they will be found on our side.

With the sanction of H.E. the High Commissioner I am recruiting 300 mounted white men in the Wodehouse District of the Cape Colony with the view of increasing the Frontier Light Horse from 200 to 300 men, and supplementing the force of mounted Infantry under Major Russell.

This would not have been necessary to the same extent, had the reinforcements from England, for which I applied, been likely to arrive.

Reasons of economy, together with inability to find Officers, alone prevents my asking for permission to raise a larger number – but it is right I should inform you that the cheapest Military force in South Africa is, without doubt, a British Regiment; and I have found that men drawn from its ranks, after a short training, are preferable for mounted duties to the usual volunteer corps.

WO 32/7704 [Printed in *BPP* (C. 2222), enc. in no. 27]

19

Lieutenant-General Lord Chelmsford to Colonel H.E. Wood

[Holograph] PMBurg
4 December 1878

I showed your letter regarding the Swazies coming down to the Pongolo R. to Sir Bartle Frere – who is going to write to Sir Theophilus Shepstone on the subject. There is no intention I find of allowing the Swazies any more country in that direction; but at the same time it is most important that we should do everything in our power to induce them to move down to the Zulu border and to remain there whilst our columns are advancing. Perhaps Mr Rudolph may be able to suggest some inducement which would be strong enough to produce the desired result – Money or arms? The Pongolo valley ought to be better guarded than by the Luneberg garrison, even though such a redoubtable hero as Schermbrucker keeps watch and ward there;[53] but unless the Swazies help us I do not see where you can look for help –

I find, on reading Chase's History of Natal, that in 1838 Andries Pretorius with a commando of 400 men took only six days to march from Rorkes drift to the hill where Retief and his party were massacred, which is 8 or 10 miles N.W. of Emtonjaneni – They entered Zululand on the 13th of December during the rainy season; and I cannot make out that they lost any horses from sickness – The road Pretorius took is the same as Glyn's column will move along,[54] and it completely turns the Mahlazatye position – I should hope therefore to give your column a good deal of indirect support when the time comes for you to take that position –

Since writing thus far I have had a talk with a Mr Bester who was one of those who went in with Pretorius – He says they took 80 waggons with them and the country was hard & open the whole way until they got to the north of the Umfelosi R.

Can you get any information for me regarding the amount of water at Rorkes drift – Is the drift often unfordible [sic] for any length of time? and will a pont or ponts be absolutely necessary if we want to keep open our line of communications by that route? I am making enquiries in every direction about this point, and I have ordered two ponts to be made in case of the drift being unfordable – There is a large working party on the Dutch road leading from Helpmakaar to Rorkes drift, and instead of your feeding the former place I should hope to be able to feed you and your column from its depôt – The High Commissioners award and demands from Cetywayo will be delivered next week at the Lower Tugela drift, perhaps on Monday – [55] We may therefore receive instructions to move forward very shortly – I wish we were better prepared; but by advancing slowly we shall create uneasiness in the mind of Cetywayo, and we may possibly induce him to attack us, which will save a great deal of trouble –

I cannot put my native contingent into the Field for want of shelter – Tents demanded were refused by the War Department and now South Africa can kindly meet our demands, all the orders have been sent all over the country –

I have no intention of taking Clery away from his present work[56] until transport arrangements have been brought into something like order – There are however a number of officers come out from home for Transport duties and they must be employed –

You had better keep Russell's Mounted Infantry under your command near Utrecht for the present – Water is still too scanty at Helpmakaar for many horses –

WC II/2/2

20

Lieutenant-General Lord Chelmsford to Sir Theophilus Shepstone

[Holograph] PMBurg
7 December 1878

. . . I have written to Col Rowlands telling him that he must not resign – [57] It would be mistaken for him from a professional point of view – As an independent Field Commander he is no doubt a failure, but I will not put him in such a position again –

I hear that he sits in his tent & writes all day – That way will not do in S. African warfare – A commander must ride about and see the country himself, or he will never be able to handle his troops properly – In the last attack on Umzocts town [?] – He ought to have held his position for a couple of days at least – To go up to a place and come down again a few hours after is waste of life for it can produce no effect on the native mind.[58] But to go up to a place and remain there which he could have done perfectly would have had an excellent effect

Can you in any ways induce the Swazies to come down as far as the Pongolo when we advance into Zululand? It will strengthen my hand enormously –

TS 35

21

Lieutenant-General Lord Chelmsford to Colonel H.E. Wood

[Holograph]

PMBurg
10 December 1878

You have done wonders with the Dutchmen and I am quite sure that the High Commissioner will be as much obliged to you from a political point of view as I am to you from a military one – [59] We will send you the printed instructions by next mail I hope –

As regards the move of the 1/13th carry out whatever you think best in the public interest – [60] Send a copy of your order here but don't wait for approval –

Glyn ought to be able to communicate with you when you reach your "6000 ft high" camp, as I have ascertained that the country south of the Umvelosi is quite open and there is a dried track to the Mhlazatye from a point about 10 or 15 miles due South from the E of Emtonjaneni (Durnford's map)

I do not believe in the Zulus professions for peace – [61] The Swazis firmly believe that the redcoats have had to retire from Sekukunis country, and as far as Griqualand West it is believed that we have had a repulse – Why then should the Zulus who believe themselves to be invincible, be suddenly in such a fright as they would lead us to suppose – It is simply a ruse I am sure – Cetywayo and his Indunas want of course to delay hostilities until the mealie crop has been gathered in; but our game is to attack them before their food supply is secured – I am only waiting now until the Natal Native Contingent is a "fait accompli". Lonsdales lot[62] ought to be together at Sand spruit valley 12 miles from Helpmekaar, on the 18th – Major Graves men will I hope turn out a few days later – [63]

Durnfords column is still in want of Europeans for 2000 men!![64] but I shall stay here for him – I shall go down to the Lower Tugela first and on along the border line to Greytown, from where I shall move to Helpmekaar – once at Helpmekaar I shall be in reach of you, and you may rely upon my paying you a visit sharp –

It may be as well to prepare your Dutchmen for a decision on the boundary question adverse to their claims, altho' as far as private individuals are concerned it will make no difference, as they will be allowed to occupy the farms they have deserted on the same terms as before only quitrent will be paid to Zulus instead of to Transvaal Govt – [65]

WC II/2/2

22

Lieutenant-General Lord Chelmsford to Colonel H.E. Wood

[Holograph] PMBurg
11 December 1878

You may remember that I wrote to you some weeks ago regarding a trader of the name of Nunn[66] who stated that he had lived for about 16 years in Oham's country, and professed to have influence over him –

He is now in PMBurg and states his intention of going back to Utrecht on Monday next (16th)

I propose to give him a letter of introduction to yourself in case you may wish to open communications with Oham through him –

He is positive that Oham will come over to our side if only we can assure him that his land will not be forfeited – [67]

On that point I spoke to Sir Bartle Frere this morning and he has desired me to tell you that you are at liberty to assure Oham, and any other Chief who professes himself as anxious not to fight against us, that if they come out of Zululand and sit quiet in such locality as we may appoint, they will be reinstated in their own lands when the Zulu question has been finally settled, and that they will be recognized as independent owing allegiance only to Her Majesty through her representative –

If Oham does come over to our side, it will go very far towards solving our difficulties – I cannot myself feel very sanguine in the matter, as I cannot see on what grounds we can assume that Oham believes our forces to be superior to those of Cetywayo; and unless he does so, why should he come over? –

12 Dec[er] Drummond sends us the following story about Oham – When Oham was at the Kings, he, in full council asked Usirayo who he was that Zululand should be embroiled by him? – What family did he belong to? was he not only a dog? He is then stated to have said that he would not assist the king with a single head of cattle to pay any fine the English might ask on account of Usirayo's outrages – In this the other princes followed suit – You must take the story for what it is worth –

I have detained Buller here until after the arrival of Bakers horse from Kokstadt who are expected tomorrow – [68]

Griffith has telegraphed to say that he can send 500 Basutos under the head chief and his two sons – [69]

If Sprigg[70] consents, I hope to hear of them starting before very long – I shall send you at least half the number –

Ronald Campbell Coldstream Gds[71] and two subalterns are waiting for conveyance to join you – They will be under Clery for transport duties –

WC II/2/2

Chapter 2
Preparing to Invade

23
Lieutenant-General Lord Chelmsford to Colonel C.K. Pearson

[Holograph] | Pieter Maritzburg
15 December 1878

If the three sons of Sirayo and the 500 head of cattle are not sent in within the 20 days your column will have to cross the river – [1] There will be no necessity to assemble carriages on the Zululand side, as I propose at first merely occupying Zulu ground without any arrière pensée of moving forward – Your troops would therefore be fed from Stanger as is now the case, & you would have only to keep up a temporary depôt as you do now at Thrings and the Lower Tugela drift – The new pont would of course have to be launched and every means taken to ensure speedy communication between bank and bank –

Fort Pearson would of course retain its garrison and your new camp would have to be pitched so that, in case of attack, you might have the benefit of its protection.

You will be glad to hear that two more battalions are under orders for Natal – One of these, and a company of Engineers, I shall send to your command – [2]

I wish I dare strengthen your mounted force – I shall not however do this until you get across the Umhlatusi river to the high ground of Kwamagwasa,[3] where I am told horses will not suffer much – When there I should be able to send you a reinforcement from Colonel Glyn's column, which will move from Rorkes drift straight to Unodwengo –

It will be as well for you at once to call upon the volunteers now under your command to give in the names of those who are willing to go across the border with you – [4]

You had also better make arrangements for forming them into one or more squadrons with a due proportion of officers and N.C. Officers, so that there may be no delay when the time comes.

You will have I am afraid a superfluity of officers, but I should only take the good ones –

Those that remain in Natal will also have to be reorganized in the same manner – They had better remain at Thrings store I should think –

The first move forward of your column should, if possible, be as far as Tyoe mission station[5] or its neighbourhood, if as I believe the road by Intumeni mission station[6] branches off from there –

The distance is I hear about 40 miles, say 4 marches – I should wish you to form an advanced depôt, well entrenched at this point, which, when the new battalion arrives, could be defended by such portion of it as you may think necessary –

Durnford's column is destined for Intumeni at first – This column will be under you, but I wish it to act separately from yours on the left flank, so that it may, as far as possible, keep up communication between your column and that of Colonel Glyn's – It will remain watching Middledrift until you have made your first step, and will in all probability cross by the Lower Tugela drift instead of Middledrift, as the latter crossing will be very difficult, and also very risky should the Zulus muster in any force opposite that point – Should Col Durnford's column move away from above Middledrift in view to crossing the Tugela at Lower drift, the colonial forces will of course be posted so as to guard that point of entry into Natal –

You will have to do your best to ascertain whether you have any formidable force of Zulus on your left flank, before you advance to Tyoe M. station, and this information must of course be sent to Durnford, who should send one battalion of his force to Thrings Store to keep up connection with you and watch the frontier line –

Should you cross the river on the completion of the 20 days, you must understand that it is not necessarily with hostile intentions – Mr Fynney should be asked to make it known in Zululand that you are going to move across the river, and that you will not permit any body of Zulus to assemble within reach of your force – Should this happen and the Zulus refuse to retire, they will of course have to take the consequences – I shall want you at first however to remain on the passive defensive, sending out however parties of mounted infantry during the day in order to make certain that no force is assembling near you, and placing outpost sentries at night to guard against a night attack – Free use should be made of spies if you can obtain the services of men who will bring in concrete information – When you cross the river Colonel Glyn will also move his troops down to Rorkes drift, and Col E. Wood will move forward, most probably beyond the hunting road –[7] The same instructions that I have given you will be given to them – Full use should be made of the border police to send information from your end of the line to the others; and you in the same way will receive information from Rorkes drift. One of your staff officers should keep a book to record the messages sent, date and hour, and another one (Guard book) to receive the messages delivered, on which should be recorded the date and hour of receipt – Eventually this lateral communication will have to be established through Zululand, should the several columns advance. –

From Tyoe, or Ekowe, your next step should be Kwagwamasa – but I do not wish you to cross the Umhlatusi R until Wood has got to the Mhlazatye, and Glyn's column is near to, or on, the head waters of that river – as then you will be able to get cross [sic] unhealthy valleys without being delayed by having to fight – There will be no difficulty I expect in keeping you informed as to the movement of the two other columns.

From Entumeni Durnford ought to be able to find a way across the river to Kwamagwasa without coming to your road.

I have given you a rough idea of what my views are regarding your column, as it may possibly guide you in getting information about the road – I understand there is a good military position near Tyoe.

I shall send you definite instructions as to crossing the river when the time arrives; this letter is only meant to prepare you for what may have to be done –

PP

24

Lieutenant-General Lord Chelmsford to Colonel H.E. Wood

[Holograph] Pieter Maritzburg
16 December 1878

In the event of Cetewayo not delivering up the three sons of Usirayo and the 500 cattle, Sir Bartle Frere wishes me to advance the several columns across the Zulu border, without however actually commencing hostilities.

How would a position near Conference hill suit you? It is rather nearer Rorkes drift than I should wish, but it will put your force near fuel and it will enable you to reconnoitre the ground towards Mhlazatye and to fix upon the position for an advanced depôt should we have to move forward – It will be necessary for Mr Rudolph to send and warn the Zulus residing near the Blood and Sand Rivers of your intention to advance, and to let them clearly understand the reason of it – They should also be warned against assembling in any force near your encampment, as such an assembly will be looked upon as an hostile act which you will have to deal with seriously – You would of course make reconnaissances far afield; but I should wish you to send officers on whom you can rely not to precipitate matters, as Sir Bartle Frere and I are both anxious not to lay the troops open to the charge of having unnecessarily brought on hostilities –

When you advance every effort should be made to induce those Zulu tribes, who are averse to war, to come under our protection – They should be sent to the rear as soon as they come in, and a special civil officer told off to locate them and feed them –

I send you copy of a letter which I am sending to Colonel Pearson relative to the movement of his column,[8] as I feel it is desirable that you should be aware of what my views are regarding the advance along the whole line –

I have already written to you regarding the general position of your advanced depôt, viz:- that it should be somewhere near the intersection of the two roads leading from Utrecht to Ulundi and from Rorkes drift to Swaziland – From there your next step must be the Mhlazatye Mountain which, when once taken, can be made a very strong position for a small force – Should they arrive in time, one company of the Royal Engineers will be sent to your column for that purpose –

With a German garrison at Luneberg and the Swazis on the north bank of the Pongolo I hope you will feel that your left flank is fairly secure – What do you propose to do with your Dutch contingent should they come out? Will you have sufficient to spare for the country between the Pongolo and the Black Umvelosi rivers? If so, they will of course give you additional security in that direction.

I shall hope to be able to send you some mounted Basutos before you commence your advance, but it is not yet quite certain whether the 500 promised by Griffith will come or not – [9] They will be useful in keeping up communications between you and Colonel Glyn during the advance of your respective columns – This will be most important, and I should feel obliged by your giving the question full consideration, so that there may be no delay in carrying it out should we advance –

WC II/2/2

25

Lieutenant-General Lord Chelmsford to Colonel H.E. Wood

[Holograph] PMBurg
16 December 1878

Have you any officers who could take up Clery's work per tem? I am most anxious to give Glyn a good staff officer before the time arrives for him to move down to Rorkes drift, and I have absolutely no one available.[10]

Ronald Campbell who was to have gone with Buller, is laid up by Natal sores & bubo, and it is doubtful when he will be fit to travel.

All the other transport officers have been told off to their respective stations – I could send you up Lt Col Law to do the work, but it is questionable whether you would care to have him – He could do the work well enough if he chose, but he is not overfond of work and his present idle life suits him down to the ground.

However if you care to put Vaughan[11] in as a temporary measure or anyone else pray do so, and let Clery get away to Helpmakaar.

WC II/2/2

26

Lieutenant-General Lord Chelmsford to Colonel R.T. Glyn

[MS copy][12]

P.M. Burg
17 December 1878

Should Cetywayo not comply with the High Commissioner's demands, and delay to deliver up the three sons of Usirayo and the 500 head of cattle by the date fixed, viz: 1st January 1879,[13] Sir Bartle Frere wishes me to advance my columns across the Zulu Border – You will see from the copies of instructions sent to Colonel Pearson and Colonel Wood, now forwarded to you, what the Columns on your right and left will be doing. I now send you a few general instructions regarding your own Column.

The order to cross the Buffalo River at Rorke's drift will be sent to you.

When received, I should wish it carried out at once. Everything ought to be ready beforehand.

I am in hopes that the two ponts will be at Rorke's drift before the end of this month, in case the river should be in flood and too full for fording.

You should at once put yourself in communication with Mr Fynn the Magistrate of Umsinga, and ask him to let it be known on the opposite side of the Buffalo River, what the orders are which you have received. He should also explain that you do not cross with any hostile intentions, but simply to show that the demands of the High Commissioner must be complied with. At the same time however, no large assembly of the Zulus must be permitted in the neighbourhood of your Encampment, and on this point Mr Fynn should also be asked to warn them. Should the Zulus neglect the warning, they will only have themselves to blame for the consequences – As regards the position for your Encampment, on the direct road from Rorke's drift to Ulundi – I understand that there is no good military position until you get into the open country beyond that of Rorke's drift on Durnford's map. To reach this point will take you two days from the Buffalo river including of course the crossing of the drift. Your first march beyond Rorke's drift would be to the nearest stream; so far as I can learn about nine miles distant. There is wood here and also at the place where your Encampment will have to be in the open country, but further on the road it does not exist, – and special arrangements will have to be made for carrying it with your column, should you go farther. Should a general advance be decided upon, it will be a question to decide as to where the advanced depôt should be, whether at your first Encampment or farther on.

Beyond the Isipezi mountain, on the upper water of the Umlatoozi river, I am told there is wood not far off – If not too far, this would be a satisfactory place for the depôt; but none of the maps are to be trusted as to distance – Wherever it may be decided to form this depôt, it will have to be strongly entrenched & made as secure as possible against sudden attack, for we should not be able to afford to leave a large garrison behind.

Your column will have to communicate with the Columns on its right and left, on this account there will be a larger force of mounted infantry attached to you. Major Russell & Capt. Barrow, with their two squadrons will eventually join you and their present commands will be augmented by Volunteers and mounted natives. The country from Rorke's drift to the White Umvelosi near Nodwengu, is all open and I hear, may be considered healthy for man and beast. Your only difficulty will be wood and supplies, both of which, I feel we shall get over successfully.

WC II/2/2

27

Lieutenant-General Lord Chelmsford to Commissary-General E. Strickland

[MS copy]

Camp at Thring's Store
30 December 1878[14]

I should feel much obliged if you could pay a visit to Stanger and Durban, and report to me on the condition of those two depôts. I do not feel satisfied about their present condition & I am anxious to have your strict assurance that there will be no break down on the important line of Durban-Lower Tugela Drift. The working of the transport will also of course engage your serious attention, as it is absolutely essential that there should be a proper system established on that line. Colonel Pearson will of course take the main part of the transport into his own hands, but there will remain that which works between Durban and Stanger and which ought to be efficiently organized so that the last named depôt may be perfectly filled up. It appeared to me that Haygate[15] was having stores sent to him from Durban which he did not require.

There is now I think no doubt that our columns will have to cross into Zululand. Cetywayo has evidently no intention of meeting our demands.

CP 27

28

Lieutenant-General Lord Chelmsford to Colonel C.K. Pearson

[Holograph] Camp Potts Spruit
31 December 1878

During my ride to this place I have come to the conclusion that after the 30 days have elapsed without the High Commissioner's demands being attended to by Cetywayo, your columns should advance as rapidly as possible, and occupy Ekowe, so as to prevent the buildings being burnt – Having occupied that post, unload all your waggons and send them back for supplies – Ekowe should be filled up as quickly as possible with as much commissariat stuff as you can cram into it – Place Ekowe in a state of defence, so as to be safe against any attack that may be made upon it. The men of the "Active"[16] should be placed in it as garrison with such an addition of redcoats and natives as you may consider desirable – The remainder should accompany the waggons back to the drift as an escort and the men should be allowed to ride in the waggons and the return journey should be made if possible in two days – I have told Mr Strickland that I wish him to accompany your column, so as to make sure Ekowe is perfectly filled up, and that the transport along the Durban-Tugela line is kept in proper working order –

{He will come out to Ekowe with the 99th, who will form the garrison of that place when you move forward – In all probability the same plan will be adopted at St Pauls[17] or Kwamagwasa, whichever you think best adopted for an entrenched depôt –

It is more than probable that I may wish to feed all the columns from the Durban base, and I want you therefore to see that each entrenched post on your line of communications, is filled up directly you occupy it – The Officers in command at Ekowe will have to keep filling up from the Lower Tugela and you, when across the Umhlatusi river, will have to see as much transport as can be spared is sent back to Ekowe, in order that the second advanced depôt may be filled up as fully and as speedily as possible –

In order to make your column as efficient as possible, I have ordered Captain Barrow to join you at once with his Mounted Infantry, and the volunteer Corps that are now here – [18] You know him as well as I do, and therefore need hardly say that I consider him the best cavalry officer in the country.}

You will most probably have to remain some time at Ekowe, or rather between that place and the Lower Tugela, as your column must not advance from there until the two left columns have made some progress – You will have plenty to do however and the troops, European & native, should be kept hard at work entrenching, or escorting supplies, or improving the roads – The latter duty is most important, as it will facilitate the supplies coming up –

{As regards Col Durnford's column crossing the Tugela, I will leave the time entirely to you – Until you are quite certain that no large body of the enemy is between Intumeni and Middledrift, he had better remain watching that latter point – But, as soon as that part of the country is clear, he will be more useful at Intumeni –

Let one of your staff officers keep a Diary of every thing that your force does, and send me a copy of it by every opportunity through the Military Secretary to the High Commissioner at PMBurg –[19] All information and reports should be sent through the same channel, by which means double reports will be unnecessary, as they will be shown to the Lt Governor, and then forwarded on to me – When communications are established between us inside Zululand, then a different procedure will have to be adopted, and I will send further instructions – As however the telegraph wire will be nearest to your column, you should send, daily if possible, a message to the officer commnd Fort Pearson, who should be instructed to forward it on to the High Commissioner – this be in addition of course to the Diary –}

PP [Printed in French, *Lord Chelmsford*, pp. 65–6 with the words between {} omitted.]

29

Lieutenant-General Lord Chelmsford to Colonel W. Bellairs

[MS copy] 31 December 1878

Send memorandum to officers commanding columns to following effect. –

"Officers commanding columns are requested to have it clearly explained to the native portion of the force under their command that any native convicted of wilfully killing a woman or child or a wounded man, will render himself liable to be hanged. No huts in Zululand are to be burnt except under the special orders of the officer commanding the column –

Any soldier, European or native, transgressing this order will render himself liable to a flogging."

CP 27

30

Lieutenant-General Lord Chelmsford to Sir Bartle Frere

[MS copy] Greytown
1 January 1879

I feel it would be almost mockery in your present position to wish you "a happy new year" –

Crealocks letter giving me the substance of what Your Excellency has written to me in your letter dated 30th December 1878[20] only reached me this morning at 7.30 a.m. having been dispatched from here by the magistrate's clerk at 10 a.m. yesterday – It was, as you may suppose received far too late for me to make any alterations in the orders already issued, as Colonel Pearson and Colonel Glyn have made arrangements to send messages from each other in one day, and the latter will send to Colonel Wood – I could not therefore have communicated with Colonel Wood in time to stop his advance, and it would not have been wise to stop Colonel Pearson and allow Colonel Wood to go in alone.

I am thoroughly satisfied from the information received during the last few days, that Cetywayo has not the smallest intention of meeting Your Excellency's demands. Any delay in the advance of our Columns would be very disadvantageous to our force; and it might certainly tempt the Zulus to make a raid into Natal, if they saw an opportunity, altho' I have never thought such a counterstroke probable at this season of the year.

On my way from Potts Spruit this morning I saw a great portion of Col. Durnford's Native Contingent – The officers speak very confidently about their men, and a very good feeling seemed already to have been established amongst them –

I was very sorry to learn of your having a neuralgic head ache, but I am not in the least surprised at it after the perpetual worry and annoyance that you have been subjected to.

I trust that before long the troops under my command may have an opportunity of settling, once and for all, the Zulu question –

I have every confidence in those under my command and I am satisfied that they will do credit to their cloth – Our cause will be a good one, in spite of all the Colenso party may say, and I hope to be able to convince them all before many weeks are over that for a savage, as for a child, timely severity is greater kindness than mistaken leniency –

As Colonel Pearson has now got Mr Robertson to accompany him,[21] there will not be the same necessity for Mr Fynney to go with his Column – He might perhaps be more useful in organizing the border natives under Captain Lucas – [22] Mr Fannin, with whom I had an interview yesterday, seemed to place great confidence in the natives located below Krantz Kop – They ought to have some European leaders told off however to them, so that they may see we intend to support them – [23]

Mr Fynn would be most useful with Colonel Glyn and I hope the Lt Governor may be able to spare him.[24] I shall if possible get to Burrups tomorrow, so as to be ready for a long march from there, through the thorns to Sand Spruit, when I shall be only one day's march from Helpmakaar –

The rain however has been so heavy during the last two days that the roads are almost impassable for wheeled transport –[25]

CP 27

31
Lieutenant-General Lord Chelmsford to Major J.W. Huskisson

[MS copy] Head Qr. Camp. Greytown
2 January 1879

I should feel much obliged by your sending on the companies of the Royal Engineers destined for Lower Tugela and the one company 99th destined for Stanger as soon as possible.

It is of the greatest importance that Col. Pearson's column should be brought up to its full strength without any unnecessary delay and I feel sure that I can trust you to send them on with the utmost despatch.

In the same way the six companies 99th when they arrive should be forwarded to Stanger. So long as the essential part of their equipment and baggage is landed, there need be no necessity for either Engineers or Infantry to be delayed. They should both leave an officer and a few men to hurry the remainder on, and should be started off with what they have got.

CP 27

32
Lieutenant-General Lord Chelmsford to Colonel H.E. Wood

[Holograph] Helpmakaar
4 January 1879

I am exercised in my mind as to how to come and see you – In the first place it is doubtful, if you cross the Blood river, where you will make your halting place – Until I know that I cannot of course come across the Buffalo. Then secondly when I know where you are, how am I to find you? and how am I to get across the river? So far as I can calculate you will be more than a days ride from here – If so, I do not see where I can stop with propriety, seeing that all the gentlemen residing on this side of the Buffalo have trekked away – [26] and moreover just at this time I cannot afford to be away 4 days from the letter bag –

I have today had a good look at Rorkes drift – There will be no difficulty in crossing – It is said that Sirayo has about 8000 men ready to oppose the crossing; I hope it may be true – We hear that you have three regiments waiting for you, numbering about 5000 – You will no doubt hear more accurately what numbers you may have to meet – [27]

Colonel Glyn will make preparations so as to cross the Buffalo on the 11th, the day after the 30 days have elapsed – I am very anxious for Sir Bartle Frere's sake that no shot be fired by us before that date – Do not therefore push on too far – You will not be able to advance towards the Umvolosi until Glyn has dispersed Sirayo who has got a strong position near Rorkes drift – [28] Could you manage to move in the direction of his country first and help to smash him up with us – We could do it without you easily, but it might fit in to your plans –

I can't proclaim martial law, but I have given you permission to remove the Zulus – [29]

WC II/2/2

33

Lieutenant-General Lord Chelmsford to Sir Bartle Frere

[MS copy]

Helpmakaar
6 January 1879

"Extract"

Report says that the Zulus cannot understand our slow and deliberate movements, & it is rumoured that Cetywayo is somewhat puzzled to know what to do. I saw three so-called messengers from Cetywayo at this place yesterday, but they had no message to give. I told them what they might expect if the demands were not complied with by the 30 days and explained clearly to them that those who did not want to fight had better come in and we would take care of them. They were all very thin, but evidently spies not messengers.[30] Orders have been issued that no more Zulus are to be allowed to come up the Biggarsberg, they will be received at Rorke's Drift. Lonsdale is charmed with his native contingent and says that his Zulus are in every respect far superior to the Fingoes.[31] He is quite prepared to go in with them, and feels satisfied that he can thoroughly depend upon them . . .

Mr Beaumont who has charge of the Border Line from the Blood river to the junction of the Buffalo & Tugela has today shown me his plan of defence which seems to me a very good one.[32] He has promised to write me out a short account of his proposals which I hope to receive in time to slip into the envelope which will take this letter. He was previously in the 75th Regiment and appears to have a good head on his shoulders. His scheme will cost a few oxen, but I consider that this expense ought to be incurred.

When we advance on the 12th it will be a good plan I think to assemble all the border natives at different fixed places and let them know through their European leaders what is happening. It will have a good effect on both sides of the water.

I am afraid Captain Lucas and Mr Fynney is not a very good combination on the Lower Tugela line.[33] However it does not really signify as we shall be stronger on that line than on the other two.

There will of course be no difficulty about the Natal Govt drawing on our treasure chest for such money as they may require provided Your Excellency sanctions it being done.

As regards border officials taking responsibility upon themselves and asking for authority afterwards, I have already told Mr Beaumont to do so as regards killing a few oxen for food. I shall ask Sir H. Bulwer to place the Border Commandants under my orders and then there will be no difficulty.

I am afraid I shall not be able to pay Wood a visit at present. There is no means of crossing the Buffalo where unfordable, and I might find myself on the wrong side without the possibility of getting back. I shall wait at all events until he has taken up his position as at present I should not know where to find him. I do not like either at the present juncture to be far away from the post, as constant references are being made from different quarters, all of which require answers.

We are all very well. I have placed Major Dartnell on my staff somewhat in the same position as Griffith was and I have placed Major Russell in direct command of all the mounted men. There was friction at first but it is, I think, over now.[34]

CP 27

34
Lieutenant-General Lord Chelmsford to Colonel H.E. Wood

[Signed MS copy]

Hd. Qr. Camp
Helpmakaar
8 January 1879

. . . On the 11th inst I should feel obliged by your making a movement in the direction of Usirayo's country South East from Bemba's Kop.

You must not advance your column towards the Umveloosi River until further orders as Colonel Glyn's column (No. 3) will be unable to give you any support on the right flank until the enemy have been forced to retire from their present position along the Buffalo river.[35]

Any assistance therefore that you can render to No. 3 column without in any way endangering your line of communications with Utrecht should be given.

Colonel Glyn will make every effort to communicate with you on the 11th inst. along the right bank of the Blood river, if you on your part will send mounted men along the same river towards him.

The country between the Blood river and the direct road from Rorke's Drift to the White Umveloosi River, should be swept clear, on the 11th inst. if possible, so as to prevent any of the enemy penetrating between No. 3 and No. 4 columns, and thus endangering your communications with Utrecht.

Daily communication must be kept up, if practicable, between Nos. 3 & 4 columns after the former crosses the Buffalo river.

WC II/2/2

35

Lieutenant-General Lord Chelmsford to Colonel H.E. Wood

[Holograph] Head Qr Camp – Helpmakaar
9 January 1879

. . . Do not endeavour to harass Sirayo, if you find that you have a force opposed to you, either in your front or left flank –

If however you can do so without risk come down to meet me on the 11th inst towards Inceceni and Itelezi hills, bringing your mounted men with you – I will come up towards you with Glyn's mounted men – This movement on my part will of course be dependent upon the state of the Buffalo R. If it happens to be unfordable for horses we shall not be able to cross in time –

If also I find that the country between Rorkes drift and Itelezi hill is not adapted for mounted men, and that there is any chance of our having to fight, either going or coming back, I shall not attempt to meet you, as I do not want to engage in any indecisive actions – Rivers permitting the mounted men will cross the Buffalo on the 11th at 5 am, and move towards the point of rendezvous at once –

Do not come further than the Itelezi hill – If we do not turn up there in reasonable time, you may assume that something has prevented our coming to meet you –

I am working entirely by the new map which was forwarded to you from here on the 5th inst – [36] Should it not have reached you I am afraid Durnford's map will mislead you, as Telezi hill is there placed north of Incenci (which is I conclude the same as Inceceni) whereas in the new map it is south of it –

On Durnford's map our point of meeting ought to be somewhere on a line with Vecht Kop, between Blood R. and Inqutu mountain –

Hoping to be able to see you on the 11th

How about the Dutchmen and amaswazies?

WC II/2/2

36

Lieutenant-General Lord Chelmsford to Sir Bartle Frere

[MS copy] Helpmakaar
10 January 1879

I am moving my camp to Rorke's drift. An express came in from Wood only this morning but contained no fresh news, except what you may have already heard, that most of the Dutchmen had left for the Utrecht & Wakerstroom border. Wood appears exercised in his mind about protecting the border to his left hand, now left without white inhabitants, but I have written to him to say that we must consider our interests first and that he must do nothing which will in any way hamper his advance. If the Dutchmen had chosen to assemble they could have perfectly well protected their own border and now if a raid is made in that direction (which Col Wood does not think probable), they will only have themselves to blame. I think it would be well if Sir Theophilus Shepstone took up his residence at Utrecht. His influence may possibly be sufficient to induce the Dutchmen to come forward and protect their own property. I cannot possibly do it without leaving the whole of Col Wood's column in its present position which would upset all my military arrangements and most probably jeopardize the whole success of the operations about to commence. I hope to meet Wood tomorrow and I shall then tell him what I have already written to him. The news which comes to me from Lt Col Durnford through Bishop Schroeder[37] is in accordance with what I have heard on this side. The whole country is in a state of bitter confusion, and our advance will complete it – The loss of oxen is becoming serious but I shall hope to be able to replenish our stock in Zululand where there must be plenty. I wish the home authorities had sent me out the reinforcements a month sooner, we want them on this line. They must see our numbers are not sufficient to spare conveniently detachments for the protection of the line of communications – Report says that Sirayo is still at his kraal with a good following.[38] I very much doubt his waiting for us to attack, as if he does, there is no means of escape for him when once our troops are in position –

CP 27

Chapter 3
Isandlwana

37
Lieutenant-General Lord Chelmsford to Sir Bartle Frere

Camp in Zululand nr. Rorke's Drift
[MS copy] 12 January 1879

We have had our first fight today – I ordered the whole force out this morning to reconnoitre the road along which we shall eventually have to advance – In passing by the Ngudu Hill we noticed that some herds of cattle had been driven up close under the Kraantz where one of Sirayo's strongholds was said to be – I ordered Colonel Glyn with 4 Companies 1/24th & 1/3d Native Contingent to work up under the Kraantz in skirmishing order [and seize the cattle] – On the approach of this force near the Kraantz, fire was opened upon them out of the caves for half an hour & ended in our obtaining possession of all the caves and all the cattle.

{Colonel Degacher who had been sent for from Camp when we found that the Kraantz was occupied by the enemy came up towards the end of the affair with ½ battn. 2/24th and about 400 2/3d Native Contingent – This force went forward to Sirayo's own Kraal which is situated under a very steep Kraantz which is filled with caves – The British soldiers & natives skirmished or rather clambered up the steep mountainside and entered all the caves which were found empty –} I ordered Sirayo's Kraal to be burnt but none of the other huts were touched – {The Native Contingent behaved very well & not a native touched a woman or child or killed a wounded man – Lt Colonel Russell[1] was sent along the Isipezi Hill road with order to get up on to the high ground above the kraantz. As he was nearly at the top about 60 of the enemy came down & fired at his men at a distance of about 100 yards fortunately without hitting anyone – His men dismounted and managed to kill 9 or 10 of the enemy amongst whom was one of Sirayo's sons, who was distinctly recognized –} I have not yet received a correct list of the enemy's loss, but I fancy it will be about 30 – On our side two natives were killed & one mortally wounded – One N.C. officer Native Contingent slightly wounded – I am in great hopes that the news of the storming of Sirayo's stronghold & the capture of so many of his cattle (about 500) may have a salutary effect in Zululand [& either bring down a large force to attack us or else produce a revolution in the country] – Sirayo's men have I am told always been looked upon as the bravest in the country & certainly those who were killed today fought with great courage. I have visited two wounded Zulus who are in our hospital & have seen that they are well looked after – Directly they are well enough I shall let them go, so that they may tell their friends how the British make war – The country is in a terrible state from the rain, and I do not know how we shall manage <u>to get our waggons across the valley near Sirayo's Kraal</u>[2] {A large working party will start tomorrow to dig deep ditches on each side of the road which runs across a broad swamp – and I hope that under this treatment it may consolidate – 16 Oxen is too few to draw even 4000 lbs and I am sending an order for sufficient oxen to be sent up so as to make each span up to 20 – Whether they are procurable remains to be seen – I am afraid our losses have been so heavy and the demands for draught oxen so great, that the Transport director[3] will find a difficulty in complying with the demand – [Might I ask Your Excellency to see that any information from Col. Pearson's Column which may reach you & which is worth sending on, is forwarded to me by post by the first opportunity. I have no faith in the border police line – It will be of great importance to me to know Col Pearson's arrangements as soon as possible – And also to have the intelligence brought in to him]} – The soldiers are in excellent health & spirits and do not seem to feel either physically or mentally the continual ducking which they get from the daily thunderstorms – {Yesterday & todays work will do both British & Native a good deal of good, & I am sure has given great confidence to our camp followers –

With best regards to Sir Henry Bulwer}

CP 27 [Extracts printed in *BPP* (C. 2242), enc. 6 in no 20. Words between [ ] omitted. Also printed in French, *Lord Chelmsford*, pp. 73–4 with words between {} omitted.]

38

Lieutenant-General Lord Chelmsford to Colonel C.K. Pearson

[Holograph] Zululand near Rorkes drift – 13 January 1879

I have already discovered that if our advance into Zululand is to be made without very serious delay, we must have strong working parties on the roads – I hope you will not hesitate to make full use of all the working tools you have with your column and keep them in constant employ by detailing mixed parties of British troops and natives. Never send the latter out without some of the former being with them and working with them – I write this caution for fear lest you should imagine that the R.E. company and Pioneer company should do all the road work – The sooner our troops understand that our success depends upon our supplies coming up and that depends upon the roads being in good order, the better. In fine weather improve them, in bad weather mend them –

I wish my column were as well off as yours in energetic officers – My transport and commissariat is very weak in that respect –

PP

39

Lieutenant-General Lord Chelmsford to Sir Bartle Frere

Head Qr Camp Zululand near Rorkes drift
[MS copy] 13 January 1879

. . . I have sent off to Colonel Wood already and have told him that he is at liberty to choose either Rudolph or Henrique Shepstone for his Political adviser. I expect he will take the former, and I hope he may, as we have so much of the Shepstone element with the different columns already. I shall certainly be able to meet Sir T. Shepstone at Rorkes drift as I do not see a chance of moving forward under a week, our supplies are not yet sufficient to warrant a forward movement & we have not yet put our road in working order. I am sending in an application for some colonial men skilled in pont work. We are at present working our pont & raft with handy men taken from amongst the Europeans of the Natal Native Contingent – These men however ought to go forward with the column as their services cannot be spared – Pont work is a specialité and if not done skillfully [sic], the pont may be lost, particularly as the Buffalo R. stream runs at a rapid pace when in flood. We shall soon have another pont ready to work, which ought to enable us to get our waggons across without any difficulty, and to start them off for our advanced depôt the same day. I shall be glad when I get Col Bray at Rorkes drift. He is not a thorough gentleman, but he is an energetic officer, and will keep everybody up to the mark from Helpmakaar to Isipezi hill when we get there. As regards my private letters to your Excellency I trust that you will send such extracts home as you think may be of use to the Sec of State & enable him to understand what is going on – [4] I hope you do not object to obtaining the information I have to give through this private channel. I can write more freely and fully when not hampered by having to pay attention to official form. I hope your Excellency approves my striking hard at Sirayo directly I got the chance? I felt that he deserved it, and also that it would bring home to the Zulu nation that we are in earnest. Every effort should be made by the Border agents to communicate with the Chiefs and Headmen who are living near the Natal and Transvaal border. I am sending in for favourable consideration today a suggestion of Mr Fynn, that if a gun and two or three assegais for every male of the tribe is given up, and the chief of the tribe and some headmen come in and make submission the tribe should be allowed to remain in its location, the Chief and headmen however being kept in Natal. This arrangement will obviate the difficulty of feeding a large number of refugees, and will be nearly as efficacious as if the whole lot were across. The border people are those whom I am anxious to see disarmed, as they are awkwardly situated on our line of advance. Mr Fynn proposes to put a European magistrate in the place of the chief as a temporary measure and I think the idea a good one. Mr Fynney, Mr Fannin & some one for the Umsinga border should be ordered to be held in readiness for the duty. I wrote to Sir Henry Bulwer about Major Dartnell some time ago. His Excellency appears to forget that he has handed over the colonial troops to me, and that I am responsible for making the best arrangements for them that I can. The police[5] hang too much on Major Dartnell and the proper commanding officer, Mr Mansell[6] does not appear capable of getting oats for his horses without Major Dartnell's assistance – I cannot admit that any reference was necessary on my part to the Lt Governor before putting Russell in order to command all the mounted troops, as had he objected I should [have] been placed in a false position. All danger of a raid into the Colony has evidently passed away for the present. The natives called as a reserve to the border force ought to be all employed on the roads. They will thus be together in case of necessity for their military services & and will be doing good and useful work in the meantime. I have had your Excellency's notice[7] read this morning to the prisoners we took & have told them to make it known to everyone they meet.

CP 27

40

Lieutenant-General Lord Chelmsford to Colonel H.E. Wood

[Holograph] Rorkes Drift – Zululand
13 January 1879

A letter from Sir B Frere this morning dated 7 January about Rudolph. Sir T. Shepstone hints that the latter does not care to meet Zulu bullets & assegais and proposes to send you his son Henrique Shepstone – High Commissioner says you are to have whichever you like best, and therefore I write to give you permission to take Rudolph, if you think he will be most useful –

Sir T. Shepstone was to leave for Utrecht viâ Helpmakaar on Saturday last (11th) – I shall have a talk to him before he goes on but I do not see that he can help me much as regards this column. He will I hope however be of immense use to you, and, by some means or other, must manage to look after your left flank when you advance –

I hope that we have shown Sirayo that we do not care for his caves, but it was a pity that we had not more of his tribe[8] to oppose us – Report says that they have gone to the Ibabanango mountain which is close to where our advance depôt will be near Isipezi hill and where we shall have to get our wood – So we may have another turn up with him before very long – I see no chance of our advancing for 7 days – Road near camp over a swamp must be drained, and supplies must be stored at Rorkes drift – at present there are scarcely any there –

The rain latterly all over Natal has been incessant and the roads are reported as impassable – Old Strickland is working grandly to make Pearsons Column fit to advance, and to push stores on to Ekowe – I wish I had as energetic a man at Helpmakaar – All may be going on as well as it is possible to make it, but I feel no confidence that such is the case –

I shall be glad when I get Col Bray at Rorkes drift – He will keep every one at work I feel sure.

I do not like remaining in this valley so long, as there is no doubt that it is a bad one for horses; but we cannot advance until we can feed ourselves.

WC II/2/2

41

Lieutenant-General Lord Chelmsford to Colonel W. Bellairs

[MS copy] Hd Qr Camp, Zululand Nr Rorkes drift
13 January 1879

. . . I shall be glad to see Col Bray at Rorkes Drift, and if you could manage to send him on in advance of his men, it would be a very good thing – Can you find an officer to take charge of the line of communication between Greytown and Helpmakaar? Bray will be placed in charge of that from the latter place viâ Rorkes drift to our advanced depôt; Hopton will look after that to Greytown, and we only want someone for the worst part of the road – He ought to be energetic and a good rider – and should have plenty of horses given to him – As in all probability there will be no troops on the line in question, a good transport Officer would do very well – He should upon arrival report to Col Bray at Rorkes Drift and on return to Greytown he should do the same to Major Hopton at PMBurg.

Has Mr Glover started? He is wanted much up here as the horses are beginning to fall sick – Pray send him off at once – I hope a new Postmaster is being sent to Helpmakaar – The present man is no use, and is not at all civil I am told – [9] There are no Post Office runners told off to carry letters between Helmakaar and Rorkes Drift! Spalding has had to engage special men –

Directly the new Asst Comy General[10] has got into the saddle he ought at once to visit Greytown and Helpmakaar and see with his own eyes how things are going at these two places –

Lieut Main RE can be placed at Major Huskisson's disposal should he want an Engineer Officer. He ought to be told however that he is not a brilliant specimen of the genus.

Our pont and raft are working well but there ought to be some special men told off to work them when we advance, as otherwise we shall have to leave some valuable men behind – There will be two ponts and one raft – Kindly see if you can get some men out of the Government, or from private employ – The latter ought to enter into an agreement

When will the reinforcements arrive?

CP 27

42

Lieutenant-General Lord Chelmsford to Commissary-General E. Strickland

Hd Qr Camp Zululand near Rorkes drift

[MS copy] 13 January 1879

I have been across the Buffalo R. today to see how the depôt was going. I find that there is absolutely nothing there and this column cannot move until there is a months supply in hand over and above the 15 days regimental supply with the column. Mr Dalton[11] is the only representative of the Commissariat Dept. at Rorkes drift, and for the first time today he has been given a sergeant of the 24th to assist him. Mr Dalton is too young to take the weight of responsibility which the charge of a column represents, altho I am sure he would do well under another. You must send up one of the new Assist Commissary Genls who are on their way out, at once to Helpmakaar, or we shall have a break down. There is no one here like Colonel Wood to keep everyone up to the mark & Helpmakaar appears to me to have been sadly neglected. Look after the interests of this column before you advance with No. 1 Column, & leave PMBurg to be, what it is, merely a forwarding station. This column will advance very shortly, & it will be a sad disgrace to the Commissariat, if it is obliged to halt short of its destination for want of supplies.

CP 27

43
Lieutenant-General Lord Chelmsford to Colonel A.W. Durnford

Hd Qr Camp Zululand near Rorkes drift
[MS copy] 14 January 1879

Unless you carry out the instructions I give you,[12] it will be my unpleasant duty to remove you from your command, and to substitute another officer for the command of No. 2 Column. When a column is acting separately in an enemy's country I am quite ready to give its commander every latitude, and would certainly expect him to disobey any orders he might receive from me, if information which he obtained, showed that it would be injurious to the interests of the column under his command – Your neglecting to obey my instructions in the present instance has no excuse. You have simply received information in a letter from Bishop Schroeder, which may or may not be true and which you have no means of verifying – If movements ordered are to be delayed because report hints at a chance of an invasion of Natal, it will be impossible for me to carry out my plan of campaign – I trust you will understand this plain speaking & not give me any further occasion to write in a style which is distasteful to me –

CP 27 [Printed French, *Lord Chelmsford*, p. 77.]

44
Lieutenant-General Lord Chelmsford to Sir Bartle Frere

Hd Qr Camp Zululand near Rorkes drift
[MS copy] 16 January 1879

News came in last evening from Wood dated 14th inst . . . .He took about 2000 head of cattle from Sirayo on the 11th on his way back to Bemba's Kop.[13] He has also taken a good number from Seketwayo and has sent word to him to say that he shall have them all back if he comes in. {Captain Barton was sent with Piet Uys and some Frontier Lt Horse to disarm a petty chief by name Niboosa[14] living on the Lower Pivan. They resisted and seven Zulu were killed. Wood states that this chief has been a most troublesome neighbour to the Transvaal – 50 adults of Seketwayo's tribe have already come in and more were expected – If Seketwayo himself comes it will relieve Wood's left flank very much – [Colonel Wood writes that he is most anxious to have Rudolph with him, but Sir T. S. offers him his son whom he does not want and says he cannot spare the former – [15] Would your Excellency kindly obtain Mr Rudolph's services for Col Wood] – Russell made a long reconnaissance yesterday as far as the Isipezi hill – The country was found quite deserted, every kraal being empty.} The description of the track taken does not sound promising. Country seamed with deep nullahs some nearly 100 yds broad, stony hills and no wood. {One memorandum I am today sending you will I hope however show that in spite of the rain and of the difficulty of the country the several columns will be able to make themselves felt in Zululand.} The plan I have laid down as necessary is not so ambitious a one as a rapid march upon Ulundi and the occupation of the King's Kraal – but I am certain it is the only safe one under the circumstances. It would be impossible to keep a long line of road passable for a convoy of waggons and if we are to advance far into the country, it would be almost certain that, instead of our supplies coming to us, we should have to return for our supplies. A retrograde movement would have a very bad effect on our native forces and would certainly encourage our enemies. [Col Wood with a roving commission will be in his element & he and Buller together will keep the Zulus in the north on the "qui vive". {Major Dartnell told me today that Capt Shepstone and the volunteers are very much annoyed at the letters in the newspapers about Lt Col Russell's appointment,[16] and requested that I might be informed that there was no truth in the statements made. They are all quite satisfied as also the Police. I am bound to say that had not Major Dartnell used his personal influence with the Police and Volunteers my action would not have been acquiesced in so readily – Dartnell will be of the greater use to me, and as your Excellency has put it in your memo to Sir H. Bulwer is really in a much higher position than if I had been able to leave him in command of the Natal mounted men.[17] I am extremely obliged to you for the memorandum in question which materially assisted to put matters in their true light – Lonsdale's regiment[18] has been reinforced and is now about 500 over its strength – Natives are still coming in by twos & threes. I am leaving however those in excess of 2200 at Rorke's Drift. They will be useful for defence and also as working parties on the roads. I wish Sir H. Bulwer would allow Mr Fynn to be with me. I have no one to consult with as regards my duties as Resident in Zululand and I am afraid that unless I am allowed his services I shall not be able to deal satisfactorily with any chiefs who are anxious to tender their submission. Mr Fynn has scarcely any work to do as nearly all his natives are in the field. Mr Beaumont could very well take his place for the time. I dont think it is right I should be left without one representative of the Natal Government at my Head Quarters as the disposal of prisoners and refugees has already cropped up[19] and Mr Fynn is 25 miles distant.[20] I was very glad to hear of Colonel Pearson getting his force safely across the Tugela. If the Zulus really intend to fight they will oppose his advance. They appear however to be acting in a very half hearted manner –]}

CP 27 [Extracts printed in *BPP* (C. 2260), enc. 2 in no. 4. Words between [ ] omitted. Printed also in French, *Lord Chelmsford*, pp. 78–9 with words between {} omitted.]

45

Lieutenant-General Lord Chelmsford to Colonel H.E. Wood

Head Quarter Camp Zululand
Near Rorkes drift
16 January 1879

[MS copy]

. . . You are working entirely in accordance with my views and in the only way, I feel sure, by which we can make ourselves felt in the country –

We must try and push every one slowly before us towards the

King's kraal,[21] or otherwise disarm the tribe and take their chiefs and some of their headmen, as hostages for good behaviour –

Russell made a reconnaissance as far as the Isepezi hill yesterday about 22 miles – Road at present quite unfit for convoys to pass –

Our first move must therefore be to the Isanblana hill where there is wood and water – I shall from there clear the Equideni forest or receive the submission of the chiefs and Headmen residing in that District. Having settled that part I shall move on to ground between the Isepezi and Umhlabumkosi but nearest to the latter where there is wood – If you are then at Ingwee we might have another meeting[22] somewhere between our two camps and again talk over the situation. The effect of two forces meeting has, I am sure, a good moral effect.

From Isepezi I should at first work towards the mission station close to the little Itala, where I shall hope to establish Durnford's column. –

I shall tell Pearson[23] not to attempt to go beyond Ekowe but to move laterally with part of his force to Entumeni. – In fact I propose to clear out the country along the Buffalo and Tugela before the three Southern columns cross the Umhlatoosi river – By this plan we shall oblige Cetewayo to keep his force together, when it will suffer from want of food and become thoroughly discontented or we shall oblige him to attack which will save us going to find him. – Under these circumstances it will not be advisable for you to go beyond Ingwee with your column. You can of course, and should make reconnaissances towards the Inhlayatye; but the great thing will be for you to make yourself thoroughly secure wherever you may take up your position. –

If you can find wood and a military position by moving further north I shall have no objection.[24] You will cover Utrecht better by such a move and if you settle Seketwayo one way or the other you will have no cause for apprehension about your rear & right flank and I know you can look after your front & left; all however that I can do is to tell you what I propose to do with the three columns in the South and I must trust to you to work the troops in the north to the best advantage – I shall hope to move to Isandlana hill in 4 days. Let me know what you think of doing. –

You must send your mounted men to me when you want information. – I have no means of sending word to you except by Natal.

WC II/2/2

46

Lieutenant-General Lord Chelmsford to Colonel H.E. Wood

[Holograph] Head Qr Camp nr Rorkes Drift
18 January 1879

I sent Russell and all his mounted men off at 3 am this morning to look up the Zulus and the cattle on the Telezi hill – Even should they not be found there, it will do good, as it will show those that remain in their kraals that we have not neglected that particular line. I wish I could send you 100 mounted men – Ours however have so much to do, as we have not any mounted natives, that I am sure, if I were to weaken their number, their horses would break down – You will see that in order to strengthen your left flank I have authorised Rowlands to bring the 250 of the 80th now at Derby down to the Pongolo, always provided that he can feed them there and that the Swazis accompany him – If they move down, I leave the question of their future movements entirely in your hands – Rowlands is of course long senior to you as a Colonel and therefore cannot serve under you, but you can place his force wherever you think it will help your left flank most, sending him the order in my name –

As you have now a roving commission and are not tied down to any particular line, I hope you will be able to rub on without difficulty –

In writing to the High Commissioner yesterday I recommended for the better security of the Natal & Transvaal border that we should rectify our boundary line – The one I consider desirable is the Ngudu range to the hunting road by the Zonguine Mt and from there along the hunting road to the Pongolo – What do you say to that line for the Transvaal? For Natal I would draw a line from the South point of the Ngudu range to a point where the Isangu joins the Umhlatoosi R and then along the latter to the sea –

We should then have possession of all the difficult country along the Natal border and the command of the Tugela & Buffalo R.

WC II/2/2

47
Lieutenant-General Lord Chelmsford to Colonel A.W. Durnford

[MS copy]

Head Quarter Camp
Near Rorke's Drift, Zululand
19 January 1879

No 3 column moves tomorrow to Insalwana Hill and from there, as soon as possible to a spot about 10 miles nearer to the Indeni Forest.

From that point I intend to operate against the two Matyanas[25] if they refuse to surrender.

One is in the stronghold on or near the Mhlazakazi Mountain, the other is in the Indeni Forest. Bengough ought to be ready to cross the Buffalo R. at the Gates of Natal[26] in three days time, and ought to show himself there as soon as possible.

I have sent you an order to cross the river at Rorkes Drift tomorrow with the force you have at Vermaaks.[27]

I shall want you to operate against the Matyanas, but will send you fresh instructions on this subject.

We shall be about 8 miles from Rorke's Drift tomorrow.

CP 27

48

Lieutenant-General Lord Chelmsford to Sir Bartle Frere

[MS copy] Head Quarter Camp, Insalwana Hill, Zululand
21 January 1879

. . . No. 3 column moved here yesterday without much difficulty. We fortunately had a fine day and did not find many bad places on the road. One nasty swamp we were able to turn with a little expenditure of labour. Half a battalion 2/24th was obliged to halt short of the camp owing to the oxen being fatigued. Otherwise all got in well.

At 1 pm I started off to reconnoitre what is called the Zulu stronghold which is almost ten or twelve miles from here.

Our road lay over a hard rolling plain, cut up at long intervals by deep watercourses which however will not be difficult to get waggons over. It ran at first almost North then North East and finally due East when we got round the Malakata range (vide Durnford's map). The so-called stronghold is a precipitous valley with krantzes on each side in which there are caves. The river[28] which runs through it tumbles over a precipice at the upper end, and the valley is thus closed in on three sides. The fourth opens out into lateral valleys some three miles down and the main valley continues on until it reaches the Buffalo river, close under the Indeni bush.

No sign of Zulus or cattle could be discovered. We mounted up on to the Malakata range which is fairly level and open, and from the different spurs we could see a long distance into the main valley. A few kraals were visible and from some we saw a few women running away with bundles on their heads, but otherwise the country was deserted. Some natives say that the inhabitants have gone to the King, others say they are in the Indeni bush. I have sent two parties of mounted men this morning to explore the country more thoroughly than I was able to do yesterday, and I have sent Lonsdale and his two battalions Native Contingent round the west side of the Malakata range with orders to climb up to the top and make a position with the mounted men. I shall know by evening therefore whether anybody is left in the country. I am going myself after breakfast with Mr Fynn, who joined me the day before yesterday, to interview the brother of Sirayo, Gamdana,[29] with whom we have both been treating. I shall then decide whether he is to be sent into Natal or not. {[I hope you will be able to pacify Sir H. Bulwer with regard to my annexing Mr Fynn. It was only after seeing how essential it was in the public interest that he should be with me, that I decided to summons him to Head Quarters.[30]}

I do not believe Mr Fannin's report about a large force in the Inkandla bush, and I am certain that the Tugela river at the present moment is not one which a force would care to dash across. Middledrift moreover is still watched by two battalions of Col Durnford's column.

No 1 column, when established at Ekowe will move a portion of its force to Entumeni, which will then be on the line of retreat of any Zulu regiment that may happen to be in the Inkandla bush.

Mr Fannin like a good many other Natal officials is an alarmist, and, not being able to appreciate what an enemy can do and what he cannot do, sees danger where there really is none.

{I enclose a memorandum which I am sending to Col. Durnford and to Col. Bray, which will shew you the arrangements I am making for moving forward, and for guarding my line of communication when I do. I shall move towards the Indeni Bush first of all so as to find out whether there are many Zulus there, and then move back again towards Isipezi.} The more I see of the Buffalo border the more convinced I am that we must hold both sides of the river, if Natal is to be made secure in the future from raiding. The same reasoning must equally apply to the Tugela River that borders on the Zulu side, is [sic] a more difficult country than the one we have been reconnoitering. With the border belt in our possession and Zululand parcelled out into small divisions under small chiefs, Natal will be quite secure.]

CP 27 [Extracts printed in *BPP* (C. 2260), enc. 2 in no. 4. Words between [ ] omitted. Also printed in French, *Lord Chelmsford*, pp. 81–2 with words between {} omitted.]

49
Lieutenant-General Lord Chelmsford to Sir Bartle Frere

[MS copy] Rorkes Drift
23 January 1879

I regret deeply to have to inform you that No. 3 column has maintained a terrible disaster –

The camp of the column was moved on Monday the 20th inst to the Isandlana Hill, about nine miles from Rorke's Drift –

On Tuesday the 21st Inst. the Natal Mounted Police and the mounted Corps under Captain Shepstone's command together with two battalions of the Native Contingent under Commandant Lonsdale[31] proceeded to search the district occupied by "Matyan" –

It was found necessary for them to bivouac out on the night of the 21st, about 10 miles from the camp of the column. I also thought it fit to strengthen the force for the purpose required, especially as Major Dartnell who was in command of the mounted troops had represented that the assistance of some Infantry was required.

The 2/24th[32] under Col. Degacher, 4 guns R.A. under Col. Harness,[33] and the Mounted Infantry & 2 cos. Native Pioneers, the whole under command of Col. Glyn left the camp at an early hour on the morning of the 22nd inst. to join the forces under Comdt. Lonsdale and Major Dartnell. I accompanied this force in person.

The troops left in camp consisted of five cos. 1/24th, 2 guns R.A. about 20 Mounted Infantry, 30 Mounted Police and 30 Natal Volunteers.[34] The whole was under command of Lt. Col. Pulleine 1/24th. There were also numerous camp followers, servants &c &c.

The rocket battery under Capt. Russell R.A.[35] and five troops Mounted Basutos, the whole commanded by Colonel Durnford R.E. arrived at the camp in the course of the day that the camp had been attacked.[36]

I had previously sent direction . . . [word illegible] the camp struck and moved to the point where the force was then operating against "Matyan". On learning that the camp was attacked, I commenced to move towards Isandlana with the Native Contingent, the mounted Infantry, and the Natal Volunteers, having the artillery and 2/24th and Natal Police to form an encampment under Col Glyn. At that time I had no doubt but that the reported attack was of small importance and that the force in camp would be quite sufficient to beat it off.

When about five miles from the camp I received further intelligence that the camp was taken and a reconnaissance party was able to see the enemy in large numbers in full possession of it.

I sent for the guns and 2/24th & Mounted Police and on their arrival about 5.30 pm I moved at once to the camp –

This I found had been in full possession of the Zulus, tents looted and destroyed wagon and oxen . . . [word illegible]

The camp had been defended with the utmost gallantry, but the soldiers had been beaten by much heavier numbers. Several officers and men have, am happy to say escaped, but by far the larger proportion died at their posts and their bodies were found on our arrival in the camp.

I did not arrive in the camp until after nightfall and with the troops who were with me bivouacked on the Isandlana Hill, among the bodies from dead soldiers and of the enemy.

A night attack was expected on the troops during last night, but none occurred, and we moved to Rorke's Drift at daylight this morning, without interruption. Large bodies of the enemy were seen in the distance, which had been on the Natal side of the Buffalo River burning kraals &c. &c.

On arrival at Rorke's Drift I found that a very determined attack had been made on the Commissariat Station there, which was occupied by a company of the 2/24th under Lt. Bromhead the whole being under Lt Chard R.E. These officers and their men made a most gallant and effectual resistance suffering much loss however.[37]

It is estimated that the attack on the Isandlana camp was made by about 15,000 to 20,000 men.

I cannot yet give details of losses, but they are very serious indeed – I shall have information in a short time as to the officers and men who escaped, but it is impossible yet to say when their last will be able to present themselves.[38]

The desperate bravery of the Zulu has been the subject of much astonishment – Though that by a most destructive fire of musketry and . . . [line missing] piles of dead and succeeded by force of recklessness and numbers –

CP 8/15

II
From Passive to Active Defence

Chapter 4
The Defence of Natal

50
Lieutenant-General Lord Chelmsford to Colonel F.A. Stanley

[MS copy of telegram] 27 January 1879

I regret to have to report a very disastrous engagement which took place on the 22nd instant between the Zulus and a portion of No 3 Column left to guard a camp about 10 miles in front of Rorke's Drift – The former came down in overwhelming numbers and, in spite of the gallant resistance made by the six companies of the 24th Regiment, 2 guns, 2 Rocket-tubes, 104 mounted men and about 800 natives, completely overwhelmed them. The camp, containing all the supplies, ammunition and transport of No 3 Column, was taken, and but few of its defenders escaped. Our loss, I fear, must be set down as 30 officers and about 500 non commissioned officers, Rank & File of the Imperial troops and 21 officers and 70 Non Commissioned Officers Rank & File of the Colonial Forces.[1]

A court of enquiry has been ordered to assemble to collect evidence regarding this unfortunate affair, and will be forwarded to you as soon as received.[2]

Full particulars, as far as can be obtained, have been sent in my despatch of this day's date which will reach you by the next mail.[3] It would seem that the troops were enticed away from their camp, as the action took place about one mile and a quarter outside it –

The effects of the reverse have already been very serious. Two whole regiments of Natives have deserted and, it is to be feared, that the rest will follow.[4]

A panic is spreading broadcast over the Colony which is difficult to allay.[5]

Additional reinforcements must be sent out. At least three Infantry Regiments and two Cavalry Regiments with horses are required and one more Company of Engineers.

The Cavalry must be prepared to act as Mounted Infantry and should have their carbines slung on their shoulder, and a sword shorter than the regulation pattern fastened to the saddle.

CP 8/29

51
Lieutenant-General Lord Chelmsford to Colonel H.E. Wood

[Holograph] PMBurg
28 January 1879

I was very much relieved to receive your letter giving an account of your successful engagement on the 24th inst – and to hear that you had received intelligence of the misfortune which happened to our column – [6]

You are now forewarned, and must be prepared to have the whole Zulu force on the top of you some of these days –

It is difficult to obtain an accurate account of what really occurred, but one informant told me that the main centre attacking column marched straight on without firing and simply bore down all opposition by sheer weight of numbers – If this account be true it shows that nothing short of some obstacle in front of the line and the flanks protected will suffice to stop men who are determined to break through regardless of loss of life –

I have had a long talk with Sir B. Frere this morning over the state of affairs – It is fortunate there is one with so cool a head and so stout a heart at the head of affairs at this present juncture –

He is of opinion that the Transvaal and the Swazies must be left to look after themselves and that you should draw down nearer to Rorkes Drift column and work hereafter in connection with that column, when it comes to be reorganized, but of course independently –

He is of opinion, and I cannot but agree with him, that we must now content ourselves with taking a certain grip of the country and thus making ourselves felt –

He considers that you should eventually move down your column to a point somewhere near where we met on the 11th inst[7] and that you should, if possible, establish your force more to the East of the Nkonyani range and upon the waterparting which runs north of the Nkudu Mountain – It was somewhere about there that Andries Pretorius advanced in 1838 when he went to avenge Retief's massacre, and I presume therefore that the country is favourable for waggons – [8]

Whether you can find wood there is another point but you may be able to ascertain –

Sir B. Frere is going to inform the Dutchmen in the Utrecht & Wakkerstroom Districts that the boundary award is torn up, and that they will in future be considered as under the British Government – [9] and you are quite at liberty to let them know of this decision at once –

Our future plan of campaign will be confined to the country south of the Umhlatoosi river and South West of the White Umvelosi river –

If we establish ourselves in good positions at different points in that part of the country, and make good use of the mounted men for reconnoitering and raids, we ought to be able to bring the Zulus down upon us again when thoroughly prepared to receive them –

I wish I could send you some mounted men – The volunteers will not serve again out of Natal, nor will the mounted police – Russell's men[10] are not fit to march – They have lost all their kit and have no waggons and no farriers –

I will strengthen your hand in every way that I can but it must be a work of time –

I have telegraphed for 3 regiments of infantry and 2 of cavalry and one company of R. Engineers – The cavalry I have said must be prepared to act as Mounted infantry and I have suggested that swords should be fastened to their saddles and their carbines slung on their shoulders –

Did Capt A. Gardiner[11] bring you the information about our mishap? You do not say how you received it –

Make the stores at Utrecht as secure as possible – The roads are now so bad that we should have great difficulty in replenishing your supplies if any accident happened to them –

Col Pearson is at Ekowe entrenching himself – and his convoy of empty waggons was eight miles distant from Lower Tugela on their return journey –

PS I have told Rowlands that, if the Swazies refuse to advance, he must be prepared to send you all his mounted men, and even companies of infantry should you ask for them –

30 January
News from Pearson at Ekowe dated 29th. He complains of the water supply being rather limited and in a letter dated 24th inst he says that the position of Ekowe is very faulty from a military point of view – [12]

I will try and send you some Mounted Basutos who belong to No 2 column – [13] They behaved very well indeed in the fight at Insalwana, and will be of great assistance to Buller, if they will only go to him willingly – They dispersed after the affair of the 22d, but have expressed a perfect willingness to serve again

They are willing, plucky fellows all armed with Swinburne Henry carbines –

WC II/2/2

52

Lieutenant-General Lord Chelmsford to Colonel H.E. Wood

[Holograph] PMBurg
29 January 1879

Colonel Lanyon is going up very shortly to Utrecht to take over the Transvaal Govt from Sir T. Shepstone –[14] He will I know do all he can to assist you – I have told him that I am most anxious to strengthen your column, and he has promised to do so in every way he can –

I have ordered Mr Wainwright[15] who is about to purchase horses in the Free State to send them all to Utrecht and I am telegraphing to accept an offer of Capt Baker Port Elizabeth to raise 200 men and told him that he is wanted to join your column – [16]

Col Lanyon also talks of being able to raise a number of mounted Griquas from Kimberley, all good shots, and I have requested him to do what he can and send them all on to you –[17]

These reinforcements however will not arrive for some time.

I wish No 3 column in the future, when reequipped and supported, to subordinate its movements entirely to those of your column – I must trust to you and Pearson to reestablish our prestige –

Colonel Rowlands has reported that 5000 Swazies are ready to march to the Pongolo, & he is evidently meditating a move down also with 5 Companies 80th Regt, two guns and some mounted volunteers – [18]

I am writing to him to say that he must be guided entirely by the information and advice you send him as to his movements – I am quite unable to say what he can do, and you are the only person who really understands the situation – Kindly send Rowlands full instructions, and remember that he is on no account to interfere with your independence, but may act, so as to assist you, in such way as you may advise him –

Colonel Pearson has entrenched himself at Ekowe with 1200 red coats and has sent back the mounted men and native contingent battalions – He is provisioned for two months – There ought therefore to be no anxiety about his holding his own – I only wish I could see my way to sending you assistance more speedily – The mounted men of No 3 column are however quite unable to move – They have lost all their equipment, transport, farriers and shoeing smiths! –

Kindly think over the present situation and let me know in what way you think No 3 column can assist your column when reinforced and reequipped –

My best thanks are due to you and Buller – I feel confident that you two are going to pull me out of my difficulties –

I was horrified when I heard that there was talk of giving you a CMG – I had written before to the Duke[19] and wrote again when I heard it, to say that the least reward you were entitled to was a K.C.M.G –

WC II/2/2

53

Lieutenant-General Lord Chelmsford to H.R.H. the Duke of Cambridge

[MS copy] P.M. Burg
1 February 1879

The sad disaster which has occurred to a portion of the force under my command will, I know well, distress Your Royal Highness extremely – It has thrown back the subjugation of Zululand to an indefinite period & must necessarily entail sacrifice of men & money in far larger proportions than was originally expected.

{Since I last wrote I have heard nothing regarding the progress which the Court of Inquiry is making, and I fear it may be some time yet before I am in possession of the proceedings – It is sitting at a distance of about 100 miles from here, & the postal arrangements are very faulty – [20]

I have gathered since from some of those who escaped, that shortly before the final fatal attack was made by the Zulus, the impression in Camp seemed to be that the affair was finished, and it is reported that Lt Colonel Pulleine and some other officers had actually returned to their tents.}

The question will no doubt be asked as to why I made no effort to bury the bodies, and why having obtained possession of the Camp again I did not retain it – The answer is clear. I had no supplies and no spare ammunition nearer than 10 miles,[21] at a post which was very open to attack & I could not afford to delay as the troops wanted food and rest –

The terrible massacre which had taken place precluded all possibility of my being able to bury those that had fallen, and to do so partially could only have the effect of bringing home to the troops the full extent of the disaster, of which they were to a certain extent kept in ignorance owing to the darkness – I felt that there was much to lose and nothing to gain by delaying the march, & I consequently did not hesitate –

The effect of the disaster upon the native population of Natal has been very great – Four out of the seven native battalions placed at my disposal by the Natal Government have disbanded themselves, and the other three are scarcely to be depended upon –[22] It is possible that many of those who have left will return after having seen their families, but the Native Contingent can never be of any use again, except for work inside the Colony.

{I have to trust therefore entirely to British troops, and the British and Dutch Volunteers – of these latter I hope to obtain a great number, as South Africa generally feels that it is a time when everyone should come forward to assist. Mr Sprigg the Colonial Secretary of the Cape Colony has behaved with great spirit – He at once sent off to Natal the three Companies 2/4th Regt which had been left at Cape Town, and he is making arrangements also to send the three Companies 88th Regt which are now at King Williams Town.

From the Transvaal we can expect no assistance. The feeling against us amongst the Boers is very bitter –[23]

One of my A.D.C.'s however, Captain Buller, Rifle Brigade, has started for the Orange Free State with a letter from Sir Bartle Frere to Mr Brand, the President,[24] and I am in great hopes that he will be able to obtain the assistance of a good number of mounted men, both European & Native.}

Colonel Pearson has entrenched himself at Ekowe, almost 36 miles from the Lower Tugela – He has 1200 British Soldiers and food for two months, and he writes very confidently that he will be able to make himself, as he calls it "quite snug".

Colonel Wood's Column covers Utrecht, and there is no cause for anxiety about him –

The Zulus have been perfectly quiet since the 22nd January,

and report says that they have felt very much the heavy loss inflicted on them – {They have had one great success, but they, at the same time, have suffered severe defeats twice since the commencement of the War; and their success was only gained at an enormous sacrifice of life – [25]

I shall proceed to the Lower Tugela after tomorrow, and I shall then be in a better position to judge what had best be done in that quarter pending the arrival of reinforcements.

The state of the roads, and slow nature of the transport of the country, is a great hindrance to rapid movements.

I do not see how any substitute for the ox waggon can be found, as horses and mules must have forage if they are to be kept in condition whereas the ox thrives upon the pastures and therefore whatever he drags behind him is all to the good –

Might I suggest to Your Royal Highness the advisability of sending out a Major General who will be competent to succeed me not only as Commanding the Forces, but also as Lt Governor & High Commissioner should anything happen to Sir B. Frere.

Sir B. Frere is, I believe, also writing on the subject. None of the senior Colonels out here possess in our opinion the requisite qualities –}

CP 28 [Extracts printed in French, *Lord Chelmsford*, pp. 120–1 with words between {} omitted.]

54

Lieutenant-General Lord Chelmsford to Colonel C.K. Pearson

[Holograph] P.M.B.
Sunday – 2 February 1879

. . . Up to what date are you rationed?

Do you wish us to try and convey more food to you? If so, can you assist the safe arrival of the convoy by sending out a portion of your force to escort it in, when we notify to you that it has left?

Have you divided your entrenchment, so that if your garrison is reduced in numbers a smaller force can defend your stores &c? No 3 column lost all its stores, ammunition, tents, transport &c on 22nd and 5 companies 1/24 and 1 company 2/24 were cut to pieces.

It is quite impossible to advance for it will require a long time to refit –

You must not run any risk with the troops now at Ekowe.

If the Zulus attack you and you give them a really good defeat which you are sure to do, then would be the time to fall back to some position beyond the bush which is now between you and the Lower Tugela so that we may feed you properly and keep up constant communications with you and the force on the Natal side –

Should the Zulus disappoint us and refuse to attack you, then combined arrangements will have to be concerted between your garrison and the Lower Tugela force so as to make your retirement secure –

I hope I have arranged so that daily communication will be kept up between us and you – In this case you will be able to give us timely notice when you propose to fall back –

It will be well to bury any ammunition you cannot carry away; under the floor of some of the rooms[26] would be a good place –

Would you be able to reach the end of the bush country in one long march? It would of course facilitate matters if you could –

Your wounded men would have to be carried back on stretchers; so that you would have to provide a proper supply, unless you happen to have any mule waggons with you –

Altho' the misfortune on the 22nd was a very severe one, the Zulus suffered very severe loss – We have beaten them five times out of six[27] & humanly speaking ought to have beaten them on the 22nd, but the force instead of being kept together was scattered about, and at least a mile from the camp they were ordered to defend!

My best thanks to you and the Naval Brigade for your successful fight at Inyazani – It was a very good business – [28] In case of another attack keep your men together – the Zulus are sure to attack in heavy masses and the close order is the one to meet it –

90 of the 2/24 at Rorkes drift post held out for 12 hours against 2500 Zulus and killed 370 of them – [29] I shudder to think of the execution your 6200 will do if they get the chance – Good luck to you all

PP

55

Lieutenant-General Lord Chelmsford to Colonel H.E. Wood

[Holograph]

PMBurg
3 February 1879

Private
The situation of affairs does not appear to me to improve, and I am fairly puzzled when I contemplate our future operations –

Our Natal native contingent may be said to have disappeared and altho' it is possible a good number may return, I very much doubt whether they will be brought to cross into Zululand again – [30] Our drivers & foreloopers will certainly not come with us and our only chance is to arm them with guns and to give them a military status. This may possibly induce men to come forward, but I do not feel very sanguine –

Pearson sent back his native contingent battalions and his mounted corps, but forgot to send back his oxen with them – He attempted to send them away without escort, and has lost 600 of them![31]

He cannot remain at Ekowe many weeks, as his food supply will not last – I do not see any advantage in his holding on there, as to feed him would require a bush fight, or battle of Inyazana, every time supplies were sent, and we have not the number of men sufficient to escort the waggons – The latter however cannot move for want of drivers, so on those grounds it would be almost impossible to send a convoy on, except of course under the most urgent case of necessity –

Pearson's force will have to fall back upon the Umsindoosi river, which is clear of the track of the bush country between Lower Tugela and Ekowe – We shall be able to feed him there, but our transport difficulty will again crop up –

My idea is that our only chance of making any real impression in Zululand is to reinforce your column to the fullest extent with mounted men and that I will endeavour to do – I propose to send the three companies of the 2/4th now at PMBurg to Utrecht, dropping one company at Newcastle – which must again be made a commissariat and advance depôt – Were any thing to happen to Utrecht, your column would find it difficult to get supplies within a reasonable distance – Here again, however, I am met with difficulties, as Col Bray left three companies with two captains and 2 sub Lieutenants, and with only 6 sergeants all told!! –

My ADC Capt Buller has gone to the Free State to see what can be done for us by Mr Brand – any mounted men, European or native, will be sent to you –

I hope you have called for the Transvaal volunteers that came to Derby, and that you will indent for the companies 80th Reg should you be able to place them to greater advantage – We may look upon the Swazies as out of the game, and it will be far better not to identify ourselves with such questionable individuals – [32]

We have had no news of you since your despatch dated 24th January –

I am anxious to hear how many men Buller will lose –[33] I hope the cattle taken may induce many to stick to him for some time longer – Mr Haines[34] has arrived here with cattle and wants to go away on leave – As he has no authority to ask for it I told Bellairs to refuse it until he could communicate with his C.O.

Send us down any scraps of information you collect regarding feeling in Zululand – We are absolutely without any here – All is apparently quiet along the Natal border, but everyone nearby expects a raid to be made; and Greytown and PMBurg are forming extra defences – [35]

Mitchell and Hime[36] are making great efforts to improvise a laager inside the town, and have done a lot of work – The townspeople altho' in a fright, are however terribly apathetic, and give little or no assistance –

When you have thought over the situation kindly let me know what your views are regarding it – Let me know particularly what you think you and your column can do, when reinforced, and how I can assist you – 1 & 3 columns will only be able to remain on the defensive, I am afraid, for some time, and perhaps make small raids now and again – The road, or track, by which either has to advance, requires numerous posts to guard the line of communications and until reinforcements arrive there are not enough for the purpose – The advance to Ekowe shows that it is a mistake to move in farther than you can get back from easily, or that you can be regularly fed –

I wish I saw my way with honour out of this beastly country, and had you as my travelling companion. Best love to Buller – You two will have to pull me out of the mire –

WC II/2/2

56

Notes by Chelmsford on the findings of the Court of Enquiry

[Holograph] n.d.[37]

Position of Insandlwana

Insandlwana is an isolated, flat-topped hill running almost due North and South – It is under 300 yards in length, and has precipitous sides along its whole perimeter, and its top is consequently inaccessible – [38]

The camp was pitched along its Eastern side facing East – The ground in front of the camp and to the right & left front of it fell away from the hill in an easy slope, & was perfectly open for a distance of at least 800 yards –

The ground which commanded it on the left was 1300 yards distance, and the stony hill on the right which dominated the camp {by about 70 feet,} was 600 yards distance from the nearest end of hill and only 100 yards broad at the point where advantage could have been taken of it. The position therefore was practically uncommanded from any point, (taking the nature of the guns with which the Zulus were armed into consideration). The rear was perfectly secure; although commanded, at the furthest effective range of the Martini Henry, the ground to its front and flanks – I consider that there never was a position where a small force could have made a better defensive stand –

{The garrison consisted of

562 [?smudged] Europeans	armed with rifles –
204 Mounted Volunteers	
450 Mounted Natives	
391 Native contingent	
Total = [?][39]}	

Assuming that it was thought desirable to occupy the whole front of Insandlwana hill, 300 yards in length; this would have given 4 rifles per running yard to the fighting line –

What force of Zulus could have successfully assaulted a front of battle so defended?

The ammunition was abundant; the soldiers were good steady shots; and every one before the disaster, felt confident that they could defeat any numbers that came against them –

Had the tents been lowered as was invariably done afterwards[40] by pulling out the tent-poles, they would also have formed an entanglement at a convenient distance from the position to be defended, which would have materially strengthened its defensive qualities –

The ground was too rocky to throw up even a shelter trench, but the waggons which were ready inspanned at 10 am (vide Lt Cochrane's[41] evidence) could if thought necessary have been formed into a laager –

Seeing however that each yard of the defensive line would have been defended by 4 rifles, it is clear that such an additional procedure was not absolutely necessary –

A shelter trench is a protection against rifle fire, but would be of no avail against a rush of Zulus –

The waggon laager was never intended to be used as a redoubt, but as a protection for the oxen –

In the march to Eshowe the troops bivouacked & fought outside the waggons – [42]

Major Clery
On the morning of the 22 Jan 1879 before leaving the camp Major Clery sent the following written instructions to Lt Col Pulleine:–

"You will be in command of the camp during the absence of Colonel Glyn – Draw in (I speak from memory) your camp, or your line of defence, (I am not certain which) while the force is out – Also draw in the line of your infantry outposts accordingly, but keep your cavalry vedettes still far advanced" – 43

Major Clery went to Col Pulleine's tent, just before leaving camp, to see that he had got these instructions, and again repeated them verbally to him –

Major Clery also believes that in the written instructions he mentioned that Colonel Durnford had been ordered to bring up his force to strengthen the camp –

Major Crealock
Lt. Colonel Crealock also had sent written instructions to Colonel Durnford "to move up to Insandlwana camp at once with all your mounted men and the rocket battery and take command of it" – 44

Capt Essex
About 8 am a report arrived in camp from a picket stationed at a point about 1500 yards distant that a body of the enemys troops could be seen approaching from the North East – i.e. from the left front of the camp –

N.B. – Insandlwana camp faced almost due East –

Upon the receipt of this news Colonel Pulleine assembled the 24th Regiment in the open space near the Head Qr. tents, which were pitched about the centre of the Isandhlwana Hill and close to it – He also sent off a mounted man with a report to Colonel Glyn – About 9 am a small body of the enemy showed itself just over the crest of the hills to the left front but returned almost immediately out of sight –

Lt Cochrane
About 10 am Colonel Durnford arrived in camp, and took over the command from Lt Col Pulleine, who several times in course of conversation repeated the orders he had received viz – "to defend the camp"

The distribution of the troops was as follows –

Native Contingent on outpost duty on the hills to the left;
Two guns N/5 RA in position on the left of the camp;
Infantry formed up in column in the open space in front of the Head Quarter {Infantry} tents –

The waggons were inspanned

Reports were coming in constantly. Some were to the effect – "That the enemy are in force behind the hills to the left"

"The enemy are in three columns"

"The columns are separating, one moving to the left rear, and one towards the General"

"The enemy are retiring in every direction" This last message was brought in by a man not dressed in uniform –

Colonel Durnford on hearing this last report said that he would go out and prevent the one column joining the force which was supposed to be engaged with the troops under the General – and he asked Lt Colonel Pulleine to give him two companies 24 Regt to go with the natives.

Col Pulleine objected, stating that he did not think he would be justified in sending away any men as his orders were "to defend the camp"

He agreed however with Colonel Durnford to send him help if he got into difficulties.

Colonel Durnford then about 11 am sent two troops of mounted natives onto the hills to the left*, and advanced himself with the two other troops and the rocket battery to the front –

Capt Essex
At this time about 11 am the impression in camp was that the enemy had no intention of advancing during the day time, but might possibly be expected to attack it during the night –

No idea had been formed regarding the probable strength of the enemy's force

*These were shortly afterwards reinforced by a third one which had been sent to assist the baggage into camp

At the same time that Colonel Durnford left the camp, a company of 1/24th under Lt Cavaye[45] was sent out on picket to a hill to the north of the camp about 2000 yards distant – This was done at Col Durnford's order –

Lt Cochrane

Colonel Durnford cantered on with the two troops of natives about five or six miles instructing the rocket battery with its escort of native contingent to follow on as best it could.

At this time a mounted man came down from the hills on the left and reported to Col Durnford that there was an immense force of the enemy behind the hills to the left.

He had hardly made the report when the Zulus appeared to his front and to his left in skirmishing order, 10 or 12 deep, with supports close behind –

They opened fire at the mounted men at about 800 yards distance – Colonel D retired in skirmishing order keeping up a steady fire for about two miles, when he came upon the remains of the rocket battery which had been cut off and destroyed –

Capt Nourse[46]

The retreat was continued slowly and in good order as far as a spruit one mile to the front of the camp –

Capt Essex

Nothing occurred in camp during Colonel Durnford's absence with the mounted men until 12 noon –

The troops had been sent to their private parades –

About noon firing was heard on the hill where Lt Cavaye's company was on picket –

Captain Gardner and Captain Essex

and shortly after Capt. G. Shepstone arrived in camp from that direction, and said that he had been sent by Colonel Durnford for reinforcements as the mounted men were heavily engaged on the hills to the left.

Lt Col Pulleine sent out first Captain Mostyn's company,[47] and a little later also those commanded by Captain Younghusband – [48] so that half of his force of British Infantry were sent away about a mile from the extreme left of the camp –

Lt Col Pulleine drew up the remaining three companies, in skirmishing order, on each side of the two guns[49] to the left front of the camp and at about ½ a mile distance from it – facing North –

Nobody therefore was left in the camp itself, but the servants, hospital orderlies, dismounted men, conductors, &c, who, altho' armed with rifles and therefore available for the defence of the camp, were too few to resist with any chance of success, (even had they been assembled, which it does not appear was done) any determined rush of Zulus round the rear of the scattered fighting line –

The position about 12 noon was as follows –

Three troops of natives on hills to left, about 1½ miles from camp –

Two companies British Infantry } in same position
One company Native Contingent }

One company British Infantry below the hill on the left –

{————————}

Three companies British Infantry and 2 guns under Lt Col P. – in position to left front of camp, and about ½ a mile distant from it –

{————————}

Two troops Natives under Col D. three miles to front of camp – [50]

{————————————————————————}

The two companies British Infantry, and the company Native Contingent, came first into action on the crest of the hill, about 12 noon but were soon after retired to a position 400 yards from the base of the hill, where they were reinforced by another company under Capt Younghusband –

The Zulus followed them down the hill at about 800 yards distance.

The ammunition of the two companies, which had first come into action, running short, Captain Essex rode back into camp to order up some more –

On his return he found that the three companies had retired again and were now about 400 yards from the left of the camp –

About this time the mounted men under Colonel Durnford were making their final stand 800 yards to the front of the camp – and the three companies and two guns under Lt Colonel Pulleine were also in action with the enemy –

At this moment the Native Contingent gave way,[51] and the Zulus swarmed into the camp on the left through the gap between the two bodies of British Infantry, who vainly endeavoured to retire and take up a final position inside the camp* They were all surrounded, and mobbed and had to fight to the last almost where they stood –

Colonel Durnford, about the time that this disaster occurred on the left, had also seen that his men were being outflanked on the right – He therefore gave the order to retire from the spruit above mentioned, to a final position inside the camp but as Lt Cochrane says in his evidence "It was too late" –

The men sold their lives dearly, and died like brave men – but the final struggle was a hopeless one –

* but as Cap Essex says in his report "It was too late".

CP 8/31 [Printed in French, *Lord Chelmsford*, pp. 144–50 with the words between {} omitted.]

57
Lieutenant-General Lord Chelmsford to Colonel H.E. Wood

[Holograph] Durban
7 February 1879

Pray congratulate Buller from me on his successful raid against the Baqulusini Kraal – It must have quite an effect in that part of the country, and will show the Zulus that we are not in the least cowed by our misfortune at Insandlana – [52]

I am very anxious to know what use you will be able to make of the force from Derby, and whether the Swazies will really come down and assist – I am inclined to doubt it myself –

I am living in hope that the Zulus will attack Pearson's force at

Ekowe and that he will then be able to withdraw a good portion of his present garrison – He has 1350 men locked up in an entrenchment, and there are consequently not enough available to take him supplies when he requires them, which I suppose will be before the end of this month – 600 men properly entrenched and properly provisioned would be ample to hold their own against any force that could be brought against them, and the remaining 700, plus those at the Lower Tugela, would be able to keep open the communications – I have written in this sense to Pearson but have not as yet received any reply – Native runners have been intercepted & killed, & my letters may have been lost –

At the present moment John Dunn's natives are carrying our letters – [53]

I am afraid it will be some time before you get any mounted men from Helpmakaar – Between ourselves Russell appears to have lost heart and has allowed his men to get out of hand I fear. The mounted infantry have no doubt had a rough time of it since they were raised, more especially, Russell's squadron –

Horse sickness has commenced at Rorkes drift and Spalding has lost two horses – It was fortunate for us that it did not come on when many horses were there.

I am looking forward to paying you a visit after I get back to PMBurg from my present trip – My best love to Buller – thank Piet Uys & his Dutchmen for the assistance he is giving –

WC II/2/2

58

Lieutenant-General Lord Chelmsford to Colonel F.A. Stanley

[MS copy] PMBurg
[8] February 1879

It is with much satisfaction that I have the honour to forward the report of the successful defence of Rorke's Drift post on the 22nd and 23rd January.[54]

The defeat of the Zulus at this post and the very heavy loss suffered by them has to a great extent neutralized the effects of the disaster at Isandhlwana and it no doubt saved Natal from a serious invasion – [55]

The cool determined courage displayed by the gallant garrison is beyond all praise, and will I feel sure receive ample recognition.[56]

As at the present moment the lesson taught by this defence is most valuable I have thought it advisable to publish for general information the report in question which I trust will meet with your approval.

CP 8/40 [Printed in *BPP* (C. 2260), no. 10 and again in enc. 2 in no. 13 and also in French, *Lord Chelmsford*, pp. 113–14.]

59

Lieutenant-General Lord Chelmsford to Colonel F.A. Stanley

[MS copy]

Durban – Natal
8 February 1879

. . . Colonel Pearson Comd. No 1 Column writes in good spirits from Ekowe, which is now a strong entrenched position with supplies until the end of the month.

Zulus hover round him, but up to date of last communication from him (the 4th) no attack has been made on him.

The arrival of the 3 Companies 88th Regiment,[57] about 350 men, will enable me to move on to the lower Tugela (Forts Pearson & Tenedos[58]) – the two companies at present between Durban & that point; 2 companies of the Buffs[59] & 5 of the 99th will be then assembled there & will be held in readiness to move in any direction at the shortest notice as soon as the necessary class of transport can be collected.

2. Durban, Stanger, P. Maritzburg & Greytown are now being placed (or are already so) in a position for defence with garrisons, which should prevent panic amongst those living around.[60]

3. At Rorke's Drift & Helpmakaar the position is quite unchanged[61] & the frontier has been quite quiet & the road running from Greytown has been quite open.

Colonel Glyn CB reports that the bodies of Lieuts Melville [sic] & Coghill 24th Regt had been found 5 miles down the river, 300 yards from the Bank – they lay close to each other & a number of dead Zulus around them showed how they had stood their ground – [62]

4. Uneasiness has been felt in the Colony at the prospect of a raid, but the latest information tends to an impression that our forces at Ekowe & Rorkes Drift are to be attacked first

5. Colonel Evelyn Wood Comd No. IV Column has forwarded me two reports copies of which I have the honour to forward – [63] He also expects to be attacked –

I beg to call your attention to the manner in which Lieut Colonel Redvers Buller carried out Colonel Wood's instructions regarding the destruction of the Bagalusini Kraal:[64] the energy & intrepidity shown by this officer & those under his command deserves in my opinion warm commendation & I have so expressed myself to Colonel Wood –

6. I regret to say that nearly half the Volunteers serving under Lieut Col: Buller are now leaving him;[65] they have done good service, but the loss of the services of mounted men such as these, is much to be deplored at this moment – Mounted men are found to be an absolute necessity in this country and I trust the efforts of H.E. the High Commissioner to obtain them from the Free State and Cape Colony may be successful –

7. The Medical Department has lost the services of two valuable officers – Surgeon Major Alcock,[66] who has been invalided, and Surgeon Major Shepherd,[67] who [sic] name is I regret to say among the list of killed on the 22nd January –

8. I have already brought to yr notice the wants of the Royal Artillery – the casualty list shows the severe loss that arms has experienced –

9. I should be very glad if a Field Telegraph could be sent out – In a country of vast distances, with so few facilities for transmission of news, it would be of great value & in the future will supplement

the main lines of telegraph according to the importance of the post.

An application of the Electric light would be of the greatest use to fortified posts and night encampments.

10. Lastly I have the satisfaction of saying the health of the troops is generally good & reports of the conduct are favourable –

11. I continue to receive the greatest possible assistance from rear Admiral Sullivan CB – C.M.G. & all those under his command –[68]

P.S. I have endeavoured in my communications not to lessen the gravity of the situation in Natal & the Transvaal & their frontiers, but at a time when it is my sad duty to forward details of our losses, I would venture to add that I have received from many natives & other sources, information, that the Zulus have been much disheartened by the severe losses they have experienced –

Mr Lloyd Political Assistant to Colonel Wood[69] writes on Feb: 1st "they are said to be much disheartened with their losses in their attack on the Rorkes Drift Column (No. 3) – the Undi Regt. – more especially the Tulwana Division of it – suffered very heavily".[70]

CP 8/48 [Printed in *BPP* (C. 2260), no. 10 and again in enc. 12 in no. 13]

60

Lieutenant-General Lord Chelmsford to Colonel F.A. Stanley

[Signed MS copy] Durban, Natal
9 February 1879

I consider it my duty to lay before you my opinion, that it is very desirable in view of future contingencies that an officer of the rank of Major General should be sent out to South Africa without delay.

In June last I mentioned privately to His Royal Highness the F.M. Comd in Chief[71] that the strain of prolonged anxiety & exertion, physical & mental was even then telling on me – What I felt then, I feel still more now.

H.E. Sir Bartle Frere concurs in this representation, & pointed out to me that the officer selected, should be fitted to succeed him in his position of High Commissioner.

In making this representation I need not assure you that it will be my earnest desire to carry on my duties for Her Majesty's Service up to the fullest extent of my powers –

WO 32/7709

61

Lieutenant-General Lord Chelmsford to Colonel H.E. Wood

Private
For family only[72]

[Holograph] Lower Tugela
13 February 1879

I was much disgusted to find by a telegram received yesterday from Bellairs that the 40 Dordrecht men intended for Buller has been detained for the defence! of PMBurg – [73] I sent back a strong remonstrance & I trust that they will be at once sent on to you – I have done all I could to strengthen your force, and it is annoying to find my efforts thwarted –

My letters telling Pearson to withdraw from Ekowe every man that was not necessary to its defence has reached him, but unfortunately he did not send his reply in duplicate, and the man who was carrying the answer did not get through on his return – I am therefore ignorant as to when he proposes to move out & cannot send any force out to meet him – The latest news however is that he is only watched by the same force he defeated at Inyezani – [74] If this be true, he will of course be able to get out quite easily – I shall be very glad when he and his 700 men reach this place, as then we can assume the offensive. –

Ekowe is provisioned up to the end of March for its present

garrison, so there is no fear of its being starved out, even if Pearson did not withdraw some of his men –

I found Fort Tenedos most elaborately defended by ditch, parapet, trous de loup, entanglements, &c, &c, but (alas that word) looked into, from one end to the other, by a long strong hill only 300 yards distant!! I have ordered a small stone wall post to be erected on the hill in question, which will make the situation quite safe, but it is fortunate the Zulus did not discover this weak point in our harness –

About 1500 oxen have also been grazing quietly on the Zulu side of the river, at a distance sometimes of three miles from the camp – I have removed the temptation for the present by bringing them back to the right bank side –

The "Active" is anchored off the Tugela mouth ready to stop any attempt at crossing by the bar – The river however has been up for some days, and there appears, so far as we can gather, no present intention on the part of the Zulus to make any raid into Natal –

I hope you thoroughly understood from my previous letters that Colonel Rowlands was in no way entitled to interfere with you in your military command – In fact I wrote to him myself to say that he was to be guided in all his movements by your advice – Pray carry this meaning of mine out to the fullest extent – I should feel most uncomfortable if I thought you were in any way hampered by the presence of Col Rowlands in your District – and I am quite prepared to order him away, if you find him a nuisance –

I hope you will find Col Lanyon of more assistance than his predecessor – [75] I am sure he is very anxious to do his best for us, and he will do all that you ask him if you will only let him know what you wish –

I shall remain here for the present in hopes of meeting Col Pearson – I am afraid all communication is cut off, as our messengers now all decline to risk their lives – I cannot blame them – but I expect that, without hearing from me again, he will take steps to withdraw –

WC II/2/2

62

Lieutenant-General Lord Chelmsford to Colonel H.E. Wood

[Holograph] Lower Tugela Drift
16 February 1879

. . . Your letter of the 3d Feb. had reference to our futile advance and dismissed the relative merits of the road advocated by Sir B. Frere and the Ingwee–Inhlazatye one – [76] I am quite ready to be guided by your advice in this matter, as you are well acquainted with the country North of the Ingutu and I am not –

If Glyn's column is joined onto your's, it will have to change its base of supplies. It could of course start with a good supply, but this would require to be replenished and that could not be done safely from Rorkes drift, unless we had very large escorts which will not be forthcoming – The question then crops up, – where is the new supply depôt to be formed? Will you answer it?

I should like however, if possible, before No 3 column joins onto No 4 that it should go to Insandlana and bury decently the bones of those poor fellows who fell there – but if there should be any risk attending this I would of course postpone it, until after we have finished our task in Zululand –

It would be an entirely separate expedition, and with three regiments might I consider be undertaken safely – In fact I am not sure whether it would not be a good plan with such a force to throw down the gauntlet to the Zulu army and allow them to try what they can do against us when prepared, even though not behind entrenchments. I do not believe that they would have got the better of the force left for the protection of the camp had it been brought together with its back to the precipitous sided hill, where their flanks could not have been turned and where they would have had an unlimited supply of ammunition –

Directly I heard your wishes that Schermbrucker's men[77] should be mounted, I telegraphed my assent to Bellairs –

Rowlands being wanted at Pretoria will leave you all his troops absolutely at your disposal – [78]

We have no signs of Pearson leaving Ekowe with any of his force and I am afraid he is making up his mind to remain there – This would be all very well if the Zulus mean to attack him but I am sure they are far too wise – However he has foodstuff for his whole force up to the second week in April and, by reducing his ration, for some time longer – So I do not feel uneasy about him – The nuisance is however that all communication is completely cut off. No native will try to get to Ekowe –

Four battalions out of the seven of the Natal Native Contingent were affiliated to columns and it was never intended that any of them should work separate from the European troops – Durnford's command was always intended for the defensive in Natal and then to join No 1 column – This was altered afterwards and I was bringing up part of his force to join No 3 column – My present view of the situation coincides pretty nearly with yours – I should let No 1 column occupy Ekowe as their most advanced post from which they could command directly all the country between their road and the sea and indirectly as far as Entumeni and between that post and the Tugela – I would give him two out of the six infantry regiments coming out and perhaps one of the cavalry regiments – [79] The other four regiments would have to go up to No 3 and No 4 columns which would work together – One regiment would be sufficient I expect for the posts of Rorkes drift, Helpmakaar, Lafnies and Landmanns drifts – and you would want me to look after Utrecht, Baltes spruit & Luneberg.

Thus we should have five regiments for the Ngwee–Nshlazatye line besides a very strong force of mounted men

I shall be back at Durban I hope on Tuesday night (18th) and at PMBurg by the end of next week – My best love to Buller –

WC II/2/2

63
Memorandum by Lieutenant-General Lord Chelmsford

Durban
[Holograph] 20 February 1879

Memorandum

The situation on the Lower Tugela line is as follows –
Fort Pearson is occupied by a small party of seamen from the "Tenedos"[80] and a company of 99th Regt –
4 companies 99th Regiment occupy an adjoining hill to Fort Pearson, connected by a narrow saddle –
The mounted infantry are at the foot of the hill on which Fort Pearson is built –
The officers and N C Officers of the 2nd Regt N.N.Contingent are encamped on the saddle which connects the two hills above mentioned but will move to Stanger immediately in anticipation of the natives again being assembled –
The N.C. Officers will be kept as a separate body and, if possible, eventually mounted.
Fort Tenedos is occupied by 40 men of the Tenedos and two Companies The Buffs –
20 of the Mounted Infantry are encamped near the Fort for purposes of patrolling.
100 of Mr J. Dunn's natives armed with breachloaders, are also on the left bank for scouting purposes; small parties being out night and day –

Ekowe is provisioned up to the 15th April for the whole Garrison, at full rations of bread & meat –

Instructions from me have been received by Col Pearson to withdraw, if possible, with every man not essential to the defence of the post, to the Lower Tugela – His reply was unfortunately not sent in duplicate and the man carrying it was shot –

I know however that Col Pearson considered 400 men would be

a sufficient force to defend Ekowe, and in my last letter to him I recommended his leaving 500 or 600 –

His total numbers are 1760; he would thus be able to withdraw 1160 men –

I should like to establish an intermediate post between Lower Tugela and Ekowe, and I understand that on the Inyazani river a suitable position might be found –

The force now available at Lower Tugela is however quite inadequate for the purpose – as all that could be spared would be four companies 99th and about 100 mounted infantry.

This force is held in immediate readiness to move forward however in the direction of Ekowe, should information be brought in, either by scouts or patrols, that a portion of Col. Pearson's force from that post is on its way back –

Until this occurs, or reinforcements arrive from England, I do not consider it would be advisable to make any effort to engage the enemy offensively on this line – or to occupy any intermediate position between Lower Tugela and Ekowe – There would be no commensurate advantage gained by such a move, as the force would not be large enough to act boldly and its advance prematurely could therefore be no assistance to the Garrison of Ekowe –

The moral effect of a force at Ekowe must make itself felt and I am therefore of opinion that the present situation on the Lower Tugela may be accepted as satisfactory –

As regards the border defence I am unable to speak so confidently – The number of natives available for defence from the mouth of the Tugela to the Impesi drift (the extreme limit of Capt Lucas' Command) did not appear to me to be sufficient, and in answer to an inquiry on the subject from the Lt. Governor of Natal, I recommended that one thousand more natives should be placed at Capt Lucas' disposal – I also recommended that the two battalions native contingent belonging to Col Pearson's column should be reassembled at once at Stanger, and should be placed in position about half way between that place and Thrings farm, as a support to Capt Lucas –

I do not consider there is much chance of Zulus crossing in force between the Tugela mouth and Tuohys drift – as a force could easily move out on their flank and rear –

Forts Tenedos & Pearson are now very strong indeed, and I am satisfied are capable of withstanding any attack that is likely to be made upon them –

The general hospital, two miles on the Tugela side of Stanger has been put into a state of defence, and is quite capable of resisting the attack of any number –

The Stanger laager is also very strong, and the defence of that place has been supplemented by the occupation of a house on a commanding piece of ground within 300 yards of the laager, which will be held by 50 men of the 88th Regiment –

Verulam has an excellent laager and apparently plenty of men to defend it effectively – a complaint however was made of an insufficiency of firearms.[81]

The safety of the Durban–Tugela Line would be very materially increased, if arrangements could be made to arm a proportion of the coolies, who are in such numbers about Verulam and its neighbourhood – [82]

At the present moment the natives are absolutely defenceless.

Were a good proportion of firearms issued out for their use, no doubt the planters would form separate defensive laagers for the protection of their own property, which would be of great value in the general system of defence – [83]

Thanks to the quiet determination and good sense of Major Huskisson Commandant of Base of Operations, {which has triumphed over the murmurings and mischievous opposition of a large number of the inhabitants of Durban,} security of that place has been arranged for as satisfactorily as it is possible to be – and every one has been made aware of the several places of defence and refuge which each will have to occupy –

The proposal [made] for a continuous line of defence round the Town is absurd, {and could only have emanated from men entirely ingnorant of the time and numbers which would be required to make such a system of defence of any avail –}

I am however of opinion that a few separate laagers, placed in suitable positions on the outskirts of the town, at distances of not more than 1000 yards apart, and visible, one from the other, could prove an effectual defence, adapted for the limited number of defenders available – This work however cannot be undertaken at present – [84]

As regards the Greytown–Fort Buckingham Line – I consider that Capt. Cherry's battalion Native Contingent which only numbers 200 men & which is entrenched with Capt. Montgomery's Battalion[85] should at once be raised to its proper strength of 1000 – 2000 natives entrenched near Fort Buckingham would be an awkward force for an invading party to pass by –

There is a laager at Hermansburg[86] which to a certain extent would cover the road to Greytown and at this latter place, in addition to the laager and its defenders, there are five Companies of the 2/4th Regt under Major Twentyman.

As regards the Greytown–Helpmakaar line I consider that the men of the two battalions Native Contingent lately serving with No 3 Column should be at once called out again, and placed so as to guard the country near the junction of the Buffalo and Tugela, and of the Mooi and Tugela rivers – The Lt Governor of Natal objects to these battalions being organized under the old conditions, and I therefore recommend that as their presence is indispensable to the proper defence of the district, they should be call'd out under the, so called, tribal system, which apparently commends itself to the Natal Government, but of the value, or details, of which I am perfectly ignorant –

This will give about 3000 natives for the defence of that line, as one Battalion under Major Bengough is now entrenched on the Sand Spruit R – [87] and with the addition of the Border Police and Levies, ought to provide adequately for the defence of this line –

There however, as elsewhere in Natal, firearms for the natives are urgently required – The stores at Helpmakaar are reported as adequately protected – An entrenchment has been thrown up round them, and there is a sufficient garrison for its defence – [88] Rorkes drift post is also reported equally secure – [89]

The Natal Mounted Police, Natal Carbineers, and the Newcastle &

Buffalo Guard volunteers ought to be sufficient to protect the border line from Helpmakaar towards Newcastle from any raiding –

The Imperial Mounted Infantry and the Basuto mounted corps I have ordered to proceed to Utrecht, in front of which place no doubt Colonel Wood will post them –

They will also materially assist in guarding the abovementioned portion of the Natal border –

Two Companies 2/4th Regt under Colonel Bray, are now at Utrecht and will ensure the proper defence of that place, which has necessarily been left with a rather weak garrison –

The main portion of Colonel Evelyn Wood's force is at Kambula Hill on the upper Umvelosi but his advanced store depôt at Balte Spruit is adequately defended having been reinforced by the men who held Utrecht up to the arrival of the 2/4th – [90]

The mobility of Colonel Wood's force has been seriously crippled by the recent departure of 80 time expired men from the Frontier Light Horse,[91] which has left Lt-Col Buller with only 120 Mounted men, exclusive of the Dutchmen under Mr Pieter Uys – [92]

Lüneberg has I trust by this time been reinforced by five Companies 80th Regiment, 2 6 lb Armstrong Guns, worked by men of the same regiment, and about 100 mounted Transvaal volunteers have joined Col Wood – [93] This will set free Commandant Schermbrucker and his 100 Germans who have hitherto been doing garrison duty – [94] These men are to be mounted, and under their gallant leader will, no doubt, in their new capacity, be more useful than before. –

Such is the position of affairs at the present moment –

The troops are at present compelled to remain on the passive defensive, but I am in hopes that Col Woods column will be shortly reinforced by mounted volunteers from the Cape Colony and the Free State, and will thus be enabled to resume its former activity – It is most important that we should resume the offensive as soon as possible, and my best efforts are being directed towards that end; but it would be folly to attempt it with inadequate means –

Were it possible to assemble a good force of natives along the Natal border, well armed with rifles, I believe that it would do much good to their "moral" [sic] to allow them to raid across the border on their own account – Even if they did not take advantage of the permission, the mere fact of being allowed to do so, when a favourable opportunity presented itself, would raise them in their own esteem and would identify them more completely with the colony they are called upon to defend –

Nothing is so demoralizing to both Europeans and Natives as remaining on the passive defensive – It at once admits an inferiority on our part, and a superiority on the side of the Enemy –

I consider, therefore, that the Natal Colonial forces, altho' told off for defence alone, should be made to understand that it may be necessary for them to cross into Zululand if only for a few hours –

I will briefly sum up the present requirements –

1) Captain Lucas force[95] to be increased by 1000 natives, 50 of whom should be mounted –

2) The Battalions of Natal Native contingent belonging to No 1 Column,[96] to be reassembled at Stanger, in view to their supporting Capt Lucas force –

3) Firearms to be sent to Verulam for use of Coolies –

4) Captain Cherry's native battalion at Krantzkop[97] now numbering 200 to be raised to 1000 –

5) Two battalions native contingent formerly serving with No 3 Column, to be reassembled under tribal system for defence of Umsinga District – [98]

6) More firearms to be sent to these native battalions –

7) Every available fighting native in the Colony to be called out, at least for the next six weeks –

CP 26/23 [Words between { } omitted from manuscript copy in GH 1423.]

64

Lieutenant-General Lord Chelmsford to Sir Bartle Frere

[Holograph] 22 February 1879

Memorandum

The complaints made by the natives lately belonging to the contingent attached to No 3 column,[99] and the reasons given for their dispersing and going to their homes, have no doubt a substratum of truth, but I do not believe that there was any serious cause for dissatisfaction up to the day of the Insandlana misfortune, except that the natives were not supplied with food on the 21st consequent upon their not returning to camp as originally intended –

There were I believe in every company officers or N.C. Officers who were capable of making themselves understood – The men were arranged by companies tribally, and had their own Indunas; several chiefs also accompanied them –

There was so much hesitation and delay on the part of the Natal Government in calling out or even in giving permission for the calling out, of the 6000 natives asked for, that it was impossible to make as good arrangements for their organization as I should have wished – Natal could not supply the requisite number of Europeans and I was obliged therefore to indent upon the Cape Colony –

Whilst fully recognizing the necessity of having an interpreter in each company, capable of explaining the orders of the commander or the wishes of the men, I entirely dissent from the axiom which it is apparently the endeavour to lay down,[100] that those officers who cannot speak the Zulu language are, not only of no use with natives, but absolutely an encumbrance –

If all the qualities required for a company leader are to be found in addition to that of speaking Zulu, there can be no question that he is the right man; but if an officer is selected purely for his linguistic knowledge, without reference to the other necessary qualities, then he can only turn out a failure –

Colonel Evelyn Wood has just had to get rid of men of the latter stamp, and has substituted British officers in their place (who are quite innocent of Zulu) with the most satisfactory results –

As the High Commissioner points out, natives when brought together, under whatever conditions, must have some recognizable and workable organization and must be subdivided into recognizable units corresponding to regiments or companies –

GH 1422, pp. 53–5

65

Lieutenant-General Lord Chelmsford to Colonel H.E. Wood

[Holograph]

PMBurg
23 February 1879

. . . I myself should much prefer to know that Buller was your second in command, ready to succeed you in the event of such a necessity, which Heaven forefend [sic] – but how can we get over Bray? Herbert[101] writes to Crealock in praise of the latter and gives him a very good character – I confess I have been much disappointed [in] him and he is not quite the gentleman – However you have got him and so long as he is under you I have no fear – Were he to succeed to the command I am afraid Buller would never serve happily under him –

I hope by this time you have got rid of Rowlands and have got hold of his troops – [102] Five companies, plus the volunteers, not to mention the two guns, will be a good addition to your force, and when Schermbrucker turns out with his 100 mounted Germans I hope you will feel pretty comfortable – If I were Cetywayo I should leave about 10000 men to watch your force at Kambula hill and send the remaining 20000 against Balte spruit and Utrecht – Are you prepared for such a manoeuvre?

I am afraid Russell will take a long time getting over to your side – No 3 column does, as you say, require waking up, but how to do it is beyond my comprehension – Nothing but an entire change could produce such a result.[103]

I shall not be able to get away from here yet-a-while – I shall have to go to Greytown and Krantzkop to see what they are doing there, & so long as Sir Bartle remains I suppose I must be near him, as the Lt Governor (between ourselves) is making himself very disagreeable.[104]

I do not see any objection to your accompanying a large mounted force on a raiding expedition, always provided that the infantry are left in a safe laager – I do not think it would be right for you to go with small raiding parties –

I was so relieved to hear that you had got over your bad attack[105] – If you shut up, I don't know what I should do –

Poor old Hassard and his adjutant Baxter went off in an ambulance today for Durban, en route for Cape Town – The former is very weak indeed from fever and I shall be glad to hear that he is alive on board ship.[106]

We had news of Pearson dated 18th[107] but cannot get a man to take a letter back – He waits to come only with 550 fighting men until I tell him the road is clear and that a force will be sent to meet him and this I cannot do; so I suppose he will hold on – He has sufficient for six weeks more, so I have no anxiety about him –

I think of sending two infantry regiments only to Lower Tugela, and of bringing four infantry & two cavalry regiments up to your part of the world. Do you approve? Best love to Buller. He made a good business of the caves, but Rowlands ought to have been in the affair I think if he had shown any promptitude – [108]

H.M.S. Shah arrived yesterday (22)[109]

WC II/2/2

Chapter 5
The Relief of Eshowe

66

Lieutenant-General Lord Chelmsford to Colonel H.E. Wood

[Holograph] PMBurg
3 March 1879

. . . I am glad you did not allow Buller to go to Insandlana, he could only have performed the burying in a perfunctory manner and it would certainly have been very bad for his men – It would moreover have been immediately seized upon as a slur upon No 3 Column who are really not able to undertake the job without first fighting Sirayo's people who are back in their caves and for which he[1] has not got sufficient strength – When reinforcements come out I will send Glyn a cavalry regiment and an infantry one on purpose to do the work and if you would send some mounted men round the Ngudu Mountain on to the heights overlooking the Insandlana camp it will ensure the work being undisturbed –

I am sorry to hear so bad an account of the Babinango route – [2] as there can be no doubt that from a strategical point of view that line is the right one for us to adopt, as it throws our whole force on to the real objective point, and by taking the Umhlutusi valley in reverse would enable Pearson to forward us supplies from the Lower Tugela – It would also give our reinforcements less distance to march to their respective columns –

Messengers have arrived from Cetywayo at Krantzkop asking for peace and saying that our fighting against each other has been quite a mistake![3] I hope to be able to give him his answer next week by sending a column forward to Ekowe – Sir B. Frere is not prepared to approve of any reply but that of unconditional surrender and general disarmament, coupled with the conditions already laid down – I shall be very glad to hear that you are able to bring the 80th companies into the Field – There is no doubt that they have hitherto been very unfortunate – [4] I hope to be able to send away one company of the 2/4th from here to Newcastle – if not more – Had I my way I should send all three at once, and 2 companies from Greytown to join your force, but I am sure that the Lt Governor would object – for fear of this . . . [illegible] from that place and this one!

I have just come back from Greytown and Krantzkop – I am collecting as many natives as I can secure out of the Government along the Tugela border and I hope to be able to send in large raiding parties with a hooroosh, directly you are in a position to resume the advance – There is plenty of cattle on the other side, and I think the natives are quite prepared to try their hand at lifting them –

Tell Buller that if I can see my way he shall have Carrington, but at present it would not be right to move him away – [5]

I shall go down to the lower Tugela in a few days to arrange with Law about the advance to Ekowe –

WC II/2/2

67

Lieutenant-General Lord Chelmsford to Sir Henry Bulwer

[Holograph] PMBurg
4 March 1879

<u>Memorandum</u>

I regret that I have not had time to reply to his Excellency the Lt Governor's memorandum of 7 February last until today – [6] I am unwilling to continue the controversy regarding the tribal and regimental system as adopted in the Natal native Contingent and I only wish to say that the tribal system as sketched out by Sir Henry Bulwer was fully carried out in Commandant Lonsdale's contingent and that the names of the officers of that Contingent were submitted to and approved by him before being appointed – I am aware that this was a mere matter of form as His Excellency could not have any personal knowledge of the officers in question; but it is important as showing that I did not, as stated by His Excellency, appoint these officers without reference to him –

The system sketched out by His Excellency the Lt Gov as to how in his opinion the native contingent should be officered, so as to retain his power over them as Supreme Chief could only answer under the supposition that very competent men are nominated to the command of the Contingent, as the representatives of the Govt. of Natal or the Lt Governor as the Supreme Chief; and that they would subordinate their own military views to those of the military commander under whom for all military purposes they are expected to act –

It appears to me to be a system fraught with great danger, as creating an imperium in imperio, and one that would be liable to lead to dangerous complications in the Field. It appears to me tantamount to appointing a military officer to command a battalion, but giving the command of the companies to civilians –

With the exception of the officers being nominated by the Lt Governor, all the other details of the system as sketched out by His Excellency were carried out –

Commandant Lonsdale has distinctly stated that no N.C. Officer in his regiment was allowed to give any orders or to interfere in any way with the natives of the several companies – they were with him simply what I always desired them to be viz – personal escorts to the company officers –

I merely used the expression "Supreme Military Chief" as representing my position with regard to the command of the Native contingents, and not as arrogating to myself a special position in the Natal Colony –

There can be no question that any force, whether European or native, which is placed under my command must, if there is to be any discipline and obedience to orders, look upon their commander for the time being as Supreme, and I feel sure that the native contingents, when in the Field, quite recognize that fact –

I cannot understand what His Excellency means by saying that "the connection between their lawful Supreme Chief and the Natal native contingent" was severed by my act – and without reference to him – Altho', as Sir Henry Bulwer justly says, the system I pressed upon him was not in accordance with His Excellency's views, still it was acquiesced in by him without meeting with his approval, at my solicitation –

As regards the complaints made by Umkungo, I have only to state that they must be looked upon as second hand, as that chief was not in the Field.

His brother Isikoto accompanied the contingent, and, according to Commandant Lonsdale's report to me on the 23rd January, expressed his perfect willingness to serve again with his men – [7]

The men were under their own native leaders – I endeavoured to obtain European officers in Natal, in order that the natives should have those with them who knew and understood them, but they were not to be found, and I was consequently forced to apply to the old Colony for those who had served under me before –

The Lt Governor has not quite appreciated my meaning as represented by him in the concluding paragraph of the memorandum under report – All I objected to was that a mass of natives should be placed at my disposal without any organization than the vague one shadowed forth under the vague term "tribal"

I have now received another memorandum written by His Excellency Sir H. Bulwer for the information of the High Commissioner, in which the tribal system as interpreted by Sir H Bulwer is more fully sketched out[8]

It recognizes the necessity of bodies of a certain strength, and of these bodies being subordinated into smaller fractions – It provides for a commander of the larger body, and for sub commanders of the fractions –

It insists upon the European leaders being recognized as the representatives of the Supreme Chief; but, in other respects, this so called tribal system is merely a feeble imitation of the regimental one – This must necessarily be the case – When large numbers are brought together to act as soldiers they must be divided and subdivided, or command & interior management becomes impossible –

I cannot but think that his Excellency the Lt Governor and myself have been arguing this question out without having thoroughly understood that the points of difference between us are not really vital ones –

Had I been in possession of His Excellency's present views six months ago I feel sure that it would have been possible to have organized the native contingents in a manner which would have been satisfactory to us both –

GH 1421, pp. 113–22 [Printed in *BPP* (C. 2318), enc. 14 in no. 1.]

68

Lieutenant-General Lord Chelmsford to Colonel H.E. Wood

[Holograph]

Durban
6 March 1879

I know well how you & Buller will rejoice over the good news from home as contained in the last telegrams, which were published yesterday – No two men in my command have supported me more loyally; and I know that you are both sincere friends as well as trustworthy "Lieutenants" – [9]

The first two regiments (infantry) that arrive I shall at once send down to Lower Tugela and if necessary a third – Ekowe must be properly provisioned and garrisoned before any general advance of natives along the Tugela line is possible, and the possession of the country between that place, the Umhlatoosi R and the sea, will have a very important effect and in a great measure I believe take pressure off the northern columns –

I shall send the two regiments of cavalry North as soon as

possible –[10] One will go to you at once and the other after we have buried the poor fellows as Insandlwana –

As reinforcements must be expected out so soon I shall remain in these parts until the column for the relief of Ekowe has been started and fulfilled its mission.

You will I fear begin to consider my repeated promises to come up to you as made of piecrust – I have however no anxiety about you, and I have in other directions – You may rest assured of my sending to you as many men as I can possibly raise, and I know that you will make the best possible use of them – The troops which will arrive about the end of this month, cannot, I reckon, be with you before the end of April and the cavalry will perhaps be even later than that – If Mr de Villiers raises his 800 Free Staters,[11] you will then have a force with which we shall be able to sweep the whole country in front of you, but Ernest Buller thinks that Mr Whitehead[12] has been too sanguine in this point – The announcement of such large reinforcements however may possibly have its effect, and make the Dutchmen anxious to participate in what, they must see, ought to be a great success.

The Cavalry commanders will want someone to coach them in the ways of the country – I shall attach a body of mounted natives to each regiment, to assist them, when marching up-country, in looking after the horses, who I suppose will rather resent kneehaltering at first, and will be inclined to take too much advantage of their liberty when out grazing – If the 17th Lancers only get a chance in the open against a large body of Zulus, they will astonish them! but I am afraid the enemy will be too wary – The *Shah* has arrived and will land her contingent this afternoon – The *Boadicea* hopes to leave Simons bay in 7 days time, as no fresh case of smallpox has appeared – We shall have about 800 Naval Brigade on shore! when she gives up her quota –[13]

My best love to Buller –

I am sending you two more companies 2/4th, one from Newcastle, the other from Utrecht –

WC II/2/2

69

Lieutenant-General Lord Chelmsford to Colonel F.A. Stanley

[Signed MS copy]

Durban
Natal
[16] March 1879

1. The date of my last dispatch was the 2nd March since which time nothing has occurred to alter the situation beyond the fact that "Uhamu", brother to the Zulu King, gave himself up on the 4th March to Captain Macleod, late 74th Highlanders, Political Agent in Swaziland; and he is now with No 4 Column.

2. It will be within your recollection that Colonel Wood for many months past has reported his belief that this important chief would separate himself from the King when opportunity offered, and Colonel Wood has always treated the natives of Uhamu's district, when it was in his power to do so, in a manner which would induce them to join us; to his and Captain Macleod's judicious management of the matter I am inclined to believe this action of Uhamu's is chiefly due.

3. Now, No 3 Column has no transport and is therefore unable to move. Colonel Wood cannot do more than keep the Northern District free from a Zulu force, I am in hopes, however, that the reinforcements of mounted men now marching to join him, will enable him to push his reconnaissances some considerable distance.

4. None of the messengers sent by us to Ekowe reached Colonel Pearson, so that, for a month, it now appears he was without news of the arrangements being made to relieve him: a messenger, however, reached us from Ekowe on the 11th instant, dated the 9th March, it was in cypher and informed Colonel Law R.A., Commanding Lower Tugela, that his flashing signals had been understood. Colonel Pearson instructed that it would be desirable to relieve the whole of the garrison as Officers and men were generally sickly and that any relieving force should bring a convoy and be prepared to fight.

Up to yesterday we were unable however to read their signals, but I am happy to say that last night I received information that communication to and from Ekowe, by means of flashing signals, was quite established.

5. As horse sickness has shown itself in the Lower Tugela valley, I have directed two Companies of the "Buffs", the 2nd Squadron Mounted Infantry and Native Mounted Contingent[14] to take up a position, and entrench it, on the high ground by St Andrew's Mission Station[15] some 3 miles in Zululand beyond Fort Tenedos.

6. The reinforcements so promptly despatched to our assistance are arriving.

The Naval Brigade, landed from H.M.S. "Shah", is already across the Frontier near Fort Tenedos. The "Boadicea" arrived yesterday,[16] and a portion of the Bluejackets and 40 marines will be landed tomorrow.

The 57th Regiment, in the "Tamar"[17] arrived on the 10th March from Ceylon in 16 days, and were disembarked the following day: they leave for the Lower Tugela tomorrow.

The "Pretoria"[18] with the 91st has arrived today and the "Dublin Castle" with the 3/60th leaves the Cape today.

7. These three Regiments will be pushed on with all speed to the Lower Tugela, and will form a portion of the relieving force, to advance on Ekowe, which will there be as follows:–

"Shah"
"Tendos"
"Buffs"
"99th Regt
"57th –"–
"91st –"–
"3/60th –"–
2nd Squadron Mounted Infantry
& other native details mounted & foot;

the garrison of that place has supplies up to the 15th April,* but before that time it will have been regarrisoned, revictualled and will become the pivot of future operations on that line.

*see *post.*, Para 24.

8. If a General Officer arrives from England (as stated in the papers to be probable) in time to take charge of the Column, I myself shall, after seeing him mark his start, return here to complete the arrangements for the disposal of the remainder of the reinforcements, and then proceed with all expedition and take command of the force on the Northern border which will consist of the following troops:

No IV Column under Colonel Wood, as before reported, at "Kambula Hill"

2/21st Regiment
2/24th do
58th do
94th do
1st Dragoon Guards
17th Lancers
2 Batteries R.A.[19]
} on the Doornberg

These forces will probably be used as two Brigades of Infantry and one of Cavalry, the whole force being under my own command, but until I know what superior Officers come out I am unable to settle details.

9. I am induced to send the two Cavalry Regiments up country, as the risk on the lower line is too great for English horses, the lower Column, however, will be strengthened by all the mounted men now coming up from Capetown [sic] under Commandants Lonsdale and Browne.[20]

10. After the events of the 22nd January it appeared to both H.E. the High Commissioner and myself to be very necessary to raise, with the least possible delay, mounted men from every available source, and I have before had the honour of reporting to you what steps were taken with this view; I now beg to submit a state [sic] showing the troops of all descriptions now under my command, or about to arrive.

11. I do not expect that any force will be raised in the Free State, indeed after the delay that has occurred, I do not desire it.[21]

12. With reference to your letter of 15 February (& 30 Jan) received yesterday, I have to apologise very much if there has been any misunderstanding relative to the raising of a Native

Contingent in Natal of about 6: to 7,000 men for Imperial purposes, and to be paid out of Imperial funds; unluckily the whole of my Military Secretary's papers were lost at Sandhlwana and I am therefore unable to refer to them, but it was my impression that the whole circumstances connected with the Officering and organization of this contingent of 7 Battalions and 5 troops of mounted natives had been laid before you.[22]

13. Owing to the views held by the Colonial Government on the subject the raising and organizing of the Contingent was too long delayed and the result was very clearly to be seen in subsequent events.

14. Six battalions and a small portion of a 7th were raised, but, soon after the 22nd January the Natives of only two battalions remained with them, (they had not been engaged with the enemy;); the Natives of the 2 battalions No 2 Regiment have since been ordered out by the Lt Governor (as supreme chief) there are now therefore, as seen by the state [sic] annexed, 4 whole Battalions of Imperial Natal Native Contingent under arms, under my command, and some mounted men – the European Officers and N.C. Officers of the 2 battalions with No 3 Column are being utilized in another manner but are still on our payment.[23]

15. The High Commissioner left PMaritizburg yesterday for the Transvaal.

I have received no information of value as to the present feeling of the Transvaal Boers, but am inclined to think that the arrival of reinforcements will cause what seemed to be open discontent and threatened rebellion, to disappear.

16. During the time the High Commissioner has been in Natal he has assisted me in every possible way in obtaining from the Natal Government, what appeared to be necessary.

17. During the past week the Lt Governor has consulted me as to what I consider necessary for the defence of Natal.

18. There has been a very large expenditure from Imperial sources for the services which, it may be considered, should be borne by the Colonial Government. Under the instructions of H.E. the High Commissioner, I have authorized the Staff Paymaster to meet such payments, on the schedule being signed by me or by my

deputy in my absence, the amounts to be adjusted hereafter; this appeared, equally to me as to Sir Bartle Frere, to be the only possible procedure under the pressure of present arrangements, and I trust my action will meet with your approval.
19. Up to the present time our endeavours to obtain a sufficient number of serviceable horses at a reasonable price £20 to £25, have been successful but I fear we shall now be forced to raise our price, if . . . [illegible] then we can procure what we want
20. Of mules there is no longer, I believe, any supply in this part of South Africa, but I have authorized the purchase of some in the Cape Colony,[24] and I have already informed you by telegraph of the advisability of sending some out.
21. The agent for Mr Donald Currie[25] was good enough to make a communication to the Naval authorities relating to his principals' desire to assist in any way our arrangements for landing horses and troops, a contact was already in existence with a Mr Crowder of Durban,[26] and it had appeared (before Mr Donald Currie's communication was received by me) to both the Admiral[27] and myself, only right that he should be continued and assisted in this contract which does not expire until the 31st instant. As, by that time, probably, the heaviest part of the work will be completed, it has been thought advisable to accept his offer to continue the contract, should he, up to that date, have given satisfaction.
22. With reference to the supposed message from Ketchwayo, reported in my last despatch as having been received by the High Commissioner I have not been furnished with a copy of the answers by H.E. the High Commissioner, but my recollection of its contents, is to the effect that nothing short of the terms before enumerated, unconditional surrender of Ketshwayo, and disarmament, would be accepted; he also informed the messengers that all communications re the subject, must be addressed to myself.[28]
23. From many different sources I have received information that the Zulu King experiences considerable difficulty in reassembling his army, their heavy losses being stated to be the reason, and, no doubt, the defection of "Oham" will have considerable influence in the politics of the country. I do not, however, place too much credence on native reports of any description, and I have no doubt

myself but that the Zulus, as a nation will be found once more in the field when we advance.

24. With reference to my statement in Para 7. of this despatch stating that Ekowe was provisioned up to 15th April, this information was based on the returns of the Commissariat Officer with Colonel Pearson and forwarded through him. Last night, however, the following message was signalled from Ekowe

"Short rations until 3rd April, Bread stuffs until 4th April, plenty of trek oxen. Captain Williams, the "Buffs"[29] died at Ekowe on 13th March."

This information will therefore necessitate the relieving column starting not later than 28th instant.

WO 32/7718

70

Lieutenant-General Lord Chelmsford to Colonel H.E. Wood

[Holograph]

Durban
17 March 1879

I have told Bellairs to inform you officially that some place on the Doornberg will be the place of rendezvous for the new brigade of 3 regts Infantry and the cavalry brigade of 2 regts[30] – and asking you to select the spot and form the commissariat depôt.

I do not think the depôt ought to be a permanent one for the reasons given in my last letter to you – [31] It will be much more convenient to have our supplies for both Brigades on one line – I have given up the idea of burying the poor fellows at Insandlwana until after our campaign is over – It must be a very long business as the skeletons will be spread over a large extent of country, and we cannot really afford to delay a day –

I hope to start with the relieving column for Ekowe on the 28th. The force will be a large one but we shall have about 120 waggons[32] to escort through a rather nasty country and this means about 4 miles in length of column – On the march and at night I see my way, but I am a little puzzled how to protect so many oxen when grazing in a bush country, and if the enemy attack us vigorously at that time it will be difficult I am afraid to drive them quickly enough into the waggon laager – We have been successful in establishing flashing signalling with Ekowe – They have rations up to the 4 April only, so it is high time a convoy & column went to their relief – It seems almost certain that we shall be attacked and I have been anxious therefore to make my column as strong as possible so that we may read the Zulus a severe lesson –

If you are in a position to make any forward movement about the 27th of this month, so that the news of it may reach the neighbourhood of Ekowe about the 29th I think it might have a good effect – I shall tell the border commandants to make demonstrations all along the line also, and if the river admits to raid across for cattle – Crealock's brother,[33] Newdigate & F. Marshall will be here about the end of the month – The former will be placed in command of the Lower Tugela column – The two others will go to Doornberg – I apply today to High Commissioner for your being given Local rank of Brigadier General. –

I shall hope to get back to Natal about the 7th of April, if all goes well with me – By that time all the reinforcements should be landed and I shall be free to move up towards Utrecht – I am afraid however you will not believe in my coming after so many false alarms –

WC II/2/2

71

Lieutenant-General Lord Chelmsford to Colonel H.E. Wood

[Holograph]

Lower Tugela
24 March 1879

. . . I quite agree with what you say about having more horses than men for mounted work in this country – Wainwright I fancy must be still buying horses, and will be kept at it continuously –

However I will make sure about it – The landing has all been satisfactorily arranged for and 34 [horses] have been brought on shore without accident. The bar rarely permits of horses being swum on shore.[34] It would not do to wait for the few chances – Knee straps & reins were ordered nearly a month ago and ought to be ready for the horses as they land –

I have already told you about the arrangements for this line and that the 57, 60 and 91st[35] are being sent here – I wish you could see for yourself the difficulties of relieving & reprovisioning Ekowe, as it is impossible to realize them except on the spot – The fact is Ekowe is just about 10 miles too far from here. The coast road which was not taken by Col Pearson is evidently the best, and is open up to the distance named. The waggon track then has to go along a twisting, narrow, ridge with deep kloofs on each side for about 6 miles, and, it is there that in all probability we shall have our first fight –

John Dunn, with whom I had a long talk today seems to think so, and advises our forming a laager of half our waggons just below the ridge on the Inyazana, and then that we should take the remaining half which would not be so much in our way when we are attacked, as if we had the whole convoy to attend to.

Fynney was also with me today and spoke about the Mhlazatye road which he said "he had seen advocated in the newspapers" – He travelled over it in 1876 when going from Pretoria to Ulundi and declares it to be quite impracticable for a long train of waggons – His own waggon he says had to have <u>three</u>! wheels locked when going down one particular hill and he added that immediately after there was an equally bad one to ascend – He does not believe that double spans would take our waggons over it – 16 miles represents the total distance which is really difficult. He has promised to put down in writing what he remembers of the road and, when I get his account, I will send it to you – It is clear that more information about that line is wanted before we commit ourselves to it – Mr Rorke or Mr Camberley[36] ought to know something about it; and perhaps your friend Oham –

Black who has visited Insandlwana describes the stench as still very sickening – [37] It would not do therefore to attempt any burying for some time to come even if I could manage it – I have read over your instructions for the column, and approve of nearly all – when we meet we will discuss those on which I am doubtful – I do not think you will be given a CMG. The Duke has received my letter deprecating its being given and seemed quite to acknowledge that it was hardly the right reward – He spoke very warmly about you –

WC II/2/2

72

Lieutenant-General Lord Chelmsford to Colonel F.A. Stanley

[Signed MS copy]

Hd Quarter Camp
Lower Tugela
25 March 1879

{Thanks for the prompt despatch of reinforcements from England. I shall in three days time be able to advance with the strong column strength as per margin to relieve the garrison of Ekowe, which has now been holding that post for upwards of 10 weeks.

As none of the Major Generals ordered out have yet arrived and Colonel Pearson, who at first commanded the column on this line, is shut up in Ekowe and as there is no other senior officer available for the duty, I have decided to take command of the relieving column myself, assisted by Colonel Pemberton 60 Rifles and Lt Colonel Law Royal Artillery.[38]

The column will not advance by the road which Colonel Pearsons column took but by one which runs nearly parallel to it but nearer to the coast: the advantage of this line is that the road runs through an easy open country for 3/4 of the distance, whereas by the other line the road runs through bush country nearly the whole way.}

The force will advance without tents and with only a blanket & waterproof sheet for each man.

Notwithstanding however this reduction of weight the convoy, carrying one months provisions for the garrison and 10 days supplies (without groceries) for the relieving column will consist of 44 carts and about 100 wagons.

With such a length of train, the greater portion of which is drawn by oxen, it will be impossible to do more than about 11 miles in the day; and even this distance according to the calculations of the colonial transport conductors will require nearly all the hours of daylight to be accomplish [sic], if due regard be paid to the interests of the oxen who will not work well in the heat of the day, and who require at least three hours for feeding –

I am desirous of bringing the transport difficulties prominently to your notice, as unless they are fully realised, it will be difficult to understand the apparent slowness which must characterize the movements of the relieving column.

It is probable that the Column will be attacked when moving along the last 10 miles of the road between this place and Ekowe.

{The track according to the information of those who know the country, runs along a narrow but open ridge, with deep ravines on each side, and is only wide enough for one wagon; it twists and turns considerably and is reported as being favourable for the attacks of an enterprising enemy.

I have suggested to Colonel Pearson by sun signal[39] that he should be prepared to make a diversion in support of the relieving column with every available fighting man that can be spared from the defence of the post.}

I should feel no doubt about being able successfully to convey the convoy and fresh garrison into Ekowe and to bring out the present garrison with its train of empty waggons were the transport of different quality.

A force moving, however, with ox transport through a difficult country is heavily hampered, if attacked determinedly by large numbers, and whilst feeling every confidence in the ability, courage and determination of those under my command I trust that should our efforts fall short of what is no doubt, expected of us, that circumstances may be duly taken into consideration.

WO 32/7722 [Extracts printed in French, *Lord Chelmsford*, p. 171 with the words between {} omitted.]

73
Memorandum by Lieutenant-General Lord Chelmsford

[Holograph] n.d. [? c. 26 March 1879]

Companies must be held together in close order – Files must loosen out, but will not be extended

Each waggon and cart with the convoy must have some ammunition boxes placed on it in such a position as to be easily got at –

The regimental reserve boxes must have the screw of the lid taken out, and each waggon or cart will have a screwdriver attached to one of the boxes so it may be ready for opening when the screw has not been taken out – [40]

The supply waggons containing stores for the garrison of Ekowe must be loaded with a proper proportion of each article of consumption –

{A commissariat officer & staff will go in charge of these waggons and will relieve the officer now at Ekowe.

The whole garrison of Ekowe will be relieved – and the post reprovisioned with at least 30 days supplies for a force of 1000 Europeans and 300 natives –

Lt Colonel Law will take command of the advanced portion of the column including the two native battalions – and will be responsible that the advance of the column is regulated to the pace of the waggons –

The two native battalions[41] will act as escort to the waggons and must give such assistance to them as they may require from time to time – A proportion of waggons should be told off to the care of each company –

The portion of the column under Lt Col Law will, if attacked, act entirely on the defensive, so as to give time to the waggons to close up into column with a front if possible 20 strong – The trek tow of the rear waggons must be fastened to the hinder part of the front and the break put on each –[42]

The rear portion of the column will act according to

circumstances, and will be free to assume the offensive should a favourable opportunity for doing so offer itself –

Each regiment must take its proper proportion of entrenching tools, and those with the advanced portion of the column must be so placed as to be easily got at when the road requires repairs –

No tents will accompany the relieving column – except one or two bell tents for hospital purposes –}

The force will form a square laager of the waggons every night with a shelter trench round it, 9 ft from the waggons, & will bivouack, as far as possible in the order of march –

The European portion of the force will bivouack between the waggons and the shelter trench; the natives, cattle and horses will be inside the laager –

The troops will be under arms at 4 am every morning; and the column will prepare for its further advance, so soon as it is daylight, and so soon as the scouts (which should be pushed forward when the force gets under arms) have reported that the enemy is not in force in the immediate neighbourhood –

No bugle sound to be permitted, except "the alarm" which will be the signal for every man to stand to his arms –

Combined parties of 6 Europeans and 6 natives will be placed ½ a mile in advance of each face of the laager at night as outlying sentries – Native scouts will however be pushed forward at least a mile.

These parties will remain quietly on the alert – No smoking; no talking above a whisper and only regarding matters of duty – Their duty is to listen – should the enemy be discovered by the native scouts they will fire volleys and fall back on the picquets who will retire quietly and give the alarm, without firing – Care must be taken not to fire upon the scouts when running in {– On each face of the laager one company will remain standing up on the watch and will be relieved every hour. Sentries however will not move about. On each face of the laager at least one officer should be on duty during the night, with a binocular which is an excellent night glass –}

Every effort must be made to complete each days march in such time as to allow the transport animals at least two hours for grazing –

{It will depend in a great measure upon the assistance given to the waggons by the officers and men of the native contingent –

Directly a waggons sticks a body of men should at once go to the wheels and help it on –

The British troops will halt every hour for at least ten minutes – When the advanced body halts the waggons will close up into a column of about 20 in front and the rearmost body will thus be able to get its ten minutes halt, altho' not at the same time as the advanced body –}[43]

CP 7/37 [Extracts printed in French, *Lord Chelmsford*, pp. 172–3 with the words between {} omitted.]

74

Lieutenant-General Lord Chelmsford to Colonel F.A. Stanley

[Signed MS copy]

Durban,
Natal
10 April 1879

In accordance with the intention expressed in my last despatch, I took personal command, on the 23 March, of the Column in course of formation at the Lower Tugela which was destined for the relief of the force under Colonel Pearson at Etshowe.

For some weeks Lieut Colonel Law R.A. had been at hand arranging details connected with this Column; in this arduous duty he was most ably assisted by his Staff Officer Captain Hart 31st Regiment, Special Service,[44] and Assistant Commissary Walton,[45] and I wish to record my appreciation of the exertions of these officers.

For some little time we had been in daily communication with Colonel Pearson by means of Flashing Signals: for this very great assistance to our operations I am indebted to Lieutenant Haines R.E., who, despite some failure and discouragement at first, persevered until complete success was attained.

By the 28th March the whole force (vide enclosure A) was

assembled on the left bank of the Tugela and organized in two Brigades, the labour of transferring the force and the necessary transport and stores was very great, and the success attained was due to the energy displayed by the detachments of the Naval Brigade under Lieutenant Abbott, R.N.[46]

Those troops who were bivouacking experienced constant rain during the two or three days previous to the advance.

I decided on advancing to the relief of Etshowe by the lower or coast road, and thus avoid the tract of bushy country around the Amatakulu until the last march, when it was my intention to move on Etshowe with the lightest possible train, in fact with only what was barely necessary for the relief of the garrison, and three days' biscuit and preserved meat for my own force.

On the 29th March the Column marched at 6 a.m., reached Nyone and formed a wagon laager which was entrenched.

On the 30th it reached the Amatakulu river and did the same.

Up to this time nothing had actually been seen of the enemy by my scouts, but reports reached me from the Border Agents[47] that bodies of Zulus had been seen moving in an Easterly direction from the Indulinda range. I fully anticipated I should not reach Etshowe without an engagement and I was only anxious that the long train of wagons should be together so that at any time on the march we might be able to fight without the chance of the camp followers and transport animals suffering: I therefore found it necessary on the 31st March to content myself with only crossing the Amatakulu river and forming a wagon laager one mile and a half beyond: the river was very high and the transfer of the train across the stream took from 6 a.m. to 3 p.m. each wagon requiring 32 instead of 16 oxen.

During this day (31st) the scouts noticed small bodies of Zulus in the vicinity of the Amatakulu bush. Captain Barrow 19th Hussars with a portion of his command pushed on some 12 miles towards the Engoya forest and burnt the kraal of Magwendo a brother of the Zulu King's.[48]

The 1st April the column marched six miles to the Gingilovo stream about one mile from the Inyazane River, a laager was formed in favourable position. From this point the road to

Etshowe, after crossing swampy ground winds through a bushy and very difficult country for some 15 miles, the last 8 or 9 being a steady ascent. The whole country is covered with very high grass, and even what appears to be open plain is really sufficiently undulating to afford easy cover to considerable bodies of natives.

Etshowe could be plainly seen from the laager, and flash signalling was at once established. Before the laager was completed a heavy thunderstorm came on, rain came on again at nightfall and lasted during the night. The laager defences were however satisfactorily completed after dark . . . [49]

The North or front face was held by the 60th Rifles; the right flank by the 57th Regiment; left flank face by the 99th Regiment and "The Buffs"; the rear face by the 91st Regiment and each angle was manned by the Naval Brigade, Blue Jackets and Marines: the gatling of the "Boadicea" being on the North East corner; two rocket tubes on the North West under Lieut Kerr;[50] 2 – 9 pounder guns under Lieut Kingscote[51] on the South West; and one gatling and two rocket tubes on the South East under Commander Brackenbury.[52] The night passed without any alarm.

On the 2nd April according to our invariable rule, the troops stood to their arms at 4 a.m. A heavy mist shrouded the country; the sun rose about 6.15 a.m.: our mounted men, as usual, were at earliest dawn scouting around. At 5.45 reports came in from them simultaneously with the picquets of the 60th and 99th Regiments, that the enemy were advancing to the attack: no preparation was necessary and no orders had to be given beyond the saddling up of the horses of the Officers of the Staff: the troops were already at their posts and the cattle had not been let out to graze. At 6 a.m. the attack commenced on the North front; the Zulus advanced with great rapidity and courage, taking advantage of the cover afforded by the undulations of the ground and the long grass: the enemy, however, did not succeed in approaching nearer than 20 yards: several casualties took place here at this time, among them Lieut Colonel Northey 3/60th[53] who, I regret to say, received a bullet wound from which he eventually died two days ago. Lieut Courtenay's[54] horse was shot as he stood beside him, Captain Barrow and Lieut Colonel Crealock being slightly wounded at the same time and Captain Molyneux's horse was shot under him. The gatling gun was of considerable value at this period of the defence.

The attack, checked here, rolled round to the West, or left face, here Lieutenant G.C.J. Johnson 99th Regiment,[55] was killed. Whilst this was being developed, a fresh force came round to the rear, probably, from the Imisi Hill, anticipating (so prisoners state) that our force would prove insufficient to defend, at the same time, all the faces of the laager: here they obstinately held their ground finding cover in the long grass and undulations. The Mounted Infantry and the Volunteers meantime having left the laager had been engaged in clearing its front face, I now directed Captain Barrow to advance across the right or East face and attack the enemy's right flank. It was now 7.30 a.m. and during one hour and a half the Zulus had obstinately attacked three sides of the laager.

Even previous to the mounted men appearing on their flank, the Zulu had, I believe, realised the hopelessness of attempting to pass through the Zone of heavy rifle fire which met them on their attempting to charge up against the rear face, but on their appearance, the Zulu retreat commenced: on seeing this the Natal Native Contingent who were formed within the entrenchment on the rear face, clearing the ditch, rushed forward with loud cheers in pursuit. Led by Captain Barrow's horsemen the pursuit was carried on several miles. This officer reports the sabres of the Mounted Infantry to have proved of the greatest service, some 50 or 60 men having been sabred.

At 8 a.m. Colonel Pearson, who, through a glass, had witnessed the fight from Etshowe, telegraphed his congratulations to us.

Bodies of Zulus were to be seen hurrying away towards the Indulinda making a stand nowhere and throwing away their arms to assist their flight.

Within a short time I directed officers and burying parties to count the enemy's loss within 1000 yards of the entrenchment – 471 were buried, 200 have been since found near the scene, but from the chance wounded men we have found five miles away and the execution done at long range by the artillery, I have no hesitation in estimating the enemy's loss at 1000 men.[56]

It appears from the statements of the prisoners taken that about 180 Companies were engaged, either in the attack or in reserve, which, estimated at sixty men per Company (less than half their strength) would give about 11,000 men. This, I am inclined to think may be the number of the force that was ordered to attack us, but this is far less than that given by the prisoners taken.

Our casualties are small considering the easy mark the laager afforded the assailants, and, had it not been for the cover afforded the troops by the broad shelter trench, I should have had to report a much heavier loss.[57]

It appears from the statements of the prisoners that the Zulus were unaware of the march of my force until 36 hours before we were attacked, neither were they aware of its strength.[58]

I attribute this ignorance, on the enemy's part, of our movements, in a great measure to the excellent manner in which the scouting duties of my force were carried out under the personal arrangements of Captain Barrow 19th Hussars who, with his small mounted force assisted by some 150 Zulus belonging to Mr John Dunn's people completely shrouded our movements.

Mr John Dunn, at my request, accompanied me and I am greatly indebted to him for the assistance he afforded me by his knowledge of the country and sound advice.

The following day, 3rd April, I left Major Walker 99th Regiment[59] with two companies of "The Buffs", two of the 91st and five of the 99th, and 400 Naval Brigade together with the Natal Native Contingent, as a garrison for the laager, which was altered in size to meet the reduced strength. The remainder of the column, carrying three days biscuit and meat, with a ground sheet between every two men and escorting 58 carts of stores for the Etshowe garrison, moved off in compact order for Etshowe. The distance to be traversed was only some 15 miles but the streams were deep and the swamps heavy and for the last 8 or 9 miles of the road, the ascent steep: in two places the road had been partly destroyed by the Zulus. It was 11.30 p.m. before the whole relief Column reached Etshowe. Colonel Pearson and a portion of the garrison came out to meet me, which would have been of great assistance had the enemy opposed our advance, but none were to be seen that day . . .

The 4th April, next day, Colonel Pearson evacuated the fort taking with him the whole of the stores etc: –

I accompanied a patrol under Captain Barrow who, with his mounted force, Dunn's scouts, and a Company of Natal Pioneers of the Etshowe garrison, proceeded to destroy a kraal of Dabulamanzi's some 8 or 9 miles off on the Entumeni Hill,[60] two of the enemy were killed and one prisoner taken. A small body of some 40 Zulus kept up a well directed fire from a neighbouring hill, but no casualty occurred on our side.

The 5th April the relieving Column left Etshowe, covering the movement of Colonel Pearson who encamped near the Inyezane the same evening, while my force bivouacked near the Imfuchini mission station.[61]

I regret to report that at 3.30 pm [sic] the following morning (6th April) a sentry of the 91st fired a shot at what he took to be a party of the enemy who did not answer his challenge: on hearing this shot the picquet of the 60th Rifles on the opposite flank of the entrenchment, retired without orders from its Officer together with Mr Dunn's scouts who had been occupying some mealie fields beyond. It was bright moonlight, and I can offer no excuse or explanation of what occurred beyond the youth of the men of the 60th for it was perfectly well known to Officers and men that these scouts were in their front. It appears that some of the 60th lining the entrenchment seeing the picquets running in, fired, probably at the native scouts but 5 of the 3/60th were wounded by their own comrades and I deeply regret to say that some nine of our native allies were bayoneted as they attempted to gain, as they thought, the shelter of the laager: one man was killed and two natives have since died of their wounds.

On the 6th April the force marched by the Ginginlovo laager and formed a new one on fresh ground one mile beyond.

On the 7th Major Walker 99th Regiment was to move from the old laager to the new ground, the atmosphere of the old laager being tainted by the results of the engagement of the 2nd April.

My reasons for ordering Colonel Pearson to evacuate Etshowe

were that I found the last 15 miles of the road of a most difficult nature, far more so than I had been led to believe by the reports furnished me before Colonel Pearson crossed the frontier in January.

Every advantage from a military point of view, in our present intention of destroying the Mangwane and old Undine kraals, can be equally gained by occupying a strong post upon the coast road; this will be done and the future operations on this line will be entrusted to Major General Crealock C.B. who will receive special instructions from me regarding the future operations of what is now the First Division of the South African Field Force.[62]

I am much indebted to Colonel Pearson for so tenaciously holding on to Etshowe after the bad news of the Insandhlwana affair had reached him. The occupation of that post, and of that one held by Colonel Evelyn Wood during a time of considerable anxiety, had no doubt a very powerful moral effect through South Africa, and diminished the effect of what would otherwise have been considered as a complete collapse of our invasion of Zululand.

I cannot close this despatch without acknowledging the assistance I received from Commodore Richards[63] with regard to all arrangements connected with the Naval Brigade which, under its respective commanders, did good and useful service.

I am much indebted to Colonel Pemberton 60th Rifles and to Lt Colonel Law Royal Artillery who were in charge of Brigades, and to the several Commanding Officers serving under their command.

The 57th Regiment under Lt Colonel Clarke[64] was conspicuous for its steadiness and for the manner in which the men controlled their fire.

Dr Tarrant Senior Medical Officer with the Column,[65] gave me every satisfaction with regard to the medical arrangements, and Assistant Commissary Walton deserves great credit for the successful exertions he made in overcoming the difficulties of supply and transport.

I have already mentioned Capt. Barrow's name as having performed very excellent service and the Commanders of the several mounted detachments under his command ably assisted him.

I have as usual to acknowledge the services of my personal Staff. Lt Colonel Crealock in the absence of Colonel Bellairs whom I was reluctantly compelled to leave behind at Durban to perform the duties of Deputy Quarter-Master General, acted as senior Staff Officer to the Column and was slightly wounded.

Captain Buller A.D.C. at my request acted as Brigade Major to Colonel Pemberton.

Captain Molyneux A.D.C. who had his horse shot under him, and Lieutenant Milne R.N. were indefatigable in their efforts to carry out my orders and give every assistance in the defence of the laager.

The Honourable W. Drummond Head of my Intelligence Department has worked indefatigably to obtain information, and I am much indebted to him for his assistance.

P.S. Owing to an extra steamer having been ordered to leave today I take the opportunity of forwarding this dispatch – but I regret I am unable to enclose until next mail Enclosures referred to from Lt. Colonel Pearson & Captain Barrow.

Owing to the press of time since I returned here 36 hours ago – the various returns of wounded & numbers engaged are hardly written out in the manner I should have wished – but the matter therein contained is correct.

WO 32/7727 [Printed in *BPP* (C. 2367), enc. 1 in no. 42.]

III

The Second Invasion

Chapter 6
Preparations and Reconnaissance

75
Lieutenant-General Lord Chelmsford to H.R.H. the Duke of Cambridge

[MS copy] Durban, Natal
11 April 1879

. . . I returned to this place two days ago after what I trust Your Royal Highness will consider a successful 10 days operations – It was an intense relief to me to get the Garrison out of Ekowe and more especially when I saw the nature of the country through which the last fifteen miles of road runs – It would have been madness to have clung on to Ekowe and General Crealock on his new line of operations along the lower or Coast road will have the benefit of a fine open country for at least 50 miles from the Tugela –

The merits of this line ought of course to have been discovered before, but I have already pointed out to Your Royal Highness how impossible it has been to obtain any really reliable information regarding the country even from those who ought to know it well – They have never been accustomed to look at any of the roads from any but a trader's point of view, and are therefore quite unable to give the detailed information which is so important when movements of troops are concerned –

The arrangements for the landing of horses, troops & stores has been admirable, and everything has been conducted with the greatest despatch and at the same time with the greatest regularity – I am much indebted to Your Royal Highness for sending out

General Clifford to assist me at the Base of Operations – He has already done much to systematize the work here, and will be perfectly invaluable as my locum tenens when I again cross the border with the Northern Force – [1]

I have formed the troops under my Command into two Divisions with a Flying Column under Colonel E. Wood whom I did not wish to disturb in his hitherto separate Command –

Crealock will command the 1st Division on the Coast line and General Newdigate on the Northern line –

I cannot adequately express my thanks to Your Royal Highness for the liberal assistance which has been afforded me –

{I cannot but look upon it as ample from the requirements of the case, but it would be well, I think, that reinforcements in the shape of drafts from the different regiments and Corps should be sent out from time to time, in order that they may be kept up to their full strength –}

The Draft for the 1/24 will be sent up to join the two remaining Companies of the Battalion[2] so soon as the losses they have sustained by the shipwreck of the Clyde have been made good – [3]

{As regards the disposal of the Colours of the regiment[4] there is not the same objection to their being in the Field in our present operations as it was in the Cape Colony –

There is no real bush work in Zululand and Regiments have been instructed to work in close order, as the only formation adopted to meet the tactics of the Enemy –}

I have asked the Prince Imperial to accompany my Head Quarters, which I am glad to find is what himself was anxious for –

I should feel much obliged if Your Royal Highness would assure the Empress that I will look after the Prince to the best of my ability, and that I am convinced I shall find him a very valuable addition to my Staff – [5]

{I trust that my replies to the questions put to me by the Adjutant General will be considered sufficient –

I believe that most of them have been already answered by the evidence, which I have already submitted, of those who were at or near Insandlwana on the 22nd Jan:[6]}

With regards to the presence of tents with the several Columns that took the field in January last, it must be remembered that we began the campaign in the height of the rainy season, and that had the troops not been adequately protected, they would in all probability have suffered severely in health – In our late operations the troops had no tents, but only waterproof sheets – These latter are essential, as the ground is generally very wet, and when the weather is fine, the dews are very heavy –

I have been much annoyed by the action of the Lieut Governor of Natal who when I had ordered the Native forces along the border to make demonstrations and if possible raids into Zululand actually sent orders without consulting me or my Staff forbidding any native to cross the border –[7]

When I made up my mind to advance upon Ekowe I felt that I might possibly have to encounter the full strength of the Zulu army and I was anxious to create a diversion in its favour by simultaneously raiding from one end of the line to the other –

The full state of the Tugela prevented this being carried out, but I consider that the action of Sir Henry Bulwer is quite indefensible & if persevered in must completely prevent my making any use of the large numbers of Natal Natives who are now in arms along the Border – I trust that Your Royal Highness after reading my official remonstrance to the Secretary of State will be able to give me full support in this matter – Sir H. Bulwer from my first arrival in Natal has thrown every obstacle in my way whilst at the same time he has endeavoured by long memoranda, minutes & dispatches to make it appear that he has given me all the assistance I have asked for –

I feel sure that had an attack been made upon Natal by the Zulus, he would have thrown the entire responsibility upon my shoulders, and I am glad to have now the opportunity of shewing how utterly delusive has been the order which placed the Colonial troops under my command –

Bishop Schroeder and Mr Fannin have been the originators of all the wild reports regarding contemplative raids – imaginary attacks upon Ekowe &c &c – and I look upon their information, based as it is upon Zulu reports, as utterly unreliable –

{I have sent messengers to one of the King's brothers, Dabulamanzi by name today that if he chooses to come in and surrender no harm shall happen to him –

Dabulamanzi has since sent his own messengers to the Lower Tugela to ascertain the correctness of my message, and I am in great hopes that he will give himself up – The surrender of such a chief will no doubt induce many others to do the same, and their defection will of course produce its effect upon the Zulu Nation at large.}

CP 28 [Extracts printed in French, *Lord Chelmsford*, pp. 180–1 with words between {} omitted.]

76

Lieutenant-General Lord Chelmsford to Major-General H.H. Crealock

[Holograph] 12 April 1879

Memorandum for guidance of Major General Crealock CB Command 1st Division South African Field Force

1) The first objective point of this Division will be the Emangwene military kraal, situated on the north side of the Umhlatoosi river –

2) This Kraal is said to number 1000 huts, and is situated in a highly populated District –

The Kraal should be burnt, and the whole district cleared out –

3) When this work is completed the Undi military kraal south of the Umhlatoosi river and about 10 miles distant from the Emangwene, should also be burnt –

4) It is probable that the King will not allow these two Kraals to be destroyed without making an effort to protect them –

{5) The road to the Emangwene kraal runs through a perfectly open country however, and a road fit for a light carriage exists between that place and the Undi Kraal –

6) There are no physical difficulties therefore, in the way of the above mentioned operations –}

7) A strong, permanent, entrenched post must be made at some

point between the Tugela and the Umhlatoosi river from which the advance should be made, and which should be held during the advance by a sufficient force –
{8) A suitable position for such an entrenched post appears to me to exist on the right bank of the Inyazani river – a rough sketch which is appended – but I have no desire to tie the Major General down to any particular spot – [8]
9) An entrenched post in Zululand should possess the following qualifications – Good command of ground all round; protected site for cattle laager; and good water within easy distance –
10) The Inyazani position possesses nearly all these qualifications, but the water is somewhat distant –
11) Two regiments could occupy the front post; the cattle and horses could be placed in the depression of ground just behind it; and the second post suited for one regiment, on the high piece of ground behind the first and separated from it by the depression just mentioned, would complete the security of the whole post –
12) A covered way on the East side along the ridge connecting the two posts would afford safe connection between the two –
13) Two months provisions for the whole Division should be stored in this entrenched post as a reserve; – and the force advancing from it to Emangwene should take with it one months supply –}
14) In order to facilitate the forwarding of supplies from the Lower Tugela to the advanced entrenched post, an intermediate post of a less permanent character should be formed about half way between the two, say near the Amatakulu river – [9]
{15) When an advance is determined upon the rear brigade, occupying the latter post, should move forward and occupy the permanent entrenched post, bringing up with it supplies sufficient for its whole strength for one month –}
16) On the completion of the operations against the Emangwene and Undi military Kraals, the Major General will have to decide for himself as to what further operations are possible or desirable –
17) The objective point of the Northern force will be Ulundi, and it is to be hoped that the 1st Division will be able to grapple successfully with the difficulties of the Umhlatoosi river between Undi and St. Pauls, and establish eventually an entrenched post

and supply depôt in the neighbourhood –[10] thus assisting in the general advance against the King's own Kraal –
18) I do not anticipate however that this movement can be made by the 1st Division until a portion of the Northern force shall have established itself on the road North of the Umhlatoosi river in the neighbourhood of Emtwyenani, from all I can gather regarding the country between Undi Kraal and St. Pauls, it would be impossible to ensure the safe conduct of convoys were the Umhlatoosi valley to be occupied by the enemy –
19) The presence of a force however to the North of it would at once render the passage of it safe, and I am in hopes that the Northern force will be able to assist the Tugela Division in this manner –
{20) It is of the highest importance that the advance upon the Emangwene and Undi military Kraals should be made as soon as possible, and that in the mean time the mounted men of the Force should make repeated reconnaissances in every direction, where bodies of the enemy may possibly re-assemble within striking distance of the present laager of the 2nd Brigade 1st Division –[11]
21) A speedy advance is mainly dependent upon supply and transport being forthcoming in sufficient quantities; and it is therefore most desirable that Major General Crealock should proceed to the Lower Tugela without delay so that he may be able to superintend the arrangements with his own eyes –}

CP 15/36 {Extracts printed in French, *Lord Chelmsford*, pp. 206–7 with words between {} omitted.]

77

Lieutenant-General Lord Chelmsford to Brigadier-General H.E. Wood

[Holograph]

Durban
[?15] April 1879

One line to congratulate you upon your successful repulse of the attack made upon Kambula laager – [12]

I am up to my ears in work & cannot say as much as I could wish, but I know you are aware how fully I appreciate all your good work – I am calling your command "a flying column" so as to keep you separate from Newdigate who will command the 2d Division S. African Field Force. –

He starts today for Dundee[13] and eventually Doornberg and is in hopes of meeting you somewhere about those parts, so that he may ascertain what you recommend in the way of arrangements for his command – I wish I could have got up to relieve you of all this trouble, but there are so many questions to settle here with General Clifford before I finally leave to join you, that it would be unwise for me to start before they are all settled –

Clifford will be invaluable and has already done wonders –

Thank all those under your command from me for their good service on the 29th – [14] I shall acknowledge it publicly in orders –

I condole with you in your loss of Ronald Campbell – I do not see how I can move Clery from Glyn until I finally dispose of the latter. You shall have him however as a staff officer if I can possibly arrange it – [15]

Dont fash yourself about Mr Rathbone and his contributions to the Press – I did not see them, but had I done so, I know you would treat them in the same way as I should with silent contempt.[16] I am glad they have given you a good service pension – The KCB must follow![17]

WC II/2/2

78

Lieutenant-General Lord Chelmsford to Sir Henry Bulwer

[Signed MS copy]

P.M. Burg
18 April 1879

I have the honour to acknowledge receipt of your Excellency's letter No 40/1879 dated 15 April 1879.[18] With reference to the line of argument adopted by your excellency in para 4 – of the letter under reply there appears to be an unfortunate misunderstanding with regard to conversation which I had the honour of holding with your Excellency at Pine Town with reference to the defence of the Natal border – It is perfectly true that I admitted a broad distinction between the natives that had been handed over to me for duty with the invading columns, and those who had been collected on the border for purposes of defence – [19]

The latter have been never regarded by me as available for regular operations in the Zulu country, but I cannot admit the accuracy of the statement that during the conversation alluded to I agreed to their exclusive employment within the border – such an argument would have been diametrically opposed to my view regarding the employment of the colonial forces called out for the defence of the border – Your Excellency will I think bear me out that ever since I have been in Natal, I have persistently pointed out to all with whom I have had to discuss the several questions connected with the defence of the colony, that no defence can be considered as satisfactory which does not provide for a resort to the offensive when the favourable opportunity arises. –

The secret instructions that I sent to the border commanders, shortly before I started with the Column for Ekowe, were to the effect that they were to make strong demonstrations along the border line; and that if a favourable opportunity offered itself, they were to make a short raid across into Zululand taking care not to compromise the retreat of their various commands.[20] I maintain that from a military point of view, the order in question did not in the slightest degree create any departure from the understanding that the native levies were to be employed exclusively for the defence of the border.

If a force placed on the defensive along a border river, which is fordable at numerous points contents itself with remaining on the defensive, without endeavouring by means of scouting in small bodies, or by raiding in large ones, to discover what the enemy is doing in its immediate front, it deserves to be surprised and overpowered –

I am so impressed with the absolute soundness of this military principle, that if your Excellency, on a fuller consideration of the question, still refuses to allow the native levies on the border to cross into Zululand in the manner, and for the purpose just indicated, I desire to place on record my firm conviction that such a decision will most materially weaken the defence of the borders, will throw increased responsibilities upon the officers entrusted with the defence of Natal, and will most probably encourage the enemy to assemble in force in the broken country along the Tugela now, so far as I can learn, almost vacated, when they find that no further raids into the country are being made –

With reference to the statement contained in para 5. of your Excellency's letter that I had adopted a course, at entire variance with the understanding then, on [sic] previously arrived at with regard to the native levies, I can only direct attention to the denial made by me, in the first portion of this letter, of any such misunderstanding having been come to –

With regard to the concluding portion of the para in question I can only say that the natives in question were placed under my command by your Excellency, and that therefore as I did not consider I was in any way departing from the understanding that they were to be employed exclusively for the defence of the border, by ordering them, should the opportunity present itself, to make a short raid into Zululand, I did not consider there was any necessity to ask for authority to do so –

I was most anxious that any intentions with regard to the employment of the border natives should not become known, and the news be taken across the border by the numerous spies that are believed to infest the colony, and I therefore refrained from making any reference whatsoever to this part of my plan when communicating my intentions to take command of the column moving on Eshowe –

In conclusion I would point out to your Excellency that the large force of native levies now assembled along the total border[21] can most materially assist in the operations against Cetywayo and the Zulu nation if permitted to cross the border. The long narrow strip of broken country extending from the Lower Tugela drift to Rorkes drift is totally unsuited to the operations of an European force –

It is however very important that no large force of the enemy should be allowed to collect in that part of the country, which has excellent grazing ground for cattle, and plentiful crops of maize and kafir corn –

Constant patrols and occasional raids, made at different parts of this long line, would of course keep any Zulus that might be living in that part of the country in a state of perpetual alarm, so they would never be certain that a general advance from that direction was not contemplated –

It would prevent them reaping their crops, it would compel them to keep their cattle well out of reach, and would most probably cause eventually the entire evacuation of the Southern border of Zululand – [22]

I am aware that the objection may be raised to this plan of operations that it is harassing the Zulu people and not Cetywayo and that consequently we are not acting up to the announcement which was made, when we first entered Zululand, that our quarrel was with the latter and not with the former – [23]

Since however the commencement of the war our troops have been attacked at different times by the whole available fighting force in Zululand, and it is therefore clear that the Zulu people themselves are not prepared to accept the distinction it was thought advisable to make.

Under these circumstances it would be unwise to neglect any opportunity that may present itself of inflicting substantial injuries upon our enemy, and I wish to place clearly on record that as the officer upon whom the responsibility for the conduct of the war rests, I can see no other way of bringing it to a speedy conclusion –

I have endeavoured, as clearly as possible, to lay my views before your Excellency in order that there may be no doubt as to the particular points upon which I an anxious to obtain a decided ruling from your Excellency in Council –

If I am considered fit to be entrusted with the conduct of the war, I contend that the command of the Colonial forces assembled along the border of Natal for its defences should be placed unreservedly in my hands, and that I should be permitted to employ them within, or without the border, in whatever manner I may consider best in the interests of the Colony, and with due regard to its protection from invasion. –

I consider that all reports regarding these forces should be sent to your Excellency through the military authorities in Natal and not direct as is now the case. – By this alteration in the existing system your Excellency will be kept equally informed of all matters connected with these forces, the danger of divided command will be done away with, and the Colonial Commanders will understand that there is but one controlling authority over them –

I would venture to press for a very speedy reply to these momentous questions, as it is impossible to say what injury may not accrue to the interests of the Colony, so long as doubt exists regarding my powers, as Commander of the Colonial forces.

GH 500, pp. 179–91 [Printed in *BPP* (C. 2318), no. 18]

79

Lieutenant-General Lord Chelmsford to Colonel F.A. Stanley

[Signed MS copy]

Pietermaritzburg
Natal
20 April 1879

1. Nothing has occurred since the 14th instant, the date of my last despatch, to show that the Zulus have recovered from the blows lately inflicted on them:[24] on the other hand, the troops under my command have made no forward move.

2. It has been persistently but erroneously stated in the local press that the forces lately under my personal command on the Lower Tugela–Inyezane line, have been withdrawn to the frontier:[25] as you will have understood from my reports such has not been the case. After the relief of Etshowe was effected it became necessary to organize the relieving force, consisting of fresh reinforcements from England and the garrison, into a Division, this was easily done by forming two Brigades with divisional Artillery and mounted men, but as a portion of the first (Pearson's) Brigade, viz:

two Companies of the "Buffs", and five Companies of the 99th Regiment, had formed part of the relieving force, these details were ordered back to join the Regiments at the Lower Tugela.

3. The 2nd Brigade under Colonel Clarke, 57th Foot, has remained in the forward and commanding position where I left it, near Gingilovo: that Officer reports that the Amatakulu Bush was scoured by major Barrow's mounted men on the 15 April and only three Zulus seen.

4. Major General Crealock has taken up his command and the whole Division will shortly be able to commence operations, if transport arrangements will allow it. A copy of my instructions to him I had the honor of forwarding last mail.[26]

Our great difficulty everywhere is still the want of drivers and leaders, and Brigadier General Wood telegraphs that he is in urgent need of 200. I have telegraphed to the Administrator, Transvaal,[27] to assist him, for we are unable to do so from Natal, under present circumstances, inasmuch as we are in want of 300.

5. The various Cavalry and Infantry Regiments, and other details are all on the march for their various points of concentration. Major General Newdigate has proceeded by Post Cart to take up his command in the north: his head quarters will, for the present, be Dundee.

6. I myself leave on the 22nd instant for Dundee where I shall, for the present, fix my Head Quarters Camp, but I intend to push on myself to see Brigadier General Wood.

7. The health of the troops is improving; the 3/60th Rifles, and Naval Brigade on the Lower Tugela line are suffering somewhat (Colonel Clarke writes) from Diarrhoea, but the proposed change of Camp to a site near the Inyezane River, 4 miles in advance, will, I expect, prove beneficial.

8. The wounded are progressing favourably and the change in the weather which has now become colder and with less rain, will I hope, materially lessen our sick list; but, as no tents accompany the troops across the frontier, we must, I fear, expect the usual results on young soldiers of such exposure.

9. Major General Clifford will fix his Head Quarters at Pietermaritzburg on my leaving.

He was present yesterday during a consultation the Lieut Governor and myself had on the subject of the defence of the Colony, which will be entrusted to him on my crossing the frontier.
10. His Excellency the High Commissioner writes cheerfully of the situation in the Transvaal.
11. As I represented by telegraph last mail,[28] it will be a necessity that drafts should be sent out periodically to replace the casualties in the Regiments in the Field.
12. The number of Officers at my disposal has enabled me to fill up some of the Brigade Staffs with well qualified Officers, but such is not the case with the Divisional Staffs, and the Head Quarter Staff is still incomplete.

I have no reserve of Officers to fall back upon. I could easily employ at this moment five or six Field Officers qualified for Staff employment, and as many Captains. I would therefore urge that this number of Field Officers to act as Assistant Adjutants General and Assistant Quarter Masters General, and Captains as Deputy Assistants should be sent out.

I should have been glad to have utilized the services of Officers who have already gained experience and done good service out here, but their presence is required with their Regiments . . .

WO 32/7732

80

Lieutenant-General Lord Chelmsford to Brigadier-General H.E. Wood

[Holograph] PMBurg
22 April 1879

A letter reached me from Sir Bartle Frere yesterday in which he expresses a hope that I may be able to spare a company or two and two guns to strengthen Rowlands force at Pretoria –[29]

I should be glad to carry out his wishes if it can be done, and I think that 2 companies 80th Regt and 2 guns should be sent to

Standerton from which place they can be moved wherever Rowlands pleases –

I have telegraphed home by the mail which leaves today for three more regiments for garrison duty – [30] The drain upon regiments in the field is so great that they ought not to be called upon to furnish any detachments – Drafts will not be of much use, as they are certain to be composed of boys – [31]

Buller seems impatient to go on – and seems to think that I am keeping you back – Should you also imagine that I am acting as drag pray disabuse yourself of that idea – Directly you feel that you can, with safety to Utrecht and the Transvaal border generally, move your column to a more forward position pray do so – You will have had a talk with Newdigate before this reaches you and will have no doubt advised him as to what he should do with the new regiments as they arrive –[32] I hope the Commissariat will be equal to the occasion, but there is a great strain about to be brought upon them – I will send you up as many youngsters and likely volunteers as I can find –

WC II/2/2

81

Lieutenant-General Lord Chelmsford to Brigadier-General H.E. Wood

[Holograph] Estcourt
25 April 1879

I am inclined to believe Magwende's statement that Cetywayo intends to invade Natal – [33] as it is what I should do myself were I in his place.

Such being the case I have to ask myself – what am I doing to prevent it? – The Natal border is watched by about 300 European mounted men, about 600 mounted natives and about 8000 native levies – As you know a force of such a description cannot be depended upon, and yet I can do nothing to strengthen it – I have advised the Lt Governor to try and induce every European that has a horse and gun to enrol himself, but I very much doubt whether it will be done – So much for the direct defence of Natal – Now for the indirect – The 1st Division is taking a road which only covers the Lower Tugela drifts – So long as we were working on the Ekowe road, the force there covered indirectly the entrance to Natal as far up the Tugela as to Middledrift, and a raiding force would feel that it might always place itself across its line of retreat – It would have been absurd however to have clung on to Ekowe as the force could not have been fed with any degree of safety –

The column at Rorke's drift when it advanced, covered indirectly also nearly all the remaining portion of the border – but I am satisfied with the wisdom of abandoning that line of advance –

If however the united forces of your troops and Newdigate's take the Inhlazatye road, Natal is in no way protected by any one of our columns –

A raiding force must necessarily advance from the Kings somewhere between St Paul's and the Babanango Mt and would of course have the same line of retreat –

If we advance from the Utrecht base by a road south of the Inhlazatye, we are at once on the line of retreat of any force raiding across the Tugela, and can really give Natal very effective assistance – If however we take the Northern road and a raid be made into Natal I feel sure that I should be blamed for my strategy and very properly so – Kindly consider then how we can best work to the South of the Inhlazatye, and yet not leave the frontier North of that mountain completely unprotected.[34]

I am willing to admit that the Babanango road is the worst of the two, but I am certain that I am right in determining that our main line of advance shall be made upon it – and with the force at our disposal, and at this season of the year we ought to have no difficulty in making any line practicable for our convoys –

I was told when at Rorkes drift that the Babanango had some bush upon it – It would be well to ascertain the correctness of this statement, as wood of course is our great difficulty.

Perhaps if Umbeline is really dead[35] the Swazis will pluck up sufficient courage to come down to the Pongolo – I would not however press them to do so – They ought to be made to understand that we can do perfectly well without their assistance –

The neighbourhood of the Ingwe Mountain will still be an advantageous position for an advanced post,[36] as it will leave the Zulus in doubt as to which line we are going to take – It will enable our mounted men also to reconnoitre a new stretch of country nearer to Ulundi –

By adopting the Babanango line also I shall carry out I hope what was always my object viz – the driving of all the Zulu population into the North East portion of Zululand, which I believe is unhealthy and not over well cultivated –

I hope this decision of mine will not upset any cherished scheme of yours – It is of course based upon purely strategical and political grounds, quite independent of any local considerations –

I am doing my best to prevail upon the Lt Gov. to allow the colonial forces to show a little activity across the border;[37] but I am not sure whether I shall succeed.

WC II/2/2

82

Lieutenant-General Lord Chelmsford to Colonel F.A. Stanley

[Signed MS copy] Dundee
1 May 1879

I have the honour to forward the accompanying letter which I yesterday received from my Commissary General.[38]

I am not prepared to take so gloomy a view of the Transport situation as that sketched out by Mr Strickland. There can be no doubt, however, that the difficulties to be overcome are very great, and the advance of the troops into Zululand cannot take place until the Transport has thrown a sufficient amount of supplies into our present advanced depôts, and has, moreover, provided the requisite amount of wagons, etc: for that advance.

The difficulties under which the Transport have laboured are, in my opinion, attributable to two causes:–

First, the insufficiency of the Transport Department generally, owing to want of a proper staff of trained Officers.

The amalgamation of Transport with supply has not worked satisfactorily.[39] The Officers of the supply branch have had more than enough work to do in their own particular sub-department, and consequently when saddled with the responsibility of Transport as well, have either had to trust to others to perform the duty, or have been obliged to leave their own legitimate duties in order to attend to it.

The work of Supply and Transport is as distinct as that of the Adjutant and Quartermaster General's department[40] and cannot be conducted by one Officer without causing one or the other sub-department to suffer.

Although in theory every Commissariat Officer is supposed to be acquainted with the details of Transport work and is supposed to be capable of superintending or executing it, in practice it is very different.

An Officer may be a most excellent Commissariat Officer in the supply sub-department and a very bad one in that of Transport: and I attribute in a great measure the breakdown of the Transport to that fact having been ignored.

A Transport Officer requires most careful training and should have the special attributes which can make that training of use to him. He should be a good judge of all animals employed as transport and should understand their care and treatment when sick or in health. He should be acquainted with the relative value of all regulation Transport-wagons, carts, etc: as also that of the different countries in which it is possible that an army may have to operate. He should have a good organizing head, so as to be able to utilize the transport at his disposal to the best advantage; and he should thoroughly understand how to manage the heterogeneous mass of civilians and natives who must necessarily be employed with hired or purchased carriage.

The want of these qualities in our Transport Officers has been much felt.

Above all things, however, one head Officer with nothing to attend to but transport duties is absolutely required.

It is a physical and mental impossibility that the Commissary General in the Field should be able to properly superintend the arrangements connected with both Supply and Transport, and I venture to express a strong opinion that even if he were able to do it, it is not desirable.

The Commissariat Officer naturally thinks of nothing but how to push forward his own supplies; and it is almost impossible for him to prevent that desire from warping his judgment when the employment of Transport has to be considered.

Hence continual friction arises between the Commissariat and the other departments who are dependent upon the former for the supply of carriage necessary to forward their own stores to the front.

The head of the Transport should therefore I contend be an Officer who can take a perfectly impartial view of the requirements of the several departments and who, under the orders of the General Commanding, will be able to regulate its employment accordingly.

The General Officer in Command must necessarily be the best judge when there are conflicting demands for transport as to which service is the most important and, whenever such a case arises, which is not very often, it should be decided by him and not by a Department personally interested in the decision.

The second cause of the failure of the Transport Department is the one so forcibly brought to notice by the Commissary General, viz:- the difficulty of obtaining and retaining an adequate supply of native drivers and leaders.

This difficulty is in my opinion attributable to the absence of any real controlling influence over the native population of Natal by the Government of the Colony.

The Lt Governor as supreme chief has vested in him the power of calling out any native to serve in the defence of the Colony, or to work on the roads.

This condition was understood and accepted by the natives who are almost entirely refugees from Zululand, on their escaping into the Colony.

The Lt Governor of Natal has exercised his power freely during the last few months and has furnished the Commissariat department with upwards of 300 drivers and leaders.

The power of the Supreme Chief, however, seems limited to the act of calling out, and does not appear to extend to keeping the natives so called out, to their engagement.

Native Contingent Battalions deserted bodily after the Insandhlwana disaster; and drivers and leaders in like manner leave their employ without any notice, and evidently do not look upon the order of the supreme chief as in any way binding upon them should the order not suit their own convenience.

The Natal Zulu has a horror of continuous service, and, as a rule, no amount of pay will induce him to remain at one particular work beyond a certain time. If, moreover, the work in question takes him away from his own home, or is one that he does not particularly fancy, or should he be to a certain extent tied down by military rules and be subject to Military discipline, no money inducement will persuade him to accept such employ. He must therefore be ordered to perform the duty. The transport service in Natal is therefore absolutely dependent upon the Lt Governor for native assistance without which it is paralysed.

That assistance has been given so far that the several magistrates have been instructed to furnish all the drivers and leaders obtainable in the districts. I have found however that such orders issued to the magistrates through the Secretary for Native Affairs,[41] take a long time in being carried out, and that the Government is unable, or unwilling to put that pressure upon the natives without which no satisfactory result can be expected.

I am quite unable, therefore, to express an opinion as to whether our present want will be met, and I can feel no certainty that, if we obtain the required number of Natives, we should be able to retain them in our service, or whether an Exodus of those natives who are still serving us may not again paralyse the movements of our Transport.

This actual state of affairs has frequently been brought to the notice of the Lt Governor but His Excellency does not appear to possess any real power to help us.

Every effort is being made by all under my command, who have any voice in the matter, to tide over our present difficulties, and I am not inclined, as I have already stated, to take too gloomy a view of our prospects.

I feel, however, that it is necessary, in justice to those upon whom the responsibility for our transport arrangement falls, to bring to your notice the present unsatisfactory state of affairs, and to submit as my conviction that it has been produced by circumstances over which they themselves have no real control.

WO 32/7736

83

Lieutenant-General Lord Chelmsford to Brigadier-General H.E. Wood

[Holograph] Dundee
1 May 1879

When the depôt and entrenched post at Conference hill is being built, would it not be well to make it of sufficient size to hold all the supplies that will be required for the whole force going forward, and thus do away with the Balte Spruit depôt? We cannot afford to have one depôt more than is absolutely necessary –

If you come over to meet me at Balte Spruit, we might go together to Conference hill and talk the matter over on the spot – My own view of a laager is to have a very large interior space with such high walls round it as to prevent any possibility of a Zulu climbing over and then to have the garrison to defend it in two large flanks. By this arrangement you can defend a large laager with a small force – [42]

We shall want to make a good reconnaissance shortly towards the Babanango mountain – If we find firewood there it will simplify our advance considerably – as we can make an entrenched post there and use it as a half-way house – I defer the discussion of the different points which you bring forward in your last letters – [43]

I am forced to make Glyn Brigadier with Newdigate, as there is absolutely no one who is better! The camp here shows that neither he nor Clery have learnt anything from Insandlwana! – [44] The latter is I fear an impostor in the Field – His place is that of Professor at a military school.[45]

Lanyon writes me word that he has done his best to help you with native drivers – I hope you have got them – Best love to Buller –

WC II/2/2

84

Lieutenant-General Lord Chelmsford to Sir Henry Bulwer

[Holograph] Utrecht
7 May 1879

I have the honour to acknowledge the receipt of Your Excellency's letter No 62/1879 dated 30 April 1879, giving cover to copy of a minute by the Border agent at the Lower Tugela regarding the feelings of the natives of the Division as to crossing the border of the colony for the purpose of making raids into the Zulu country – [46]
2) The report of Mr Fynney is diametrically opposed to that which I received from the Border commanders during my numerous visits to that part of the colony –
3) From what however I have ascertained from Major Dartnell regarding the feelings of the natives on the same subject in the Umsinga District, and from the evident reluctance on the part of Mr Wheelwright in the Umvoti District to attempt a raid with the natives under his command,[47] I am quite satisfied of the correctness of Mr Fynney's report, and of the feelings being general along the whole Natal border –
4) So long as the Natal Native thought that there was no chance of his being made to cross the border against his own wish, he was continually begging to be allowed to make a raid –
5) immediately however he saw that there was a chance of being taken at his word, fright took the place of boastful confidence –
6) With such men it would be absurd to attempt any military

operations across the border; and I should certainly have never pressed so strongly that the Border forces should be placed at my disposal for the purpose had I been informed earlier of the real feelings amongst these natives –

7) Whilst however admitting that the Natal Natives now defending, or rather placed along the border for the defence of, Natal, do not possess that martial spirit at present which would render them effective soldiers, I feel bound to represent that I do not consider it is the fault of the individual –

8) Man for man I believe the Natal Zulu to be quite equal to the Zulu proper, and I am certain that he only requires to be properly armed, organized and disciplined, to make him equal, if not superior, to the enemy we are now fighting –

9) Altho' I admit that the battalions of the Native Contingent now in the Field, and those at Krantzkop and Sand Spruit,[48] are not as perfectly armed, organized or disciplined as they should be, still there can be no doubt, that owing to what has been done in that direction, they are infinitely superior as regards efficiency, and I believe would prove themselves far more courageous across the border, than the native levies now within it –

10) Your Excellency will, I think, be prepared to admit that the efficiency of the Border levies should be made as perfect as circumstances will allow; and, also, that, as at present constituted, they have not answered the expectations of those who were anxious to see them called out under the tribal system – as, whilst those under the regimental system are quite ready to move across the border unsupported by British troops, those under the tribal system are not –

11) I would recommend therefore that every effort be made to organize the Border reserves as far as possible under some kind of regimental system –

12) That they should have more European officers attached to them, and that they should have a larger supply of firearms served out to them –

13) I am expecting several thousand Enfield rifles from England, which I shall gladly place at Your Excellency's disposal for distribution when they arrive –

14) It was, I think, a mistake that the border natives were informed when called out, that they should not be made to cross the border against their own wish, as it was calculated to lower their "moral", and to make them imagine they were inferior, man for man, to the enemy –
15) This mistake should, I consider, be at once rectified; and I should feel obliged to Your Excellency causing it to be notified to one and all, that if the military authorities consider it advisable in the interests of Natal that a native force should make a raid into Zululand, they are all bound to obey the order –
16) I need hardly again assure Your Excellency that, with the knowledge I now possess of the feelings of the Natal border forces, it will only be under very exceptional circumstances that I should venture to call upon them to perform this service –
17) I consider however that they should be made fully to understand their obligations in this respect; – and that every endeavour should be made by those who are commanding them to increase their self confidence, and to improve their "moral" –

As at present organized it is evident that the Natal levies are not worth the food we are giving them –
18) It would not be prudent however to disband them as the knowledge of their inefficiency is confined to ourselves; and the moral effect of some 10000 natives under arms along the border, must produce an effect on the opposite side, and make the chances of a raid into Natal appear somewhat hazardous in the eyes of the Border Zulus – [49]
19) Altho' the Natal Mounted Police and volunteers are now in the Field watching the Border, I cannot consider that the European portion of the Natal population have done as much as they ought for the defence of the Colony –
20) As I have several times pointed out the true defence of Natal lies in the border; and every available horseman ought to be placed in such a position as would enable him to place himself there at a few hours notice –
21) Defensible laagers are very useful for the protection of life, but they can be, as at present placed, of no use in preventing a raiding party of Zulus penetrating for a considerable distance inside the colony –

22) The garrison of the laagers therefore should be reduced to the minimum, and should consist of men who are physically unfit to take the Field –
23) All the young, able bodied, Europeans who possess a rifle and a horse should understand that their duty lies outside the walls of the laager –
24) I am aware that the Natal Government has no authority over any Europeans but those who have consented to serve as Police or volunteers –
25) Still I consider that some appeal should be made to the participation of those who have hitherto refused to join any of the Colonial Forces; and that, in the present juncture, the Natal Government should, either by persuasion or force, compel every available European within the colony to assemble, armed & mounted, near the border for the protection of their own interests and to give confidence to the Natal natives –

GH 500, no. 2526/1879, pp. 195–206

85

Lieutenant-General Lord Chelmsford to Brigadier-General H.E. Wood

[Holograph]

Utrecht
11 May 1879

If we are to wait for our advance until the Commissariat throw into our advanced depôts a sufficient supply of oats or mealies for our horses, I believe we shall never advance at all – Will not the country supply Kafir corn and mealies enough for our colonial horses? We could take a certain amount of oats & mealies with us, but they should not be touched until we have failed to find a Kafir corn field or two, sufficient for our daily requirements – Would you kindly instruct the officers who go out on reconnaissance to report on this subject –

Bettington[50] took a line from Conference hill south of Bembas kop and appears to think that a waggon track is to be made by it –

He came back on a line apparently due East (?) to Koppie Allein – If we could cross the Blood river at this latter point we should save a good many miles; and Bishop Schroeder writes me word that the road runs over the north end of the Ngutu Mt, which seems to show that an advance in that direction is practicable – I will have it carefully explored by the mounted men at Conference hill, and let you know the result –

I am glad you put Col Malthus straight – I have sent on copy of your letter to him to Newdigate, with an endorsement to the effect that I entirely concur in what you suggest – [51]

I suggested to Baker, who was over here two days ago, that it would be well for him to take as many men as he could mount, and make a reconnaissance across the Blood river – He is doing nothing for his money –

The Commissariat having reported that the KDG[52] cannot be fed at Ladysmith, they have been ordered on to Dundee, 40 miles further!! I hope to be in time to stop them, but I am afraid it is too late –

WC II/2/2

86

Lieutenant-General Lord Chelmsford to Brigadier-General H.E. Wood

[Holograph] Utrecht
12 May 1879

It is no use thinking of an advance until we have thoroughly ascertained which is our best line –

I am sure there must be a practicable track from Conference hill over the N. end of the Ngutu if we could only find it, as I have heard from so many sources of waggons being taken that way – However all I want is the nearest road to Ulundi south of the Umveloosi and that I feel sure you & Buller will find out for me before long –

Bullers report of his reconnaissance did not come by yesterdays post – I cannot make out the line he mentions viz the Itytyozi valley as in my map that river rises in the Telezi hills and falls into the Umvelosi west of the Inhazatye Mt – [53]

WC II/3/1

87

Lieutenant-General Lord Chelmsford to Brigadier-General H.E. Wood

[Holograph] [?14 May 1879][54]

There is no intention to ignore you and I am sure none of my staff have any desire to do so –

I do not see however how you can look after the Utrecht District when I am here, and at the same time absolve me of the responsibility – I have no desire to take over the command, nor would it be right that I should do so; but as regards instructions which may appear desirable to me, if they invariably go through you first valuable time may be lost and the opportunity of carrying them out may be missed – For instance the question of ammunition for the posts at Burghers laager and Luneberg – [55] When the DAG spoke to me about it I considered it would be well to throw in an extra quantity so as to avoid any possibility of its being required when we are away – Had I sent it through you first it could not have left under escort of the Kaffrarian horsemen[56] this day – I therefore told Bellairs to issue the order and send it on to you for information – You cannot expect me to sit quiet here and take no interest in what is going on round me – I am the one to be hanged if anything goes wrong, but I am quite satisfied to leave my neck in your hands – Therefore pray do not imagine that there is any intention to ignore your position – Head Qr Staff officers are no doubt inclined to forget the proper channel occasionally, but if they do, take for granted that it is an oversight and not intentional –

I have forbidden any kraals being burnt for fear lest we should want them for firewood – If however we advance by Bullers Itytyozi valley those kraals near Newdigate will not be required –[57]

Where is Buller's report of the reconnaissance he made on the 10th and 11th – It has not reached me –

WC II/3/1

88

Lieutenant-General Lord Chelmsford to Colonel F.A. Stanley

[Signed MS copy] Newcastle Natal
14 May 1879

I have already sent you by telegram (yesterday) that the troops are in position[58] & are only waiting for sufficient supplies & transport to advance.

I arrived here yesterday from Utrecht so as to be in telegraphic communication with MGeneral Clifford on this subject; from what I gather from him, it will, I fear, be out of my power to advance before the 1st June.

Major General Crealock commanding No. 1 Division reports that he hopes to have 2 months supplies in 3 weeks time on the Inyezane River at a point some 30 miles in advance of our frontier,[59] thence he will be able to carry on the operations I referred to in my memorandum to him, a copy of which I forwarded for your information last month.[60]

Since the date of my last dispatch, I have visited the posts on the northern line and have now fixed my Head Quarters at Utrecht, where they will probably remain until the 2d Division under Major General Newdigate is ready to advance.

In the meantime the mounted men with Staff Officers are occupied in pushing reconnaissances into the enemy's country with a view of reporting on the different lines of advance & the cavalry are about to be utilized in the same manner.

Of the Zulu movements I have but little to report. From native sources we hear the army is to be called up at once, but at present they are occupied in reaping their crops: rumour speaks of the disinclination of the nation to continue the War but I consider no reliance can be at present placed on such a statement.[61]

When at Maritzburg I had a conversation with Bishop Colenso – when he offered to request permission of the Zulu King to bury the dead at Sandhlwana: I promised to forward a statement of his views on this point to the High Commissioner, but at the same time I explained to him the reasons why I could not recommend the acceptance of his offer.

I now have the honour to forward the answer I had the honour to send his Lordship on hearing from Sir Bartle Frere.[62]

WO 32/7739 [Printed in *BPP* (C. 2374), enc. 1 in no. 32]

89

Lieutenant-General Lord Chelmsford to Brigadier-General H.E. Wood

[Holograph]

Utrecht
16 May 1879

. . . Cetywayo has sent messengers to Lower Tugela column asking for peace; but giving no promises and offering no guarantees – I have told them to come to you and have in the meantime telegraphed to Sir Bartle at Kimberley for instructions –[63] If Buller reports favourably of the Vechtkop–Ngutu Line, it would be well I think if you moved your force to a position on the Ngutu or near to it – We should then be able to improve the road before our general advance and you would be able to thoroughly reconnoitre the road further on – We might also perhaps manage to bury the dead round Insandlwana before moving forward, which would give great satisfaction everywhere – Kindly consider these questions, and let me have your opinion upon them – If you are favourable, the sooner the movements are made the better –

I should like myself to accompany the burying party to Insandlwana, if you think it can be managed, and it will give me an opportunity of seeing the first part of our line of advance from Vechtkop –[64]

Newdigate reports that his 2 months supplies will be ready in 14 days –

There are 14 waggon loads of supplies, principally biscuit and flour, at Newcastle – I am trying to ascertain whether the transport to bring them is here; if so and the Commissariat can spare the waggons, I shall send for the stuff – No more will be sent from the Base at Newcastle – Everything is to be directed to Dundee from Ladismith –

WC II/2/2

90

Lieutenant-General Lord Chelmsford to Brigadier-General H.E. Wood

[Holograph] Utrecht
19 May 1879

If the reconnaissance now out bring back a report that the Ngutu-Isipezi line is quite practicable for waggons, and that there is some firewood on the road, it would be very advantageous for our advance that you should move down on it – Gosset writes today that the largest number of waggons they can collect will be 250 – To carry supplies for 60 days with horses at half rations there should be 350 waggons in Newdigates camp – The only chance therefore to get up a proper supply to the Babanango or other intermediate post will be by making two trips and to do this safely and comfortably your column ought to be on the spot – Longcast says that he knows the country well from Isipezi hill to Emtonjaneni, and that it is a ridge nearly the whole way, with no dongas or swamps to cross – If you could get as far as the Babanango by the dotted line track leading from the Inlazatye road across the Itytyozi river, (Intelligence map March 1879),[65] which Drummond declares to be quite practicable for waggons, it would facilitate matters immensely –

The disadvantage would be that you uncover completely the Transvaal N.W. border and that you will be a long distance removed from Newdigates force – If however Newdigate were to advance simultaneously with you, with as many waggons as he could load up, the last objection would be removed and you could make yourself quite snug and safe in your new position and be able to do a lot of good work patrolling in a new district and reconnoitering our future line of advance – "Chi va piano, va sano e va lontano" is a good proverb,[66] and I am not sure that a partial advance, such as I advocate, will not be better than a general one –

PS

When we begin to advance I intend to send the KDG to Rorkes drift, where there is plenty of grain, and make them go to Sandlwana to bury the dead – The move will have a good effect in a military point of view, over and above that which will be produced in the colony and in England by our doing what many think ought to have been done long ago –

WC II/2/2

91

Lieutenant-General Lord Chelmsford to Colonel F.A. Stanley

[MS copy]

Head Quarter Camp
Landman's Drift[67]
25 May 1879

No further communication has been received from the Zulu King since I had the honour of addressing you on the 21st inst.[68] This fact, however, I consider [will] not affect the sincerity of his intention to treat for peace, as General Crealock informed him that the messengers should be sent to my camp on the Northern border, which would cause delay, and the High Commissioner's subsequent message will probably cause him to consult the great council before again sending to me.

In the meantime General Clifford has been pushing on supplies from the Base to the advanced depôts on the S. Eastern and Northern frontiers, and General Crealock has been systematically passing large weekly convoys forward from the Lower Tugela Depôt to his advanced post, 30 miles from the frontier on the Inyezane.[69]

During the past week reconnaissances have been made by Lieut Colonel Buller CB in one direction, and Lieut Colonel Harrison R.E.[70] in another, and the information obtained has enabled me to decide on the most practicable line to reach the Ibabanango mountain, which is our first objective point.

Major General Marshall, by Major General Newdigate's orders, made a reconnaissance to the field of Sandhlwana, and buried a large number of the remains of our brave comrades who fell on the 22nd January.

40 carts and wagons were also removed by the Army service Corps attached to the force . . .

I consider the arrangements were judiciously made, and that the prompt action taken by General Newdigate so soon after the arrival of the Cavalry, will have an excellent effect. I can but regret, however, that the burying of the dead was not carried out to the fullest extent possible.

I need scarcely say that the earliest opportunity will be taken to complete this sad duty.[71]

The Head Quarter Wing of the King's Dragoon Guards moves tomorrow to Koppie Allein, a post 12 miles distant on the Blood River.[72]

The 2nd Division will follow the day following and continue to advance on or before the 1st June.

I met Colonel Lanyon, the Administrator of the Transvaal, at Utrecht on 23 inst. I explained to him my inability at the present juncture to detach any of Her Majesty's troops to assist him in the operations against Sekukuni which he is about to commence.

His Excellency is raising a considerable force of Volunteers and Native Levies for this object, and I have, with the concurrence of the High Commissioner and full approval of Colonel Lanyon, left him to carry on this duty, being fully persuaded of his ability to do so.[73] I hope, if possible, to send him some officers to assist him in administrative duties.

Colonel Lanyon having temporarily taken over military command of the Transvaal, I am enabled to utilize Colonel Rowland's services with the 1st Brigade 1st Division, the command of which has become vacant by Colonel Pearson's state of health.

CP 13/19 [Printed in *BPP* (C. 2374), enc. 6 in no. 32.]

92

Lieutenant-General Lord Chelmsford to Brigadier-General H.E. Wood

[Holograph]

Landmans Drift
27 May 1879

I am very sorry to hear that you came to Koppie Allein to meet me this day – I am afraid that I did not explain myself sufficiently clearly to Buller – I wanted him to tell you not to come over today but tomorrow when I was going to move my Head Qrs to the new camp of the 2d Division – [74]

I have telegraphed to Clifford asking that DCG Morris may be allowed to come up with our advancing force as senior Commissariat Officer – [75] I did not like to "jump" him without reference to the I G of L of C & B[76] as he is one of his staff –

Newdigate is going to buy his first experience of S. African marching – [77] I hope it will open his eyes to the necessity of attending to transport details, as, when he comes to have 300 waggons to look after the task will be a heavy one –

We shall have to talk over our marching arrangements before we start, if, as you propose, the two columns are to march on the same day, keep within reasonable distance of each other and laager within reach one of the other –

If the waggons have not to move in single file it will be fairly easy to keep together, otherwise your rear waggons must check the progress of the head of the 2d Division –

It was difficult going to Ginginlovo with 120 waggons to make more than seven miles in the day! What shall we do when we have 300? I am sending you a company of R.E. and one of Pioneers, in exchange for Major Moysey,[78] whose place is in the senior command – As you go first you must necessarily repair drifts &c and you will find them useful – I am in despair about our postal arrangements – I have begged Clifford to send transport carts & mules to carry our mail bags to Ladysmith from Landmans drift – He has promised to do his best, but when will they come?

I hope you appreciate my having sent you all four Gatlings![79]

WC II/2/2

93

Lieutenant-General Lord Chelmsford to Brigadier-General H.E. Wood

[Holograph (pencil)]

Stony Koppie Camp[80]
28 May 1879
1–45 pm

Your letter just came in – I send you Careys[81] reconnaissance report which leads me to believe that our road from here does run between the Incenci and Itilezi, as far as the beaten track which runs S.E towards the Babanango.

I am going out myself tomorrow to try for a road that way –

Carey did not take it as he understood his instructions were to find B[82] which he believed to be to the left of the beaten track –

Would you or Buller come out towards the neck between the Incenci and Itelezi and then we can compare notes, & you will be able to point out where B really is –

I cannot state positively now when this column will be able to cross the Blood river, but I hope by the 1st June – [83] DCG Morris who is coming with us will let me know this evening which carriage there is – It all depends upon that and upon filling up our waggons at Conference hill –

I am sending you a company of RE & of Pioneers – [84] which will help you to improve the road, but we must make sure of our lead first –

Please return reconnaissance reports

WC II/2/2

94
Lieutenant-General Lord Chelmsford to Brigadier-General H.E. Wood

[Holograph (pencil)]

Malafelugu Kraals [?]
2–30 pm
East of range between Telezi and Incenci
29 May 1879

I thought that I had given you the rendezvous between Telezi and Incenci and not between the latter Mt and the Mcanda –

I am now on a ridge which runs parallel to the one which I expect you recommend and which lies to the North of this one –

This ridge seems to be good going the whole way to where Bullers road would meet it, but as that road has not been accurately laid down as yet, it is difficult to say positively that it does so – So far as I can make out from the Intelligence Map March 78[85] the ridge runs between the Tombokulu and Ityotyozi rivers – We have not had time to go as far as the junction of these two rivers, but it seems all plain sailing up to that point –

Bullers road as far as I can [make] it out in my map passes between the Tombokulu and Umvumyana rivers –

I shall send out an officer to make sure about this track and also to go over the one you recommend – The former would be several miles shorter if it is practicable the whole way –

WC II/2/2

95
Lieutenant-General Lord Chelmsford to Brigadier-General H.E. Wood

[Holograph]

Stony hill camp
30 May 1879

We are unlucky about meeting – I did not reach the saddle between Incenci and Itelezi till past 10 am which I had reckoned would have given you plenty of time – I was under the impression that you were as near to that point as we are –

Carey has verified the track I wrote to you about yesterday[86] and the 2nd Division will move along it, I hope, starting on the 1 June –

It now only remains to decide where your force will cut in to that line – Your column and Newdigate's will be moving parallel one with the other, and it might perhaps be well, if that arrangement were continued up to Babanango, provided the two columns are always near enough to mutually assist one another –

This column will take two marches to reach the Ityotyozi, and I reckon you are about the same distance.[87]

I am riding over this morning to Conference hill to talk to Colonel Davies[88] about patrolling when we move on – With a wing of the K.D.Gs he ought to be able to detect any big force coming down upon us from the North –

I have been thinking over the arrangements for the empty waggons coming back from Babanango and refilling with supplies – I am inclined to think that it will be an advantage for half to refill at Landmans drift, and half at Conference hill as this camp is about half way between each depôt.

I shall have to ask you to take command of the troops & convoys returning, as I know that you and Hughes between you will have the refilling done in the shortest possible time –

The waggons I reckon ought not to take more than four days returning and may perhaps do the distance in three – The infantry might be allowed to ride on the empty waggons when returning, each company being allowed ten waggons to carry themselves and their equipment on – Two regiments with mounted men ought to be sufficient, if escorted some distance by the 17 Lancers and if met by the wing KDGs from Conference hill – The Malifekya kraal road is a very safe one as it runs along a high ridge from which the whole country round can be seen – I shall hope to be able to tell you positively today when this column can start –

WC II/2/2

96

Lieutenant-General Lord Chelmsford to Colonel F.A. Stanley

[Signed MS copy]

Head Quarter Camp
Blood River
31 May 1879

Memorandum

Having noted lately in the Natal newspapers that an absurd report has been circulated to the effect that I had received instructions from the Horse Guards regarding the disposal of the two Cavalry Regiments, and exception also having been taken to the distribution of those two Regiments,[89] it may be well that I should place on record my reasons for bringing them both up to the South West border of Zululand –

Looking to the importance of bringing so fine a body of men and horses as quickly as possible into the Field, and to the difficulties of supplying them with food and grain, a mere glance at the map of Natal and Zululand would lead to the conclusion that one, at least, of the two Cavalry regiments should be sent, either to the Lower Tugela, in order to operate actively with the 1st Division; or to some point on the Natal border for the purpose of protecting the Colony from invasion.

My reason for not adopting the first plan was as follows –

The coast country is very unhealthy for horses; and that fatal disease called "Horse Sickness"[90] does not disappear from that part of Zululand until the middle, and sometimes not until the end of June.

Serious loss was therefore to be anticipated had a Cavalry regiment been placed on that line.

Secondly, the Country itself between the Tugela and the Umhlatoosi rivers affords a very circumscribed area for Cavalry operations.

The narrow strip of open country, suitable for Cavalry, is never more than ten miles broad and in parts much less; consequently a regiment on that line could have no proper freedom of action, its movements would have been crippled and its usefulness considerably curtailed.

As regards its employment for the defence of Natal, there is only one portion of the border, viz:- the country north of Greytown, where Cavalry could be employed, and having on each side of it the broken country of the Inanda location[91] and of the Mooi River Valley, could easily, and would no doubt, be avoided by a raiding force of the enemy.

A cavalry force placed in the Umvoti district would, I consider, have been completely thrown away.

The country in which the Cavalry Brigade has been acting, and in which it would be called upon to act, is specially adapted for that arm of service.

It has plenty of open ground in every direction and can consequently work to the greatest advantage, and with the smallest amount of risk.

The line of advance from the Blood River to the Babanango virtually covers, at least, two thirds of the Natal frontier, as a force of the enemy moving from Ulundi to invade Natal must necessarily pass close to that mountain.

When an advanced post is formed near that mountain, the Natal border will be even more efficiently protected, whilst, at the same time the main object of the campaign, viz:- the subjugation of Zululand, will not be delayed.

An invasion of Natal by the Zulus can in fact be prevented far better by a counter-invasion of their own country than it can be by any passive defence system along the Natal border[92] and it was in that view, in addition to the other considerations already mentioned, that I decided upon moving the Cavalry so far from the Base.

Having thus explained my reasons for a decision entirely my own, and uninfluenced by any orders, or suggestions, from the Horse Guards it may be as well that I should also explain why, having brought both Cavalry regiments so far, I have decided to leave the largest part of one of them behind –

The Line of our advance from the Blood River to Babanango runs, almost in a bee line, in a South Easterly direction, over the neck between the Inceni and Itelezi mountains, between the

Ityotyozi and Tombakala rivers, to the Southern slopes of that mountain. As the 2nd Division and Flying Column have only transport sufficient to carry one month' s supplies, an entrenched post will be formed near the Babanango, our wagons will be emptied of their contents and sent back to Landman's drift and Conference Hill for a further supply, under strong escort; and the larger portion of the mounted force which will remain at Babanango, will be occupied during this enforced halt in patrolling and reconnoitering the country towards Ulundi, Kwamagwasa, and the Inkandla bush.

In order to afford additional security to the advancing columns and to the convoys going and returning, I have placed two squadrons of the King's Dragoon Guards at Conference Hill post, which is on the Blood River, close to the road leading from Utrecht to Ulundi by the Inhlazatye mountain, with orders to patrol constantly in a North Easterly, Easterly, and South Easterly direction. They will thus cover the left flanks of the columns moving towards Babanango, or the right flank of the convoy returning, and they will moreover watch a portion of Zululand in which large bodies of the enemy have been always in the habit of collecting – and from which the most daring raids into the Transvaal have been made.[93]

The other squadron of the King's Dragoon Guards has been placed at Rorke's Drift, and will be able to watch the greater portion of the country belonging to Sirayo, who is one of our most determined enemies, and cover, to a great extent, the right flank of the advancing columns.

On the return of the convoy to Babanango, unless the situation alters unexpectedly, a strong force moving without tents with as few impediments as possible, will advance on Ulundi; a strong garrison consisting of the three arms being left at the Babanango post.

Fort Newdigate on the Blood River[94] and another entrenched post midway between that Fort and the Babanango,[95] will be held by a small detachment (two companies) in order to ensure a regular postal communication between the Column and Landman's Drift.

WO 32/7744

Chapter 7
Ulundi

97
Lieutenant-General Lord Chelmsford to Colonel F.A. Stanley

Camp 7 miles beyond Blood River under Itelezi Mountain
[MS copy] 2 June 1879

Prince Imperial acting under orders of the Assistant Quarter Master General[1] reconnoitered on 1st of June road to camping ground of 2nd June accompanied by Lieutenant Carey 90th Reg. D.A. Quarter Master General and his six white men and friendly Zulus all mounted. Party halted and offsaddled the road about 10 miles from this camp, but as the Prince gave the order to mount a volley was fired from long grass around the Kraals.[2]

The Prince Imperial and two troopers are reported missing by Lieut. Carey who escaped and reached this camp after dark. From the evidence taken there can be no doubt of the Prince being killed. 17th Lancers and ambulance are now starting to recover the body but I send this off at once hoping to catch mail.[3]

I myself was not aware that Prince had been detailed for this duty.

CP 11/8 [Printed in French, *Lord Chelmsford*, p. 242.]

98

Lieutenant-General Lord Chelmsford to King Cetshwayo

[Signed MS copy sent by Hon. W. Drummond to Brigadier-General Wood, 5 June 1879]

Camp
4 June 1879

Message from Lord Chelmsford to Zulu King –

{Your three messengers by name Umsuelo Umtyibela – and Umpokotyayo – arrived this day at Genl. Woods camp where I personally heard their words – asking why war had been made – and I gather they wished to take back to the King the terms on which Peace would be made – [4]

My answer is this –}

1) If Ketshwayo wishes for Peace he must give substantial proof of being in earnest –

2) he must at once restore all horses, oxen, arms ammunition and other property taken during the War –

3) one or more Regiments to be named by me must come under a flag of truce and at a distance of one thousand yards from my camp lay down their arms as a token of submission –

[[4) If this is done, I will order a cessation of hostilities pending discussion of final terms of peace.]]

Until this is done, Her Majesty's Armies will continue to advance –

{The next message from the King must be brought by one of his officers who was present at the delivery of the Ultimatum in December last at the lower Tugela – Usitwango[5] or other well known messenger of the King must accompany him –}

{A copy sent by Hon. W. Drummond to Brig. Wood 5 June}

CP 13/37 [Printed in *BPP* (C. 2454), B in enc. in no. 33. Words between [ ] omitted from MS copy but printed in *BPP*. Extracts also printed in French, *Lord Chelmsford*, p. 247 with words between {} omitted.]

99

Lieutenant-General Lord Chelmsford to Brigadier-General H.E. Wood

[Holograph]

Camp right bank of Ityontyozi R
5 June 1879
4 am

I have not left a post on this river as the ground was too hard to make any progress worth speaking of yesterday –

As also it now appears that we have to pass close by the Inthlabamkosi to get to Babanango we must alter our line of communications with Koppie Allein, as the former hill by the route over the Ingutu that Harrison proposed is very much shorter than the one we are now taking –

Bullers road according to his and your report[6] ought to have left Inthlabamkosi about 7 or 8 miles to our right, and we ought now to have been within two marches of Babanango – I am very uneasy about our wood supply, as the calculation was only for 7 days, and it will be now, I fear, the 10th or 11th before we shall reach Babanango, and according to your report it seems doubtful whether we shall find our supply near the road to Ulundi –

We must moreover make our new line of communications secure and for waggons to pass by it will entail having working parties to enable them to get up the Southern slopes of the Ngutu –

Kindly talk over these points with Harrison and let me have your opinion as to how these difficulties are to be overcome –

We might find sufficient mealie cobs and cow dung out of the kraals to carry us along, but the collection of this in sufficient quantities means time – You must help this Division somehow or other –

I am sending Drummond with my written answers to Cetywayo – [7] and I have told him to propose to the messengers in order to show their sincerity, that two of them should go to the King and that one should stay behind –

WC II/2/2

100

Lieutenant-General Lord Chelmsford to Colonel F.A. Stanley

[Holograph] Head Qr Camp on Upoko river Zululand
8 June 1879

I have the honour to acknowledge receipt of your letter dated War Office 1st May 1879 . . . with regard to the cost and value of the native levies which have been raised in this country at Imperial charge – [8]

Of the 7000 natives originally intended to be raised only 4000 are at the present moment under arms; as the two battalions belonging to the No 3 Column, which disbanded themselves after Insandlwana, have never been brought together again, and one of the battalions ordered to be raised for No 2 Column under Colonel Durnford never reached a higher number than 200, while the other battalions of this column are not up to their full strength of 1000 strong – [9]

With regard to their value as fighting units I am free to confess that I cannot rank them very highly – I do not however attribute any blame in this matter to the individuals, who, man for man, are I believe quite as courageous, and possess quite as fine a physique, as the Zulu proper –

Steady behaviour under fire on the part of troops in the Field, depends almost entirely upon drill, discipline, organization and good officers –

These advantages, owing to the hurried manner in which the Native Contingents were necessarily raised, have been hitherto enjoyed by them to a very limited extent, and they are only now beginning to feel their effects –

The four native battalions now serving in Zululand, are very superior in every respect to what they were when we first took the Field, and I have great confidence that they will behave fairly well, when next tested –

However this may be, the presence of these battalions with the columns to which they are attached is absolutely indispensable to their efficiency; as there is much work which native levies alone can properly perform – They are excellent scouts, indefatigable & quick witted; perform all fatigue duties most cheerfully; and can be employed with mounted men when necessary, in consequence of their wonderful marching powers – Many of the men are employed as spies; and all cheerfully & willingly perform any duty they may be detailed for such as bringing in wood, repairing roads, searching difficult country, building entrenched posts, &c, &c –

If it be admitted, as I maintain, that the true way to defend Natal from the Zulus is to invade Zululand then no doubt the colony should bear its portion of the expense –

Natal has at the present moment a large number of natives assembled on its borders for defensive purposes, many of whom, as I lately reported, are in receipt of pay drawn by the Natal govt from the Imperial chest – The Natal–Zulu border is so extended, and the country generally so difficult and broken, that none but natives could possibly watch and guard it effectively – and I do not consider in the present state of affairs that it would be wise to reduce their numbers however large they appear to be – The charge however is purely a colonial one and will I presume be so treated.

CP 10/42 [Printed in *BPP* (C. 2482), enc. in no. 13]

101

Memorandum by Lieutenant-General Lord Chelmsford

[Holograph]

Head Quarter Camp
Ntoneni river – Zululand
8 June 1879

Memorandum

I have only just received H.E. Sir Henry Bulwer's remarks upon the peace terms proposed to be offered to Cetewayo – [10]

Altho' I quite admit that the surrender of 10,000 stand of arms will not, in itself have any practical permanent effect, unless the future importation of arms be effectively prevented, still I consider that such a surrender of arms would be a proof of the desire of the nation for peace, and would also be a token that Cetewayo and his people acknowledge that they have been defeated –

I do not understand Sir H. Bulwer's objection to a fine – We are surely entitled to demand an indemnification for the expenses of the war, and cattle is the only shape in which it can be paid –

I feel, very strongly that the fine demanded should be paid at once, as I fear, if allowed to be spread over several years, that it will keep up the soreness of defeat, and may possibly end in political complications by the payment being eventually evaded, or repudiated altogether; when Cetewayo or any other chief in Zululand sees that we have not the requisite number of troops in the country to enforce it –

I have not yet, on the line I have been advancing upon, discovered what I consider a suitable position for a post to be occupied pending negotiations, or perhaps permanently. The essential requisites of wood and water have at present only been found near our present camp,[11] the country in front of which would require a considerable force to watch, and where small parties going out for the above-mentioned essentials, would always be liable to annoyance from the enemy.

I am convinced from what I have now seen of the part of Zululand which lies opposite the Natal & Transvaal borders that it is essential to the future safety of those Colonies there should be a rectification of their frontiers.

As regards Natal, the frontier should I consider be extended up to the Umlatoosi R from the sea to its source on the Southern slopes of the Babanango Mt. from the source of the Umlatoosi R to the Northern slopes of the Inthlabamakosi, from there along the Swazi trading road until it strikes the Utrecht-Ulundi road and so North up the Mundhla to the boundary line beaconed off in 1864, which would represent the Transvaal boundary –

Such a rectification of our boundary would give us an open country to our front, and a broken country to our rear, which could be easily defended by our natives, if supported at certain intervals by strong military posts –

It would give us the use of the forests of Qudeni, Inkandhla Entumeni and Ingowe, and of the coal field near the Mundhla, and North of that point –

With such a boundary as a base, should any military invasion of Zululand at any future time become necessary the difficulties to be overcome would be much diminished –

The shortest lines from our Base would be available viz. Durban – PMBurg, Greytown Rorkes drift – Inthlabamakosi; and Port Durnford-Umhlatoosi River –

Police posts would be required at the mouth of the Emlalazi, at Ekowe, Entumeni, Inthlabamakosi, & Mundhla –

I am not well acquainted with the country between Mundhla and the Pongolo R. and I cannot therefore name at once the positions of the Police posts along that line, which would appear to be the most desirable –

If Cetewayo be allowed to remain as Supreme Chief in Zululand I consider this rectification of the frontiers an absolute military necessity; for in my opinion he will never rest satisfied until he has revenged his defeat by an invasion of Natal or the Transvaal –

So long moreover as he remains on the throne, so long the military system will, by some means or other, be maintained, in spite of any promises he may make to the contrary; and I believe on this point he will have the Zulu nation on his side, as it is so deeply imbued with military instinct, and so proud of its military traditions –

I cannot conceive therefore any permanent peace in S. Africa, or any security to Natal or Transvaal, if Cetewayo be allowed to remain on the throne –

On the other hand should Cetewayo be deposed, and the land parcelled out amongst some of the principal Zulu chiefs, ruling independently, but under the control of the British Government, I foresee a bright future not only for Natal and the Transvaal, but also for Zululand itself –

CP 13/44 [Copy dated 9 June 1879 printed in *BPP* (C. 2482), sub-enc. 2 in no. 8.]

102

Lieutenant-General Lord Chelmsford to Colonel F.A. Stanley

[MS copy] Camp on the Upoko River, Zululand
10 June 1879

I have received your private letter dated 8 May,[12] and cannot conceal from you that it has distressed me very much.

I quite feel that you have every right to complain of the baldness of the telegram which was sent regarding the additional three regiments I asked for but that was not my fault. I send herewith copy of the telegram I sent to General Clifford, and which he altered so as to leave out all the explanation I had put in.[13] The demand for more Army Service Corps and for more supplies was made by him in my absence and on the recommendation of the Commissary-General,[14] and it would have been better had he sent this part of the telegram in his own name. I will write to him today and beg that whatever message he sends home as General Officer Commanding the Base shall be sent in his own name and not in mine, so that you may distinguish between my direct messages and those of the General Officer who is filling my place at the Base.

I cannot understand what you mean by considerable anxiety existing as to the indefinite prolongation of the War.

Do people at home imagine that a country so large as Zululand, and peopled by such warriors as the Zulus have proved themselves to be, can be conquered off-hand? We have now been 5 months in the Field, and looking to all the difficulties which surround military operations in this country, I cannot but consider in spite of the untoward results of the Insandlwana, Intombi and Inhlobani[15] affairs, that the forces under my command have made as much progress towards a final result as could reasonably be expected.

I can only look upon the paragraph of your letter which touches upon the possibility of an officer of superior rank being sent out to command the forces under my orders should three more regiments still be demanded in the light of a threat. If I am fit to command 17,000 men in the Field I cannot understand by what powers of reasoning I am not equal to command 20,000. Rest assured however that should Her Majesty's Govt and the Duke of Cambridge come to the conclusion that they no longer have confidence in me as Commander of the Forces, I shall be quite ready to serve in a more subordinate capacity under whomsoever may be selected to succeed me.

His Royal Highness in a letter of the same date as your own received also this day,[16] alludes to my not having given as much information regarding my future plans as I ought to have done, and as I am now writing to you, I think it best to explain how impossible it is for a General conducting operations in this country to lay down his plans beforehand in the same deliberate manner as would be the case were he commanding an army operating in a European country.

The maps of Zululand are almost useless for military purposes as the country has never been surveyed with any pretensions to accuracy; and even the trading tracks through the country have been inserted more by guess work than from any real knowledge of their exact direction.

At the outbreak of the Zulu war in January last I was not aware of the untrustworthy character of the maps, or of the information regarding the country, furnished by traders and others who had travelled in Zululand, being so inaccurate.

It was only by degrees, as we ourselves became better acquainted with the country, that we discovered how dangerous it would be to lay down any plan of operation which was based upon any information other than that afforded by our own officers gained by bold reconnaissances.

For instance {when I had decided to abandon the line of advance North of the Umvelosi River, advocated by General Evelyn Wood, and to move both columns, from the Base of the Blood River, to Ulundi by the Babanango Mountain,} I had the greatest difficulty ascertaining by what line the two columns could advance, and it was only a very few days before the arrival of sufficient supplies and transport at the advanced depôt, that by repeated reconnaissances, pushed far into the enemy's country, the excellent line we are now following was discovered.[17]

Were I to have sent home a plan of campaign based upon insufficient information, which would have most probably had to have been altered most materially, I should have laid myself open to severe and just criticism. It must also be remembered that until I arrived at Dundee and Balte Spruit at the beginning of last month, I had never crossed the Buffalo river, and had been unable to personally decide as to the advanced posts which should be occupied and as the exact point where the troops should be assembled previous to advancing.

How was it possible for me on my return from the relief of Ekowe in the month of April, to write fully as to the exact plan of campaign I intended to adopt.

I did send home copy of my memorandum to General Crealock regarding the operations I wished him to undertake, as I was able to do so from personal knowledge of the country.[18]

With regard to the operations in the North, I could do no more than decide upon the number of freshly arrived troops that should be sent in that direction, and move up myself there as soon as possible.

His Royal Highness seems to regard with some alarm the distance between the columns commanded by General Crealock and Newdigate respectively. This was unfortunately a geographical necessity. There is no way for a column to enter Zululand between the Lower Tugela & Rorke's Drift – and consequently no possibility of opening up communications with General Crealock's column until the northern columns shall have got in to the Lower Tugela-Ulundi line, either at Kwamagwasa or Entonjaneni. The columns I am now commanding are within about 50 miles of those two places, and it is possible, altho perhaps not probable, that we may be able to exchange communications on arriving there with the Lower Tugela column.

At all events should General Crealock be opposed by any considerable force of the enemy occupying the valley of the Mflatoosi, it will be very easy for us to afford him indirect, if not direct, support by pushing a force in the direction of St Pauls.

It will be seen therefore that I did not overlook the advantage of our two columns being in communication with the 3rd one operating on the Lower Tugela line, and I still hope that I may be able to carry it out, altho by a rather circuitous route rendered necessary by the nature of the country.

The Commissariat have had great difficulty in forwarding sufficient supplies for General Crealock's Division at its present strength and of course any addition to it would only have increased them. That line was, I fear, unhealthy for horses and it has turned out to be for men also. It has also the disadvantage of having the Muhlatoosi river about midway, the valley of which contains very difficult ground, which I have always doubted a column being able to cross, unless assisted by one operating on the northern bank of that river.[19]

It was with these considerations in view that I decided to send a considerable portion of the reinforcements to operate on the Northern border, and I have no reason to regret the decision I came to.

His Royal Highness also finds fault also with me for asking that mules should be sent from S. America and then telegraphing that they can be procured at the Cape.[20] As General Officer Commanding the Forces I am of course responsible for the acts of every department serving under me. At the same time it is impossible for me to do the work of the Heads, and it would be dangerous in most cases to neglect to approve of what they recommend.

In the case under reference I received a most urgent telegram just as I was leaving for the Lower Tugela saying that unless mules were sent for from S. America the whole Transport would come to a standstill. This course was strongly advocated by D.C.G. Palmer,[21] ACG Healy[22] and supported by Colonel Bellairs who at that time occupied the position during my absence from PMBurg now filled by General Clifford. The telegram was sent and I went to Ekowe. On my return I found General Clifford had entered upon his duties and one of the first things almost he spoke to me about was the question of mule supply. He had ascertained what the Commissariat and Transport officers might also, and ought to have ascertained, that the supply of mules from Cape Town and its neighbourhood would be quite equal to our demands. I consider therefore that in this instance I am perfectly justified in throwing all the responsibility for the mistake upon the shoulders of the Commissariat Department, the more especially, as the urgent request was made to me by the Commissariat officer who had been sent out by the War Office to succeed Mr Strickland, in the event of the latter breaking down, and was supported by the officer who was selected to take especial charge of the transport.

As it is more than probable with such a large number of newspaper correspondents in camp, that many false impressions may be circulated and sent home regarding our present operations either intentionally or ignorantly, I trust that so long as I am allowed to retain command of the Forces in S. Africa, that you will not accept them as true should they be damaging to my reputation as a General until I have been given an opportunity if possible of refuting them. It is trying enough to have to conduct operations in a country where there is complete absence of roads, where firewood is obtainable at only long intervals and has to be carried for a large force, and where the grass is becoming so dry as to render grass fires a serious danger. But when is superadded to these, and many other difficulties the presence of a number of men belonging to a press which has been generally hostile to me, who are always ready without sufficient data for their guidance to express opinions on every conceivable military subject ex cathedra, I cannot help feeling after reading your letter under reply that they may be able to distort the truth or misrepresent it, in such a manner as to increase the uneasy feeling regarding my proceedings which has evidently taken possession of your mind, and from which I fear His Royal Highness is not altogether free.

Their presence in the camp will make no difference to myself, and you may depend upon my pursuing "the even tenour of my way" uninfluenced by the knowledge that I am surrounded by those who will not be sparing in their criticism if everything is not rearranged exactly to their liking.

CP 28 [Printed in French, *Lord Chelmsford*, pp. 259–64 with words between {} omitted.]

103

Message from Lieutenant-General Lord Chelmsford

[MS copy] 11 June 1879

Message from the Lieut. General Commanding the Forces to any Zulu Chiefs desirous of tendering their submission –

Should any chief desire to tender his Submission to the English the Lt. General Commanding will receive it on the following conditions.
(1) The chief, with such small personal following as may befit his rank, must surrender his person either to the Lt General himself, or, if more convenient to the chief, the O.C. Rorke's Drift,[23] to Mr. Fynn RM. Umsinga, or any other magistrate or border agent whom he may select. He will be there located at such spot in English territory as the Lt. General or the Government may direct, until the conclusion of hostilities .
(2) The arms of the chief himself and his personal following must be surrendered in token of the submission of his whole tribe, and of their willingness to do likewise when called upon.
(3) Should, for military reasons, any portion of H.M. troops enter the district of a chief who has submitted, the headman left in charge of his tribe must give himself up to the Officer Commanding it, and orders to that effect must be left by the chief.
(4) Under these conditions the Lt. General Commanding is willing to spare the lives of, and afford protection to the people of any Chief who submits.

CP 13/6 [Printed in French, *Lord Chelmsford*, p. 275.]

104

Memorandum by Lieutenant-General Lord Chelmsford

[MS copy] 15 June 1879

I agree with Colonel Lowe[24] that the poor condition of the horses is due to want of a proper quantity of fodder – At the same time however I consider that the opportunity afforded by a weeks halt in a valley full of excellent grass and large fields of Kafir corn has not been properly taken advantage of.[25]

The Cavalry Officers serving in this command have been slow to recognize the necessity of adopting colonial customs as regards the horses, and have hesitated to run them loose to graze – This has now been rectified and I am certain that the horses will now improve in appearance. Much valuable time however has been lost and I am afraid that the condition lost will not be easily recovered –

The oats served out have been of very inferior quality but 8 lbs is the largest quantity that can be issued, having regard to the amount of transport available.

WO 32/7752 [Printed in French, *Lord Chelmsford*, pp. 275–6.]

105

Lieutenant-General Lord Chelmsford to Colonel F.A. Stanley

[Signed MS copy]

Head Quarter Camp
Upoko River
Zululand
16 June 1879

I have received no further communication from Ketshwayo since the departure of his messengers from my camp on the 6th inst:;[26] the 14th was the earliest day I could have received an answer to my message, and judging by native custom and Ketshwayo's dilatoriness in answering former communications, I am not inclined to consider that even several days further delay on his part, will show that he is not still desirous of coming to terms.

2. I reported in my last despatch[27] that Brigadier General Wood had returned to the advanced depôt[28] with a convoy of empty wagons: he returns here today with 600 wagons containing 6 weeks' supplies.

A portion of the force will advance tomorrow to a point between the Isipizi and Inthlabamkosi Mountains, where the tracks from

Rorke's Drift and the Transvaal frontier join. Here I intend forming a post (Fort Marshall) garrisoned by 4 companies 2/4th Foot, a squadron of Cavalry, 2 guns, and a detachment of natives both foot and mounted. The distance from this post to that at Rorke's Drift (garrisoned by 3 Companies 2/24th Foot and 1 squadron King's Dragoon Guards) is about 25 miles; and to Fort Newdigate, on the Nondweni River, on Transvaal frontier road, is 16 miles; the latter post has a garrison of 2 Companies 2/4th Foot and 1 squadron Cavalry and a detachment of natives, foot and mounted; this last post is 21 miles distant from Koppie Allein on the Blood River.

3. The 2nd Brigade will be now broken up and the remaining Regiments of the Division, viz:- 1/24th, 58th and 94th will form the Brigade under Colonel Glyn C.B.

Colonel Collingwood[29] will remain in charge of the two forts, Forts Marshall and Newdigate.

4. Major General Marshall will take charge of the whole line of communication in the enemy's country and such portion of the garrisons which are left in the frontier posts for the purpose of patrolling.

5. Lieut Colonel Black 2/24th from Rorke's Drift has been actively patrolling the enemys' country around, and reports that it is clear between that portion of the frontier and this place.

6. Colonel Buller made a reconnaissance from here on the 14th and 15th inst: on the other flank towards Intabankulu . . .

I consider credit is due to him and those under his command for the manner in which the duty was performed.

7. The advance will be continued from the Isipizi Hill on the 19th inst:.

8. The weather has been wet and cold during the past week, but the health of the troops has been very good. The average daily sick for week ending 6th June was 16.81 in a total strength of 3963, and that ending 13th June, 12.16 in a total of 3132 N.C. Officers and men . . .

9. It will be seen by the Enclosed report that the English horses are not thriving, my remarks on the subject will be found attached to the report itself.[30]

10. General Crealock reports that the portion of his division at the Lower Tugela is now moving forward. His presence there up to

the present time has been, he considers, absolutely necessary to superintend the sending on of convoys and equipment of the Division. You will have already heard by telegram thro' General Clifford, more particulars of his movements than I am at present able to furnish.[31]

11. I hear from Colonel Lanyon, Administrator of the Transvaal, that he expects to have 800 Mounted Volunteers in a few days, and he himself hopes to proceed very shortly to the scene of operations against Sikukuni.

Zulus have from time to time shown themselves in the neighbourhood of Lüneberg since the march of Br General Wood's Column from that portion of the frontier. The force of Burghers expected by Colonel Lanyon to be raised by Pretorius should have secured this district: As it is, the mounted force at Colonel Bray's disposal is inadequate for the area to be patrolled.

On the 4th June Commandant Schermbrucker with 38 mounted men and 40 natives, pursued a raiding party 9 miles from the Pivan Laager – 18 Zulus were killed and 5 wounded.

Major Blake 4th K.O. Regt[32] commanding at Lüneberg reported on 7th June, that a Zulu force estimated at 3000 was in the vicinity of, and had to be swept away from, Niebur's Farm: his interpreter Mr H. Filter and six native policemen were cut off when reconnoitering.[33] The 25 mounted men of the King's Own Regt under Captain Moore[34] and 18 of Schermbrucker's horse were insufficient to act against the enemy. They were supposed to be Bagalusini men from the Hlobane Mountain and have now retired.

WO 32/7752 [Printed in *BPP* (C. 2454), enc. 1 in no. 42 and repeated in no. 51.]

106

Lieutenant-General Lord Chelmsford to the Hon. W. Drummond

[Signed MS copy] 16 June 1879

Prisoner Umsangi may be allowed to return to his own District –

He should be told to go to Seketwayo and say the King, having sent in Messengers stating that he was anxious for peace, has been told that he must send to my headquarters a high Induna and, as an earnest of his sincerity, the two small cannon captured at Isandhlwana.

Until the King sends an Ambassador and complies with the preliminary conditions, the army under my command in every part of Zululand has orders to advance and make raids as was done the other day along the Umvelosi valley.[35]

Cetewayo has the power to stop further fighting provided he agrees to the terms I have laid down, but permanent peace can only be secured by the people themselves agreeing to the conditions which I shall dictate to the King.

Under these conditions

Young men will be allowed to marry whenever it suits them; and they will no longer be liable to be called away from their kraals to assemble in Military bodies.

WO 32/7752 [Printed in *BPP* (C. 2454), enc. 6.B in no. 51.]

107

Lieutenant-General Lord Chelmsford to Brigadier-General H.E. Wood

[Holograph] Camp Babanango Spruit
20 June 1879

Kindly give orders that the kraals which you use for fuelling near your camp shall not be burnt, and that no kraal within reach of our camp shall be touched.[36] Yesterday a kraal your fellows burnt set fire to the grass near our base camp and we had to send a party down to put it out – They also burnt in one hut a large quantity of mealies –

If you will leave the kraals near this camp, we will do the burning before we leave –

WC II/2/2

108

Lieutenant-General Lord Chelmsford to General Sir Garnet Wolseley

[MS copy]

Head Quarter Camp
Emtonjaneni
Zululand
28 June 1879

Memorandum

Your telegram sent through General Clifford from Port Elizabeth just received. – [37]

Plan of operations in this part of Zululand is almost developed. The two columns under my command, commanded respectively by General Newdigate and General Evelyn Wood are now within 17 miles of Cetewayo's military Kraal, Ulundi – I am now forming a strongly entrenched post, consisting of two wagon redoubts, flanking a central cattle laager, in which I shall leave all spare oxen, horses, mules, wagons, and impedimenta – The garrison will consist of two companies 1/24th Regt, 60 volunteers, 100 native contingent, 60 mounted native Basutos, and a number of British Infantry whom it is thought desirable by the Doctors to leave behind as likely to knock up from the exposure of bivouacking. Garrison will number at least 400 Rifles amongst the regular troops, and there will be in addition some 40 European Conductors who are all armed with rifles –

The remainder of the Force[38] . . . will move forward on Ulundi without tents, and with ten days' provisions, and I expect that its advance will be opposed before crossing the Umvolosi River, which is about ten miles from our present position – The road runs through a thorn bush country which gets more difficult as it gets near the river. There is no water between this position and the Umvelosi River, and the road will only admit of one wagon moving along it at a time – As the two columns require 200 wagons to carry their supplies, ammunition, entrenching tools &c. the operation presents some little difficulty, which no doubt however will disappear when we become better acquainted with the grounds –

Three strong columns of the Enemy were seen to leave Ulundi

Kraal this morning, and move in the direction of the Umvelosi River – A certain force is still in Ulundi itself. As this force could only first be seen by the aid of telescopes, it is impossible to form any correct idea of its real strength – All who saw the columns, however, describe them as being from 8 to 12 men in breadth, and as extending over a great length of the road on which they were seen advancing –

I shall be guided by circumstances as to the future movements of the force –

It is possible the Enemy may determine to attack us before we are ready to attack them. Should they do so, it will simplify matters very much. Should they on the other hand give no signs of moving towards us, and our reconnaissances show that they occupy a position commanding the drift across the Umvelosi in very considerable force, I may possibly feel inclined to delay my attack for a day or two until hunger has had its effect, for the Zulu Commissariat, when a big force is collected in one spot, is very deficient, and the want of food may force them to make an attack on us against their inclination –

With regard to the orders issued to Major General Crealock's column in April last, they were to the following effect: – [39]

Form an entrenched post on the Inyezane River, and through [sic] into it two months' supplies for your whole force; – then from there, move along the coast road across the Umhlatoosi River and attack and burn the Mangweni Kraal, which is near Empangeni Mission Station. Then, if possible, move against old Undine Kraal and burn that. – From that point you will be able to judge whether you can again cross the Umhlatoosi river and reach St. Paul's on the main Ulundi road. – My own impression is that you will be hardly able to do so, until the Northern columns reach the neighbourhood of Kwamagwasa; as from all I can hear, the valley of the Umhlatoosi is very difficult for ox wagons to cross, and the bush in it very thick. – Unless assisted, therefore, by a force on the left bank, should there be any large body of the enemy opposing you, it would be difficult for you to make your way across, and more difficult to keep open your communications –

When giving these instructions to Major General Crealock, I was under the impression that the force under his command would be able to advance by the middle of May. Difficulties of every kind, however, cropped up unexpectedly, and the necessary supplies and transport were not provided as quickly as I hoped –

Separated as I necessarily was at such a distance from General Crealock, it would have been impossible for me to control his movements, even had I desired to do so –

I gave him therefore fully to understand, that I must trust entirely to him to work his force in the manner which he considered most advantageous, and as far as possible to keep the coast district between the Tugela and the Umhlatoosi river clear of the enemy –

General Crealock's reports and diaries, which I believe are in the possession of General Clifford, will show best what he has done, and what he is now doing –

It may be as well at once to set aside an idea which I hear is gaining ground, that General Crealock's column was expected to co-operate with the two under my command – As I have already stated, I expected it would have been able to move before these two columns were able to do so, and thus make a diversion in favour of the latter; but I always considered that this force must trust entirely to its own resources, and not rely upon any help from the coast column, which was virtually an independent force –

The sickness amongst the oxen must necessarily cramp the movements of General Crealock's column very considerably, and I am afraid he will hardly be able to carry out all that was laid down for him –

Should Port Durnford[40] turn out a success, it will be well to see whether the communications between it and the main Ulundi road cannot be improved –

Could a good wagon track be made between Port Durnford and some point on the road between Ekowe and St. Paul's, it would, from a strategical point of view, be very advantageous; as a force stationed at the latter place, or Kwamagwasa, would have a double line of communications, which would be useful in the event of one of these positions being selected as a post to be occupied, either permanently or until the conditions of peace have been fulfilled –

As regards my future operation after Ulundi and the surrounding military Kraals have been destroyed, it is difficult to write confidently – I very much question being able to hold on to the Ulundi valley even if it were advisable, which I doubt.

Our supplies will not last beyond a certain time, and it would be difficult to replenish them from such a distance as Landman's Drift. The grass also will be getting scarce and dried up, and much of it is sure to be burnt. It will be desirable, therefore, to decide upon some advantageous position which can be permanently occupied in the enemy's country, which will command as much of it as possible, and to which supplies can be safely and speedily carried –

This post might be occupied by a battalion and a squadron of cavalry with two guns, and a few native horsemen and footmen – The rest of the column, minus the troops occupying the smaller posts keeping open the line of communications, could then be withdrawn nearer to our own border, and the oxen be allowed to rest until the rains commence –

It is difficult to find a position suitable in every respect, and not one of those already established on our line of communications fulfil all the necessary conditions – I am inclined to think that Kwamagwasa would be the most advantageous one, if only it could be supplied from the coast line.[41] Otherwise I fear the distance from Landmans Drift, and the difficulty of keeping open the communications would be too great –

I am writing on the supposition that we shall be unable to inflict such a decisive defeat upon the enemy as will oblige Cetewayo to agree to any terms that may be imposed upon him, and force the people also to submit to them.

I am, however, hopeful that the enemy will stand, and thus give the troops under my command the opportunity they are longing for.

WO 32/7771 [Printed in French, *Lord Chelmsford*, pp. 277–81.]

109

Lieutenant-General Lord Chelmsford to King Cetshwayo

[MS copy] 30 June 1879

{Lord Chelmsford sends the following to Ketshwayo –}

1) If the Induna "Mundula"[42] brings with him (1000) one

thousand Rifles – taken at Sandhlwana – I will not insist on 1000 men coming to lay them down if the Zulus are afraid to come – He must bring the 2 canon [sic] and the remainder of the cattle. I will then be willing to negotiate –
2) As he has caused me to advance by the great delay he has made – I must now go as far as the Umvelosi River to enable my men to drink – I will consent, pending negotiations to halt on the further (Ulundi) bank of the river – & will not burn any Kraals – until the 3d July – provided no opposition is made to my advance to the position on the Umvelosi – by which day the 3rd July – by noon the conditions must be complied with –
3) If my force is fired upon – I shall consider negociations are at an end – and to avoid any chance of this – it is best that Mundula come to my camp tomorrow at daybreak or tonight, & that the Zulu troops withdraw from the River and its neighbourhood to Ulundi –
4) I cannot stop General with coast army until all conditions are complied [with;] when they are so – I will send as speedily as possible a message to him –
{*Sent 2 pm*}

CP 21/2 [Printed in *BPP* (C. 2482), enc. A in enc. in no. 32 and in French, *Lord Chelmsford*, pp. 252–3, with the words between {} omitted.]

110

Lieutenant-General Lord Chelmsford to Major-General the Hon. Sir H.H. Clifford

[MS copy]

Camp on Umvelosi River
2 July 1879

Memorandum[43]

I have received this day from General Clifford copy of a telegram sent by him to Sir Garnet Wolseley in reply to a confidential telegram containing apparently advice about keeping up communications.[44]

I have read this telegram with much surprise & much regret

General Clifford states that he could long ago have organized what Sir Garnet had suggested had he been allowed to do so.

I labour under the disadvantage of not knowing what was proposed: but it is evident from the context it refers to something which it is considered ought to have been done inside the enemy border and especially to Rorkes drift. General Clifford seems to imagine that when sitting at his desk at PMBurg he is capable of looking after my lines of communication in the enemys country.

I am satisfied that he can do nothing of the sort, & that even those within our border are not looked after as they could be were General Clifford free to travel up & down them as an Inspector General should.

The mistake made has been the amalgamating of the two duties of commandant of the Base and Inspector General of the Lines of Communication.

To perform both properly is a physical impossibility.

I quite agree with General Clifford that it is a mistake to divide the authority over lines of communication, & had he been free to perform the duties of Inspector General up to my most advanced depôts, I should certainly not have restricted his responsibility in the manner I thought necessary. General Clifford apparently imagines that someone must have advised me to adopt this (ill advised?) course.

I can only state that I am quite ready to defend what I have done and to accept the entire responsibility for having done it.

I believe that I understand the proper workings of the system: and I am quite sure that General Clifford himself has quite failed to do so if he supposes that he was in a position to do justice to the charge of communications from Landmans drift to the Umvelosi.

I venture to differ entirely from General Clifford when he says that he holds in his hand perfect command over two hundred and ninety miles of communication. The telegraph wire alone does not to my mind constitute "perfect command" over the communications – Personal superintendence is an important factor in the arrangement.

I consider General Clifford has no right to say that had he been charged with the duty in question everything would have been carefully provided for – He could not possibly have personally supervised it, & consequently must have entrusted it to some one under his command who would virtually be the responsible person.

The appointment of General Marshall therefore was really carrying out what General Clifford himself would have done, but with this exception that the full responsibility rested on the shoulders of the man who was doing the work and not upon those of an officer 300 miles to the rear[45]

General Clifford seems to infer that communications in the enemy's country have not been properly established. I am not aware of the grounds on which he bases this statement: but if he alludes to the postal service not being as regular as it might be, I must conclude that he has hardly appreciated the principal duty of posts on the line of communications – Postal service can hardly be looked upon as the most important duty of such posts.

General Clifford is right when he says that he does not consider I attach much importance to keeping up my communications in rear, but he should have added the words "so far as regards the postal service" – of course I should have been glad to ensure a daily postal service could it have been done without working the cavalry horses too much; but I have endeavoured to impress upon the officers commanding the several posts on the line that their first duty is to keep the country clear of small bodies of the enemy who might possibly intercept our own postal messengers and render the line insecure.

General Clifford has no right to say that General Marshal [sic] has not been "left the force necessary to carry out the duty" if by it he means to imply that I might have given him more –

He has all the K.D.G.'s and one squadron of the Lancers besides one hundred of mounted volunteers.

What he means by saying "his communication is cut off" I am at a loss to understand. Our communications have never been cut off for a day since I left Landmans Drift & up to today not a Zulu has been seen in the neighbourhood of any of the posts –

I cannot answer for what is taking place with the coast column, but as there is telegraphic communication to Fort Chelmsford, I cannot believe that communication, so far as news is concerned, is not properly established on that line also.

General Clifford appears to be strangely ignorant of the situation of the forces under my command when he talks of their being placed in a critical position – He is absolutely unacquainted with the country, except thro' the medium of very inaccurate maps & has no knowledge of the enemy we are at war with except apparently through a very distorted medium –

The position is certainly not one of Genl. Clifford's advising, and I should have been very foolish had I trusted to the advice of one who seems to think that South African warfare can be carried on according to the strict rules laid down for an European campaign –

Judging from the very indifferent postal communication that up to quite recently had been established between Ladysmith and Landman's Drift which was entirely under General Clifford, I cannot say that I should have been hopeful of seeing better arrangements carried out than now exist, had he been entrusted to carry them out through the medium of some of his subordinates.

CP 17/34 [Printed in French, *Lord Chelmsford*, pp. 231–4.]

III

Lieutenant-General Lord Chelmsford to Colonel F.A. Stanley

[Signed MS copy]

Head Quarter Camp
Entonjaneni
Zululand
6 July 1879

My last despatch . . . dated June 28th[46] will have placed you in full possession of the situation, on that date, of that portion of Her Majesty's Forces under my immediate and personal command and of our relations with Ketshwayo.

These forces were about to leave this place for the valley of the Umvelosi with ten days' provisions and about 200 wagons, the remainder of the stores, together with all the tents and wagons etc.

etc.* being left behind in an entrenched position here. I was at that time aware that a very considerable force was collected on the left bank of the River and I reported that until I received from Ketshwayo compliance with the demands I had already communicated to you, I should continue my advance to Ulundi.

The advance was commenced on the 30th June and the camps of the Flying Column and 2nd Division were formed that day at a distance of 9 or 10 miles from the Umvelosi River.

Two messengers from Ketshwayo were seen by me about midday – I have the honour of enclosing a copy of the message sent to him, which, at their request, was reduced to writing,[47] likewise a copy of the written communication received by me through Mr Fyn, the white man with the Zulu Chief.[48] The messenger brought with them the sword of the late Imperial Prince Louis Napoléon, which for safe custody was sent back to the post here: the messengers were desired to take charge of the cattle which had been sent in to me at Entonjaneni, as I wanted to return them now I was advancing, but they refused to take them on the plea of the delay it would cause in their return to the King.[49]

On the following day (1st July) our advance was continued over a difficult country when the wagon track passed through bush of Cactus and Mimosa trees: after considerable labour on the part of the Troops in clearing the road and levelling the drifts the Column reached the vicinity of the river Umvelosi: about 1 p.m. The enemy's picquets fell back on our approach and no opposition took place that day to our taking our positions on the right bank; at one time indeed large bodies of Zulus were seen to move from Ulundi to certain positions in our front, which made me anxious to get our Camps formed as speedily as possible. By dark our position was perfectly defensible and our cattle and horses had been watered at the river.[50]

On the ensuing day (2nd July) the camp of the 2nd Division closed up to that of the Column under Brigadier General Wood, and one entrenched camp, with a small stone fort was formed on a

* 6000 oxen 800 mules 400 wagons

plan that would enable a small garrison to defend it, having the remainder of the force free to operate unencumbered by any wagons, in such manner as might be deemed desirable.

The Zulu force did not show itself this day: no messengers arrived from the King: a large herd of white cattle was observed being driven from the King's Kraal towards us but was driven back again shortly afterwards.[51]

As no message had been received from Ketshwayo the following morning (3rd July) and as considerable annoyance was offered to our watering parties by Zulus firing on them, I arranged for a reconnaissance to be made by Lieut Colonel Buller C.B. with his mounted men,[52] as soon as the time allowed for meeting my demands had expired. The cattle sent in by Ketchwayo on 29th June were driven across the river to him during the morning.[53]

Lieut Colonel Buller crossed the river by the lower drift to the right of our camp, and was soon in possession of the high ground on our front and the Indabakaombie Kraal.[54] The object of Lt Col Buller's reconnaissance was to advance towards Ulundi and report on the road and whether there was a good position where our force could make its stand if attacked.

I was also anxious if possible to cause the enemy to show his force, its points of gathering, and plan of attack.

Lt Col Buller completely succeeded in the duty entrusted him: having collected his mounted men near Indabakaombi from the thorny country near the river, he advanced rapidly towards Ulundi, passing Nondwengo on his right: he had reached the vicinity of the stream Untukuwini about three quarters of a mile from Ulundi, when he was met by a heavy fire from a considerable body of the enemy lying concealed in the long grass around the stream – [55] Wheeling about, he retreated to the high ground near Nondwengo where he commenced to retire by alternate portions of his force in a deliberate manner – the Zulus were checked, but in the meantime large bodies of the enemy were to be seen advancing from every direction, and I was enabled with my own eyes to gain the information I wished for as to the manner of advance and points from which it would be made in the event of our force advancing to Ulundi – though the Zulus advanced rapidly and endeavoured to get round his flank, Col. Buller was able to retire his force across the river with but a few casualties;[56] he informed me of a position which on the following day my force occupied, and which subsequent events showed was admirably adapted for the purpose I had in view.

I consider that this Officer deserves very great credit for the manner in which he conducted this duty.

That night the Zulus were moving about in large bodies as testified by the sound of their War songs, but they in no manner interfered with us.

At 4 a.m. the 4th July the troops were silently roused, the Bugles however sounding the Reveille at the usual hour, 5–15 a.m.

I left the camp with all the wagons, oxen etc: garrisoned by the 1/24th Regiment and casualties. Colonel Bellairs C.B. D.A.G. at my special request remained in command of them.

At 6.45 a.m. the force . . . crossed the river:[57] Lt Col Buller's mounted men going by the lower ford seized the high ground on our front without opposition.

Passing over a mile of very bushy ground, the force marching in a hollow square – ammunition and entrenching tool carts, etc: in the centre, the guns moving also in the square in such positions as to enable them to come into action on each face without delay – reached the high ground between the Kraals Indabakaombi and Nondwengo at 7.30 a.m.. The mounted men were now out, covering our front and flanks, while the 17th Lancers covered our rear.

By this time our advance from camp was evidently observed and dark clusters of men could be seen in the morning light on the hill tops on our left and left front; to our right where the largest number of the enemy were believed to be, we could see but little as the mist from the river and the smoke from their Camp fires hung heavily over the bush below.

Leaving Indabakaombi to our left (this Kraal was burnt by our rear guard)[58] I advanced to the position referred to by Lt Col Buller, this was about 700 yards beyond Nondwengo, and about the same distance from the stream that crossed the road half way to Ulundi;[59] this was high ground uncommanded from any point and with but little cover, beyond long grass, near it.

At this point I wheeled the square half right so as to occupy the most favourable part of the ground.

The portions of the Zulu Army on our left and left front were now formed in good order and steadily advancing to the attack: masses also appeared from the thorn country on our right and passed round to Nondwengo and to our rear, thus completing the circle round us.

The battle commenced about 8.45 a.m. by our mounted men on the right and left becoming engaged: slowly retiring until the enemy came within our range, they passed into our square which now opened fire with Artillery and Rifles.

Shortly before 9 a.m. the Zulu Army attacked us on every side.

The Nondwengo Kraal, a vast assemblage of huts probably numbering 400 in number, afforded good cover for concealing the movements of a force which appears to have been the Ulundi, Ngobamakosi, Uve, and Umbakanli Regiments: no order was to be seen in their movements, which was caused (so state prisoners) by these Regiments having been taken by surprise by our early and silent advance: hurrying up from their bivouacks they had no time to form up separately, but, in a cloud advanced to the attack beyond the cover of the Kraal; the fire by which they were met however from our right face proved too heavy and the bulk of these Regiments, failing to advance, rapidly passed to their left & joined the Umcityu Regiment which was pressing up to the attack in a determined manner. As the ground here fell suddenly and cover was afforded them in this advance men were killed within 30 yards of the companies of the 21st Regiment forming the rear face at this point.

The fire of the enemy from a few minutes to nine to 9.20 was very heavy, and many casualties, I regret to say, occurred, but when it is remembered that within our comparatively small square, all the cavalry, mounted men, Natives, Hospital attendants, etc: were packed, it is a matter of congratulation that they were not heavier.

The fire from the Artillery and Infantry was so effective that, within half an hour, signs of hesitation were perceivable in the movements of the enemy: I then directed Colonel Drury-Lowe to take out the 17th Lancers, passing out by the rear face he led his regiment towards the Nondwengo Kraal, dispersing and killing those who had not time to reach the shelter of the Kraal or the bush below; then wheeling to the right charged through the Zulus who, in full flight, were endeavouring to reach the lower slopes of the mountains beyond.

Numbers of the enemy in this direction who had not taken part in the actual attack were now firing and momentarily strengthened by those flying were enabled to pour in a considerable fire on the advancing Lancers below them. Our cavalry did not halt however until the whole of the lower ground was swept and some 150 of the enemy killed: many of those they had passed in their speed, had collected in a ravine to their rear, these were attacked and destroyed by our mounted natives.[60]

The flight of the Zulu army was now general – the slopes of the hills were however beyond the reach of our already fatigued Cavalry, and having no fresh troops to support him, Colonel Drury Lowe exercised a wise discretion in rallying his men.

Lt Col Buller meanwhile had posted the Mounted Infantry so as to fire into the flank of the retiring enemy, and the remainder of his mounted men, making for the country beyond, killed some 450 in the pursuit.

Our 9 pounder guns were shortly afterwards moved from the rear and front faces of the square, and made excellent practice on the enemy retreating over the hills to the East on our left rear, and between Ulundi and the River Umvelosi.

As soon as our wounded had been attended to, and were fit to be moved the force advanced to the banks of the stream near Ulundi while the mounted men and Cavalry swept the country beyond.

Ulundi was fired at 11.40 a.m. and the Kraals of Qikazi and Umpambongwena, shortly afterwards.

At 2 p.m. the force commenced to return to its camp on the Right Bank of the Umvelosi which it reached about 3.30 p.m. – by sunset every Military Kraal undestroyed up to this time, in the valley of the Umvelosi, was in flames – not a sign of the vast army that had attacked us in the morning was to be seen in any direction.

By the statements of the prisoners . . . it would appear that nearly the whole of the available Zulu army was under Ketshwayo's command this day. By Mr Fyn's statement it would appear he considered it to be 20,000, by others it is put down at 25,000 or even more, and was larger than that assembled at Kambula, it must have been formed on a circumference of some 10 miles . . . [61]

It appears that Ketshwayo himself arranged the disposition of the forces and that they considered they would have no difficulty in defeating British Troops if they advanced in the open, away from their wagons.[62]

I feel I have a right in saying that the results of the Battle of Ulundi, gained by the steadiness of the Infantry, the good practice of the Artillery, and the dash of the Cavalry and Mounted Troops will be sufficient to dispel this idea from the minds of the Zulu Nation and of every other tribe in South Africa for ever.

It is difficult to compute accurately the loss of the Zulus on this occasion as the extent of ground over which the attack was made, and the pursuit carried on, was so great, but judging by the reports of those engaged it cannot be placed at a less number than 1500 killed.

The loss of the Zulus, killed in action, since the commencement of hostilities in January, have been placed at not less than 10,000 men, and I am inclined to believe this estimate is not too great.[63]

I regret to state that in addition to the casualties in killed and wounded,[64] The Honble W. Drummond (in charge of my Intelligence Department) is reported missing; it appears he was last seen riding alone near Ulundi, at a time when a considerable number of Zulus were still hovering about.[65]

On the 3rd July Major Upcher[66] commanding the Forts here reported that Lieutenant Scott-Douglas of the 2/24th Regiment in charge of the signalling stations, had not returned here . . . [67]

I fear it must be considered certain that Mr Drummond, Lieut Scott-Douglas and the Corporal of 17th Lancers, have fallen into the hands of the enemy.

I hope to enclose the name of the Corporal before the Post closes . . .

In order that my account of the battle of Ulundi may reach you with as little delay as possible, I have taken upon myself to disregard the instructions I have received, and am sending this despatch direct, furnishing a copy to Sir Garnet Wolseley who is with General Crealock's Division.[68] I trust that this action will meet with your approval.

[As I trust that the request to be allowed to resign my command, made to you in a separate communication,[69] may be favourably received,] I avail myself of what probably may be a last opportunity to bring to your notice the names of the following Officers who have specially assisted me during the recent operations in Zululand:-

Major General E. Newdigate C.B.
Brigadier General E. Wood V.C. C.B.
Colonel Drury Lowe 17th Lancers
Lt Colonel Redvers Buller C.B. 60th Rifles
Lt Colonel Crealock 95th Regt, Mly Secretary
Captain W.C. Molyneux 22nd Regt Senior A.D.C.
Captain E. Buller Rifle Brigade Commandant at Head Quarters
Lieut A. Milne R.N. A.D.C.
Dr Scott, Medical Officer in charge of Head Quarters[70]
Colonel Bellairs C.B. D.A.General
Major Grenfell 60th Rifles D.A.A.G.[71]
Lt Colonel East D.Q.M. General[72]
Lt Colonel Harrison R.E. A.Q.M.General
Dy Commissary General Morris

I have requested Major General Newdigate and Brigadier General Wood to furnish me with the names of any Officers whom they themselves are anxious to bring to my notice but it is probable that this list will not be in time to accompany my despatch.

I feel bound to express my obligations to my Interpreter Mr H.W. Longcast, who has since my first taking the Field last January, always been at my side, and who by his intimate knowledge of the Zulu character and of their country has proved of the greatest value to me, and during the late operations afforded great assistance as a guide to the leading Column.

WO 32/7763 [Printed in *BPP* (C. 2482), enc. in no. 32. Words between [ ] omitted from *BPP*.]

Chapter 8
Extrication from a False Position

112

Lieutenant-General Lord Chelmsford to General Sir Garnet Wolseley

[Holograph copy of telegram] Entonjaneni
6 July 1879

Your instructions sent through General Crealock received last night – [1] They appear to contemplate my being forced to retire and probably do not hold good after the severe defeat inflicted on the Zulu army.

I have returned to Entonjaneni, as the Zulus, having dispersed in all directions, it is not possible to strike another blow at them for the present – I was also anxious to get the men under cover again as the nights are very cold with heavy dews –

With your approval I purpose to send back 2d Division to Fort Newdigate with the wounded numbering some 90 odd,[2] and to bring up another convoy of supplies should it be required; the Flying Column to proceed to join you viâ Kwamagwaza and St Pauls, a strong post being left at the former place, which like all other posts on this line of communications will be garrisoned by troops of the 2d Division – The posts I now hold secure the best grass lands in this part of the country, but these are beginning to fail – A hasty evacuation of the country I now occupy seems to me inadvisable at the present moment, and I await your further instructions before carrying it out – The cattle of this column will not live on the sea coast –

CP 21/1

113

Substance of telegrams despatched from Lieutenant-General Lord Chelmsford to General Sir Garnet Wolseley via Landman's Drift and Pietermaritzburg to Port Durnford

[MS copy] 7 July 1879

I am warned that cold rains are to be expected end of this month and beginning of next when the oxen will probably die in large numbers owing to the hard work they have done. Although I am making preparations to get up another convoy if required, it is extremely doubtful if the oxen would be able to bring it up, and I doubt the advisability of keeping too large a force in this part of the country.

---

9 July 1879

We have had sixty hours cold rain. My losses in cattle and horses have been heavy. I hope to reach Saint Paul's with flying column about fourteenth. The 2nd Division marches tomorrow. Unless instructions to the contrary are received from you, it will proceed to Fort Newdigate, and after giving over wounded and sick to an escort from Koppie Allein will encamp in Upoko valley, where grass and water are plentiful, and where wood can only be obtained, short of the Dornberg. It will there await further orders from you, in the meantime harassing the enemy as much as possible – I expect to reach Kwamagwasa on the eleventh.

On following day I shall build a Fort,[3] and if the weather continues fine, I hope to be at Saint Paul's on afternoon of fourteenth. Road so far is reported good.

WO 32/7771 [Printed in *BPP* (C. 2482), A in no. 47]

114
Lieutenant-General Lord Chelmsford to Colonel F.A. Stanley

[Holograph] n.d. [c. 9 July 1879][4]

I have the honour to acknowledge receipt of your Despatch . . . dated 29 May 1879.[5]

With reference to its penultimate para, the substance of which was communicated to me by telegram,[6] and to my letter of 5 July asking permission to resign my present command[7] I beg to forward for your consideration the enclosed copy of a General Order issued by General Sir G. Wolseley on arrival in this country[8]

You will see that I have been deprived by this General Order of the position given to me by Her Majesty of Lt General commanding the Forces in S. Africa, altho' the Commission which I hold conferring upon me that command has never, to my knowledge, been cancelled; – and that I have been placed in charge of a force which in numbers is actually inferior to that of the 1st Division under Major General Crealock who was before the publication of that order under my direct orders –

I am not of course aware whether the change that has been made in my military position is in accordance with any private instruction that may have been furnished to Sir G. Wolseley by H.M. Govt, but it certainly does not agree with the instructions contained in your despatch of 29th May – I should have been quite prepared, in accordance with those instructions "to submit and subordinate" my plans to Sir Garnet Wolseley's "control"; but I could not accept the inferior command to which he has considered it within his power to reduce me, except under a firm conviction that such sacrifice of dignity & position was required in the public interest – Under such circumstances I should have been ready to set on one side all private interests and would have gladly filled any position in which it was thought I could be useful to my country.

Since however the recent battle of Ulundi such necessity has ceased to exist; and I feel that under present circumstances I am not called upon to make any self-sacrifice, or to accept, without any authority being shown for the change, a command inferior to that which I have held for the last eighteen months and the greater portion of which has been in the Field –

In this view I have forwarded to Sir Garnet Wolseley a telegram, copy of which is enclosed,[9] and I purpose, after receiving reply to the latter portion of it, to make my way to PMBurg either by the Coast line or by Landmans drift, and from there to England, with as little delay as possible –

I shall thus extricate myself from a false position, in which, I am inclined to think, it was not the intention of H. M. Govt to place me in; and I shall moreover relieve the army estimates of the charges due on arrival of my pay and allowances as Lt General commanding the Forces in S. Africa and of those of my personal Staff –

I trust that this step will meet with your approval and with that of H.R.H. the commander in chief –

CP 21/7

115

Lieutenant-General Lord Chelmsford to General Sir Garnet Wolseley

[MS copy] Camp near St Paul's
14 July 1879

I have to thank you very sincerely for your kind letter, dated 12th inst. wh. reached me this forenoon & for the flattering terms in which you speak of our success at Ulundi.[10] I am also much obliged to you for offering to facilitate in every way my wish to get away from S. Africa.[11] With regard to the irregularity (as you call it) of Crealock signing himself "Military Secretary", I am solely to blame. The view I took of my position (wh. according to your view is an erroneous one) was that you came out as High Comm. & Commander-in-Chief replacing Sir Bartle Frere in both capacities, but that I retained the same position as regards yourself as I did to the latter, and that your appointment did not in any way cancel the one I secd. when I was sent out to S. Africa. This view is apparently embodied in the S. of S.'s despatch to me which I see has been published in the Natal newspapers – [12] I of course expected that you as a General officer shd. regulate the plan of campaign, & that I shd. receive instruction from you on the subject – but I did not anticipate that I am to be deprived of my commission as the General Commg. the Forces in S. Africa and of the services of the chief officer of my personal staff. Neither from you nor from him have I recd. any intimation that it was intended to supersede me, & I cannot but think, if such were the intentions of the Govt. that I ought to have been informed. Crealock will of course cease to sign himself Military Secy., but I think some notification ought to have been sent to me that he had been deprived of his appt. as the C. in C. and the Lt. Gen. Commg. have hitherto each had officers on their staff in that position, and there was therefore no irregularity in Crealock signing himself as such.

With regard to my plan of campaign it is of course, like any other, fair grounds for criticism – I am anxious, however, to let you know that had I to begin operations again I shd. make no change whatsoever in my operations with the distribution of my troops.

I do not wish to claim success as a proof that I was right but am quite prepared to argue out the question on purely military & political grounds.

I have been keeping some prisoners in anticipation of your wishing to send messengers to some of the chiefs, & I am sending them off today to the several chiefs you mention in your letter.[13]

I shall hope to be able to meet you at Empangeni in the next few days but I am doubtful at present whether the road viâ the old Ondine is practicable for the mule waggons. A reconnaissance tomorrow will I hope, settle the question – [14] The most difficult part of operating in Zululand is that until you have seen a road or track for yourself it is almost impossible to say whether it wd. be safe to take troops & waggons by it. In hopes of shortly seeing you & again thanking you for the kind terms in wh. you have spoken of our success.

CP 28 [Printed in French, *Lord Chelmsford*, pp. 299–300.]

116

Memorandum by Major-General Lord Chelmsford

[Holograph] ? February 1880

Memorandum C.[15]
{Page 219}[16]
Mr Forbes sets forth very fairly the difficult nature of the problem which confronted me; but he has entirely misapprehended the reason which induced me to commence operations, and has also done injustice to Sir Bartle Frere in assuming that he was anxious to hasten events so as to anticipate official orders –

Sir Bartle and myself were both fully impressed with the gravity of the situation, and the extreme probability which existed of a serious raid of Zulus being made into Natal or the Transvaal –

The peculiar nature of the Natal and Transvaal border, its great extent and the fewness of the troops to watch it, rendered to my mind any attempt to defend it directly almost impossible, and I came to the conclusion, the accuracy of which I still maintain, that the best chance of saving the two Colonies from the consequences of such an inroad, was to invade Zululand ourselves –

Natives have a decided objection to any force, however small, being found in their rear; and I calculated on this feeling being sufficient to protect our frontier effectually –

I consider that I have a right to point to results as a proof of the accuracy of this view –

Mr Forbes has condemned without having that knowledge of the secret springs which so often have to guide a General in command –

The writer's premise being false, his conclusions naturally fall to the ground –

Every military undertaking, conducted in an unknown country against an unknown enemy, must be deemed 'precarious'; but a commander must weigh chances, and adopt that course which to his mind is best under the peculiar circumstances of the situation –

The double duty of offence and defence by the determination to invade Zululand ceased, and thus, practically, {nearly} the entire force was available for offensive purposes – Had I declined to move the safety of the Transvaal and of Natal would not have been secured –

I am not aware that I ever gave an 'apology for the collapse' that I had underrated the enemy and the difficulties of the country – and therefore to prove that those pleas are inadmissible is tantamount to whipping a dead horse –

I was well aware that I might have to meet very heavy odds, and I had expressed my opinion in a public despatch that these odds would certainly be in the proportion of ten to one, and might possibly rise to 30 or 40 to 1 –[17]

I have already mentioned that for military purposes the information regarding the character of the country was of little value; and it is clear that no reconnaissances could be made into Zululand until after war was declared – and therefore 'no such provision' was 'within the scope of the military art' at the time when it was needed –

{Page 219 & 220 –}

Mr Forbes again lays down his premisses, the inaccuracy of which I have already pointed out, and then proceeds to lay down 'what course of invasive action' it behoved me to pursue –

My reason for the plan of campaign adopted is given in the following extract from one of my despatches –

'Unless then his (the Zulu) country, or stronghold, is attacked by several columns, each strong enough to hold its own, moving in from different directions, he has always the power to evade the blow, and to prolong the war to an indefinite time' – [18]

I believed, and still believe, that the three columns which invaded Zululand were strong enough to hold their own, and I am confirmed in this belief by the action at Insandlwana, which, in spite of the faulty disposition of the troops, it is now known was very nearly being a complete success instead of a sad disaster –

{Page 220}

In a country like Zululand, as in Afghanistan, there is no possibility of 'intercommunication and mutual support' – each column as I have already said was supposed to be strong enough to fight alone, and I have never heard that either Colonel Pearson or Colonel E. Wood felt any doubt in their own minds on this point –

I certainly never lost sight of the fact that the enemy occupied the interior lines, but on the contrary I had placed on record in one of my despatches that 'he has the advantage of being able to march in one day at least three times as far as the British soldier and he has no commissariat train to hamper him' – [19]

The event, was I contend, no proof of the faultiness of the strategy –

Had Insandlwana camp been successfully defended, of the possibility of which now there can be no doubt, the opening of the campaign would have been a complete proof of the accuracy of my calculations, for each of the three columns would have defeated the enemy severely –

{Page 221}

It is very easy to lay down that 'for strategical purposes or purposes of respective comparative safety, the advance of the columns should have borne due relation to each other' – but anyone who has made war in a country like Zululand must know that the rapid communication of intelligence between two columns situated as No. 1 and No. 3 were respectively was simply an impossibility – There was no telegraph at the commencement of the campaign farther than PMburg, and the postal arrangements in spite of all my efforts to get them improved, were faulty in the extreme –

The statement made regarding the site of the camp at Insandlwana is absolutely untrue – [20]

The camp was laid out by Major Clery acting under Colonel Glyn's orders and no remonstrance was made either by the last-named officer or by Major Dartnell – I have always maintained that for a defensive position the site of the camp was as good as it could be and that the perpendicular faced hill at its back gave it a strength against a Zulu attack which no other camp that I have seen in Zululand possessed –

{Page 222}

I am averse to entering into any discussion regarding the fatal catastrophe of Insandlwana –

I believe that the evidence which has been obtained regarding the events of that unfortunate day is quite sufficient to show, as I have already stated, that the Zulus were very nearly defeated, and it is to me absolutely certain that had the force been drawn up with its back to Insandlwana hill the enemy would have been defeated with heavy loss and the 550 mounted men which belonged to the camp would have made the defeat a complete one –

Mr Forbes, in his quotation from my despatch, leaves out after the words 'Had the Force but taken up a defensive position' the words 'inside the camp' – This was the fault that cost the unfortunate garrison so dear, and marred the whole prospect of the campaign –

It was never intended that the waggons were to be used as a laager for the Insandlwana camp. They were under orders to return to Rorkes drift for further supplies – Para 20 of the Regulations for Field Forces in S. Africa did not lay down that the laager was to be formed (as was subsequently done) in every camp but only when there was any possibility of attack – [21]

{Page 223}

In accordance with this order when information came in that the enemy was reported to be in force on the left, the waggons might then have been utilised, and at all events the tents should have been struck –

It was owing to this precaution not being taken that I believed the camp was in no danger, as Lt Milne reported to me that up to 11 oclock am on the 22nd January, 1879, the tents were still standing –

With the exception of the one message that was despatched to me from the camp at 8 am by the hands of Capt Allan Gardiner,[22] none was received by me and none, so far as I can gather, was sent –

It is absolutely incorrect to say that 'The early days of this period,' viz between Insandlwana and the commencement of the final invasion, 'were spent in aimless despondency' –

Colonel Wood's column was reinforced as fully and as quickly as possible and he was instructed to do as much as he could to harass the enemy –

Consequently in the month of February the Bagulisini military kraal was burnt by Col. Buller and his horsemen, and {Manyoba's} caves were attacked – [23]

Early in March Oham was brought into Utrecht –

So admirably in fact had Colonel Wood carried out my wishes that Cetewayo at the end of March sent a large force to attack him, which force was completely defeated at Kambula –

The mounted men under Major Barrow on the Lower Tugela line were also not idle, and by their activity kept the enemy at a distance from the border –

I consider therefore that I have a right to assume that the presence of the two columns in Zululand and the activity of Colonel Wood and Colonel Buller were the real cause of no raids being made into Natal or the Transvaal –

{Page 224}

The Etshowe garrison had only fives days supplies remaining when it was relieved –

I do not know what authority Mr Forbes quotes as regards the amount of supplies and transport available on the Lower Tugela when the force advanced to relieve Etshowe. His estimate certainly does not tally with mine –

Pearson's column was quite unfit for immediate active operations – The time of engagement for his transport had long expired, and most of the contractors refused at the time to renew it – There was a great deal of sickness amongst the force, open and latent, and in fact it required to be reorganised –

{Page 225}

The last 15 miles of the road to Etshowe was practically a defile – It was only broad enough for a single waggon, the inclines were steep and continuous –

Sir Garnet Wolseley tried to reopen this road, but the difficulties were too great and Col Clarkes column when it advanced, moved by the coast road –

Mr Forbes estimate of the time it would have taken to reach Ulundi from Etshowe viz one week, shows how little he can have appreciated the difficulties of that particular line – which bye the bye I believe he never visited –

How on arrival at Ulundi we should have been 'master of the situation and could have been reinforced and reprovisioned from behind as occasion demanded' I should like to see set forth more in detail –

I cannot accept the statement but as utterly false and erroneous –
{Page 225 & 226}

Mr Forbes statement that I 'deliberately pigeonholed' 6,500 men and 'restrained them from directional offensive' is again utterly untrue – and Mr Forbes in the last para on the following page says and says truly that I 'left the 1st Division entirely to the independent discretion of its General' –

The second affirmation made by Mr Forbes on the same page is not true – I never for one moment imagined it possible that I could give a hand to Crealock and advance to Ulundi in co-operation with him –
{Page 227}

The attack on General Crealock is mere spite and is based on none but hearsay evidence –

Stores were sent to Conference Hill because Evelyn Wood affirmed positively that there was no practicable waggon trail to Babanango except by the one which his column took viz round the Mundhla Hill –

I did not reach Landmans Drift until late in the evening of the 24 May –

On the 25th Newdigate was ordered to march to Koppie Allein and reconnaissances were ordered by me to try and discover a nearer trail across the Ngutu mountains –

On the 29th May a good trail was discovered between the Itelezi and Incenci hills which saved us at least two marches –

The supplies at Conference hill were never moved back, but when General Wood returned to Koppie Allein with empty waggons half of them loaded up at the supply dept and half at Landmans drift – Conference hill is about 8 miles from Koppie Allein with a good road between the two –
{228–229}

Mr Forbes {in these two pages} harps upon the advantage of the Lower Tugela line (which he has never seen!)
{230}

The proposal to advance by detachments & form depôts was directly opposed to General Wood's views and to my own – Wood wrote to me very strongly on this point and implored me not to send his column in separately, but to let it join on to Newdigates! – So much for Mr Forbes proposal –

Rorkes drift was abandoned by me as a line of advance on account of the Greytown-Helpmakaar road, after Insandlwana, being considered dangerous by the native waggon drivers & leaders who when the news of the disaster reached the Colony, abandoned their wagons and ran away –

It had also the disadvantage of being exposed on the right flank to attack from the Indeni Forest direction which it was impossible to watch properly –

The Rorkes drift post however kept all that part of the country clear by repeated reconnaissances and thus guarded the right flank of the advancing column – [24]

CP 24/5 [Printed in French, *Lord Chelmsford*, pp. 333–9 with the words between {} omitted.]

Notes

Publication details of all books mentioned in the Notes are given in the Bibliography.

Introduction

1 J.P.C. Laband and Jeff Mathews, *Isandlwana*, pp. 38, 60.
2 J.P.C. Laband, *Kingdom in Crisis: The Zulu Response to the British Invasion of 1879*, p. 57.
3 Intelligence Branch of the War Office, *Narrative of the Field Operations connected with the Zulu War of 1879*, pp. 146–51.
4 J.P.C. Laband and P.S. Thompson, *Field Guide to the War in Zululand and the Defence of Natal 1879*, pp. 14–15.
5 War Office, *Narrative of Field Operations*, p. 172; Intelligence Division of the War Office, *Precis of Information Concerning Zululand*, p. 58.
6 War Office, *Narrative of Field Operations*, p. 174. The excessive expense of the Abyssinian War of 1867–8 (£8,800,000, or £5,300,000 more than the original estimate) led to the expectation that colonial operations should be conducted economically in future. Garnet Wolseley showed this could be done with the Red River Expedition of 1870, which cost less than £1,000,000, and with the Second Ashanti War of 1873–4, which cost about £800,000. (See E.M. Spiers, *The Late Victorian Army 1868–1902*, p. 276.)
7 Ibid., p. 296.
8 War Office, *Narrative of Field Operations*, p. 167; John Young, *They Fell Like Stones: Battles and Casualties of the Zulu War, 1879*, pp. 29, 37–9, 52–67, 88, 100–2, 112–17, 127–8, 161, 170–1, 212–13.
9 For the British press, see the *Daily Telegraph*, 3 March 1879; the *Saturday Review*, 22 February, 8 and 15 March 1879; the *Standard*, 3 and 8 March 1879; and the *Observer*, 9 March 1879. For the Natal press, see the *Colonist*, 15 February 1879 and the *Natal Witness*, 27 February 1879. For comment on attacks on Chelmsford in the colonial press, see S. Clarke, *Zululand at War: The Conduct of the Anglo-Zulu War*, pp. 96–9: J.N. Crealock to Alison, 2 March 1879.
10 The acme of aggressive journalism was by the war correspondent Archibald Forbes, who later put together his criticisms in 'Lord Chelmsford and the Zulu War', *The Nineteenth Century*, February, 1880. The element of personal spite should be noted, however, for Chelmsford had alienated Forbes by refusing his request for the Zulu War medal.

11 Clarke, *Zululand at War*, pp. 26–9.
12 For parliamentary debates between February and July 1879, see *Hansard's Parliamentary Debates* (Third Series), vols. CCXLIV–CCXLVII: 2nd–5th vols. of sessions of 1879.
13 See, for example, the letters from the Duke of Cambridge to Sir Bartle Frere printed in Clarke, *Zululand at War*, pp. 112, 114: 6 March and 22 May 1879.
14 CP 24/1: Speech at Cape Town by Chelmsford, n.d. [early August 1879]. Holograph on Government House statepaper.
15 Chelmsford defended his conduct during the debate in the Lords on 19, 30 August and 2 September 1880. See *Hansard* (Third Series), vol. CCLV: 4th vol. of 2nd session of 1880, pp. 1544–67; ibid., vol. CCLVI: 5th vol. of 2nd session of 1880, pp. 636–7, 1025–35.
16 S. Clarke, *Invasion of Zululand 1879: Anglo-Zulu War Experiences of Arthur Harness; John Jervis, 4th Viscount St Vincent; and Sir Henry Bulwer*, pp. 24, 29.
17 Lieutenant-Colonel A. Harness, 'The Zulu Campaign from a Military Point of View', *Fraser's Magazine*, 101, April, 1880.
18 W.H. Clements, *The Glamour and Tragedy of the Zulu War*.
19 Major the Hon. G. French, *Lord Chelmsford and the Zulu War*, p. xvi.
20 See ibid., pp. 360–7 for French's specific replies to Clements's charges.
21 D.R. Morris, *The Washing of the Spears: A History of the Rise of the Zulu Nation under Shaka and its Fall in the Zulu War of 1879*, p. 620.
22 CP 26/36: General Gossett to Lady Chelmsford, 7 June 1906.
23 Sir R. Coupland, *Zulu Battle Piece: Isandhlwana*.
24 Most of the other popular histories written during this period were little more than reworkings of the familiar material. See, for example, R. Furneaux, *The Zulu War: Isandhlwana and Rorke's Drift*, D. Clammer, *The Zulu War* and A. Lloyd, *The Zulu War*.
25 Adrian Preston (ed.), *The South African Journal of Sir Garnet Wolseley 1879–1880*. The original journal is held in the Public Record Office, Kew.
26 J. Mathews, 'Lord Chelmsford: British General in Southern Africa, 1878–1879' . Mathews built on his earlier work, 'Lord Chelmsford and the Problem of Transport and Supply during the Anglo-Zulu War of 1879'.
27 Mathews, 'Lord Chelmsford', p. 341.
28 *Encyclopaedia Britannica*, 11th edition, vol. 6, pp. 23–4; P. Townend (ed.), *Burke's Peerage, Baronetage and Knightage*, p. 481.
29 *Vanity Fair*, 3 September 1881; *The Times*, 10 April 1905; Sir Sidney Lee (ed.), *Dictionary of National Biography. Supplement. January 1901 – December 1911*, vol. III, p. 498.
30 CP 18/34: Chelmsford to General Whitmore, draft of a letter sent on 2 January 1881 for the consideration of the Duke of Cambridge.
31 Lee, *Dictionary of National Biography. Supplement. January 1901 – December 1911*, vol. III, p. 500; Townend, *Burke's Peerage*, p. 482.

32 Enc. in CP 18/34: Statement of foreign, staff and active service of Major-General Lord Chelmsford, 1 January 1881.
33 Mathews, 'Lord Chelmsford', p. 40.
34 Discussion below on the officer caste is drawn primarily from Spiers, *The Late Victorian Army*, pp. 94–9, 104–5, 113–14.
35 CP 18/35: Chelmsford to Whitmore, 2 January 1881. The purchase price of a commission in the Foot Guards was £1,200 (E.M. Spiers, *The Army and Society 1815–1914*, p. 11).
36 Townend, *Burke's Peerage*, pp. 481–2.
37 Mathews, 'Lord Chelmsford', pp. 38–9.
38 Ibid., p. 38; Clarke, *Zululand at War*, p. 30; Morris, *Washing of the Spears*, p. 257.
39 Coupland, *Zulu Battle Piece*, p. 45.
40 See Note 32 above.
41 Mathews, 'Lord Chelmsford', pp. 26–7, 39–41, 341–2; Clarke, *Zululand at War*, pp. 29–30; Morris, *Washing of the Spears*, p. 257; Lee, *Dictionary of National Biography. Supplement. January 1901 – December 1911*, vol. III, p. 498.
42 Mathews, 'Lord Chelmsford', p. 350; Clarke, *Zululand at War*, pp. 29–30.
43 Captain W.E. Montague, *Campaigning in South Africa: Reminiscences of an Officer in 1879*, pp. 132–3.
44 L.H. Addington, *The Patterns of War since the Eighteenth Century*, p. 110.
45 Colonel C.E. Callwell, *Small Wars: Their Principles and Practice*, pp. 21–3, 25–9. Callwell's work summarized many years of discussion concerning the professional implications of Britain's characteristic mode of warfare in the second half of the nineteenth century. For a modern treatment, see Spiers, *Late Victorian Army*, pp. 272–304: 'Colonial Campaigning'. See also G. Harries-Jenkins, 'The Development of Professionalism in the Victorian Army', *Armed Forces and Society* 1, 4, 1975, pp. 484–5; and H.L. Wesseling, 'Colonial Wars: an Introduction' in J.A. de Moor and H.L. Wesseling (eds.), *Imperialism and War: Essays on Colonial Wars in Asia and Africa*, pp. 2–8.
46 Sir M. Howard, 'Colonial Wars and European Wars' in ibid., p. 219.
47 P. Burroughs, 'Imperial Defence and the Victorian Army', *The Journal of Imperial and Commonwealth History*, XV, 1, October 1986, pp. 58, 66, 72.
48 G. Harries-Jenkins, *The Army in Victorian Society*, pp. 6–7.
49 C. Wilkinson-Latham, *Uniforms and Weapons of the Zulu War*, pp. 21–3.
50 See H. Strachan, 'The Early Victorian Army and the Nineteenth-Century Revolution in Government', *English Historical Review*, XCV, 1980, pp. 782–809, passim.
51 T.F. Gallagher, 'Cardwellian Mysteries: The Fate of the British Army Regulation Bill, 1871', *The Historical Journal*, XVIII, 2, 1975, pp. 327–48, passim; R.C.K. Ensor, *England, 1870–1914*, pp. 8–16; C. Barnett, *Britain and her Army, 1509–1970: A Military, Political and Social Survey*, pp. 304–14; Mathews, 'Chelmsford', pp. 19–27.

52 For example, the standard height of a soldier, which had been fixed in 1870 at 5ft 8in, had fallen by 1881 to 5ft 4in (Wilkinson-Latham, *Uniforms and Weapons*, p. 17).

53 H. Bailes, 'Technology and Imperialism: A Case Study of the Victorian Army in Africa', *Victorian Studies*, 24, 1, Autumn 1980, p. 103; Burroughs, 'Imperial Defence', pp. 70–1.

54 Spiers, *Late Victorian Army*, pp. 3, 5–8, 31–2; Mathews, 'Lord Chelmsford', pp. 17–18, 22–3.

55 Preston, *Wolseley's South African Journal*, p. 5.

56 Mathews, 'Lord Chelmsford', pp. 300–1, 313, 322, 324.

57 Laband & Thompson, *Field Guide*, pp. 9, 13–14.

58 Major W. Ashe & Captain the Hon. Wyatt Edgell, *The Story of the Zulu Campaign*, pp. 188–9; H. Strachan, *European Armies and the Conduct of War*, pp. 84–5; Spiers, *Late Victorian Army*, pp. 285–6.

59 Ibid., pp. 67–9, 109–11, 157; J.P.C. Laband, 'Introduction', *Companion to Narrative of Field Operations connected with the Zulu War of 1879*, pp. 5–6.

60 P. Gon, *The Road to Isandlwana: The Years of an Imperial Battalion*, p. 147.

61 Crealock himself presented a problem. He attempted to shield Chelmsford by withholding information from him, and was suspected of wielding undue influence over him. Yet he was not noted for his efficiency, and his abrasive personality decidedly exacerbated the strained relations between the military and the Natal government. See Clarke, *Zululand at War*, pp. 25–7, 52–5; and *Invasion of Zululand*, pp. 46–7.

62 See Mathews, 'Lord Chelmsford', pp. 265–7; Clarke, *Zululand at War*, pp. 52–3.

63 This officer was Captain J.F. Maurice, who had also been an instructor of tactics at Sandhurst, and who had worked with the intelligence Branch of the War Office (Laband, 'Introduction', *Companion to Narrative*, pp. 9–10).

64 Callwell, *Small Wars*, pp. 32–3, 47.

65 See F. Fynney, *The Zulu Army and Zulu Headmen. Compiled from Information Obtained from the Most Reliable Sources, and Published by Direction of the Lieut.-General Commanding for the Information of Those under his Command*; and *Regulations for Field Forces in South Africa 1878*.

66 See Clarke, *Zululand at War*, pp. 121–2; Clery to Alison, 18 March 1879, p. 126; Clery to Alison, 13 April 1879.

67 G. Regan, *Someone Had Blundered . . . A Historical Survey of Military Incompetence*, pp. 22–6, 77.

68 Mathews, 'Lord Chelmsford', pp. 44, 47.

69 For Frere's policy in southern Africa and his readiness to risk war with Zululand, see Laband, *Kingdom in Crisis*, pp. 4–14, passim.

70 Captain H. Hallam Parr, *A Sketch of the Kafir and Zulu Wars*, pp. 166–8, 171; J.P.C. Laband & P.S. Thompson, *War Comes to Umvoti: The Natal-Zululand Border, 1878–9*, pp. 15–17; with S. Henderson, *The Buffalo Border 1879: The Anglo-Zulu War in Northern Natal*, pp. 19–20.

71 Laband & Thompson, *Field Guide*, pp. 13–14, 17; Laband, 'Bulwer, Chelmsford and the Border Levies: The Dispute over the Defence of Natal, 1879' in J.P.C. Laband & P. Thompson, *Kingdom and Colony at War: Sixteen Studies on the Anglo-Zulu War of 1879*, pp. 150–3. See also, Mathews, 'Lord Chelmsford', pp. 64–70, 112.
72 Laband & Thompson, *Field Guide*, p. 17.
73 TS 95 (Uys Papers, vol. VI): O.C. Oftebro to G.C. Cato, 28 November 1878; J.E. Carlyle, 'The Zulu War', *British Quarterly Review*, 69, 1879, pp. 438–9; Hallam Parr, *Kafir and Zulu Wars*, pp. 170–1.
74 Laband, *Kingdom in Crisis*, pp. 12–14.
75 N. Dixon, *On the Psychology of Military Incompetence*, p. 28; M. van Creveld, *Command in War*, pp. 5–6.
76 H. Whitehouse, *Battle in Africa, 1879–1914*, pp. 7, 12.
77 Callwell, *Small Wars*, pp. 57–8; Bailes, 'Technology and Imperialism', pp. 89, 103.
78 Callwell, *Small Wars*, pp. 59, 64, 66.
79 For ox-drawn transport, see War Office, *Narrative of Field Operations*, p. 171: 'Transport in South Africa'; and Lieutenant-Colonel I.H.W. Bennett, *Eyewitness in Zululand: The Campaign Reminiscences of Colonel W.A. Dunne, CB, South Africa, 1877–1881*, pp. 43–5.
80 Clark, *Invasion of Zululand*, pp. 211–14: Sir Henry Bulwer to Edward Bulwer, 8 December 1879.
81 Mathews, 'Problems of Transport and Supply', pp. 1–9, 42–3; 'Lord Chelmsford', pp. 71–84, 111–12, 243–4, 344; Bennett, *Eyewitness in Zululand*, pp. 49–54; Bailes, 'Technology and Imperialism', pp. 93–4; Spiers, *Late Victorian Army*, pp. 76–8.
82 See CP 26/9: His Excellency the Lieutenant-General Commanding, *Special Instructions Regarding the Management of Ox Transport on the Line of March, and for Conducting the Line of March when Troops March with Ox Wagon Transport, and for Forming Wagon Laagers* (Durban). See also, Whitehouse, *Battle in Africa*, pp. 14, 18; Bailes, 'Technology and Imperialism', p. 89; Strachan, *European Armies*, pp. 81–2.
83 Instead, Chelmsford advocated partial entrenchments and laagers for animals only. See *Regulations for Field Forces in South Africa 1879*, p. 3.
84 For details concerning Chelmsford's supply-trains, see Laband & Thompson, *Field Guide*, p. 11.
85 Mathews, 'Lord Chelmsford', pp. 42–9.
86 Callwell, *Small Wars*, pp. 108–12.
87 Harness, 'Zulu Campaign', pp. 478–9.
88 Laband, *Kingdom in Crisis*, pp. 122–4.
89 Mathews, 'Lord Chelmsford', pp. 43–4.
90 For Chelmsford's suggestions on how precisely the Zulu border should be 'rectified', see Documents 46 and 101.

91 CP 27: Chelmsford to Wood, 11 January 1879; TS 36: Frere to T. Shepstone, 21 January 1879.

92 GH 601, no. 12A/79: Notification by His Excellency the High Commissioner, 4 January 1879.

93 Ashe and Wyatt Edgell, *Zulu Campaign*, pp. 306–7; *Illustrated London News*, 24 October 1879, p. 314: Sir E. Wood on the Zulu Campaign.

94 Callwell, *Small Wars*, pp. 40–1, 146, 245–8, 403; Harness, 'Zulu Campaign', p. 478.

95 A574 (NAD): Lord Chelmsford (the General's father), to Biggs Andrews, QC, 15 May 1878, discussing Thesiger's Pondoland campaign.

96 TS 34: Thesiger to T. Shepstone, 2 November 1878.

97 J.P.C. Laband, 'The Cohesion of the Zulu Polity and the Impact of the Anglo-Zulu War: A Reassessment', in Laband and Thompson, *Kingdom and Colony*, pp. 2–7.

98 TS 35: Chelmsford to T. Shepstone, 28 November 1878.

99 Callwell, *Small Wars*, pp. 37–9, 90–1, 93, 103–4, 106.

100 Strachan, *European Armies*, p. 83.

101 Burroughs, 'Imperial Defence', p. 61; Strachan, *European Armies*, p. 82. For detailed discussion on the characteristics of these various weapons, see Laband & Thompson, *Field Guide*, pp. 10–11; Major D. Hall, 'Artillery in the Zulu War – 1879', *Military History Journal*, 4, 4, January 1879, pp. 152–61; Wilkinson-Latham, *Uniforms and Weapons*, pp. 53–7; D. Featherstone, *Weapons and Equipment of the Victorian Soldier*, pp. 24–7, 36, 52, 58–62, 74, 83–5, 95–6, 106–9.

102 For description of the various types of fortification and prepared defence employed by the British during the war, and their specific functions, see CP 26/158: Major W.C.F. Molyneux, *Notes on Hasty Defences as Practised in South Africa* (private circulation), pp. 1–9, passim; J. Plé, *Les Laagers dans la Guerre des Zoulous*, pp. 1–15, passim; Ashe and Wyatt Edgell, *Zulu Campaign*, pp. 196–7; Callwell, *Small Wars*, pp. 277–85; Major G. Tylden, 'The Waggon Laager', *Journal of the Society for Army Historical Research*, XLI, 168, 1963, pp. 200–4; Laband & Thompson, *Field Guide*, pp. 25–7; J. Laband, 'British Fieldworks of the Zulu Campaign of 1879, with Special reference to Fort Eshowe' in Laband and Thompson, *Kingdom and Colony*, pp. 68–79, passim.

103 C. de B. Webb & J.B. Wright (eds.), *A Zulu King Speaks: Statements Made by Cetshwayo kaMpande on the History and Customs of his People*, pp. 29–31; C. Vijn, *Cetshwayo's Dutchman: Being the Private Journal of a White Trader in Zululand during the British Invasion*, pp. 31, 96–7.

104 Webb & Wright, *Zulu King Speaks*, pp. 30–1.

105 CP 8/49: Report by Bishop Schreuder on conversation with the *induna* Ulankana son of Undikile, 10 February 1879.

106 For the Isandlwana campaign and the battle of Rorke's Drift, see Laband, *Kingdom in Crisis*, pp. 57–8, 72–113; and Laband and Mathews, *Isandlwana*, pp. 1–69, passim.

107 For the situation in Natal after Isandlwana, and circumstances of Pearson's and Wood's columns up to the end of March, see Laband, *Kingdom in Crisis*, pp. 114–22, 124–46, passim.
108 Laband, 'Introduction', *Companion to Narrative*, pp. 13–14; I. Knight, *Zulu: Isandlwana and Rorke's Drift, 22nd–23rd January 1879*, pp. 122–3.
109 For the battle of Gingindlovu and the relief of Eshowe, see Laband, *Kingdom in Crisis*, pp. 170–82.
110 For the battle of Khambula, see ibid., pp. 147–69.
111 For the period between the relief of Eshowe and the battle of Ulundi, see ibid., pp. 183–206, passim.
112 See Laband and Thompson, *Buffalo Border*, pp. 67–73.
113 For the dispute over Chelmsford's raiding policy and the command of the border levies, see Laband, 'Bulwer, Chelmsford and the Border Levies' in *Kingdom and Colony at War*, pp. 150–65.
114 Mathews, 'Lord Chelmsford', pp. 308–12.
115 WP 27/17: Adria Lady Chelmsford to General Wood, Bath, 3 June 1879.
116 F. Emery, *The Red Soldier: Letters from the Zulu War, 1879*, p. 224: letter by an anonymous gunner in the Royal Artillery first printed in the *Aberystwyth Observer*, 26 July 1879.
117 See J.P.C. Laband and J. Mathews, 'The Slaying of the Prince Imperial, 1 June 1879' in *Battlefields of South Africa* (Times Media with Jonathan Ball, Johannesburg, 1991), pp. 52–7.
118 See R.T. Stearn, 'War Correspondents and Colonial War, c. 1870–1900' in J.M. MacKenzie (ed.), *Popular Imperialism and the Military, 1850–1950*, pp. 139–61, passim.
119 See French, *Lord Chelmsford*, pp. 224–34.
120 See Laband, *Kingdom in Crisis*, pp. 190–202.
121 For the final stages of the British advance on the Mahlabathini plain and the battle of Ulundi, see J.P.C. Laband, *The Battle of Ulundi*, pp. 7–48, passim.
122 Mathews, 'Lord Chelmsford', pp. 336–9; Laband, *Kingdom in Crisis*, pp. 235–6.
123 Preston, *Wolseley's South African Journal*, pp. 54–5: 12 July 1879.
124 CP 21/9: Wolseley to Chelmsford, Camp near Port Durnford, 12 July 1879.
125 Quoted by D. Russell, '"We carved our Way to Glory": The British Soldier in Music Hall Song and Sketch, c. 1880–1914' in MacKenzie, *Popular Imperialism*, p. 58.
126 See CP 22/30, CP 24/2–4 for correspondence relating to Lord Strathnairn's criticisms in the House of Lords of Chelmsford's conduct.
127 For Wolseley's chagrin at Chelmsford's favourable reception by the court, society and the 'old fashioned set' in the army, see Preston, *Wolseley's South African Journal*, pp. 106–7: 4 September 1879.
128 See French, *Lord Chelmsford*, pp. 306–15, 324–67, 378–83; Lee, *Dictionary*

of National Biography. Supplement. January 1901–December 1911, vol. III, p. 500.

129 E.C.L. Durnford, *Isandhlwana, Lord Chelmsford's Statements Compared with Evidence*; F.E. Colenso, assisted by Lieutenant-Colonel E.C.L. Durnford, *History of the Zulu War and its Origin*; and E.C.L. Durnford (ed.), *A Soldier's Life and Works in South Africa, 1872–1879: A Memory of the Late Colonel A.W. Durnford, Royal Engineers.*

130 French, *Lord Chelmsford*, pp. 316–23; R.W.F. Droogleever, *The Road to Isandhlwana: Colonel Anthony Durnford in Natal and Zululand 1873–1879*, pp. 243–6.

131 See CP 22/5–7, 38–48, 52–3 for Chelmsford's correspondence on this matter.

132 French, *Lord Chelmsford*, p. 384.

133 There are eight holograph versions of this defence in CP 24/5.

I. Chapter 1: Planning the Campaign

1 Chelmsford spent July in Cape Town as the guest of the High Commissioner, Sir Bartle Frere, in order to discuss the situation in southern Africa (*Times of Natal*, 26 August 1878).

2 Since March 1878 Chelmsford had been in command of operations in the 9th Frontier War against the Gcaleka and Ngqika Xhosa on the eastern marches of the Cape Colony. The war, which had begun in September 1877, was effectively over by the end of June 1878, but mopping-up operations were to continue until August. See Mathews, 'Lord Chelmsford', pp. 42–8.

3 In December 1877 the Natal government offered to mediate in the longstanding territorial dispute between the Zulu kingdom and the Transvaal, since April 1877 a British possession. The Boundary Commission began its sittings at Rorke's Drift on 17 March 1878. Frere received its report on 15 July 1878. Since it upheld Zulu claims at the expense of the Transvaal's, it was a severe embarrassment to Frere, who was at a loss as how best to respond. He eventually released the report on 11 December 1878 in conjuction with his ultimatum to the Zulu king, thus effectively nullifying its provisions. See Laband, *Kingdom in Crisis*, pp. 10–13.

4 HMS *Active* was a 3,078 ton, 270 foot corvette built of iron and sheathed wood, completed in 1873. Its station was the Cape of Good Hope.

5 On 31 August 1878 Chelmsford proclaimed nine miles of the west bank of the Mzimvubu River British territory, and its occupation was effected by 'B' Company, 1/24th Regiment. The intention was both to overawe the Mpondo people on Natal's southern border and to secure the natural harbour at the river mouth for British interests. See *BPP* (C. 2220), enc. 1 in no. 72: Thesiger to Frere, 2 September 1878.

6 The earthwork Fort Buckingham, overlooking the Thukela near Kranskop,

was built in 1861, modified in 1863–4 and abandoned after 1868. It was in ruins by 1878 and not restored.

7 The Natal Volunteer Corps, first raised in 1855, consisted in late 1878 of the Durban Volunteer Artillery, the three corps of Colonial Volunteer Infantry and the eleven corps of Natal Mounted Volunteers. The Corps was drawn predominantly from English-speaking colonists who elected their own officers and provided their own uniforms and horses. The Natal government issued them with weapons. See Laband and Thompson, *Field Guide*, pp. 9–10, 13–14.

8 The Natal Mounted Police, a small standing body of quasi-military police, was created in 1874. See H. P. Holt, *The Mounted Police of Natal*, pp. 12, 15–41, passim.

9 The Natal Native Contingent (NNC) consisted of black levies drafted from the Natal Native Reserves by the district magistrates. See Laband and Thompson, *Field Guide*, pp. 9, 14.

10 The Frontier Light Horse were raised in the Cape Colony in 1877 for service in the 9th Frontier War and were maintained at imperial expense. The senior officers were seconded regulars, and the men enlisted for six months. See Major G. Tylden, 'The Frontier Light Horse, 1877–79', *Journal of the Society for Army Historical Research*, 18, 1939, pp. 224–5.

11 The earthwork Fort Williamson, built in 1861 on the lower Thukela, but in disrepair by 1870, was superseded in November 1878 by the construction of Fort Pearson, half a mile upstream.

12 Frontier Light Horse.

13 Captain Edward Robert Prevost Woodgate, 4th Regiment. Service in Abyssinian War, 1867–8; 2nd Ashanti War, 1873–4. In Zululand served with No. 4 Column as General Staff Officer and then as Principal Staff Officer. AAG to Wood's Flying Column. Present at Khambula and Ulundi. Promoted Brevet Major.

14 Captain Howard Molyneux Edward Brunker (1844–1914), 26th Regiment. Service in Abyssinian War. In Zululand served with the Frontier Light Horse with No. 4 Column. Present at Zungwini and Hlobane. In April appointed DAQMG on lines of communication at Durban. Promoted Brevet Major.

15 Captain Charles Lacon Harvey (1839–1922), 71st Light Infantry. With the British National Society for Aid to the Sick and Wounded in Franco-Prussian War, 1870–1; service in the Transvaal, 1878. In Zululand Principal Staff Officer to No. 5 Column until March 1879. Brigade Major of the 1st Brigade 1st Division and subsequently DAQMG to the 1st Division. Promoted Brevet Major.

16 Colonel S.P. Jarvis, CMG. 82nd Regiment. Service in Indian Mutiny, 1857–9; Red River Expedition, 1870. Embarked for Natal in 1879 in charge of drafts.

17 See Document 5.

18 12 April 1877.

19 In February 1838 Zulu forces of King Dingane kaSenzangakhona (c. 1795–1840) attacked the Voortrekker laagers along the Bushmans (Mtshezi) River in an attempt to annihilate the white settlers who were infiltrating Zulu territory. The Boers beat the Zulu off after heavy loss, and henceforth called the district Weenen, or Weeping. See J. Bird (compiler), *The Annals of Natal 1495–1845*, vol. I, pp. 370–4. Chelmsford's reference to 1837 above should properly be 1838.

20 This is reference not only to the territory either side of the Blood (Ncome) River, long in dispute between the Zulu and the Transvaal Boers, but also to the open frontier along the upper reaches of the Phongolo. The Zulu had been expanding into this region since the 1860s, as had white settlers. From 1877 the Zulu had steadily built up pressure against the settlers, and in September 1878 were warning them to vacate their farms. Possibly Chelmsford also had in mind the minor border incidents of 28 July and 17 September 1878 when small parties of Zulu violated Natal territory. See Laband, 'Mbilini, Manyonyoba and the Phongolo River Frontier: A Neglected Sector of the Anglo-Zulu War of 1879' in Laband and Thompson, *Kingdom and Colony*, pp. 183–9; Laband and Thompson, *Umvoti*, p. 23; *Buffalo Border*, 30–1.

21 On 20 December 1878 the Natal government instructed the chiefs living along the Zulu border to furnish a quota of fighting-men to take the field under white levy-leaders whenever a Zulu raid threatened. As these levies did not constitute a standing force, they did not require government upkeep. See Laband and Thompson, *Field Guide*, p. 14.

22 In 1876 Sekhukhune of the Pedi had successfully fought off the Transvaal Boers' attempt to impose their authority. The British, as the rulers of the Transvaal from April 1877, renewed the campaign in February 1878, but with singular lack of success. Full-scale operations came to a halt in October 1878 and were not resumed until after the conclusion of the Anglo-Zulu War. See P. Delius, *The Land Belongs to Us: The Pedi Polity, the Boers and the British in the Nineteenth Century Transvaal*, pp. 181–250, passim.

23 In November 1869 German Lutherans from the Hermannsburg Mission Society in Natal established themselves between the Phongolo and Ntombe rivers and named their settlement Luneburg. See Laband, 'Mbilini', pp. 185–6.

24 Luneburg had a stone laager built around the church. On 19 October 1878 two companies of the 90th Light Infantry arrived to strengthen the laager and fortify the adjoining graveyard, and during November built the nearby earthwork Fort Clery.

25 Standerton is a hundred miles away to the northwest of Utrecht, on the Transvaal highveld.

26 A stone settlers' laager existed at Utrecht, as well as an adjoining military earthwork, built in December 1877 by men of the 80th Regiment.

27 Mbilini kaMswati (1845–79) was a renegade Swazi prince who, since 1866,

had settled in the northwest of Zululand and given his allegience to the Zulu king. His widespread raiding activities, which kept this frontier region in turmoil, undoubtedly furthered Zulu expansionist aims. His latest raid, on 7 October 1878, sent the Luneburgers into a panic and required British intervention. During 1879 Mbilini was a commander in the successful Zulu actions at Ntombe and Hlobane, and was mortally wounded in a skirmish on 5 April 1879. See Laband, 'Mbilini', pp. 189–91, 198–202.

28 The tour had taken a fortnight and covered a distance of 370 miles over rough country. See Clarke, *Zululand at War*, p. 56: J.N. Crealock to Alison, 23 October 1878.

29 The Norwegian Mphumulo mission station and the nearby American Board Maphumulo mission station.

30 During November 1878 two companies of the 3rd Regiment built the earthwork Fort Pearson at the site as the depot for No. 1 Column.

31 By the end of November 1879 black Special Border Police, under white Border Agents, had been placed along the Buffalo (Mzinyathi) and Thukela rivers. Their strength never amounted to more than 190 men. See Laband and Thompson, *Field Guide*, pp. 14–15.

32 Sir Bartle Frere had written on 7 October 1878 to Colonel Wood requiring that he should defend the uneasy Luneburgers. Wood had consequently despatched the Utrecht garrison of two companies, 90th L.I. to Luneburg, where they arrived on 19 October. See Laband, 'Mbilini', p. 191.

33 The Kaffrarian Rifles, who numbered about 40 mounted men, had been recruited from the German settlers of the Eastern Cape and had served initially in the 9th Frontier War as the Frontier Armed and Mounted Police. See Wilkinson-Latham, *Uniforms and Weapons*, p. 64.

34 Shepstone and his disciples in the colonial administration believed in a system of indirect rule over the indigenous black population through the supervision of white magistrates. They jealously guarded their prerogatives from the interference of imperial officials or officers. See N. Etherington, 'The "Shepstone System" in the Colony of Natal and beyond the Borders' in A. Duminy and B. Guest (eds.), *Natal and Zululand from earliest Times to 1910; A New History*, pp. 170–92, passim.

35 Sir T. Shepstone in particular believed that the chiefdoms incorporated in the early nineteenth century into the Zulu kingdom were eager to throw off the king's authority. Although divisions certainly existed in the Zulu kingdom, the British overestimated them. See Laband, 'The Cohesion of the Zulu Polity under the Impact of the Anglo-Zulu War: A Reassessment' in Laband and Thompson, *Kingdom and Colony*, pp. 2–3, 25.

36 Frederic Thesiger, 1st Baron Chelmsford, died on 5 October 1878.

37 Chelmsford wrote this memorandum after an interview with Strickland following receipt of his letter of 5 November 1878 (*BPP* (C. 2234), enc. 1 in no. 19: Strickland to Chelmsford, Pietermaritzburg, 5 November 1878).

38 Nos 1 & 3 Columns.

39 No. 5 Column.
40 This map in not among the Chelmsford Papers.
41 Presumably this map was Lieutenant-Colonel A.W. Durnford's 'Sketch of Zululand &c. Compiled from Original Sources and from Personal Observation & Information, Natal, September 1878'. A copy is to be found in CP 25/6.
42 The Frontier Light Horse, for example, were raised in the Cape, or 'Old' Colony.
43 See CP 9/77: Wood to Chelmsford, Utrecht, 19 November 1878. Mr Potter Junior of Derby was one of the few Boers prepared to turn out if called, but even he clearly found the pay unsatisfactory.
44 Major Edward Hopton (1837–1914), 88th Regiment. Service in the Crimean War, 1855–6; Indian Mutiny; Ninth Frontier War, 1877–8. Assisted in the organization of transport for the war in Zululand; February to April 1879 commanded three companies of the 88th Regiment in reserve at Fort Tenedos and was involved in the organization of transport and the bringing up of supplies when the 88th Foot subsequently formed part of 1st Brigade, 1st Division. Promoted Brevet Lieutenant-Colonel.
45 Deputy Commissary-General Emilius Hughes (1844–1926), Commissariat Department. Senior Commissary Officer of No. 4 Column; then Assistant Commissary-General of Wood's Flying Column. In July 1879 remained in commissariat charge of troops at St Paul's after reorganization of the forces after Ulundi. Created CMG. Promoted Commissary.
46 The seven battalions of the Natal Native Contingent.
47 Colonel Durnford, who commanded the 1st Regiment, Natal Native Contingent (three battalions), had more ambitious plans for his men than Chelmsford, who initially saw them in an entirely support role. Durnford armed, dressed and drilled his men to a higher standard than envisaged by the General and hoped they would be allowed to act as an independent striking force. See Droogleever, *Road to Isandhlwana*, pp. 165–7.
48 Captain MacLeod was in Swaziland attempting to persuade King Mbandzeni that, should war break out between the British and the Zulu, he should intervene on the British side since they would support Swazi territorial claims in the Phongolo region. See P. Bonner, *Kings, Commoners and Concessionaires: The Evolution and Dissolution of the Nineteenth-Century Swazi State*, p. 151.
49 In fact, the Zulu army, which had been partially mobilized in mid-October 1878, had soon dispersed, and by the end of November the *amabutho* were all reported to have left the king and to be on their way home. See Laband, *Kingdom in Crisis*, pp. 27–9.
50 During September-October 1878 the Frontier Light Horse had taken part in the unsuccessful campaign against the Pedi in the northeastern Transvaal. See Tylden, 'Frontier Light Horse', pp. 225–6.
51 Kingwilliamstown in the Eastern Cape.

52 Deputy Commissary-General William Frederick Wright, Ordnance Store Department. In charge of the Ordnance Store Department during the Ninth Frontier War and proceeded in same capacity with Chelmsford's Headquarters to Natal, where he was stationed at Durban and subsequently Pietermaritzburg. Created CB.

53 In early December 1878 two companies of the 1/13th L.I. and the Kaffrarian Rifles under Commandant Schermbrucker relieved the two companies of the 90th L.I. at Luneburg.

54 Chelmsford's reading of John Centlivres Chase, *The Natal Papers: A Reprint of All Notices and Public Documents Connected with that Territory Including a Description of the Country and a History of Events from 1498 to 1843* was defective. The accounts reprinted in Part II, pp. 56–71 are clear that the Boer commando under Andries Pretorius did not cross the Buffalo at Rorke's Drift, but forty miles upstream. On 16 December 1838 the Boers defeated the Zulu at Blood River, and by 20 December were encamped at emGungundlovu, King Mpande's capital, which was four miles northwest of Mthonjaneni. The following day the Boers visited kwaMatiwane, the hill of execution outside the entrance to emGungundlovu where, on 6 February 1838, Dingane had ordered the killing of Piet Retief (who was trying to negotiate the cession of land to the Voortrekkers) and his party. See Bird, *Annals of Natal*, vol. I, pp. 438–57.

55 In fact, it was not until Wednesday, 11 December 1878 that John Shepstone, the Acting Secretary for Native Affairs in Natal, met the representatives of the Zulu nation at the Lower Thukela Drift. He presented them with Frere's ultimatum which required (among other things) that the Zulu dismantle their military system. This could not have been done – as Frere well knew – without disrupting the social, economic and political structure of the nation. Consequently, as anticipated, King Cetshwayo mobilized his army for war, and allowed the ultimatum to expire unanswered on 10 January 1879. See J.P.C. Laband, 'The Ultimatum Tree, 11 December 1878' in *Battlefields of South Africa*, pp. 26–9.

56 Major Clery, who had commanded the Luneburg garrison during October, was temporarily diverted from Colonel Wood's No. 4 Column to serve as Colonel Glyn's Principal Staff Officer. See Clarke, *Zululand at War*, pp. 59–60: Clery to Alison, Utrecht, 6 December 1878.

57 Chelmsford had placed Colonel Rowlands in command of all Imperial and Colonial troops in the Transvaal on 13 August 1878. Rowlands's subsequent operations against Sekhukhune had been a failure, and were called off at the end of October 1878. See K.W. Smith, 'The Campaigns against the Bapedi of Sekhukhune, 1877–1879', *Archives Year Book for South African History, 1967 (II)*, pp. 31–4.

58 On 5–6 October 1878 Rowlands had taken but immediately evacuated a Pedi stronghold, and done so again on 27 October. See War Office, *Narrative of Field Operations*, pp. 9–10.

59 Colonel Wood had succeeded in persuading Piet Uys to raise a small force of mounted men from the Utrecht District of the Transvaal (the Dutch Burghers) to serve under Lieutenant-Colonel Buller, in command of the mounted men of No. 4 Column. See CP 9/27: Wood to Chelmsford, Utrecht, 27 November 1878.

60 Two companies of the 1/13 L.I. were in garrison at Luneburg. The remainder of the battalion, fresh from the operations against Sekhukhune, were being concentrated at Utrecht, the December base of No. 4 Column.

61 During November 1878 Cetshwayo's protestations regarding his desire to avoid war with the British, carried by his messengers into Natal, grew in number and vehemence in direct relation to the British build-up along his borders. Numbers of his leading chiefs sent similar placatory messages on their own account. See Laband, *Kingdom in Crisis*, pp. 31–2.

62 3rd Regiment NNC.

63 Major Shapland Graves. 3rd Regiment. During December 1878 he was Commandant of Colonial Defensive District No. VI (Durban and Victoria Counties). He took command of the 1st Battalion, 2nd Regiment NNC during the advance of No.1 Column on Eshowe, and was present at Nyezane.

64 In the NNC there were to be – ideally – one captain, two lieutenants and six NCOs (all whites drawn mainly from Natal and the Cape) to each company of 110 blacks. See Droogleever, *Road to Isandhlwana*, p. 173.

65 The boundary award was only made public on the morning of 11 December 1878, when its import was muted by the delivery of the British ultimatum. It recommended that the Blood River form the boundary between the Transvaal and Zululand, even though some Boer farms were staked out to the east of the river. See E. H. Brookes and C. de B. Webb, *A History of Natal*, pp. 130–1.

66 Herbert Nunn was a white trader who in the 1860s had taken up residence with Hamu. The prince relied on him for advice and trading goods, including firearms and gin. He advised Hamu to collaborate with the British, and acted as go-between.

67 Hamu had begun negotiating with the British as early as September 1878. See Laband, *Kingdom in Crisis*, p. 31.

68 Major J.F. Baker, late of the Ceylon Rifles, raised Baker's Horse in the Cape in 1878 for service in the 9th Frontier War. (See Wilkinson-Latham, *Uniforms and Weapons*, p. 58.) They were disbanded at the close of hostilities, but re-activated for service in Zululand. Some 230 men strong, they served with the the No. 4 Column and Wood's Flying Column. Present at Khambula and Ulundi.

69 Commandant Charles Duncan Griffith was from 1871 the High Commissioner's (later the Cape Governor's) Agent in Basutoland, and commanded the Frontier Armed and Mounted Police during the 9th Frontier War. In the event he sent Chelmsford no Sotho. The only Sotho

who fought for the British were the fifty or so amaHlangwe under Hlubi, living in Weenen County, Natal. As a troop in the Natal Native Horse they served initially with No. 2 Column, and subsequently with No. 4 Column. See P. Thompson, 'Weenen County and the War, 1878' in Laband and Thompson, *Kingdom and Colony*, pp. 255–6.

70 John Gordon Sprigg was a Cape politician in favour of confederation, and Frere consequently requested him to form a ministry in 1878. He continued as Cape Premier until 1881.

71 Captain the Hon. Ronald George Elidor Campbell (1848–79), Coldstream Guards. Adjutant, 1871–8. Principal Staff Officer to No. 4 Column. Killed in action at Colonel Wood's side at Hlobane. Second son of Earl of Cawdor.

Chapter 2: Preparing to Invade

1 The second and third requirements of the British ultimatum stipulated that Cetshwayo must surrender the sons and brother of Sihayo involved in the border incident of July 1878, and pay a cattle fine for not having done so earlier. See SNA 1/6/3, n.n.: Original draft of the ultimatum, signed by Bulwer on 4 December 1878.

2 The 99th Regiment embarked from England for service in South Africa in late November 1878. By early January 1879 the 99th was with Pearson's Column with detachments in garrison at depots along the coastal line. The 2nd Company, Royal Engineers, joined Pearson at the same time. The 2/4th Regiment embarked for Natal in early December 1878, and was despatched to northern Natal and to Colonel Wood's area of operations.

3 KwaMagwaza was an Anglican mission station established in Zululand in 1860. In 1879 it was standing abandoned, all the missionaries having left Zululand under threat of the coming conflict.

4 The Natal Mounted Volunteers were called into service on 25 November 1878. However, they were bound only to defend Natal itself and could not be called upon to serve in Zululand unless they volunteered to do so, which almost all did. See Laband and Thompson, *Field Guide*, pp. 9–10, 13.

5 The abandoned KwaMondi mission station at Eshowe in Zululand, founded in 1860 by Pastor Ommund Oftebro of the Norwegian Mission Society.

6 The abandoned Norwegian mission station at Ntumeni, founded in 1852.

7 The Hunting Road, or Jagt Pad, crossed the Buffalo River between its confluence with Blood River and Rorke's Drift to the south, and proceeded north-east into Zululand and across the Phongolo River into Swaziland.

8 See Document 23.

9 They did not.

10 Major Clery joined No. 3 Column as Principal Staff Officer.

11 Captain Henry Vaughan, Royal Artillery. Director of Transport to No. 4 Column, January to April 1879. Present at Hlobane, Khambula and Ulundi. Promoted Brevet Major.

12 Transmitted to Colonel Wood for his information, 19 December 1878.

13 In fact, 10 January 1879.

14 Chelmsford left Pietermaritzburg on Thurdsday, 26 December 1878 to inspect his dispositions at Durban and the lower Thukela. He intended to be with No. 3 Column at Helpmekaar by 6 January 1879. See Mathews, 'Lord Chelmsford', pp. 108–9.

15 Assistant Commissary Bernard Heygate (1854–98), Commissariat Department. Supply Officer to No. 1 Column. Subsequently employed on the coastal line of communications. Present at Nyezane and throughout the blockade of Eshowe.

16 The men of HMS *Active*, under Commander H.J.F. Campbell, RN, formed part of the Naval Brigade with No. 1 Column.

17 The abandoned Anglican St Paul's mission station, just south-east of KwaMagwaza.

18 The Natal Volunteer units at Potspruit were the Alexandra Mounted Rifles, the Durban Mounted Rifles and the Natal Hussars. See Laband and Thompson, *Umvoti*, p. 106.

19 Captain Henry Hallam Parr, 13th Regiment. Since 1877 he had been Sir Bartle Frere's Military Secretary. Frere gave him permission in January to join Colonel Glyn's staff, and Parr was away with him on reconnaissance during the battle of Isandlwana. He returned in May to his duties with Frere.

20 This letter is apparently not among the Chelmsford Papers.

21 The Revd Robert Robertson was an Anglican missionary to Zululand who established, among others, the mission station at KwaMagwaza. Frustrated in his attempts to convert the Zulu, he became a leading detractor of the Zulu monarchy and called vociferously for its overthrow by Britain. He accompanied No. 1 Column. Present at Nyezane and throughout the blockade of Eshowe.

22 Lucas, Gould Arthur (1832–1914). Captain 73rd Regiment. Resigned his commission, 1858. Service in Eighth Frontier War, 1850–3; Langalibalele expedition, 1873. Resident Magistrate, Alexandra County, Natal, 1860; of Klip River County, 1860–75; and of Alexandra County, 1876–89. Commandant, Colonial Defensive District No. VI, December 1878–September 1879.

23 These were the Border Guard levies which, in Defensive District No. VII, had an estimated potential of 2,000 men (Laband and Thompson, *Umvoti*, p. 121).

24 After considerable reluctance, Bulwer permitted Fynn in mid-January to accompany Chelmsford into Zululand as his personal interpreter and political adviser. See Laband and Thompson, *Buffalo Border*, pp. 41–2.

25 1878 had been a year of drought and the spring rains had come late. As if in compensation, the summer of early 1879 was exceptionally wet.

26 The combination of the long-standing drought and fear of Zulu raids once

war began persuaded most of the Boers along the Buffalo border to move away with all their livestock, sometimes as far as the Orange Free State. See Laband and Thompson, *Buffalo Border*, pp. 38–9.

27 In fact, Sihayo did not defend the crossing, and his available fighting-men numbered at most a few hundred since most had answered the king's call to muster at oNdini. For the same reason, there were no regular *amabutho* facing Wood, only the local Qulusi irregulars. See Laband and Thompson, *Buffalo Border*, p. 42 and Laband, *Kingdom in Crisis*, p. 58.

28 Sokhexe, Sihayo's chief homestead, was on the western side of the Nquthu Heights, six miles from Rorke's Drift, below cliffs full of defensible caves.

29 Wood wished for security reasons to remove all Zulu from the neighbourhood of his base at Balte Spruit. Frere had been reluctant that such action should anticipate hostilities, and in any case preferred that the Zulu should stay where they were as British subjects. See WC II/2/2: Chelmsford to Wood, 23 December 1878.

30 They were indeed genuine emissaries, despite the prevailing British suspicion that all royal messengers must be spies. For Cetshwayo, though mustering his army, nevertheless persisted in his efforts to negotiate a settlement, and sent seven separate messages to the British between the delivery of the ultimatum and the opening of hostilities. See Laband, *Kingdom in Crisis*, p. 40 and Laband, 'Humbugging the General? King Cetshwayo's Peace Overtures during the Anglo-Zulu War' in Laband and Thompson, *Kingdom and Colony*, pp. 45, 47.

31 Lonsdale had led Mfengu levies during the Ninth Frontier War.

32 Beaumont had established five Border Guard posts overlooking the Buffalo border line. At each there was a white levy leader with a standing reserve of 100 black levies, backed up by a further 200 with whom they would rotate for duty. In addition, he had assigned strategic places of rendezvous for the part-time levies whom the chiefs were to provide in times of emergency. By the end of the war the number of levies called out in Defensive District No. I was 3,731 men. See Laband and Thompson, *Buffalo Border*, p. 35.

33 Fynney, as Border Agent, had to report intelligence of hostile activity to Captain Lucas, the Commandant of Colonial Defensive District No. VI. But Lucas, although always eager to take military action, was a cavalier administrator, causing Fynney much frustration. See P.S. Thompson, 'Captain Lucas and the Border Guard: The War on the Lower Thukela, 1879' in Laband and Thompson, *Kingdom and Colony*, pp. 167–72.

34 Chelmsford desired a unified command over all the mounted troops at his disposal, both British and colonial. The difficulty was that, in terms of para. 144 of his own *Regulations for Field Forces in South Africa*, colonial officers were not entitled to hold command over regular forces. This meant that he was unwilling to appoint Major Dartnell, the commander of the Natal mounted men and their preferred choice, and chose instead Major J.C. Russell, who commanded No. 1 Squadron, Mounted Infantry. Chelmsford

compromised on 7 January 1879 by placing Major Dartnell on his Headquarters Staff as commander of the Natal Mounted Police and Volunteers, but giving Major Russell effective command of all the mounted men in the field during operations. See *Times of Natal*, 10 January 1879.

35 The Zulu position in strength along the Buffalo River was imaginary.

36 This would have been the much improved 'Military Map of Zulu Land, compiled from most recent information by the Intelligence Branch of the Quartermaster-General's Department'. See WC II/4/1 for a clean edition, printed in March 1879. For an annotated edition printed in June, see CP 25/8.

37 Bishop Hans Schreuder.

38 Sihayo was indeed at Sokhexe, but his small following presented no threat.

Chapter 3: Isandlwana

1 Major Russell now held the local rank of lieutenant-colonel.

2 This was the valley of the Batshe River.

3 Captain E. Essex.

4 The Secretary of State for War, Colonel Stanley. These extracts were later printed in the *British Parliamentary Papers*. See Documents 44 and 48.

5 The Natal Mounted Police.

6 George Mansell had been appointed First Inspector of the Natal Mounted Police in October 1878. Major Dartnell, their commandant, was on Chelmsford's staff. See Document 33.

7 See *BPP* (C.2242), enc. 2 in no. 9: Notification by Frere, 11 January 1879.

8 The Qungebe people.

9 Henry Lee had been postmaster at Helpmekaar since 1876. He was not to be replaced until August 1879.

10 Presumably Deputy Commissary-General Henry John Brownrigg, Commissariat Department. He proceeded to Helpmekaar in January 1879 in charge of the commissariat and transport on the north-west frontier. Was subsequently Commissary-General of the 2nd Division.

11 Acting Assistant-Commissary James Langley Dalton. Commissariat Department. Service in Eighth Frontier War, 1850–3; Ninth Frontier War. Present at Rorke's Drift, where it seems he did more to organize its defence than the regular officers present. Severely wounded. Afterwards Senior Commissariat Officer at Fort Napier in Pietermaritzburg. Awarded VC.

12 On 8 January Chelmsford had instructed Durnford to send two of his strongest battalions to Sandspruit to support Glyn and not to advance across Middle Drift until Pearson had occupied Eshowe. However, in terms of the discretion he considered Chelmsford had allowed him, Durnford prepared on 13 January to advance across the Thukela with all his force to forestall an unsubstantiated Zulu plan to invade Natal. Chelmsford's countermand arrived at 2 a.m. on 14 January. See Droogleever, *Road to Isandhlwana*, pp. 190–1.

13 No. 4 Column encamped at Bemba's Kop on 10 January 1879. Wood marched with part of his force down the left bank of the Blood River to within 12 miles of Rorke's Drift before returning to his base on 13 January.
14 Mbuso was an *induna* of the Qulusi. Barton's force attacked him on 13 January 1879 and captured 538 cattle, though he and most of his people escaped to ebaQulusini, the Qulusi *ikhanda*. See Laband, *Kingdom in Crisis*, p. 126.
15 See Document 39.
16 On 10 January 1879 the *Times of Natal* printed the General Order of 7 January 1879 concerning Russell's appointment, and the *Natal Mercury* made editorial comment on the same day. On 13 January the *Times of Natal* also carried editorial comment, and on 17 January printed a letter by 'Fairplay', written on 14 January.
17 See Documents 33 and 39. Frere's memorandum is not with the Government House (Natal) Papers, and has not been traced.
18 3rd Regiment NNC.
19 On 17 January 1879 Gamdana kaXongo, a Qungebe *induna* and brother of Sihayo, gave himself up with a few of his adherents (the majority refused to follow him and continued to resist). Those who surrendered were relocated for the duration in Weenen County. See Laband, *Kingdom in Crisis*, p. 72.
20 In fact, Bulwer relented. Fynn was allowed to join Chelmsford at Rorke's Drift and accompany him into Zululand, and Beaumont temporarily shouldered Fynn's duties and established his headquarters at Fynn's Umsinga magistracy. See Document 30. See Laband and Thompson, *Buffalo Border*, pp. 41–2.
21 oNdini in the Mahlabathini plain.
22 Chelmsford had conferred with Wood on 11 January on the left bank of the Blood River at Nkonjane Mountain, about twelve miles north of Rorke's Drift. See War Office, *Narrative of Field Operations*, p. 50.
23 See Pearson Papers: Chelmsford to Pearson, 16 January 1879.
24 On 18 January Wood advanced his camp east from Bemba's Kop to the White Mfolozi, building Fort Tinta on 21 January.
25 Matshana kaMondisa, the Sithole chief, lived in the Qudeni bush. During December 1878 he began tentatively to negotiate with the British, but nothing came of it. In January 1879 he played a vital role in the Isandlwana campaign by luring part of No. 3 Column away from the camp (see Laband, *Kingdom in Crisis*, p. 78). Chief Matshana kaSitshakuza of the Mchunu lived in the Buffalo River valley. Both chiefs surrendered to the British on 20 August 1879 at Rorke's Drift.
26 Downstream from Rorke's Drift.
27 No. 11 Battery, 7th Brigade, Royal Artillery; five troops of Natal Native Horse; three companies 1/1st NNC.
28 Mangeni River.
29 See Document 44.

30 See Documents 30 and 44.
31 This force, under the command of Major Dartnell, consisted of 150 Natal Mounted Police and Volunteers and about 1,600 NNC (1 and 2/3rd NNC).
32 Six companies of the 2/24th Regiment.
33 N Battery, 5th Brigade, RA.
34 In fact, a company of the 2/24th was left in camp besides the six companies of the 1/24th, giving a total of 19 officers and 580 men. The mounted men totalled 115 officers and men; while Chelmsford omitted altogether the two companies respectively of the 1/3rd and 2/3rd NNC (or 19 officers and 391 men). He also left out the 50 officers and men of the Royal Engineers, Army Service Corps, Army Hospital Corps and Natal Native Pioneer Corps. See Laband and Mathews, *Isandlwana*, p. 38.
35 Captain Francis Broadfoot Russell, Royal Artillery. Commanded No. 11 Battery, 7th Brigade, R.A., first at Fort Napier in Pietermaritzburg from 1878, and then with No. 2 Column. Killed in action at Isandlwana.
36 In addition to the single officer and 9 men of the Rocket Battery and the 6 officers and 259 men of the Natal Native Horse mentioned by Chelmsford, there were also 7 officers and 240 men of the 1/1st NNC in Durnford's command. See Laband and Mathews, *Isandlwana*, p. 38.
37 Besides the company of the 2/24th, various detached or ill personnel were involved in the defence of Rorke's Drift, making a total of 8 officers and 131 men, of whom 35 were invalids. The attacking Zulu force was between 3,000 and 4,000 strong. The defenders lost 17 men killed and 1 officer and 7 men wounded, while the Zulu lost about 600 killed. For a detailed account of the battle, see J.P.C. Laband, '"O! Let's Go and Have a Fight at Jim's!": The Zulu at the Battle of Rorke's Drift' in Laband and Thompson, *Kingdom and Colony*, pp. 111–30, passim.
38 The camp was defended against nearly 20,000 Zulu by 1,768 officers and men, of whom approximately half were black. The British lost 1,357 men and the Zulu not less than 1,000. See Laband and Mathews, *Isandlwana*, pp. 60–1.

II. Chapter 4: The Defence of Natal

1 See Document 49 and notes.
2 On 24 January 1879 Chelmsford summoned a court to enquire into 'the loss of the camp'. The Court of Enquiry sat from 27 to 29 January. Much of the evidence heard was not recorded, since it was deemed irrelevant or repetitious. The court found that most of the blame for the disaster could be attributed to the imprudent actions of Colonel Durnford and to the behaviour of the NNC. The evidence was printed in WO 33/34, *Zulu War, Miscellaneous, 1878–9*, pp. 234–42. See Mathews, 'Lord Chelmsford', pp. 217–19.
3 See *BPP* (C. 2252), enc. 2 in no. 22: Chelmsford to Secretary of State for War, 27 January 1879.

4 The two battalions of the 3rd Regiment NNC had been habitually ill-treated by their officers and lost their morale after Isandlwana. In the face of growing desertions, Lonsdale decided to disarm and strip them of all their government issue. He then disbanded them on 24 January. See Laband and Thompson, *Buffalo Border*, pp. 44–5.
5 Since Natal now seemed thrown open to Zulu invasion, colonists flocked to private and government laagers, improvised defences were thrown up at Pietermaritzburg and Durban, and many families trekked out of Natal to the safety of the Orange Free State. See P.S. Thompson, 'Town and Country and the Zulu Threat, 1878–9: The Natal Government's Arrangements for the Protection of Settlers' in Laband and Thompson, *Kingdom and Colony*, pp. 232–4.
6 On 24 January Wood led a mounted patrol against the Qulusi and local irregulars between the Ntendeka range and Zungwini. He took 3,000 of them by surprise and put them to flight. However, the news of the Isandlwana disaster, which reached Wood during the skirmish, caused him immediately to fall back on his camp. See Laband, *Kingdom in Crisis*, pp. 127–8.
7 At Nkonjane hill on the left bank of the Buffalo. See Document 45.
8 In fact, between 26 and 31 January Wood was to retire north-west to Khambula, at the headwaters of the White Mfolozi.
9 Chelmsford is referring not to the Boers of the Utrecht and Wakkerstroom Districts of the Transvaal as such, but to those who had settled east of the Blood River and whom the boundary award had placed in Zululand. See Document 21.
10 No. 1 Squadron, Mounted Infantry.
11 Captain Alan Coulston Gardner, 14th Hussars. Served as Staff Officer in No. 3 Column and subsequently in the same capacity in Wood's Flying Column. Present at Isandlwana. Promoted Brevet Major.
12 See CP 7/5: Pearson to Chelmsford, 24 January 1879; and CP 7/8: Pearson to Chelmsford, 28 [sic] January 1879.
13 Hlubi's Troop or Sikali's three Troops, Natal Native Horse.
14 Lanyon took over as Administrator of the Transvaal in March 1879 from Shepstone, who had not been a success and was pensioned off.
15 Assistant Commissary Ernest Charles Wainwright (1854–81), Ordnance Store Department. Placed in charge of the depot at Fort Tenedos in January 1879, and was Commissary of Ordnance to No. 1 Column until the formation of the 1st Division. Remained in charge at Fort Pearson until invalided home in September suffering from fever.
16 See Document 22.
17 Nothing came of this.
18 Rowlands's No. 5 Column, which consisted of 1,565 officers and men, was stationed in the Phongolo region both to keep an eye on the Pedi and to protect the Wakkerstroom District from Zulu inroads. The column

consequently did not advance from its posts at Derby and Luneburg except to take part in localized strikes. The Swazi, despite promises, never moved down in support. See Laband, 'Mbilini', p. 194.

19 The Duke of Cambridge.

20 The Court of Enquiry sat at Helpmekaar. The proceedings were completed by 29 January 1879 and Chelmsford forwarded them to the Secretary of State for War on 8 February. See Dcoument 50.

21 Supplies of ammunition were in any case short at Rorke's Drift, while Helpmekaar, the next nearest depot, was 25 miles from Isandlwana.

22 In fact, only the two battalions of the 3rd NNC were permanently disbanded, and the remaining five battalions of the 1st and 2nd NNC were reorganized. See Laband and Thompson, *Field Guide*, p. 9.

23 The Boers were resentful of the British annexation of 1877 and the failed Sekhukhune campaign of 1878, and desired the restoration of their independence. See C.F. Goodfellow, *Great Britain and South African Confederation, 1870–1881*, pp. 138–44, 156, 171–3.

24 Johannes Henricus Brand, President of the Orange Free State, 1864–88. A much respected statesman, Brand was aware of the advantages to be gained by his fledgling republic from good relations with Britain.

25 The Zulu victory at Isandlwana was matched by their defeats at the battles of Nyezane and Rorke's Drift, and in a number of skirmishes against Wood's forces. Zulu losses were probably already in excess of at least 2,000.

26 Within the entrenchments at Eshowe there were the buildings of the mission station, three of which were used for stores, and the church, which served as a hospital.

27 In calculating British successes, Chelmsford was including not only the battles of Nyezane and Rorke's Drift, but some of Wood's successful skirmishes in north-western Zululand, which occurred on 12, 18, 20 and 24 January 1879. He would not yet have learned of Wood's succesful strikes on 26 January and 1 February. See Laband, *Kingdom in Crisis*, pp. 126–8, 134.

28 For the battle of Nyezane on 22 January 1879, see ibid., pp. 116–21. The 95 officers and 2,687 men of No. 1 Column successfully threw off the ambush laid by between 4,000 and 6,000 Zulu. The British lost 2 officers and 9 men killed, with 1 officer and 14 men wounded. Nearly 400 Zulu were found dead on the field.

29 See Document 49 and notes and also Document 58.

30 See Documents 50 and 53.

31 The two battalions of the 2nd NNC and 233 mounted men left Eshowe for Fort Tenedos on 29 January 1879. Remaining in garrison were 1,339 whites and 355 blacks. On 30 January Pearson despatched about a thousand cattle back to Natal since there was not sufficient pasture within reach of the fort, but the Zulu captured 900 of them. See War Office, *Narrative of Field Operations*, p. 54.

32 Following Isandlwana, the Swazi decided (despite their prevarications to

the contrary) to stand on the defensive behind their own borders until they could be certain that the British would be the winners. See Bonner, *Swazi State*, pp. 152–3.

33 Eighty time-expired men from the Frontier Light Horse, who had enlisted for six months, left for their homes. See Document 59.

34 Lieutenant Charles Edward Haynes, Royal Engineers. Served in Zululand with No. 1 Column, the Eshowe Relief column and the 2nd Division.

35 The Greytown Laager had been begun in 1854 and strengthened during 1877–8. Following Isandlwana, the Greytown garrison improved the laager's field of fire by demolishing nearby buildings, and threw up an earthwork adjacent to it. The hastily improvised Pietermaritzburg Laager consisted of fortified buildings connected by barricades.

36 Lieutenant-Colonel Charles Bullen Hugh Mitchell (1836–99), Royal Marine Light Infantry. Receiver General of British Guiana, 1877; Colonial Secretary of Natal from January 1878. In December 1878 appointed Commandant of the Colonial Defensive Sub-District of Pietermaritzburg and elected Leader of the City Guard. He was in charge of putting Pietermaritzburg on a defensive footing after Isandlwana, and appointed Captain Albert Henry Hime, R.E. (the Colonial Engineer of Natal from May 1875) Commandant of Ward Laager No. 1.

37 Since the report of the Court of Enquiry was submitted to Chelmsford on 29 January 1879 and he only forwarded it to the Secretary of State for War on 8 February, he would have had just over a week in which to make preliminary notes. However, from internal evidence (see footnotes 40 and 42 below) it seems that this version was only completed in April, after the relief of Eshowe.

38 In fact, it is relatively easy to scramble to the top of Isandlwana.

39 See Document 49.

40 This is a likely reference to the Eshowe Relief campaign and to the battle of Khambula, which suggests these notes may have been made in April.

41 Lieutenant William Francis Dundonald Cochrane, 32nd Light Infantry. Served with No. 2 Column as Orderly Officer to Durnford and survived Isandlwana. He subsequently served with Wood's Column in command of the Natal Native Horse and was present at Hlobane, Khambula and Ulundi.

42 Further evidence that these notes were written in April.

43 The note read as follows:

'You will be in command of the camp in the absence of Colonel Glyn. Draw in your line of defence while the force with the general is out of camp. Draw in your infantry outpost line in conformity. Keep your cavalry vedettes still well to the front. Act strictly on the defensive. Keep a waggon loaded with ammunition ready to start at once, should the general's force be in need of it. Colonel Durnford has been ordered up from Rorke's Drift to reinforce the camp.' (Clarke, *Zululand at War*, p. 83: Clery to Colonel

Harman, 17 February 1879.)

44 In fact, Durnford was not ordered to 'take command of the camp'. The order read:
'You are to march to this camp *at once* with all the force you have with you of No. 2 column. Major Bengough's Battalion is to move to Rorke's Drift as ordered yesterday.' See Mathews, 'Lord Chelmsford', p. 151 and Document 47.

45 Lieutenant Charles Walter Cavaye, 24th Regiment. Service in Ninth Frontier War. Served with No. 3 Column in Zululand and commanded E Company, 1/24th at Isandlwana, where he was killed.

46 Captain C. Nourse, 1/1st NNC. With No. 2 Column at Isandlwana and made good his escape.

47 Captain William Eccles Mostyn, 24th Regiment. Service in Ninth Frontier War. Commanded F Company, 1/24th at Isandlwana, where he was killed.

48 Captain Reginald Younghusband, 24th Regiment. Service in Expedition to Little Andaman Island, 1867; Ninth Frontier War. Commanded C Company, 1/24th at Isandlwana, where he was killed.

49 The two 7-pounder guns of N Battery, 5th Brigade, RA.

50 For modern interpretations of British dispositions between noon and about 1 p.m., see Laband and Thompson, *Field Guide*, pp. 56–7; and Laband and Mathews, *Isandlwana*, pp. 40, 43.

51 It seems that the disorganized withdrawal of the British firing-line on the camp was the consequence of its being outflanked, rather than because the NNC had given way.

52 On 1 February 1879 Buller, in a mounted raid, destroyed the ebaQulusini *ikhanda*, which was the rallying-point of Zulu resistance in north-western Zululand. See Laband, *Kingdom in Crisis*, p. 134.

53 John Dunn's adherents who, with him, were refugees in Natal, served the British as scouts and messengers.

54 See WO 32/7737: Lt. J.R.M. Chard to Col. R.T.Glyn, 25 January 1879.

55 In reality, the defence of Rorke's Drift merely diverted a large Zulu raiding party from going about its short-term business of ravaging the Buffalo River valley. See Laband, '"O! Let's Go and Have a Fight at Jim's!"', pp. 111, 115–16.

56 Eleven Victoria Crosses and four Distinguished Conduct Medals were awarded (J.W. Bancroft, *Rorke's Drift*, p. 158: Appendix A).

57 These companies of the 88th Regiment had been in garrison at King William's Town, guarding the Eastern Cape frontier.

58 The earthwork Fort Tenedos, directly across the Thukela from Fort Pearson, was built in January 1879 by men of No. 1 Column.

59 The 3rd Regiment.

60 Besides local volunteer units, there was a company of the 88th Regiment to man the improvised defences of Durban and the Durban Redoubt, an earthwork begun in 1842. Stanger had a stone-walled laager, built in 1878, and garrisoned by a company of the 99th Regiment. There were three

companies of the 2/4th Regiment to hold the fort and laager at Greytown, and in Pietermaritzburg a company of the 88th Regiment occupied Fort Napier, commenced in 1843 as the headquarters of the British garrison in Natal.

61 The garrison at Rorke's Drift consisted of seven companies of the 2/24th and detached personnel; while Helpmekaar was held by two companies of the 1/24th, four companies of the 2/4th and Battery N, 5th Brigade, RA.

62 Lieutenant Teignmouth Melvill, Adjutant of the 1/24th Regiment. Service in Ninth Frontier War. Lieutenant Nevill Josiah Aylmer Coghill, 24th Regiment. Service in Ninth Frontier War. ADC to Frere, but given permission to join No. 3 Column as an extra ADC to Col. Glyn. Both officers died attempting to save the Queen's Colour at Isandlwana. On 4 February a patrol from Rorke's Drift found the bodies on the Natal bank of the Buffalo and the Colour in the river. See J. Mathews, 'Fugitives' Drift, 22 January 1879' in *Battlefields of South Africa*, pp. 40–3.

63 See CP 9/95: Wood to Chelmsford, 30 January 1879; and CP 9/96, Wood to Chelmsford, 31 January 1879.

64 See Document 57.

65 See Document 55.

66 Surgeon-Major Nathaniel Alcock.

67 Surgeon-Major Peter Shepherd, MB. Attached to the 24th Regiment and killed on the fugitives' trail from Isandlwana while assisting the wounded.

68 Rear-Admiral Francis William Sullivan, CB, CMG, Royal Navy. Commodore of the naval flotilla in Durban.

69 Llewellyn Lloyd, Political Assistant to Col. Wood. Killed in action on Hlobane.

70 The Zulu reserve, consisting of the uThulwana, iNdlondlo and iNdluyengwe *amabutho* (the 'Undi Regt.'), as well as the uDloko *ibutho*, went on to attack Rorke's Drift. The uThulwana seem to have suffered the greatest punishment. See Laband, '"O! Let's Go and Have a Fight at Jim's!"', pp. 112, 119.

71 The Duke of Cambridge.

72 Written by Wood.

73 This contingent of mounted men, recruited at Dordrecht in the Eastern Cape, was intended to replace the time-expired men who had returned home. See Document 55. Pietermaritzburg was no longer in any danger of attack, though the improvised laager, erected after Isandlwana, was not dismantled until July 1879.

74 The Zulu blockade of Eshowe was assigned to men of all the *amabutho* living in the coast country, augmented by local irregulars. About 500 of them kept watch, while the remaining 5,000 or so were barracked in local *amakhanda*, ready to form an army to prevent the relief of the British garrison. See Laband, *Kingdom in Crisis*, p. 138.

75 Sir T. Shepstone.

76 See CP 9/98: Wood to Chelmsford, Kambula Hill, 3 February 1879.

77 On 9 February five companies of the 80th Regiment relieved the Luneburg garrison, and Schermbrucker's Kaffrarian Rifles went to join Wood at Khambula.

78 On 26 February Colonel Rowlands and his staff left for Pretoria to carry out defensive measures against the disaffected Transvaal Boers. His troops in the Derby and Luneburg district (the former No. 5 Column), which consisted of 800 men of the 80th Regiment, 300 mounted men, 300 native levies and 2 6-pdr guns, were attached to Wood's command.

79 The infantry regiments being despatched to Natal were the 2/21st Fusiliers, 57th Regiment, 58th Regiment, 3/60th Rifles, 91st Highlanders and 94th Regiment; the cavalry were the 1st Dragoon Guards and the 17th Lancers.

80 HMS *Tenedos* was a 1,755 ton corvette built of wood in 1870. It was from the North America and West Indies station.

81 The brick-walled Verulam Laager was built in late 1878. Some 300 local whites were available to defend it, though only 200 Sniders and a few muzzle-loaders were in store.

82 Indentured Indian labourers ('Coolies') began to arrive in Natal in 1860 to work on the coastal sugar plantations, and were assigned to estates from Verulam, north of Durban, to Umzinto to its south. See J. Brain, 'Natal's Indian, 1860–1910: From Co-operation, through Competition, to Conflict' in Duminy and Guest, *Natal and Zululand*, pp. 249–53.

83 In the event, the only colonial defensive post along the Durban-Thukela line to be created (besides the existing laagers at Stanger and Verulam) were a stockade at Kearsney on the Hulett estate, and the fortified gaol at Williamstown, or Umhlali. For once the post-Isandlwana panic had subsided, colonists preferred to rely on the military for their protection.

84 For a full discussion on the sharply conflicting schemes put forward for the defence of Durban by the miltary and municipal authorities, see P. Thompson, 'The Defence of Durban, 1879' in Laband and Thompson, *Kingdom and Colony*, pp. 295–336.

85 Cherry's battalion was formerly the 3/1st NNC, but was reorganized as the 3rd Battalion NNC. It was encamped at the earthwork Fort Cherry (hurriedly thrown up in late January 1879) with the 1st Battalion NNC, formerly the 1/1st NNC, under Commandant Alexander Montgomery.

86 The stonework Hermannsburg Laager was built in 1878 by Dutch-speaking settlers. They took shelter there from January until mid-April 1879 and furnished a mounted force of between 50 and 80 men, who patrolled the vicinity.

87 The stonework Fort Bengough was built during the fortnight after Isandlwana and garrisoned by the 2nd Battalion NNC under Maj. Bengough. In early May it joined the advance of the 2nd Division.

88 An entrenched laager was formed at Helpmekaar on the night of Isandlwana, but was replaced during the following few weeks by a strong

earthwork fort, built by the 5th Co., Royal Engineers and men of the 2/4th Regiment. A variety of units garrisoned the fort, which was finally abandoned in late October 1879.

89 In late January and early February the 5th Co., RE replaced the makeshift barricades at the Rorke's Drift post with a strong, stone-walled enclosure. The fort was garrisoned by men of the 2/24th and abandoned in April for Fort Melvill nearby.

90 Balte Spruit began as a stone laager built by the Boers in 1877, and was improved during January 1879 by the Royal Engineers under Colonel Wood's command.

91 See Documents 55 and 59.

92 Dutch Burghers.

93 Ferreira's Horse, Raaff's Transvaal Rangers and Weatherley's Border Horse. These mounted irregulars and the other units mentioned above had formed part of Colonel Rowlands's command. See Document 62.

94 Kaffrarian Rifles.

95 The Border Guard in Colonial Defensive District No. VI.

96 Formerly 1 and 2/2nd NNC, reorganized as 4th and 5th Battalions NNC.

97 3rd Battalion NNC.

98 Men from the disbanded 1 and 2/3rd NNC were reincorporated in the Weenen Contingent. See Thompson, 'Weenen County', pp. 263–5.

99 See Document 55.

100 The axiom was Sir H. Bulwer's.

101 Presumably Robert George Wyndham Herbert, Under-Secretary of State at the Colonial Office, 1871–92.

102 The former No. 5 Column. See Document 62.

103 Colonel Glyn, who remained until May in command of the troops at Rorke's Drift (the remnants of No. 3 Column), was quite unenterprising and content to remain on the defensive. See Laband and Thompson, *Buffalo Border*, pp. 44–6, 60–1, 110.

104 Bulwer was hotly disputing the function of the border levies as envisaged by Chelmsford, and asserting his authority over them as colonial, as opposed to imperial, troops. See J. Laband, 'Bulwer, Chelmsford and the Border Levies: The Dispute over the Defence of Natal, 1879' in Laband and Thompson, *Kingdom and Colony*, pp. 152–5.

105 Wood had been delirious of a fever brought on by want of sleep and consequent neuralgia, and had been confined to bed for the 36 hours preceding 16 February (CP 9/102: Wood to Chelmsford, Kambula Hill, 16 February 1879).

106 Colonel Fairfax Charles Hassard, CB, Royal Engineers. Commanding Royal Engineers in South Africa and Field in 1879. During late January 1879 he supervised the erection of a proper fort at Helpmekaar and sat on the Court of Enquiry into Isandlwana. He seems both to have lost his nerve and to have become ill, and was invalided to Cape Town, where he

remained in command until the end of the war. Lieutenant John Cordy Baxter, Royal Engineers. Accompanied Headquarters Staff in January 1879 as Hassard's adjutant. Was invalided with him to Cape Town.

107 See CP 7/22: Pearson to Chelmsford, 18 February 1879.

108 On 13 February 1879 Buller attacked Manyonyoba kaMaqondo's caves in the Ntombe valley from which that *induna* had been raiding Luneburg and its environs. Success was only partial, for Manyonyoba remained ensconced, though losing much of his livestock to the British. Rowlands had not been available as he was preparing for a similar raid on Talaku Mountain on 15 February. See Laband, 'Mbilini', pp. 196–7.

109 HMS *Shah* was a 5,700 ton frigate, built of iron and cased teak and completed in 1873. She sailed from St Helena on learning of Isandlwana with No. 8 Battery, 7th Brigade, RA and one company, 88th Regiment.

Chapter 5: The Relief of Eshowe

1 Colonel Glyn, in command at Rorke's Drift.

2 Wood's letter of 25 February, to which this is in reply, is not among the Chelmsford Papers and has not been traced.

3 Two messengers from Cetshwayo crossed the Thukela at Middle Drift on 1 March and made initial contact with Bishop Schreuder. See Laband, 'Humbugging the General', p. 50.

4 They were formerly under Colonel Rowlands's command. See Documents 62 and 65.

5 Carrington and his mounted infantry were to remain in the Transvaal throughout the war.

6 See *BPP* (C.2318), enc. 7 in no. 1: Memorandum by Sir. H. Bulwer, 7 February 1879.

7 Mkhungo kaMpande and his brother Sikhotha were half-brothers of Cetshwayo and the full brothers of Mbuyazi, against whom Cetshwayo won the succession struggle of 1856. Mkhungo and Sikhotha took refuge in Natal in 1857 with their followers, the iziGqoza, and in 1878 were living in the Weenen Division. The iziGqoza contributed to the 1/3rd NNC and 273 of them fought at Isandlwana, 54 being killed. The 3rd NNC was disbanded in late January, but the colonial authorities required black levies for defence. They called on the iziGqoza, who gained the assurance that they would not again be organized or drilled in European fashion, nor be sent to Zululand. In April 200 of them became part of the Weenen Contingent in Colonial Defensive District No. I. See Thompson, 'Weenen County' , pp. 263–5 and P. Colenbrander, 'The Zulu Kingdom, 1828–79' in Duminy and Guest, *Natal and Zululand*, pp. 106–7.

8 See CSO 1926, no. 1356/79: Memorandum by Bulwer, 28 February 1879.

9 Both Buller and Wood had been created CMGs for their services in the Ninth Frontier War. However, in January 1879 Chelmsford had pressed

Wood's claim to the KCMG with the Duke of Cambridge (see Document 52), and the award of the lesser honour prompted the disappointed Wood to threaten 'to decline the honour'. See CP 9/108: Wood to J.N. Crealock, 7 March 1879.

10 The 1st Dragoon Guards and the 17th Lancers, which had arrived in Durban in detachments between 7 and 12 April 1879.

11 Josias Eduard de Villiers, land surveyor and member of the Volksraad of the Orange Free state, 1875–82. He did not succeed in raising this force. See Document 69.

12 Percy Whitehead of the Middelburg cobalt mine was a prominent spokesman for the mining industry in the Transvaal, closely consulted by the British administration.

13 HMS *Boadicea* was a 3,913 ton iron-built corvette completed in 1877. She landed 200 additional men for the Naval Brigade in Durban on 15 March. Over 2,600 officers and men disembarked at Durban during the first weeks of March and passed to camp sites around the town before moving up to the front.

14 Natal Native Horse.

15 St Andrew's was an Anglican mission station founded in 1860 by the Revd Robert Robertson.

16 See Document 68.

17 HMS *Tamar* was a 4,857 ton iron-built troopship, built in 1863.

18 The *Pretoria* was a Union Line steamer of 2,040 tons used as a troopship.

19 11th Battery, 7th Brigade, RA.

20 Commandant George Hamilton-Browne ('Maori Brown'). Commanded 1/3rd NNC with No. 3 Column and was on reconnaissance during Isandlwana. He disbanded the 3rd NNC at Rorke's Drift and formed its white NCOs into a mounted unit which became the nucleus of the Natal Horse. In March he was ordered to the Cape Colony to assist in raising Lonsdale's Mounted Rifles. Present at Gingindlovu.

21 See Document 68.

22 See Document 6.

23 They were formed into the three troops of Natal Horse (de Burgh's, Cooke's and Bettington's). The first two later served with the 1st Division, and the third with the 2nd Division.

24 See Document 102.

25 Donald Currie of Donald Currie & Co., Steam Ship Owners, Smith Street, Durban.

26 Samuel Crowder of S. Crowder & Co., Landing & Shipping Agents, The Point, Durban.

27 Rear-Admiral Sullivan.

28 See Document 66 and *BPP* (C.2318), enc. 2 in no. 9: Frere to Chelmsford, 3 March 1879.

29 Captain Herbert John Mainwaring Williams, 3rd Regiment. Served with No. 1 Column. Present at Nyezane. Died of fever during the blockade of Eshowe.

30 The 2nd Division, which began to concentrate in late April at Landman's Drift on the Buffalo to the south of the Doornberg, eventually consisted of two brigades of two infantry regiments each and a cavalry brigade.
31 See WC II/2/2: Chelmsford to Wood, Durban, 14 March 1879.
32 The column Chelmsford led out from Fort Tenedos on 28 March consisted of 5,700 men and 122 wagons.
33 Major-General H.H. Crealock.
34 The height of the notorious sandbar made Durban harbour inaccessible to most ocean-going vessels. Horses had consequently to be brought ashore in lighters.
35 These regiments all formed part of the Eshowe Relief Column.
36 James M. Rorke, who farmed at Knostrope near Helpmekaar, was with Wood in an advisory capacity. By 'Camberley', Chelmsford means William Calverley, a white trader who acted as an adviser to Hamu. He was killed in action at Hlobane.
37 Major Wilsone Black, 24th Regiment. Service in the Crimean War and Ninth Frontier War. When No. 3 Column crossed into Zululand was appointed DAQMG to Chelmsford, with special charge of roads. From May 1879 in command of the garrisons at Rorke's Drift and Helpmekaar. Conducted several reconnaissances to the Isandlwana battlefield, including the one in question on 14 March. Created CB. Promoted Brevet Lieutenant-Colonel.
38 Colonel Wykeham Leigh Pemberton (1823–1910), 60th Rifles. Indian Mutiny 1857–8. Durban March 1879 in command of 3/60th. Commanded the 2nd Brigade, Eshowe Relief Column. Present at Gingindlovu. Invalided at end of April and proceeded to England in June in charge of the body of the Prince Imperial. Lieutenant-Colonel Law commanded the 1st Brigade, Eshowe Relief Column.
39 The heliograph was essentially a hinged mirror on a tripod, which could flash coded messages up to 90 miles on a sunny day when there was intervisibility.
40 It was believed that one of the reasons for the British defeat at Isandlwana was the inadequate supply of ammunition. However, this shortage was more the consequence of the failure to organize a system of runners to the firing-line than of the inaccessibility of screw-drivers necessary to open the boxes. See J.A. Verbeek and V. Bresler, 'The Role of the Ammunition Boxes in the Disaster at Isandhlawana, 22nd January 1879,' *The Journal of the Historical Firearms Society of South Africa*, 7, 6 December 1977, pp. 22–30.
41 The 4th and 5th Battalions NNC.
42 This section of the manuscript is badly smudged and full of interpolations.
43 Chelmsford later refined these instructions and published them preparatory to the advance of the 2nd Division. See CP 26/9 with its holograph emendations: *Special Instructions regarding the Management of Ox Transport on the Line of March, and for Conducting the Line of March when Troops*

March with Ox Wagon Transport, and for Forming Wagon Laagers. By His Excellency the Lieutenant-General Commanding ("Mercury" Press, West Street, Durban).

44 Captain Arthur Fitzroy Hart, (1844–1910), 31st Regiment. Service in Second Ashanti War. Staff Officer to 2nd Regiment NNC with No. 1 Column; then Staff Officer with Eshowe Relief Column; next Brigade-Major of the 2nd Brigade, 1st Division; and finally Principal Staff Officer of Clarke's Column. Present at Nyezane and Gingindlovu. Promoted Brevet Major.

45 Assistant Commissary Clifford Elliot Walton (1839–91), Commissariat Department. From February 1879 stationed at Fort Pearson in charge of commissariat and transport, first for No. 1 Column, and then for Eshowe Relief Column, which he accompanied. Subsequently with the 1st Division and superintended the establishment of the depot at Fort Durnford and the re-embarkation and pre-audit of stores at the end of the campaign. Present at Gingindlovu. Promoted Commissary.

46 Lieutenant T.F. Abbott, Royal Navy. On shore from HMS *Shah* between 8 March and 21 July 1879. In charge of transporting the Eshowe Relief Column across the Thukela. Subsequently advanced with the 1st Division to Port Durnford.

47 Fannin and Fynney.

48 Prince Makwendu kaMpande, a half-brother of Cetshwayo, lived near the lower reaches of the Mlalazi River. He was of little influence.

49 The wagon-laager was made 140 yards square to give sufficient room inside for 2,000 oxen, 300 horses, 150 white and 130 black mounted irregulars and 2,150 black infantry. It was enclosed by a shelter-trench, 172 yards square and about 15 yards in front of the wagons, to which the 3,240 white infantry would advance during combat. For a detailed account of the battle of Gingindlovu, see Laband, *Kingdom in Crisis*, pp. 171–8.

50 Senior Lieutenant (Gunner) Frederick Ralph Carr, Royal Navy. Commanded *Boadicea's* Naval Brigade in Zululand, which formed part of the rear-guard of the Eshowe Relief Column. Present at Gingindlovu and at the relief of Eshowe.

51 Lieutenant Anthony Kingscote, Royal Navy. On shore from HMS *Active* and commanded the Naval Brigade from the *Tenedos*. Senior Officer Commanding on the lower Thukela. Formed part of the advance guard of the Eshowe Relief Column and commanded two 9-pounder guns at Gingindlovu. Promoted Commander.

52 Commander John William Brackenbury, Royal Navy. On shore from HMS *Shah* and commanded its Naval Brigade. With the Eshowe Relief Column, and subsequently advanced with the 1st Division to Port Durnford. Present at Gingindlovu. Created CMG.

53 Lieutenant-Colonel Francis Vernon Northey, 60th Rifles. Service in Indian Mutiny and Red River Expedition. Commanded the 3/60th in the 2nd

Brigade of the Eshowe Relief Column. Present at Gingindlovu and died of his wounds.

54 Lieutenant Edward Reginald Courtney, 20th Hussars. Staff Officer to Major Barrow, in command of the mounted troops in both No. 1 Column and the Eshowe Relief Column. Present at Nyezane and Gingindlovu.

55 Lieutenant George Charles Jefferyes Johnson, 99th Regiment. Served with Eshowe Relief Column and killed in action at Gingindlovu.

56 This figure could well have been an under-estimation, especially when it is remembered that few of the wounded would have survived. Most likely, nearly 1,200 Zulu died.

57 The British lost 2 officers and 11 men killed, and 4 officers and 44 men wounded.

58 On the contrary, the Zulu knew of Chelmsford's advance the moment he began to march, and the British saw the Zulu signal fires burning on the hills. The Zulu, however, were not able to concentrate their forces around Eshowe until the evening of 1 April. See Laband, *Kingdom in Crisis*, pp. 170–3.

59 Major Albert Lancelot Walker, 99th Regiment. Service in Third China War, 1860. Officer Commanding at Stanger on line of communications during the first phase of the war in Zululand. Accompanied the Eshowe Relief Column and subsequently served as DAG in the 1st Division throughout its operations. Promoted Brevet Lieutenant-Colonel.

60 The eZulwini *umuzi* at Ntumeni, which this force destroyed, had escaped burning during an earlier raid on 1 March by the Eshowe garrison (see Laband, *Kingdom in Crisis*, pp. 139, 178). Prince Dabulamanzi kaMpande was a half-brother of Cetshwayo. He led the Zulu force that attacked Rorke's Drift and served as one of the senior commanders at Gingindlovu under the supreme command of Somopho kaZikhala. He surrendered to the British after prolonged negotiations on 12 July 1879.

61 The Lutheran Emvutshini mission was established in 1859 by the Hermannsburg Mission Society and abandoned in 1877.

62 See Document 76.

63 Captain Frederick William Richards, Royal Navy. Commodore on the West Coast of Africa from March 1879. On shore from 19 March to 11 June and accompanied the Eshowe Relief Column. Present at Gingindlovu. Created CB.

64 Lieutenant-Colonel Charles Mansfield Clarke (1839–1932), 57th Regiment. Service in Indian Mutiny, 1858; Second Maori War, 1863–6. Took part in relief of Eshowe and commanded 2nd Brigade, 1st Division in its advance on Port Durnford. Subsequently commanded Clarke's Column which advanced to oNdini with Wolseley in late July and was employed in the pursuit and capture of Cetshwayo in August. In September Clarke's Column returned to Natal via Middle Drift, enforcing the submission of the border Zulu chiefdoms (see Laband and Thompson, *Umvoti*, pp. 85–6). Present at Gingindlovu.

65 Brigade Surgeon T. Tarrant, MD, Army Medical Department. Senior Medical Officer of No. 1 Column, and in turn of the Eshowe Relief Column, the 1st Division and the camp and convalescent home at Pinetown, Natal. Present at Gingingdlovu.

III. Chapter 6: Preparations and Reconnaissance

1 Later known officially as the Second Division of the South African Field Force.

2 These two companies had been stationed at Helpmekaar since 22 January 1879 and arrived at Dundee on 9 May.

3 The *Clyde*, a steamer of 1,480 tons built in 1870 and owned by Temperleys, Carter and Drake, carrying 15 officers and 526 men of the 1/24th, was wrecked on 3 April 1879 on Dyer Island (home for penguins and seals, and the cause of many a shipwreck), three miles off the Cape shore between Danger Point and Quoin Point, about 70 miles southeast of Simon's Town. The troops were taken on in HMS *Tamar*.

4 The Queen's Colour was lost in the Buffalo River on 22 January 1879 and recovered on 4 February.

5 The widowed former Empress Eugenie of France had been reluctant for her only son, Louis Napoleon, the Prince Imperial, to place himself in danger by volunteering for service in Zululand. Lord Beaconsfield, the prime minister, had concurred. However, the Prince had appealed directly to Queen Victoria, with the upshot that he arrived in Durban on 31 March as a 'spectator'. Chelmsford was impressed with the plucky and enthusiastic young man and, in order to keep a close eye on him, invited him to join his personal staff as an extra aide-de-camp. See Morris, *Washing of the Spears*, pp. 516–19.

6 See CP 8/56: Adjutant General to Chelmsford, 6 March 1879, with Chelmsford's draft answers to his questions. Chelmsford submitted the evidence gathered by the Court of Enquiry on 8 February 1879. See Documents 50, 53, 56 and 58.

7 See Document 70 and CSO 1926, no. 1880/79: Minute by Bulwer, 9 April 1879.

8 The earthwork Fort Chelmsford was commenced on this site on 29 April 1879.

9 This was the earthwork Fort Crealock, built on 23 April 1879 on the left bank of the Matigulu River.

10 A small redoubt was built on the hill adjacent to St Paul's mission on 28 July 1879 to guard the new base for operations following the battle of Ulundi.

11 The Gingindlovu Laager was an entrenched camp formed on 6 April by the retiring Eshowe Relief Column. It was a mile to the south of the laager where the battle of 2 April had taken place.

12 On 29 March 1879 Wood, with a force of 2,086 officers and men, repulsed and routed the main Zulu army of about 20,000 men (many of them the

veterans of Isandlwana) with the loss of 3 officers and 26 men killed and 5 officers and 49 men wounded. The Zulu lost about 2,000 killed. The battle of Khambula marked the turning-point of the war, for the Zulu never regained either the initiative or their morale. For a detailed account, see J. Laband, 'The Battle of Khambula, 29 March 1879: A Re-examination from the Zulu Perspective'in Laband and Thompson, *Kingdom and Colony*, pp. 80–110, passim.

13 Newdigate left Durban on 15 April.

14 At the battle of Khambula.

15 Major Clery was Glyn's Principal Staff Officer. He could not be released to take up the position with Wood in place of Captain R. Campbell, who had been killed on Hlobane, until Glyn had assumed his new command of the 1st Brigade, 2nd Division. see Clarke, *Zululand at War*, p. 170: J.N. Crealock to Alison, 14 April 1879.

16 In CP 9/117: Wood to Chelmsford, 20 April 1879, Wood wrote: 'I am pained beyond power of expression by the unjust and ungenerous abuse of you in the London Papers . . . Wellington was abused in unmeasured terms when he fell back on the Torres Vedras; but I had hoped in these days we were more enlightened.'

17 See Documents 52 and 68.

18 See *BPP* (C.2318), no. 18: Bulwer to Chelmsford, 15 April 1879.

19 The Natal Native Contingent, Natal Native Horse and Natal Native Pioneers, as opposed the the various Natal border levies.

20 See Document 70.

21 Numbers constantly fluctuated, but in the border Colonial Defensive Districts Nos I, VI, and VII the various Border and River Guards, and Border and Reserve Levies amounted to about 8,000 men. See Laband and Thompson, *Field Guide*, pp. 14–15.

22 Subsequent major British raids were mounted across the border from Rorke's Drift on 21 May, from Ngonweni, Elibomvu and Middle drifts on 20 May, and from Tollner's and White Rock drifts on 28 May 1879. Smaller raids also continued to take place. See Laband and Thompson, *Buffalo Border*, pp. 72–3; *Umvoti*, pp. 56–63; and Thompson, 'Captain Lucas', p. 175.

23 See *BPP* (C.2242), enc. 2 in no. 9: Notification by Frere, 11 January 1879.

24 The battles of Khambula and Gingindlovu.

25 See, for example, the *Natal Witness*, 19 April 1879: corresponent with Pearson's Column, 11 April 1879.

26 See Document 76.

27 Colonel Lanyon.

28 See *BPP* (C.2318), no. 18: telegram, Chelmsford to Stanley, 21 April 1879.

29 See CP 6/7: telegram, Frere to Chelmsford, 18 April 1879.

30 See *BPP* (C.2318), no. 18: telegram, Chelmsford to Stanley, 21 April 1879.

31 The Army Enlistment Act of 1870, which aimed at increasing the size of the army reserve through the introduction of short service (six years in the

regular army coupled with six in the reserve) had led to increasing numbers of young and physically immature recruits. See Mathews, 'Lord Chelmsford', pp. 23, 25.

32 Newdigate conferred with Wood at Khambula on 22–3 April before proceeding to Dundee. The 2/21st and 94th Regiments reached Dundee by way of Greytown on 29 April. See War Office, *Narrative of Field Operations*, pp. 89–90.

33 Makwendu, who surrendered with 130 adherents to the 1st Division on 21 April, was interrogated before being relocated to Natal. See Laband, *Kingdom in Crisis*, pp. 191–2.

34 In the event, the decision was taken that the existing garrisons in the area could contain the Zulu, and the Flying Column moved south on 5 May to join the 2nd Division. In Wood's absence the Qulusi, with aid from the Wakkerstroom Boers, raided the district repeatedly between 4 and 21 June. However, these raids never proved more than an irritant. See Laband, 'Mbilini', pp. 202–4.

35 Mbilini, the 'Hyena of the North', was mortally wounded in a skirmish on 5 April 1879.

36 One was never built.

37 See Document 78.

38 See WO 32/7736: Strickland to Chelmsford, Pietermaritzburg, 26 April 1879.

39 Throughout the nineteenth century there were repeated attempts to remedy the British army's transport and supply problems. In 1867 transport and supply were placed under one Department of Control; in 1872 they were separated into two branches; and in 1875 the Control Department was abolished and the Commissariat and Transport Department set up. However, this new Department was no better than its predecessors and proved to be inefficient, understaffed and unable to adapt to southern African conditions. See Mathews, 'Transport and Supply', pp. 1–9; 'Lord Chelmsford', pp. 71–4.

40 The duties of the Adjutant-General's department involved the issuing of orders, and all matters relating to drill and discipline; those of the Quartermaster-General's department the movement and quartering of troops, military positions and reconnaissances. See T.G. Fergusson, *British Military Intelligence, 1870–1914: The Development of a Modern Intelligence Organization*, pp. 47–8.

41 John Wesley Shepstone, Assistant Resident Magistrate, Pietermaritzburg County, 1863–6; Resident Magistrate, Umvoti County, 1867–76; Acting Secretary for Native Affairs in Natal, 1876–84.

42 Conference Hill served as depot for both the 2nd Division and the Flying Column. During May the 94th Regiment and a company of Royal Engineers built a pair of earthwork redoubts 60 yards apart with a rectangular space between for stores, protected by stone walls connecting the redoubts. Balte Spruit continued to operate during May as a depot.

43 See CP 9/116: Wood to Chelmsford, Kambula Hill, 18 April 1879.

44 Chelmsford was shocked at the lack of defensive measures at Dundee, and insisted that a strong fort be built to protect the stores and to serve as an anchor for defence. Named Fort Jones after Captain W. Parke Jones, RE, who designed it, it was made of stone and earth with two flanking towers at opposite corners, and was surrounded by a deep ditch. It was garrisoned by companies of the 2/24th. See Laband and Thompson, *Buffalo Border*, p. 67.

45 Clery had held such a position at the Royal Military Academy, Sandhurst, 1872–5. In 1888 he returned to academic life as the Commandant of the Staff College. His lack of success in the field as commander of the 2nd Division in the Second Anglo-Boer War bore out Chelmsford's strictures. See Clarke, *Zululand at War*, p. 280.

46 See GH 1326, no. 62/1879: Bulwer to Chelmsford, 30 April 1879; also, SNA 1/1/33, no. 8: Fynney to J.W. Shepstone, 19 April 1879 and minute by Shepstone, 24 April 1879.

47 See CSO 1926, no. 1880/79: Wheelwright to Lieuenant-Colonel Mitchell, 2 April 1879.

48 The 1st and 3rd Battalions NNC were at Kranskop; the 2nd was at Sandspruit, on its way to serve with the 2nd Division; and the 4th and 5th were with the 1st Division.

49 However, on 25 June 1879 about a thousand of the Magwaza and Ntuli living along the border mounted an entirely successful raid at Middle Drift, throwing the Natal border region into alarm and disarray. See Laband and Thompson, *Umvoti*, pp. 67–77.

50 Major Rowland Albemarle Bettington. Settled in South Africa in 1872, but gave up farming to serve in the Ninth Frontier War. Adjutant in 1879 to 2/1st NNC. In April took command of No. 3 Troop, Natal Horse (Bettington's Horse), which comprised many NCOs of the disbanded 3rd NNC. Advanced with the 2nd Division. Present at Ulundi.

51 This letter is not among the Chelmsford Papers.

52 The King's (or 1st) Dragoon Guards left Pietermaritzburg on 28 April for Dundee.

53 Chelmsford's map, doubtless the 'Military Map of Zulu Land', was correct.

54 The date is conjectured as 14 May since Wood's letters had been taking three days to reach Chelmsford, and the letter under reply is dated 11 May. (See WC II/3/1: Wood to Chelmsford, Camp Sengonyama, 11 May 1879, 9.30 pm.)

55 In May a small force of Utrecht Boers (Burghers), under Commandant J.A. Rudolph, was stationed at the Burghers' (or Pivaan) Laager, which antedated the war. Two companies of the 2/4th had been in garrison at Luneburg since 9 April.

56 The Kaffrarian Rifles.

57 Newdigates's headquarters were at Landman's Drift on the Buffalo River.

58 The 1st Division was divided between Forts Tenedos, Crealock and

Chelmsford; the 2nd Division was at Landman's Drift, and the Flying Column at Wolf Hill.

59 Fort Chelmsford.

60 See Document 76.

61 By the end of May the Zulu *amabutho* were responding to the king's call to muster once more at oNdini. See Laband, *Kingdom in Crisis*, pp. 190–1.

62 See WO 32/7739: Chelmsford to Revd John Colenso, Bishop of Natal, Utrecht, 12 May 1879: ' . . . I do not believe the work could have been done without risking the health of those employed in the task until quite lately: and now I feel I could not detach the requisite number of troops without seriously interfering with the operations now going on'.

63 Frere instructed on 19 May that any messengers must be directed to Chelmsford for his response (*BPP* (C.2374), enc. 5 in no. 32: Frere to Chelmsford, 19 May 1879).

64 On 19 May Major-General Marshall set out from Dundee for Rorke's Drift with much of the Cavalry Brigade attached to the 2nd Division. On 21 May they visited the Isandlwana battlefield and began the burial of the dead. Chelmsford did not accompany the expedition. See Laband and Thompson, *Buffalo Border*, pp. 70–3.

65 'Military Map of Zulu Land'.

66 'Slow and steady wins the race' (Italian proverb).

67 The camp, which the 2nd Division established during May at Landman's Drift, consisted of three earthwork forts built in echelon with about 50 yards between each one. The cavalry and artillery camps were between two of the forts, and the cattle laager, formed of the Division's wagons, in the other space. A large hospital area was also laid out.

68 See *BPP* (C.2374), enc. 4 in no. 32: Chelmsford to Stanley, Utrecht, 21 May 1879.

69 Fort Chelmsford.

70 Colonel Richard Harrison, Royal Engineers. Service in Indian Mutiny; Third China War. In May 1879 appointed AQMG at Headquarters, and in that capacity was in charge of the QMG's Department during the advance on oNdini. When Brigadier-General Wood was invalided to England, was appointed to command the Flying Column. Present at Ulundi. Created CB.

71 The partial burial of the dead at Isandlwana on 21–22 May was resumed by the garrison at Rorke's Drift on 20 June, but it was not until March 1880 that the task was finally completed. See Laband and Thompson, *Buffalo Border*, p. 75.

72 Near Koppie Alleen the 58th Regiment built Fort Whitehead (named after their colonel). It consisted of two earthwork redoubts, 250 yards apart. After the 2nd Division moved on in June, companies of the 2/24th garrisoned the fort.

73 Since Chelmsford would spare no troops, and those in the Transvaal were

insufficient until reinforced for a direct assault on the Pedi stronghold, Lanyon decided to force the Pedi to remain on the defensive by means of patrols. See Smith, 'Campaigns against the Bapedi', pp. 37–8.

74 At Koppie Alleen.

75 Deputy Commissary-General Edward Morris (1833–1923), CB, Commissariat Department. In April 1879 appointed DCG of lines of communication and base. Subsequently served with Chelmsford as Commissary-General to the 2nd Division and the Flying Column. Present at Ulundi.

76 Major-General Clifford, who was Inspector General of Lines of Communication & Base.

77 The 2nd Division began to move forward on 27 May from Dundee, Landman's Drift and the Doornberg to concentrate at Koppie Alleen.

78 Major Charles John Moysey (1840–1922), Royal Engineers. Royal Engineer officer in charge of the Transvaal (1878) before commanding the Royal Engineers in Wood's Column. Present at Ulundi. Promoted Brevet Lieutenant-Colonel.

79 No. 10 Battery, 7th Brigade, RA, under Brevet Lieutenant-Colonel J.F. Owen, was the first Mounted Gatling Field Battery in the British army.

80 Near Koppie Alleen.

81 Captain Jahleel Brenton Carey (1847–83), 98th Regiment. Service Honduras Expedition, 1867; Second Ashanti War. Served as DAQMG to the 2nd Division. As a result of the Prince Imperial's death on 1 June 1879 while accompanying a patrol of which Carey was in command, he was tried by court martial. The verdict of guilty was not confirmed. See Morris, *Washing of the Spears*, pp. 531–4, 539–43.

82 See the discussion in WC II/2/2: Chelmsford to Wood, 21 May and 24 May 1879, where 'B' is a position placed on a defective map.

83 On that day the 2nd Division moved forward to Thelezi Hill.

84 The 5th Company, RE, under Brevet Major W.P. Jones; and the Natal Native Pioneers under Captain J. Nolan.

85 A slip for 79, since the Intelligence map was published in March 1879.

86 See Document 94.

87 The Flying Column was at Munhla Hill.

88 Colonel Henry Fanshawe Davies, Grenadier Guards. Service in Crimea War; Indian Mutiny and Third China War. Served with the 2nd Division in command of the garrisons at Conference Hill and Landman's Drift.

89 See the *Times of Natal*, 28 May 1879: editorial.

90 An acute viral infection in horses transmitted by nocturnal midges.

91 The Inanda Native Location, created in 1847, was south-east of Greytown.

92 However, note the major Zulu raid at Middle Drift on 25 June 1879.

93 Chelmsford would have had Mbilini's exploits in mind.

94 Chelmsford must have meant Fort Whitehead on the Blood River, for Fort Newdigate was on the Nondweni River, and it was not begun until 6 June 1879.

95 By this Chelmsford could have meant either the real fort Newdigate or Fort Marshall, built on 18 June.

Chapter 7: Ulundi

1 Colonel R. Harrison.

2 The Zulu scouting party, which ambushed the Prince Imperial's patrol at Sobhuza's *umuzi* near the Tshotshosi River, consisted of between thirty and forty men drawn from the iNgobamakhosi, uMbonambi and uNokhenke *amabutho*. See J.P.C. Laband and J. Mathews, 'The Slaying of the Prince Imperial, 1 June 1879' in *Battlefields of South Africa*, pp. 55–6.

3 The Prince's naked body was found the next morning. It had eighteen wounds, all in the front, and the belly had been ritually slit open. The Prince's remains were escorted back to Natal and embarked on 11 June for England. See Morris, *Washing of the Spears*, pp. 534–5.

4 Mgcwelo, Mtshibela and Mphokothwayo had left the king on 30 June and had at first made for Khambula, believing Wood still to be there. See Laband, 'Humbugging the General', p. 55.

5 Sintwangu was an *inceku* (or high official in the king's household) and a well-known royal emissary. He had attended the ultimatum ceremony on 11 December 1878 as the king's eyes and ears. He had negotiated with Major-General Crealock on 28 May 1879, and was to do so again on 30 June. See Laband, *Kingdom in Crisis*, pp. 194, 196, 198.

6 See CP 16/28: Wood to Chelmsford, Mundhla Hill, 28 May 1879.

7 See Document 98.

8 See *BPP* (C.2482), enc. in no. 13: Stanley to Chelmsford, 1 May 1879.

9 Official returns (War Office, *Narrative of Field Operations*, p. 170) gave the respective strengths of the NNC battalions as follows: 1st, 960; 2nd, 1,066; 3rd, 879; 4th, 1,134; 5th, 887.

10 On learning of Cetshwayo's plea for peace, delivered at Fort Chelmsford on 15 May, Chelmsford had suggested additional terms for Zulu surrender over and above those contained in the ultimatum, namely: that all captured weapons and prisoners be surrendered, and that 10,000 stands of firearms be handed over, as well as 10,000 cattle or 20,000 sheep. See CP 13, no. 18: J. Crealock to Mitchell, 21 May 1879. For Bulwer's response, see *BPP* (C.2482), sub-enc. 1 in enc. 1 in no. 8: Memorandum by Bulwer, 29 May 1879.

11 Fort Marshall was built there on 18 June.

12 This letter does not seem to be among the Chelmsford Papers.

13 See Document 80.

14 Commissary-General Strickland.

15 Official returns (War Office, *Narrative of Field Operations*, pp. 157–8, 160) gave British losses at 52 officers and 1,277 men at Isandlwana on 22 January; 2 officers and 60 men at Ntombe on 12 March; and 15 officers and 79 men (excluding about 100 black levies) at Hlobane on 28 March 1879.

16 For the Duke's letter of 8 May severely criticising Chelmsford's conduct of operations, see Mathews, 'Lord Chelmsford', pp. 302–3.
17 See Document 99.
18 See Document 76.
19 The 1st Division's advance ground to a halt at Fort Richards near Port Durnford, begun on 1 July. Fort Argyll, an advanced post on the southern bank of the Mhlatuze River, was only commenced on 24 August 1879.
20 See Document 69.
21 Deputy Commissary-General Charles Palmer (d. 1886), Commissariat Department. Service in Eighth Frontier War; Crimean War. In February 1879 placed in charge of accounts and returns in Pietermaritzburg. Was afterwards for a short time in charge of the Commissariat Department, but suffered a paralytic stroke and was invalided.
22 Assistant Commissary-General Richard Calvert Healey, Commissariat Department. Service in Second Ashanti War. In January 1879 in charge from Fort Tenedos of commissariat and transport of No. 1 Column. Afterwards Director of Transport and President of the Remount Committee at Headquarters. Then Commissary-General to the 1st Division. On breaking up of the Division, took charge of the line of communication and posts from the lower Thukela and Port Durnford to Ulundi. Superintended removal of stores and evacuation of Zululand on the southern line.
23 Lieutenant-Colonel W. Black.
24 Colonel Drury Curzon Drury-Lowe, 17th Lancers. Service in Crimean War and Indian Mutiny. Commanded 17th Lancers when they formed part of the Cavalry Brigade of the 2nd Division. Present at Ulundi.
25 The 2nd Division remained halted in the valley of the Phoko, or Ntinini, Stream from 7 to 17 June.
26 See Document 98 for the message they carried from Chelmsford to Cetshwayo.
27 CP 16/36: Chelmsford to Stanley, Head Quarters Camp, 9 June 1879.
28 Fort Newdigate.
29 Colonel William Pole Collingwood (1829–98), 21st Fusiliers. Service in Ceylon Rebellion, 1848; Crimean War 1854–5; Indian Mutiny, 1858; Third China War, 1860; DQMG in Ireland, 1874–7. On special service in 1879 and commanded 2nd Brigade, 2nd Division on march to Ulundi. In June took command of Forts Newdigate and Marshall. Created CMG.
30 See Document 104.
31 CP 15/21: telegram, H. Crealock to Chelmsford, Fort Pearson, 13 June 1879. See also CP 15/61: H. Crealock to J. Crealock, 10 June 1879, enclosing the Staff Diary of the 1st Division for Chelmsford's information.
32 Brevet Major Walter Francis Blake, 4th Regiment. Served throughout the war in garrison at Helpmekaar, Utrecht and Luneburg.
33 Heinrich Filter, Major Blake's Zulu interpreter, was the seventeen-year-old son of the Revd P. Filter, who arrived as pastor in 1870 to take charge

of the Hermannsburg mission congregation who had established Luneburg in 1869. Young Filter was speared to death in sight of the Luneburg Laager and his anguished mother. See Laband, 'Mbilini', pp. 185, 202–3.

34 Captain Henry Moore, 4th Regiment. Stationed from April to September 1879 in garrison at Luneburg.

35 On 15 June Buller and the mounted men of the Flying Column crossed the Mfolozi to Thabankhulu Mountain, capturing 300 cattle and 100 sheep and burning 24 *imizi*. On 7, 8 and 10 June he had led similarly successful raids on the Zulu in a 25-mile radius of the British camp in the Phoko valley. See Laband, *Kingdom in Crisis*, pp. 188–9.

36 The Flying Column was encamped by the Mhlatuze River, 5 miles in advance of the 2nd Division.

37 Wolseley instructed Chelmsford to report directly to him instead of to the authorities in England. Wolseley left Port Elizabeth on 26 June and landed at Durban two days later. See Preston, *Wolseley's Journal*, pp. 45–6: 26 June; 28 June 1879.

38 Approximately 5,500 men.

39 Compare with Document 76 for the original instructions.

40 The 1st Division reached Port Durnford on 28 June. The 'port' was merely an open sandy beach where the surf broke with less than its usual violence. The intention was to establish a landing place so that the Division could be supplied by sea.

41 Fort Albert was eventually built on 11–12 July on a hill next to the KwaMagwaza Mission.

42 Muwundula kaMamba, *induna* of the kwaNodwengu *ikhanda* and brother of the eMgazini chief, had been a prominent member of the Zulu deputation which had received the British ultimatum on 11 December 1878, and had fought at Isandlwana.

43 Lieutenant-Colonel Gossett, who arranged the Chelmsford Papers, annotated this memorandum as 'A stinger for Genl Clifford'.

44 See CP 17/29: telegram, Clifford to Chelmsford, 24 June 1879 (recd 2 July 1879).

45 The Cavalry Brigade, under Major-General Marshall's command, had the function of guarding and keeping open the lines of communication in Zululand. See Document 105.

46 See *BPP* (C.2482), enc. 1 in no. 23: Chelmsford to Stanley, Entonjaneni, 28 June 1879.

47 See Document 109.

48 Cornelius Vijn was a lame twenty-three-year-old Dutchman who had come to Natal in 1875. He traded in Zululand and was trapped there by the outbreak of war. Cetshwayo used him to write letters on his behalf to the British. But unbeknown to the king, the dicated message of 30 June carried Vijn's postscript to the effect that in his opinion it was the intention of

Cetshwayo and his people – if not the chiefs – to fight on (see *BPP* (C.2482), Aa in enc. in no. 32: Message from the Zulu King to Chelmsford, 30 June 1879). After the battle of Ulundi, Vijn came into Wolseley's camp on 10 August with a last despairing message from Cetshwayo. He agreed, on the promise of a reward, to persuade the king to surrender, but was unsuccessful. See Laband, *Kingdom in Crisis*, p. 241.

49 On 27 June Chelmsford had accepted a herd of 150 cattle as an indication that he was still willing to negotiate. The king's messengers, Mfunzi and Nkisimana, refused to accept them back for the additional reason that the cattle had apparently been 'doctored' to ensure the defeat of the British, and the Zulu feared that the magic would be turned on them instead. See Laband, 'Humbugging the General', p. 57.

50 Chelmsford glosses over the fact that the inexperienced 2nd Division twice panicked in the face of Zulu activity, first firing blindly on the Flying Column to their front, and then hastily forming laager over a mile short of the camp on the White Mfolozi. See Laband, *Ulundi*, p. 13.

51 As a last, desperate peace offering, a hundred of the royal cattle were driven towards the British camp, but the young men of the uMcijo *ibutho* turned them back, insisting they would rather fight. See Laband, *Kingdom in Crisis*, p. 211.

52 Approximately 500 mounted men of the Flying Column.

53 The return of the cattle (which, in fact, Cetshwayo had sent on 27, not 29 June) indicated that negotiations were at an end. See Laband, *Kingdom in Crisis*, p. 212.

54 In fact, the kwaBulawayo *ikhanda*.

55 Buller had fallen into an ambush cunningly laid by about 4,000 Zulu, among whom the uMxhapho *ibutho* was prominent. Only their poor marksmanship saved the British from heavier casualties. See Laband, *Ulundi*, pp. 16–18.

56 See ibid., pp. 18–19. Buller lost 3 men killed and 4 wounded, as well as 13 horses. Three Victoria Crosses were subsequently awarded for real acts of gallantry during this sortie.

57 The total strength of the force was 4,166 white and 958 black officers and men, 12 pieces of artillery and 2 Gatling guns. The garrison left behind numbered 529 white and 93 black troops. See War Office, *Narrative of Field Operations*, pp. 114, 164–5.

58 Rather, kwaBulawayo.

59 The Mbilane stream.

60 Natal Native Horse.

61 The size of the Zulu army was probably between 15,000 and 20,000 strong, with over 5,000 in reserve. See Laband, *Ulundi*, p. 26.

62 See ibid., pp. 26–7. Cetshwayo was not in personal command of his army. Having instructed his generals, he left oNdini on the night of 3 July and was at his kwaMbonambi *ikhanda* four miles away to the north-east throughout the battle. His brother, Ziwedu kaMpande, and other notables witnessed the fighting.

63 A figure of not more than 8,000 is probably more realistic, though any accurate count is not possible. The fact that many Zulu who escaped the field would not have survived their bone-shattering bullet wounds makes actual body-counts conducted by the British incomplete.

64 The British lost 3 officers and 10 men killed, and 69 men wounded. See War Office, *Narrative of Field Operations*, p. 160.

65 Drummond's body was later found in the charred ruins of oNdini. He had been among the mounted officers who had raced for the honour of being the first at Cetshwayo's capital (Captain Lord William Beresford had won), and had lost his way among the huts. See Laband, *Ulundi*, p. 41.

66 Brevet Major Russell Upcher, 24th Regiment. Commandant of Durban, September 1878. Was marching to Rorke's Drift when he received the news of Isandlwana, and retired on Helpmekaar. Assumed command of the 1/24th from 23 January to 11 May 1879. With the 2nd Division on the march to oNdini, and was left in command of the Mthonjaneni laager during the battle of Ulundi.

67 Lieutenant Henry James Scott-Douglas, 21st Fusiliers. Chief of Signalling Staff of 2nd Division. He and Corporal William Cotter, 17th Lancers, set out from Mthonjaneni on 30 June to carry despatches to Fort Evelyn (built 23–24 June). On their return they lost their way and were ambushed in the dark and killed near KwaMagwaza.

68 See Document 108. Wolseley had attempted to land at Port Durnford on 2 July, but the heavy surf had made it impossible, and on 4 July he had been forced to return to Durban. He reached Fort Pearson by land the following evening, only to learn to his chagrin of Chelmsford's victory. See Preston, *Wolseley's Journal*, pp. 50–2: 2–5 July 1879.

69 See CP 28: Chelmsford to Stanley, n.d. (5 July 1879): 'I have during the last 18 months, done a considerable amount of work and I trust that my request to be relieved of my command may be considered as a reasonable one. Should Sir Garnet Wolseley offer no objection I prefer to return in anticipation of your sanction.'

70 Surgeon-Major Frederick Beaufort Scott, MD (1838–1903), Army Medical Department. Medical Officer in charge of Headquarters and served on Chelmsford's Personal Staff. Subsequently Senior Medical Officer at Port Durnford. Present at Ulundi.

71 Brevet Major Francis Wallace Grenfell (1841–1925), 60th Rifles. Ninth Frontier War, 1877–8. 1879 served as DAAG and DAQMG on Headquarters Staff. Accompanied No. 3 Column and 2nd Division. Present at Ulundi. Promoted Brevet Lieutenant-Colonel.

72 Lieutenant-Colonel Cecil James East (1837–1908), 57th Regiment. Service in Crimean War; Indian Mutiny; Lushai Expedition, 1871–2. DAQMG, Intelligence Branch of War Office. Joined Chelmsford in June 1879 as DQMG to the Forces in South Africa. Senior Staff Officer and continued in same capacity with Wolseley during pacification of Zululand. Present at Ulundi. Promoted Brevet Colonel.

Chapter 8: Extrication from a False Position

1 See CP 21/1: telegram, Wolseley to Chelmsford via Fort Pearson, 5 July 1879.

2 The wounded numbered 70, if included is Lieutenant George Astell Pardoe, 13th Regiment, who died of his wounds at Fort Marshall on 14 July.

3 Fort Albert. It was initially named Fort Robertson after the Revd R. Robertson of the KwaMagwaza Mission nearby.

4 This is the original draft of despatch WO 32/7770, Camp Entonjaneni, 9 July 1879.

5 See CP 19/13: Stanley to Chelmsford, 29 May 1879.

6 See CP 19/12: telegram via St Vincent, Stanley to Chelmsford, 28 May 1879: 'Her Majestys Government have determined to send out Sir Garnet Wolseley as Administrator in that part of South Eastern Africa in the neighbourhood of the seat of war with plenary powers both Civil and Military . . .

The appointment of a senior officer is not intended as a censure on yourself but you will as in ordinary course of service submit and subordinate your plans to his control . . . '

7 See CP 28: Chelmsford to Secretary of State for War, n.d. [5 July 1879].

8 See Clarke, *Zululand at War*, p. 263, note 3: General Order No. 62.

9 See WO 32/7770: telegram, Chelmsford, Intonjaneni, to Wolseley, Fort Chelmsford, n.d. [9 July 1879].

10 See CP 21/9: Wolseley to Chelmsford, Camp near Port Durnford, 12 July 1879.

11 Chelmsford wished 'to leave Cape Town by one of the first steamers in August', accompanied by five members of his personal staff (WO 32/7770: Chelmsford to Lieutenant-Colonel H. Brackenbury, RA, Camp, 5 miles west of St Paul's, 14 July 1879). Wolseley permitted him to 'proceed to England, in anticipation of his resignation being accepted', and allowed three of his staff to accompany him, namely, Lieutenant-Colonel Crealock, Captain Molyneux and Captain Buller (WO 32/7770: Extract from General Order No. 130 by Wolseley, 16 July 1879).

12 See CP 19/13: Stanley to Chelmsford, 29 May 1879. This despatch was published by the *Natal Witness* on 8 July 1879.

13 The chiefs named in CP 21/9: Wolseley to Chelmsford, Camp near Port Durnford, 12 July 1879, were Ntshingwayo of the Khoza, King Cetshwayo, Manqondo of the Magwaza, Mnyamana of the Buthelezi and Zibhebhu of the Mandlakazi.

14 Chelmsford met Wolseley at St Paul's on 15 July.

15 This memorandum is an attempted rebuttal of some of the criticisms raised by Forbes in 'Lord Chelmsford', pp. 216–34, passim. In CP 24/5 there are two earlier, pencilled drafts of this memorandum (memoranda A and B), as well as detailed and extremely lengthy notes (memorandum D) in which Chelmsford attempts to refute Forbes point by point.

16 This, and the page numbers below, refer to the specific pages in Forbes's article which Chelmsford is discussing.

17 See Document 5.

18 *BPP* (C.2222), enc. 2 in no. 12: Thesiger to Stanley, 11 November 1878.

19 Ibid.

20 Forbes rhetorically enquired of the position of the camp 'whether one more inherently vicious could have been found on the most industrious search'.

21 In fact, para. 20 of *Regulations for Field Forces in South Africa 1878* laid down that troops in encampments were to be under arms morning and evening. Para. 18, however, stipulated that oxen should be placed in a wagon laager at night; while para. 19 stated clearly that the 'camp should be partially entrenched on all sides'. Neither of these regulations were adhered to at the Isandlwana camp.

22 Captain A.C. Gardner. This message is held by the Regimental Museum of the South Wales Borderers and Monmouthshire Regiment, Brecon. It reads: 'Staff Officer.
Report just come in that the Zulus are advancing in force from left front of Camp.
8.5. a.m. H.B. Pulleine
Lt Col'

23 On 1 February Buller destroyed the ebaQulusini *ikhanda* (see Document 57) and raided Manyonyoba on 13 February (see Document 65). Despite several further British attempts to drive him out of his caves in the Ntombe valley, Manyonyoba continued to resist until 22 September 1879. See Laband, 'Mbilini', pp. 196–7, 202, 205–7.

24 Chelmsford's responses to Forbes's criticisms stop short with those made on p. 230 of the article. For Chelmsford's detailed refutation of Forbes's further points on pp. 231–4, mainly concerning the landing of stores at Port Durnford and the withdrawal after the battle of Ulundi, consult CP 24/5: Memorandum D. For a comprehensive and effective answer to Forbes's criticisms (far superior, it must be noted, to Chelmsford's), see Harness, 'The Zulu Campaign', pp. 477–88, passim.

Biographical Notes

Other persons mentioned in the transcripts are identified in the Notes.

NOTE ON FORMAT: Name; dates; rank, regiment, orders and decorations at beginning of Anglo-Zulu War; record of past service; service during 1879; battles where present; orders & decorations and promotion in recognition of service during Anglo-Zulu War. Subsequent career not noted.

Baker, Francis James (1841–1915). Formerly Captain, Ceylon Rifles. Resigned his commission, 1871. Commandant of Baker's Horse, which he raised in the Eastern Cape in February 1879. Served with the Flying Column. Present at Khambula and Ulundi.

Barrow, Percy Harry Stanley (1848–86). Captain, 19th Hussars. Brigade Major of Cavalry at the Curragh from 1877 until March 1878, when he went to South Africa on special service to form a mounted infantry squadron. In 1879 served first with No. 1 Column in command of No. 2 Squadron, Mounted Infantry, then with the Eshowe Relief Column in command of the Divisional Troops. Commanded the mounted men of the 1st Division, and subsequently the Mounted Infantry with Clarke's Column. Present at Nyezane and Gingingloviu, where he was wounded. CMG. Brevet Major.

Barton, Geoffrey (1844–1922). Captain, 7th Fusiliers. Service in 2nd Ashanti War, 1874. On special service throughout 1879, first as Staff Officer to Colonel Durnford of No. 2 Column and commander of the Natal Native Horse, and subsequently as commander of the 4th Battalion NNC, successively with the Eshowe Relief Column, the 1st Division and Clarke's Column. Present at Isandlwana and Gingindlovu. Brevet Major.

Barton, Robert Johnston (1849–79). Captain, Coldstream Guards. Service as second-in-command, Frontier Light Horse, in Ninth Frontier War, 1877–8. In 1879 commanded Frontier Light Horse with No. 4 Column. Killed in action at Hlobane.

Beaumont, William Henry (1851–1930). Formerly 75th Regiment. Came to Natal in 1871. From 1875 Clerk in the Governor's Office and First Clerk to the Colonial Office, Natal. Resident Magistrate, Newcastle Division, February 1878. Encouraged the building of laagers in his Division for the protection of settler families. In 1879 Acting Commandant of Colonial Defensive District No. I while its commander, Major Dartnell, was serving with No. 3 Column. After Isandlwana organized the reluctant settlers in the defence of his Division.

Bellairs, William (1828–1913). Colonel, Staff, CB. Service in Crimean War, 1854–6. Staff appointments in the West Indies, Ireland, Canada and Gibraltar, 1857–77. DAG in the 9th Frontier War, 1877–8. On special service in 1879 as DAG and QMG on the Headquarters Staff. Remained in Pietermaritzburg until General Clifford's arrival allowed him to join the 2nd Division in the field. Commanded the force left in camp on the banks of the White Mfolozi during Ulundi.

Bengough, Harcourt Mortimer (1837–1922). Brevet Major, 77th Regiment. Service in Crimean War, 1854–5. On special service in 1879 in command of 2/1st NNC with No. 2 Column. Following Isandlwana, proceeded to Umsinga to protect the border and built Fort Bengough. There his battalion regained its morale and was reconstituted in March as the 2nd Battalion NNC. In May it joined the 2nd Division in its advance, and then served with Baker Russell's Column until the end of August. Present at Ulundi. Brevet Lieutenant-Colonel.

Brackenbury, Henry (1837–1915). Brevet Lieutenant-Colonel, Royal Artillery. Service in Indian Mutiny, 1857–9; Franco-Prussian War, 1870–1 with British National Society for Aid to the Sick and Wounded; Second Ashanti War, 1873–4. Appointed Wolseley's military secretary in 1875 and accompanied him to Natal. Proceeded on special service to South Africa in 1879 in same capacity on Wolseley's staff.

Bray, Edward William (1823–1891). Colonel, 4th Regiment, CB. In command in 1879 of 2/4th Regiment. Spent the war in garrison along the western frontiers of Zululand in Utrecht, Newcastle, Balte Spruit and Luneburg. In September assisted Baker Russell's Column in the final pacification of the Ntombe valley.

Bromhead, Gonville (1845–1891). Lieutenant, 24th Regiment. Left in command of the detachment of the 24th Regiment at Rorke's Drift when No. 3 Column advanced to Isandlwana. Subsequently commanded detachments in garrison at Dundee, Landman's Drift and Koppie Allein, and commanded Wolseley's personal escort at Ulundi. Present at Rorke's Drift. VC. Brevet Major.

Buller, Ernest Henry (1839–88). Captain, Rifle Brigade. On special service in 1879 as ADC to Chelmsford and Commandant at Headquarters. Acted as Staff Officer to the 2nd Brigade, Eshowe Relief Column. Present at Gingindlovo. Brevet Major.

Buller, Redvers Henry (1839–1908). Lieutenant-Colonel, 60th Rifles, CB. Service in Third China War, 1860; Red River Expedition, 1870; Second Ashanti War, 1873–4; Ninth Frontier War, 1878. On special service in 1879 and commanded mounted troops of No 4 Column and Wood's Flying Column. Present at Hlobane, Khambula and Ulundi, and numerous skirmishes. VC, CMG, ADC to the Queen. Colonel.

Bulwer, Sir Henry Ernest Gascoyne (1836–1914). GCMG. Official Resident in Ionian Islands, 1860–4; Receiver-General of Trinidad, 1866; Administrator of Government of Dominica, 1867–9; Governor of Labuan and Consul-General of Borneo, 1871; Lieutenant-Governor of Natal, 1875–80.

Cambridge, Duke of, George William Frederick Charles (1819–1904). Succeeded his father, seventh son of King George III, as 2nd Duke, 1850. Field Marshal, GCH, KG, GCMG, GCB, KP. Service in Crimean War, 1854–5. Commander-in-Chief of the British Army, 1856–95.

Carrington, Frederick (1844–1913). Brevet Major, 24th Regiment. Instructor of musketry, 1870. Raised mounted infantry to serve in Griqualand West (the Diamond Fields), 1875; trained mounted infantry to serve in Transvaal as Carrington's Horse (Transvaal Mounted Infantry), 1877; raised Frontier Light Horse and commanded it during Ninth Frontier War, 1877–8; commanded Carrington's Horse in Transvaal against Sekhukhune, 1878–9. Remained in Transvaal throughout 1879. Brevet Lieutenant-Colonel.

Cetshwayo kaMpande (c.1832–1884). King of the Zulu. Defeated brother Mbuyazi, rival for the succession, 1856; recognized as heir to his father, King Mpande kaSenzengakhona, 1861, and henceforth exercised most of his royal prerogatives. Succeeded to the throne on Mpande's death, 1872.

Chard, John Rouse Merriott (1847–97). Lieutenant, Royal Engineers. Senior officer present at defence of Rorke's Drift. Accompanied advance of 2nd Division. VC. Brevet Major.

Clery, Cornelius Francis (1838–1926). Major, Half-pay. Service in Griqualand West, 1877; Transvaal, 1878. Instructor of Tactics at the Royal Military College, 1871 and Professor, 1872–5. DAQMG on Headquarters Staff at Dublin, 1875–7 and at Aldershot, 1877–8. On special service in 1879, when first joined No. 3 Column as Principal Staff Officer to Colonel Glyn, and then served with Wood in the same capacity. Present at Ulundi. Brevet Lieutenant-Colonel.

Clifford, the Hon. Sir Henry Hugh (1826–83). Major-General, Staff, VC, KCMG, CB. Service in Eighth Frontier War 1850–3; Crimean War, 1854–5, Third China War, 1860. AQMG at Aldershot, 1860–4 and at the War Office 1865–8. AAG and ADC to Duke of Cambridge. On special service in May 1879 and appointed Inspector-General of Line of Communication and Base. During second invasion in command of the base and lines of communication between it and all forces operating in Zululand, as well as of all forces defending Natal.

Colenso, John William (1814–83). First Anglican Bishop of Natal, 1853. Translated much of the Bible into Zulu, compiled the first Zulu-English dictionary and produced Zulu readers for use in schools. When confronted with difficulties in converting the Zulu, he questioned the literal interpretation of the Bible, was found guilty of heresy and excommunicated. However, the civil courts allowed him to retain his bishopric, and a schism opened up in the Anglican community when a rival Bishop of Maritzburg was consecrated in 1869. Colenso forfeited support among the colonists by his campaign to expose the unfair trial of the Hlubi chief, Langalibalele, in 1873. He protested against the war with the Zulu in 1879, which he felt the British had deliberately and unjustly provoked. His views necessarily brought him into conflict with the military authorities.

Crealock, Henry Hope (1831–91). Major-General, Staff, CB. Service in Crimean War, 1854–5; Indian Mutiny, 1858; Third China War, 1860. DQMG in Ireland, 1874–7. On special service in 1879 and commanded 1st Division from its formation in April until the end of the campaign. CMG.

Crealock, John North (1837–95). Brevet Lieutenant-Colonel, 95th Regiment. Service in Indian Mutiny, 1857–8; Ninth Frontier War, 1878. Assistant Military Secretary to Chelmsford, 1878. In 1879 continued on Chelmsford's Personal Staff and promoted Military Secretary. Senior Staff Officer to Eshowe Relief Column. Present at Gingindlovu (slightly wounded) and Ulundi. Returned to England with Chelmsford. CB.

Dabulamanzi kaMpande (c.1839–86). Half-brother of King Cetshwayo. Lived at his eZulwini *umuzi* near Ntumeni. Led the Zulu force that attacked Rorke's Drift and served as one of the senior commanders at Gingindlovu under the overall command of Somopho kaZikhala. Surrendered to British on 12 July after long negotiations.

Dartnell, John George (1838–1913). Brevet Major, retired by sale of commission, 1864. Service in Indian Mutiny, 1858. Commandant, Natal Mounted Police, 1874, and Inspector of Volunteer Forces, Natal. In 1879 on Chelmsford's Headquarters Staff during first invasion as commander of Natal Mounted Police and Natal Mounted Volunteers. Accompanied No. 3 Column, and away skirmishing during Isandlwana. Commandant of Colonial Defensive District No. I, December 1878–July 1879.

Degacher, Henry James (1835–1902). Lieutenant-Colonel, 24th Regiment, CB. Commanded 2/24th Regiment throughout campaign of 1879. Commanded No. 3 Column, and away skirmishing during Isandlwana. Subsequently commanded Rorke's Drift post, which he fortified, and later built Fort Melvill nearby. In April moved with half the 2/24th to Dundee, where he remained in command while the battalion was scattered at posts along the border to protect the lines of communication and the Dundee District during the advance of the 2nd Division.

Drummond, the Hon. William (1845–79). Second son of 9th Viscount Strathallan. Natal civil servant. On Chelmsford's Headquarters Staff in charge of the Intelligence Department. Killed in oNdini after Ulundi.

Dunn, John (1830–95). Entered Zululand as a trader and hunter in 1853 and, gaining Cetshwayo's confidence, became his adviser and supplier of guns. Rewarded with a large chiefdom in the south-east of the country. In 1878 advised Cetshwayo against war. When accused of treason by the king's other advisers, crossed over to Natal in late December 1878 and threw in his lot with the British. Dunn rode with the Eshowe Relief Column to organize reconnaissance and advise on laagering procedures. Accompanied the 1st Division in command of John Dunn's Scouts, and played an important role in negotiating the submission of the coastal chiefs. Present at Gingindlovu.

Durnford, Anthony William (1830–79). Brevet Colonel, Royal Engineers. Posted to Ceylon in 1851 and served also in Malta, Gibraltar, Ireland and England.

Posted to Natal in 1871. Chief-of-Staff to Lieutenant-Colonel Milles during Langabilalele Expedition, 1873, and blamed by colonists for debacle of Bushman's River Pass. Civil Engineer for the Colony of Natal, 1873–5. Sat on Zululand Boundary Commission, 1878. Raised and commanded 1st Regiment NNC and took command of No 2 Column. Killed in action at Isandlwana.

Essex, Edward (1847–1939). Captain, 75th Regiment. On special service to Natal, November 1878. Transport officer to No. 3 Column, and escaped from Isandlwana via Fugitives' Drift to Helpmekaar. Director of Transport to the 2nd Division. Present at Isandlwana and Ulundi. Brevet Major.

Fannin, John Eustace (1834–1905). Grew up in Natal and fluent in Zulu. Led an itinerant life, alternating between intermittent employment in the Natal civil service, land surveying, military service and farming. Special Border Agent Umvoti, and commander of Border Police, November 1878–October 1879. Responsible for latest intelligence of events in Zululand.

Forbes, Archibald (1838–1900). A drop-out from Aberdeen University, he enlisted and rose to acting quartermaster-sergeant in the Royal Dragoons. In 1867 he left the army and pursued journalism. From 1870 he was the war correspondent to the *Daily News*, and reported the Franco-Prussian, Carlist, Serbian, Russo-Turkish and Afghan wars. Arrived in Natal in April 1879 and reported the advance of the 2nd Division, though relations between him and Chelmsford's Headquarters Staff were strained. He was present at Ulundi, and by his 'ride of death' brought news of the battle ahead of Chelmsford's official despatch. He claimed the South African Campaign Medal for his exploit, but since he had carried only a private letter and not an official one, Chelmsford was instrumental in denying him the decoration. Forbes revenged this rebuff by publishing attacks on Chelmsford's generalship.

Frere, Sir Henry Bartle Edward (1815–84). GCB, GCSI, KCB. His posts in India, 1834–67, included Political Resident to Rajah of Satara (1846–50); Chief Commissioner of Sind (1850–9); member of the Council of the Governor-General (1859–62) and Governor of Bombay (1862–7). In 1867 returned to England as a member of the Indian Council, and in 1875–6 accompanied the Prince of Wales on his Indian tour. Baronetcy and GCB in 1876. In 1877 appointed Governor of the Cape and High Commissioner for South Africa. Planned war against Zululand to further the confederation of southern African states under Britain. Wolseley's appointment in May 1879 took the affairs of Natal and Zululand out of his hands, and Frere was recalled in August 1880.

Fynn, Henry Francis, Jnr (1846–1915). Brought up in Natal and fluent in Zulu. Entered Natal civil service in March 1864 as Clerk and Interpreter to the Resident Magistrate, Newcastle; Clerk of the Court, Richmond District, 1865; Resident Magistrate, Umsinga Division, 1876. Interpreter to the Zululand Boundary Commission, 1878. Personal interpreter and political adviser to Chelmsford, January 1879, and accompanied No. 3 Column into Zululand. With Chelmsford on the day of Isandlwana. Subsequently resumed magisterial duties in Umsinga. Negotiated surrender of Zulu chiefs along Buffalo border, August 1879.

Fynney, Frederick Bernard (*c.* 1840–88). Natal Government Interpreter, 1876–7; Administrator of Native Law and Special Border Agent, Lower Tugela Division, 1878–9. Responsible for intelligence of events in Zululand, and in command of Border Police, Colonial Defensive District No. VI. Compiled *The Zulu Army and Zulu Headmen. Published by Direction of the Lieut.-General Commanding*, Pietermaritzburg, 1878, which was to prove very influential in forming British perceptions of Zulu political organization and military capability.

Gardner, Alan Coulston (1846–1907). Captain, 14th Hussars. On special service in 1879, first as Staff Officer in No. 3 Column, and subsequently in same capacity in the Flying Column. Present at Isandlwana and escaped via Fugitives' Drift. Brevet Major.

Glover, Benjamin Lucas (1848–1904). Veterinary Surgeon, 1st Class, Royal Artillery. In 1879 served with N Battery, 5th Brigade, and accompanied No. 3 Column. Away skirmishing during Isandlwana. Subsequently established a sick horse depot at Fort Pearson. Proceeded to Transvaal to assist in obtaining remounts, and was then employed in inspecting animals at military posts in northern Natal.

Glyn, Richard Thomas (1831–1900). Colonel, 24th Regiment, CB. Service in Crimea, 1854–5; Indian Mutiny, 1857–8; Ninth Frontier War, 1877–8. Given command of No. 3 Column, December 1878. Away skirmishing during Isandlwana. Subsequently in command of the post at Rorke's Drift. In May took up command of the 1st Brigade, 2nd Division. Present at Ulundi in command of the Infantry Brigade.

Gossett, Matthew William Edward (1839–1909). Brevet Major, 54th Regiment. Service in Indian Mutiny, 1857–8; Ninth Frontier War, 1878. On special service as ADC on Chelmsford's Personal Staff, 1878–9. Accompanied No. 3 Column and away with Chelmsford on day of Isandlwana. Subsequently AAG and AQMG to 2nd Division. Present at Ulundi. Brevet Lieutenant-Colonel.

Hamu kaNzibe (*c.* 1834–87). Full and elder brother to King Cetshwayo, though through *ukuvuza* custom heir not to his father, King Mpande, but to his father's deceased brother, Nzibe. *Induna* of uThulwana *ibutho* and chief of the Ngenetsheni people in north-western Zululand. Brooked no interference from Cetshwayo in his chiefdom, and had his eyes on the crown. Opposed to risking war with Britain, and in September 1878 was already negotiating his defection. Finally went over to the British in March 1879, dealing a heavy blow to Zulu morale.

Harness, Arthur (1838–1927). Brevet Lieutenant-Colonel, Royal Artillery. Commanded N Battery, 5th Brigade throughout 1879. Accompanied No. 3 Column. Away skirmishing on day of Isandlwana. Subsequently stationed at Helpmekaar, and served on Court of Enquiry into the Loss of the Camp at Isandlwana. In April joined 2nd Division. Served in June on court martial of

Captain Carey. In August joined Baker Russell's Column amd patrolled in search of fugitive Cetshwayo. Present at Ulundi. CB.

Hassard, Fairfax Charles (1822–1900). Colonel, Royal Engineers, CB. Service in Crimean War, 1854–6; Ninth Frontier War, 1877–8. In 1879 joined Chelmsford's Headquarters Staff as Officer Commanding Royal Engineers in South Africa and Field. In the aftermath of Isandlwana, dug in at Helpmekaar, and built a proper fort. Served on Court of Enquiry into the Loss of the Camp at Isandlwana. Then suffered a nervous breakdown, and surrendered his command to Colonel Bray. Proceeded to Cape Town by order, and remained there in command until the end of the war.

Hime, Albert Henry (1842–1919). Captain (on temporary reserve list), Royal Engineers. Service in Third China War, 1860. Colonial Engineer of Natal and Member of Executive Council from May 1875. Commandant in 1879 of the First Ward Laager of Pietermaritzburg when the city was organized for defence after Isandlwana.

Huskisson, John William (1832–1906). Major, 56th Regiment. Service in Indian Mutiny, 1858. On special service, December 1878–October 1879, as Commandant of Durban, AQMG at the Base and Commandant of Colonial Defensive Sub-District of Durban. Superintended disembarkation of troops at Durban, and responsible for organizing the defence of Durban after Isandlwana. Brevet Lieutenant-Colonel.

Lanyon, William Owen (1842–87). Colonel, 2nd West India Regiment. Service in Second Ashanti War as ADC to Wolseley, 1873–4. Administrator of Griqualand West, 1875–9. Resident of Pretoria and Administrator of the Transvaal, March 1879–April 1881.

Law, Francis Towry Adeane (1835–1901). Lieutenant-Colonel, Royal Arillery. Service in Indian Mutiny, 1857–8; Third China War, 1860; Ninth Frontier War, 1877–8. On special service in 1879 on Chelmsford's Headquarters Staff as Officer Commanding Royal Artillery. After Isandlwana, served on Court of Enquiry into the Loss of the Camp. Then appointed Commandant of the Lower Tugela District, and prepared the column for the relief of Eshowe. Commanded 1st Brigade, Eshowe Relief Column. Subsequently Officer Commanding Royal Artillery, 1st Division. Present at Gingindlovu. CB.

Longcast, Henry William (1850–1909). Of Irish settler stock, orphaned in Natal. Adopted and brought up at the KwaMagwaza mission by the Revd R. Robertson. Lived in Zululand until just before the outbreak of war. Interpreter and Guide to Chelmsford from November 1878 to July 1879. Present at Gingindlovu and Ulundi.

Lonsdale, Rupert de la Tour (dates unkown). Lieutenant (retired, 1874), 74th Regiment. Service in Ninth Frontier War, 1878, when commanded Fingo levies. In 1879 Commandant, 3rd Regiment NNC with no. 3 Column. Away skirmishing on day of Isandlwana. The 3rd NNC was disbanded after Isandlwana, and Lonsdale proceeded to Cape Town to raise a troop of irregular horse, Lonsdale's Mounted Rifles. They served first with the 1st

Division, and were subsequently divided between Clarke's and Baker Russell's Columns.

Louis Napoleon, Prince Imperial of France (1856–79). Only son and heir of the exiled Napoleon III, who died in 1873. The Prince graduated in 1875 from the Royal Military Academy, Woolwich, but did not take a commission. He wished for active service and was permitted to join the forces in Zululand as a spectator, and was attached as an Extra ADC on Chelmsford's staff. To occupy him, Chelmsford attached him to the QMG's Department to map the road ahead of the 2nd Division. Killed when his patrol was ambushed on 1 June 1879 near the Tshotshosi River.

MacLeod, Norman Magnus (1839–1929). Captain, 74th Highlanders (resigned 1872). Natal Special Agent for Indian Immigration and Protector of Immigrants, 1874–5. Civil and Political Assistant to O.C. Utrecht, Border Agent to Swazis and Justice of the Peace for Utrecht, Wakkerstroom and Lydenburg, 1878. Between November 1878 and August 1879 unsuccessfully attempted to persuade King Mbandzeni of the Swazi to intervene against the Zulu on the side of the British.

Main, Thomas Ryder (1850–1934). Lieutenant, Royal Engineers. Service in Ninth Frontier War, 1877–8. In 1879 served with No.1 Column, and subsequently with the 2nd Brigade, 2nd Division. Present at Nyezane, blockade of Eshowe, and Ulundi.

Malthus, Sydenham (1831–1916). Lieutenant-Colonel, 94th Regiment. Commanded the 94th, which arrived in Durban in April 1879 and formed part of the 2nd Division. Built the post and depot at Conference Hill in May, and commanded it until the advance on Ulundi began in June. Subsequently commanded the regiment when it formed part of Baker Russell's Column. Present at Ulundi. CB.

Marshall, Frederick (1829–1900). Major-General, Life Guards. Service in Crimean War, 1854–5. Proceeded to Natal in February 1879 to command the Cavalry Brigade attached to the 2nd Division. When the brigade was disbanded after Ulundi, Wolseley placed him in command of advanced posts and lines of communication. CMG.

Milne, Archibald Berkeley (1855–1938). Lieutenant, Royal Navy. With HMS *Active's* contingent of the Naval Brigade. Attached as an ADC on Chelmsford's Personal Staff. Present with Chelmsford on day of Isandlwana, at Gingindlovu and at Ulundi, where he was slightly wounded.

Molyneux, William Charles Francis (1845–98). Captain, 22nd Regiment. Service in Ninth Frontier War, 1878. ADC to Chelmsford at Aldershot, and proceeded with him to South Africa in 1878 in same capacity. Invalided home in July 1878. Returned on special service with reinforcements after Isandlwana. In March 1879 rejoined Chelmsford's Staff as Senior ADC, and served during relief of Eshowe and second invasion. Present at Gingindlovu and Ulundi. Brevet Major.

Newdigate, Edward (1825–1902). Major-General, Staff. Service in Crimean War,

1854–5; Red River Expedition, 1870. Arrived on special service with reinforcements in Natal, April 1879, and took command of 2nd Division until it was disbanded in July. Present at Ulundi. CB.

Pearson, Charles Knight (1834–1909). Colonel, Half-pay, CB. Service in Crimean War, 1854–5. On special service in 1879. First commanded No. 1 Column, January–April, and then 1st Brigade, 1st Division, until invalided home in May. Commanded at Nyezane and blockade of Eshowe. KCMG.

Pulleine, Henry Burmester (1839–79). Brevet Lieutenant-Colonel, 24th Regiment. Service in 9th Frontier War, 1877–8, and raised Transkei Rifles and Frontier Light Horse. Commandant of Durban, then Pietermaritzburg, December 1878; President, Remount Depot, January 1879. Subsequently commander of 1/24th with No. 3 Column. Killed in action at Isandlwana.

Rowlands, Hugh (1829–1909). Colonel, Half-pay, VC, CB. Service in Crimean War, 1854–5; Transvaal, 1878. Commanded forces throughout first Sekhukhuni campaign of 1878 and present in every action under fire. On special service in 1879 and commanded No. 5 Column until 26 February, when left for Pretoria to carry out defensive measures against Boers. Succeeded Pearson in May as commander, 1st Brigade, 1st Division.

Rudolph, Gerhardus Marthinus (1828–1906). A voortrekker in Natal and Zulu linguist. Joined Natal civil service as a Clerk and Interpreter, 1855. Appointed Landdrost of Utrecht, Transvaal Republic, 1874. Continued as Landdrost after British annexation of Transvaal, 1877. Local Boers held him in some suspicion for his pro-British attitude.

Russell, Baker Creed (1837–1911). Brevet Lieutenant-Colonel, 13th Hussars, CB. Service in Indian Mutiny, 1857–9; Second Ashanti War, 1873–4. Accompanied Wolseley on special service to Zululand in 1879 on his Staff. In July took command of a column (Baker Russell's Column) made up of part of the disbanded Flying Column. Proceeded north-west out of Zululand, enforcing Zulu submissions as he went. KCMG.

Russell, John Cecil (1839–1909). Brevet Major, 12th Lancers. Service in Second Ashanti War, 1873–4. In 1879 on special service and given command (with local rank of Lieutenant-Colonel) of No. 1 Squadron, Mounted Infantry in No. 3 Column. Away skirmishing during Isandlwana. In March 1879 transferred to No. 4 Column. After the debacle on Hlobane, 28 March, was transferred to Pietermaritzburg as Commandant, Remount Establishment. Present at Hlobane. Brevet Lieutenant-Colonel.

Schermbrucker, Friedrich Xavier (1826–1904). Born in the Kingdom of Bavaria and a lieutenant in the Bavarian army, 1852. Service as volunteer with British in Crimean War, 1854–5. Joined German Legion for service in the Cape, 1856. Left military service in 1857 and earned living as farmer, auctioneer and butcher in British Kaffraria. Elected member of the Cape Legislative Assembly, 1868. Left to seek his fortune in the diamond- and gold-fields, 1870. Settled in Bloemfontein, Orange Free State, as a journalist, 1873. Political differences and financial difficulties caused him in 1877 to take up command of Frontier Armed and Mounted Police in Ninth Frontier War. In 1879 commanded this unit, renamed the Kaffrarian Rifles, with No. 4 Column. Formed part of Luneburg garrison, December 1878–February 1879, and again after June 1879. Present at Hlobane and Khambula.

Schreuder, Hans Paludan Smith (1817–1882). Norwegian Lutheran missionary in Zululand since 1851. Consecrated Bishop in the Church of Norway, 1866. Broke with the Norwegian Missionary Service in 1872 and launched independent mission, centred at Ntumeni. When missionaries withdrew from Zululand in 1877, took up position at his Natal station, kwaNtunjambili, near Kranskop. In 1879 served British as source of intelligence through continuing contacts with Cetshwayo and information fed by his Christian converts still in Zululand.

Sekethwayo kaNhlaka (*c.* 1814–83). Chief of the Mdlalose, *induna* of the kwaNodwengu *ikhanda* and member of Cetshwayo's inner council. Began negotiating his submission with Wood, January 1879, but foiled by king's armed intervention. Submitted to Baker Russell, 25 August 1879.

Shepstone, Henrique Charles (1840–1917). European and Coolie Immigration Agent, Natal, 1864–9; Resident Magistrate, Alfred County, 1870–3; and of Umlazi Division, Durban County, 1874–6. Secretary for Native Affairs, Transvaal, 1877–8.

Shepstone, Theophilus, Jnr (1843–1907). Attorney. Member of Natal Legislative Council for Pietermaritzburg Borough, 1872–87. Captain and Officer Commanding Natal Carbineers, 1872–80. Advanced with No. 3 Column, but away skirmishing during Isandlwana. Subsequently in garrison at Fort Pine with Natal Mounted Volunteers. Then commanded No. 3 Troop, Natal Horse (Bettington's Horse) and Shepstone's Native Horse (formerly Edendale Horse) with the 2nd Division. Finally, served with Shepstone's Native Horse in Baker Russell's Column. Present at Ulundi.

Shepstone, Sir Theophilus (1817–93). KCMG. Diplomatic Agent to the Native Tribes, 1845–55; Secretary for Native Affairs, Natal, 1856–76; Administrator of the Transvaal 1877–79.

Sihayo kaXongo (*c.* 1824–1883). Chief of the Qungebe. Favourite of Cetshwayo. The trans-border raid by his sons and brother in July 1878 was one of the *casus belli*, and he was blamed by many leading Zulu for bringing ruin on Zululand. The storming of his Sokhexe homestead by No. 3 Column on 12 January 1879 was the first action of the war.

Spalding, Henry (1840–1907). Major, 104th Bengal Fusiliers. Service in Indian Mutiny, 1857–8; Ninth Frontier War, 1878. On special service in 1879 as DAQMG, Headquarters Staff, during first invasion. In temporary command of lines of communication when No. 3 column advanced. On 22 January, believing post at Rorke's Drift to have fallen, retired on Helpmekaar to secure stores behind a wagon laager. Performed transport duty throughout the remainer of the war. On Chelmsford's Headquarters Staff as DAQMG during second invasion, but was employed at base.

Stanley, Frederick Arthur (1841–1908). Colonel, ADC to the Queen. Secretary of State for War in Lord Beaconsfield's second cabinet, April 1878–April 1880. Succeeded in 1893 as 16th Earl of Derby.

Strickland, Edward (1821–1889). Commissary-General, Commissariat Department, CB. Service in Ontario Rebellion, 1838–9; Cephalonia, 1847–8; Crimean War, 1854–5; Second Maori War, 1864–6. As District Commissary-General on Chelmsford's Headquarters Staff in 1879, in charge of Commissariat in Natal and entrusted with organization of Transport Service. Commissary-General in the Field on Chelmsford's Headquarters Staff during second invasion. KCB.

Twentyman, Augustus Charles (1836–1913). Brevet Major, 4th Regiment. Service in Abyssinian War, 1867–8. Commander in 1879 of Imperial Forces in Colonial Defensive District No. VII. Coordinated British raids between March and May across the middle Thukela in support of the advance of the Eshowe Relief Column and of the 2nd Division. Brevet Lieutenant-Colonel.

Upcher, Russell (1844–1936). Brevet Major, 24th Regiment. Commandant of Durban, September 1878. While marching to join No. 3 Column received news of Isandlwana, and retired on Helpmekaar. Assumed command of the 24th Regiment from 23 January to 11 May 1879. Advanced with 2nd Division, but left in command of the Mthonjaneni laager during Ulundi.

Uys, Piet Lafras (1827–79). Natal voortrekker. On British annexation of Natal, moved in 1847 to the Utrecht District. Farmed in the Blood River district and was an influential personality. In 1879 he raised a small force of some 30 Dutch Burghers to operate with the Irregular Horse of No. 4 Column. Killed in action at Hlobane while successfully rescuing his eldest son.

Wheelwright, William Douglas (1847–1924). Service in Langalibalele Expedition, 1873. Resident Magistrate, Drakensberg Location, 1875; and then Ulundi District. Acting Resident Magistrate, Weenen County, 1877; Resident Magistrate, Umvoti County, 1878. Commandant of Colonial Defensive District No. VII, December–July 1879, and raised Border Guard levies for its defence. Refused to allow his levies to accompany imperial forces on raids into Zululand. From mid-July instrumental in persuading Zulu chiefs of middle border to tender their submissions.

Wolseley, Sir Garnet Joseph (1833–1913). Lieutenant-General, Staff, GCMG, KCB, KCMG, CB. Service in Second Burma War, 1852–3; Crimean War, 1854–5; Indian Mutiny, 1857–8; Third China War, 1860; commanded Red River Expedition, 1870; commanded in Second Ashanti War, 1873–4 and selected his staff, known afterwards as the 'Wolseley Circle' or the 'Ashanti Ring'. Administrator of Natal, 1875. High Commissioner of Cyprus, 1878. Sent to South Africa in May 1879 on special service as High Commissioner in South Eastern Africa, Governor of Natal and the Transvaal, and Commander-in-Chief of the Forces in South Africa with local rank of General. Arrived too late for Ulundi, but pacified Zululand after

Chelmsford's departure. His September settlement of Zululand proved a recipe for civil war. GCB.

Wood, Henry Evelyn (1838–1919). Brevet Colonel, Staff, VC, CB. Service in Crimean War, 1854–5; Indian Mutiny, 1858; Second Ashanti War, 1873–4; Ninth Frontier War, 1878. On special service in 1879 in command of No. 4 Column and the renamed Flying Column. Local rank of Brigadier-General, 8 April 1879. Present at numerous skirmishes and at Hlobane, Khambula and Ulundi. KCB.

Glossary

Modern spelling, where it differs from Chelmsford's, is in square brackets.

assegai	Zulu spear
Boer	Dutch-speaking white settler
conductor	driver of a wagon carrying stores
coolie	then a common, but now an offensive mode of referring to an Indian living in South Africa
donga	dry eroded watercourse running only in times of heavy rain (cf. Anglo-Indian nullah)
drift	shallow fordable point in a river
forelooper [voorloper]	leader on foot of a span (team) of oxen pulling a wagon
ibutho (pl. *amabutho*)	Zulu age-grade regiment
ikhanda (pl. *amakhanda*)	major military centre where *amabutho* were stationed
induna (pl. *izinduna*)	person appointed by the Zulu king to a position of command
inspan	to yoke or harness a team of draught animals and make a wagon ready for travel
kaffir [kafir]	mode of reference to a black now regarded as offensive, but then often used in Natal to describe a black living in the colony, rather than in the Zulu kingdom
kaffircorn [kafir corn]	sorghum
kloof	a deep ravine or valley, usually wooded, or a gorge between mountains
kop	prominent hill or peak
kraal	enclosure for livestock, or cluster of African huts (a homestead or *umuzi*)
kraantz; krantz [krans]	overhanging sheer cliff-face or crag, often above a river
laager	defensive formation of parked wagons, but also any defensive enclosure, whether of barricades, masonry, etc.
mealie	maize

pont	large, flat-bottomed ferry-boat worked by ropes or cables to convey passengers, animals and wagons across rivers
span	team of draught animals
spruit	a tributary watercourse feeding a larger stream
trek tow [trektou]	a heavy draw rope, or trace, usually of twisted oxhide (riem), attached to the disselboom (shaft) of the wagon and upon which the yoked oxen pull
voortrekker	Boer pioneers who, dissatisfied with British rule, left the Cape Colony for the interior of South Africa

Gazetteer

First column: present spelling; second column: contemporary spelling where it differs from the present.

Mountains

Babanango	Babinango; Ibabanango
Bemba's Kop	Bembas kop
Biggarsberg	
Conference Hill	
Doornberg	Dornberg
Hlazakazi	Mhlazakazi
Hlobane	Inhlobani
Isandlwana	Insalwana; Insandhlwana; Insandlana; Insandlwana; Isanblana; Isandlana; Sandhlwana; Sandlwana
Khambula	Kambula
Koppie Alleen	Koppie Allein
Kranskop	Krantz Kop; Kranz Kop
Leolu	Lulu
Little Thala	Little Itala
Malakatha	Malakata
Misi	Imisi
Mthonjaneni	Emtonjaneni; Entonjaneni
Mundla	Mundhla
Nceceni	Inceceni; Incenci; Inceni
Ndulinde	Indulinda
Ngoye	Engoya; Ingowe
Ngweni	Ingwe; Ingwee; Ngwee
Nhlabamkhosi	Inthlabamakosi; Inthlabamkosi; Umhlabumkosi
Nhlazatshe	Inhazatye; Inhlayatye; Inhlazatye; Inlazatye; Mahlazatye; Mhlazatye; Nshlazatye
Nkanda	Mcanda
Nkonjane	Nkonyani
Nquthu	Inqutu; Ngudu; Ngutu; Nkudu
Ntabankulu	Intabankulu
Ntendeka	Ityenteka

Nteneshane	Emtwyenani
Siphezi	Isepezi; Isipezi; Isipizi
Thelezi	Itelezi; Itilizi; Telezi
Tinta's Kop	
Vegkop	Vecht Kop
Zungwini	Zonguine

Forests

Ngoye	Engoya; Ingowe
Nkandla	Inkandhla; Inkandla
Ntumeni	Entumeni
Qudeni	Equideni; Indeni

Rivers

Bivane	Pivan
Blood (Ncome)	
Buffalo (Mzinyathi)	
Gingindlovu	Gingilovo
Matigulu	Amatakulu
Mfolozi	Umfelosi; Umvelosi; Umveloosi; Umvolosi
Mhlathuze	Mflatoosi; Muhlatoosi; Umhlatoosi; Umhlatusi; Umhlutusi; Umlatoosi; Umlatoozi
Mlalazi	Emlalazi
Mooi (Mpofana)	
Msunduze	Umsindoosi
Mvunyane	Umkumyana; Umvumyana
Nondweni	
Ntinini (see Phoko)	Ntoneni; Teneni
Ntukwini	Untukuwini
Nyezane	Inyazana; Inyazane; Inyazani; Inyezane; Inyezani
Nyoni	Nyone
Phoko (see Ntinini)	Upoko
Phongolo	Pongolo
Sandspruit	Sand spruit; Sand Spruit
Sanqu	Isangu (runs into Mhlathuze)
Thukela	Tugela
Tshotshosi	Ityontyozi; Ityotyozi; Itytyozi
Vumankala	Tombakala; Tombokulu

Drifts

Laffnie's Drift	Lafnies drift
Landman's Drift	Landmanns drift
Lower Drift	Lower Tugela drift
Middle Drift	Middledrift
Mpisi Drift	Impesi drift
Rorke's Drift	Rorkes drift
Toohey's Drift	Touhys drift

Towns

Cape Town	
Derby	
Dordrecht	
Durban	
Estcourt	
Greytown	Grey Town
Kimberley	
Kokstad	Kokstadt
Ladysmith	Ladismith
Luneburg	Luneberg; Lüneberg
Middleberg	
Newcastle	
Pietermaritzburg	Pieter Maritzburg; P.Maritzburg; PMBurg; Maritzburg
Pinetown	
Standerton	
Stanger	
Utrecht	
Verulam	
Weenen	

Administrative Districts and Native Locations

Griqualand West	
Inanda Location	
Tugela Location	
Umsinga Division	Umsinga District
Umsinga Location	
Umvoti County	Umvoti District
Wakkerstroom District	Wakerstroom

Forts, Posts, Laagers and Camps

Balte Spruit Laager	Baltes spruit
Burrup's Hotel	Burrups
Conference Hill (depot/fort)	
Dundee (depot)	
Eshowe (fort)	Ekowe; Etshowe; Tyoe
Fort Albert	
Fort Buckingham	
Fort Chelmsford	
Fort Cherry	
Fort Crealock	
Fort Evelyn	
Fort Marshall	
Fort Newdigate	
Fort Pearson	
Fort Tenedos	
Fort Whitehead	
Fort Williamson	
Gingindlovu Laager	Gingilovo; Ginginlovo
Helpmekaar (depot/fort)	Helpmakaar
Hermannsburg Laager	Hermansburg
Khambula Camp	Kambula Hill
Koppie Alleen depot	Koppie Allein
Landman's Drift (camp)	
Munhla Hill (camp)	Mundhla
Pivaan (Burghers') Laager	Pivan Laager
place unidentified	Malafelungu Kraals/ Malifekya kraal
Potter's Store	
Potspruit Camp	Potts Spruit
Rorke's Drift (post)	Rorkes drift
St Paul's (camp/fort)	St Pauls
Stanger Laager	
Thring's Post (fort)	Thrings; Thring's store
Vermaak's farm (camp)	Vermaaks
Wolf Hill (camp)	

Mission Stations

Emvutshini Mission	Imfuchini Mission
Empangeni Mission	
Eshowe Mission	
KwaMagwaza	Kwamagwasa; Kwamagwaza; Kwagwamasa
Maphumulo	Mapumulu (American)
Mphumulo	Umpumulu (Norwegian)
Ntumeni	Entumeni; Intumeni
St Andrew's Mission	
St Paul's	St Pauls

Zulu Military Homesteads (*amaKhanda*)

kwaGqikazi	Qikazi
emLambongwenya	Umpambongwena
kwaNdabakawombe	Indabakaombi; Indabakaombie
oNdini (1st)	Ondine; Undi; Undine
oNdini (2nd)	Ulundi
emaNgweni	Emangwene; Mangwane; Mangweni
kwaNodwengu	Nodwengu; Nondwengo; Unodwengo
ebaQulusini	Bagulusini; Baqulusini

Zulu Regiments (*amaButho*)

uMbonambi	Umbakanli
uMcijo	Umcityu
uNdi (uThulwana, iNdlondlo & iNdluyengwe)	Undi; Ulundi
uThulwana	Tulwana
uVe	Uve

People

Mfengu	Fingoes
Qulusi	Bagalusini
Sotho	Basutos
Swazi	Amaswazi; amaswazies; Swazis; Swazies

Individuals

W. Calverley	Camberley
King Cetshwayo kaMpande	Cetewayo; Cetewayo; Cetywayo; Ketshwayo
King Dingane kaSenzangakhona	Dingan

Prince Hamu kaNzibe	Hamo; Oham; Uhamu
Capt. N. MacLeod	McLeod
Prince Makwendu kaMpande	Magwende; Magwendo
Chief Matshana kaMondisa	Matyan; Matyana
Chief Matshana kaSitshakuza	Matyan; Matyana
Mbilini kaMswati	Umbeline; Umbelini
Mbusa	Niboosa
Mgcwelo	Umsuelo
Mkhungo kaMpande	Umkungo
Mphokothwayo	Umpokotyayo
Msengi	Umsangi
Mtshibela	Umtyibela
Muwundula kaMamba	Mundula
Bishop H. Schreuder	Schroeder
Chief Sekethwayo kaNhlaka	Seketwayo
Sekhukhune	Sekukuni; Sikukuni
Chief Sihayo kaXongo	Sirayo; Usirayo
Sikhotha kaMpande	Isikoto
C. Vijn	Fyn

Bibliography

1 Manuscript Sources

Official Papers

(a) *Public Record Office, Kew*

War Office, Papers Relating to the Anglo-Zulu War:

WO 32/7699	Report on Transvaal and Natal Borders.
WO 32/7702	Requirements for Invasion of Zululand.
WO 32/7704	Organization of Forces.
WO 32/7709	Chelmsford's request for Relief.
WO 32/7718	Report on Disposition of Forces.
WO 32/7722	Report on Preparations for Relief of Ekowe.
WO 32/7727	Report on Relief of Etshowe.
WO 32/7732	Report on Disposition and Condition of Forces.
WO 32/7736	Organization of Transport.
WO 32/7737	Report on Defence of Rorke's Drift.
WO 32/7739	Reasons for Delay.
WO 32/7744	Disposition of Cavalry Regiment.
WO 32/7752	Report on Operations.
WO 32/7763	Report on Battle of Ulundi.
WO 32/7770	Chelmsford's Resignation.
WO 32/7771	Wolseley's Instructions.

(b) *Natal Archives Depot, Pietermaritzburg*

Colonial Secretary's Office, Natal:

CSO 1926: Zulu War: Special Border Agent Reports.

Government House, Natal:

GH 500	General Officer Commanding, South Africa: Despatches.
GH 601	Despatches from High Commissioner.
GH 1326	High Commissioner: Copies of Despatches.
GH 1421–2	Zulu War: Memoranda.

Master of the Supreme Court, Pietermaritzburg:

Estates, 1840–1959

Secretary for Native Affairs, Natal:

SNA 1/1/33 Letters Received.
SNA 1/6/3 Papers Relating to Cetewayo.

Private Papers

(a) *National Army Museum, Chelsea*

6807–386 The Papers of General Lord Chelmsford:

5 Commissariat and preparations for advance into Zululand.
6 Transvaal and attitude of Boers.
7 Advance of No. 1 Column.
8 Advance of No. 3 Column.
9 Activities of No. 4 Column.
10 Defence of Natal.
11 Death of Prince Imperial.
13 Zulu peace proposals.
15 Activities of 1st Division.
16 Advance of 2nd Division.
17 Correspondence with Major-General Clifford.
18 Appointments.
19 Correspondence with Secretary of State for War.
21 Correspondence with General Wolseley.
22 Correspondence received after Anglo-Zulu War.
24 Drafts of speeches.
25 Maps.
26 Miscellaneous documents and printed papers.
27 Letter book, 29 December 1878–21 January 1879.
28 Letter book, 29 January–14 July 1879.

6810–38 Collection of Correspondence between Lord Chelmsford and Colonel Pearson.

(b) *Killie Campbell Africana Library, Durban*

KCM 89/9 The Papers of Field Marshal Sir Henry Evelyn Wood:

26 Correspondence, September–December 1878.
27 Correspondence, January–June 1879.

(c) *Natal Archive Depot, Pietermaritzburg*

A574 Chelmsford letter, 15 May 1878.

A96 Sir Theophilus Shepstone Papers:

31–6 Letters received, 1878–9.
95 Uys Papers, vol. IV, 1879–91.

A598 Sir Evelyn Wood Collection:

II/2/2 Incoming letters, 1878–9.
II/3/1 Outgoing letters, 1878–9.

2 Official Printed Sources

Blue Books for the Colony of Natal, 1862–79

British Parliamentary Papers
LII of 1878–9 (C. 2220), (C. 2222), (C. 2242). S.A. Correspondence, 1878–9.
LIII of 1878–9 (C. 2252), (C. 2260), (C. 2367). S.A. Correspondence, Appointment of Wolseley
LIV of 1878–9 (C. 2318), (C. 2367), (C. 2374), (C. 2454). S.A. Correspondence *re* Military Affairs
L of 1880 (C. 2482). S.A. War. Correspondence, 1879–80.

Hansard's Parliamentary Debates (3rd Series), vols. CCXLIV–CCXLVII.

Natal Government Gazette, vols. XXX–XXXI, 1878–9.

3 Newspapers and Periodicals

Daily Telegraph, 1879.
Graphic, 1879.
Illustrated London News, 1879.
Natal Almanac, Directory and Yearly Register 1878–80.
Natal Colonist, 1878–9.
Natal Mercury, 1878–9.
Natal Witness, 1878–9.
Observer, 1879.
Saturday Review, 1879.
Standard, 1879.

The Times, 1905.
Times of Natal, 1878–9.
Vanity Fair, 1881.

4 Books

(books published in London unless noted otherwise.)

Works of Reference

Branford, J. and Branford, W., *A Dictionary of South African English* (Oxford University Press, Cape Town, 1991).
Chesneau, R. and Kolesnik, E. M., *Conway's All the World's Fighting Ships, 1860–1905* (1979).
Davis, H.W.C. and Weaver, J.R.H., *The Dictionary of National Biography, 1912–1921* (1927).
Dictionary of South African Biography (Human Sciences Research Council, Pretoria, 1968, 1972, 1977, 1981, 1987), vols. 1–5.
Hart, Major-General H.G., *The New Annual Army List, Militia List and Indian Civil Service List* (1878, 1879, 1884), vols. 39, 40, 45.
Jones, H.M., *A Biographical Register of Swaziland to 1902* (University of Natal Press, Pietermaritzburg, 1993).
Lee, Sir S. (ed.), *Dictionary of National Biography. Supplement. January 1901–December 1911* (Oxford, 1920), vol. III.
Lloyds Register of Shipping for 1879.
Montague-Smith, P. (ed.), *Debrett's Correct Form* (1978).
Navy List: 1879 (1879).
Townend, P. (ed.), *Burke's Peerage, Baronetage and Knightage* (1963).
Spencer, S. O'B., *British Settlers in Natal, 1824–1857: A Biographical Register* (University of Natal, Pietermaritzburg, 1981, 1983, 1985, 1987, 1989, 1992), vols. 1–6, Abbott-Fyvie.
Stephen, Sir L. and Lee, Sir S. (eds.), *The Dictionary of National Biography* (reprinted 1937–8), 21 vols.
The Natal Who's Who, 1906 (The Natal Who's Who Publishing Company, Durban, 1906).
Who Was Who, 1897–1915 (1935).
Who Was Who, 1916–1928 (1929).
Who Was Who, 1919–1940 (1941).

Contemporary Accounts and Reminiscences

Ashe, Major W. and Wyatt Edgell, Captain the Hon. E.V. *The Story of the Zulu Campaign* (1880).

Bird, J. (compiler), *The Annals of Natal 1495–1845* (T. Maskew Miller, Cape Town, 1888).

Callwell, Colonel C.E., *Small Wars: Their Principles and Practice* (3rd edit, 1906).

Chase, J.C., *The Natal Papers: A Reprint of All Notices and Public Documents Connected with that Territory Including a Description of the Country and a History of Events from 1498 to 1843* (Godlonton, Grahamstown, 1843).

Colenso, F.E., assisted by Durnford, Lieutenant-Colonel E., *History of the Zulu War and its Origin* (1880).

Durnford, E.C.L., *Isandhlwana, Lord Chelmsford's Statements Compared with Evidence* (1880).

– (ed.), *A Soldier's Life and Work in South Africa, 1872–1879: A Memory of the Late Colonel A.W. Durnford, Royal Engineers* (1882).

Fynney, F., *The Zulu Army and Zulu Headmen. Published by Direction of the Lieut.-General Commanding* (Pietermaritzburg, 2nd edit. revised, April 1879).

Hamilton-Browne, Colonel G., *A Lost Legionary in South Africa* (c. 1911).

Holt, H.P., *The Mounted Police of Natal* (1913).

Intelligence Branch of the War Office, *Narrative of the Field Operations Connected with the Zulu War of 1879* (1881).

– *Precis of Information Concerning Zululand* (1895).

MacKinnon, J.P. and Shadbolt, S., *The South African Campaign, 1879* (1880).

McToy, E.D., *A Brief History of the 13th Regiment (P.A.L.I.) in South Africa during the Transvaal and Zulu Difficulties* (Devonport, 1880).

Molyneux, Major-General W.C.F., *Campaigning in South Africa and Egypt* (1896).

Montague, Captain W.E., *Campaigning in South Africa: Reminiscences of an Officer in 1879,* (Edinburgh and London, 1880).

Moodie, D.C.F. (ed.), *The History of the Battles and Adventures of the British, the Boers and the Zulus in Southern Africa, from 1495 to 1879, Including Every Particular of the Zulu War of 1879, with a Chronology* (George Robertson, Sidney, Melbourne and Adelaide, 1879).

Norbury, Fleet-Surgeon H.F., *The Naval Brigade in South Africa during the Years 1877–78–79* (1880).

Norris–Newman, C.L., *In Zululand with the British throughout the War of 1879* (1880).

Parr, Captain H. Hallam, *A Sketch of the Kaffir and Zulu Wars* (1880).

Plé, J., *Les Laagers dans la Guerre des Zoulous* (L. Baudoin, Paris, 1882).

Regulations for Field Forces in South Africa 1878 (Pietermaritzburg, November 1878).

Tomasson, W.H., *With the Irregulars in the Transvaal and Zululand* (1881).

Vijn, C. (tr. from the Dutch and edited with preface and notes by the Rt. Rev. J.W. Colenso, D.D., Bishop of Natal), *Cetshwayo's Dutchman: Being the Private Journal of a White Trader in Zululand during the British Invasion* (1880).

Wood, Field Marshal Sir E., *From Midshipman to Field Marshal* (1906), vol. II.

Later Edited, Annotated Contemporary Accounts

Bennett, Lieutenant-Colonel I.H.W. (ed.), *Eyewitness in Zululand: The Campaign Reminiscences of Colonel W.A. Dunne, CB: South Africa, 1877–1881* (1989).
Child, D. (ed.), *The Zulu War Journal of Colonel Henry Harford, C.B.* (Shuter & Shooter, Pietermaritzburg, 1978).
Clarke, S. (ed.), *Invasion of Zululand 1879: Anglo-Zulu War Experiences of Arthur Harness; John Jervis, 4th Viscount St Vincent; and Sir Henry Bulwer* (Brenthurst Press, Houghton, 1979).
– (ed.), *Zululand at War: The Conduct of the Anglo-Zulu War* (Brenthurst Press, Houghton, 1984).
Emery, F., *The Red Soldier: Letters from the Zulu War, 1879* (1977).
Knight, I. (ed.), *"By Orders of the Great White Queen": Campaigning in Zululand through the Eyes of the British Soldier, 1879* (1992).
Preston, A. (ed.), *Sir Garnet Wolseley's South African Journal, 1879–1880* (A.A. Balkeman, Cape Town, 1973).
Webb, C. de B. and Wright, J.B. (eds.), *A Zulu King Speaks: Statements Made by Cetshwayo kaMpande on the History and Customs of his People* (University of Natal Press and Killie Campbell Africana Library, Pietermaritzburg and Durban, 1978).

Secondary Works

Addington, L.H., *The Patterns of War since the Eighteenth Century* (Croom Helm, London and Sidney, 1984).
Ballard, C., *John Dunn: The White Chief of Zululand* (Ad. Donker, Craighall, 1985).
Bancroft, J.W., *Rorke's Drift* (Spellmount and Ashanti Publishing, Tunbridge Wells and Rivonia, 1991).
Barnett, C., *Britain and her Army 1509–1970: A Military, Political and Social Survey* (1974).
Battlefields of South Africa (Times Media with Jonathan Ball, Johannesburg, 1991).
Benyon, J.A., *Proconsul and Paramountcy in South Africa: The High Commissioner, British Supremacy and the Sub-Continent, 1806–1910* (University of Natal Press, Pietermaritzburg, 1980).
Bonner, P., *Kings, Commoners and Concessionaires: The Evolution and Dissolution of the Nineteenth-Century Swazi State* (Ravan Press, Johannesburg, 1983).
Brookes, E.H. and Webb, C. de B., *A History of Natal* (University of Natal Press, Pietermaritzburg, 1965).
Clammer, D., *The Zulu War* (1973).
Clements, W.H., *The Glamour and Tragedy of the Zulu War* (1936).
Coupland, Sir R., *Zulu Battle Piece: Isandhlwana* (1948).
Delius, P., *The Land Belongs to Us: The Pedi Polity, the Boers and the British in the Nineteenth Century Transvaal* (Ravan Press, Johannesburg, 1983).

De Moor, J.A. and Wesseling, H.L. (eds.), *Imperialism and War: essays on Colonial Wars in Asia and Africa* (E.J. Brill, Leiden, 1989).

Dixon, N., *On the Psychology of Military Incompetence* (1986).

Droogleever, R.W.F., *The Road to Isandhlwana: Colonel Anthony Durnford in Natal and Zululand 1873–1879* (1992).

Duminy A. and Ballard, C. (eds.), *The Anglo-Zulu War: New Perspectives* (University of Natal Press, Pietermaritzburg, 1981).

– and Guest, B. (eds.), *Natal and Zululand from Earliest Times to 1910: A New History* (University of Natal Press and Shuter and Shooter, Pietermaritzburg, 1989).

Edgerton, R.B., *Like Lions They Fought: The Zulu War and the Last Black Empire in South Africa* (Southern, Bergvlei, 1988).

Ensor, Sir R., *England, 1870–1914* (Oxford, 1968).

Farewell, B., *Queen Victoria's Little Wars* (Norton, New York, 1972).

Featherstone, D., *Weapons and Equipment of the Victorian Soldier* (Poole, 1978).

Fergusson, T.G., *British Military Intelligence, 1870–1914: The Development of a Modern Intelligence Organization* (1984).

French, Major the Hon. G., *Lord Chelmsford and the Zulu War* (1939).

Furneaux, R., *The Zulu War: Isandhlwana and Rorke's Drift* (1963).

Gon, P,. *The Road to Isandlwana: The Years of an Imperial Battalion* (Ad. Donker, Johannesburg, 1979).

Goodfellow, C.F., *Great Britain and South African Confederation, 1870–1881* (Oxford University Press, Cape Town, 1966).

Harries-Jenkins, G., *The Army in Victorian Society* (1977).

Hurst, G.T., *Short History of the Volunteer Regiments of Natal and East Griqualand: Past and Present* (Knox Publishing, Durban, 1945).

James, L., *The Savage Wars: British Campaigns in Africa, 1870–1920* (1985).

Keegan, J., *The Mask of Command* (1987).

Knight, I., *Brave Men's Blood: The Epic of the Zulu War, 1879* (1990).

– *Zulu: Isandlwana and Rorke's Drift, 22nd–23rd January 1879* (1992).

– *Nothing Remains but to Fight: The Defence of Rorke's Drift, 1879* (1993).

Laband, J.P.C., *The Battle of Ulundi* (Shuter & Shooter and KwaZulu Monuments Council, Pietermaritzburg and Ulundi, 1988).

– *Kingdom in Crisis: The Zulu Response to the British Invasion of 1879* (Manchester, 1992).

Laband, J.P.C. and Mathews, J., *Isandlwana* (Centaur Publications and KwaZulu Monuments Council, Pietermaritzburg and Ulundi, 1992).

Laband, J.P.C. and Thompson, P.S., *War Comes to Umvoti: The Natal–Zululand Border, 1878–9* (Department of History, University of Natal, Research Monograph No. 5, Durban, 1980).

– *Field Guide to the War in Zululand and the Defence of Natal 1879* (University of Natal Press, Pietermaritzburg, 2nd revised edition, 1987).

– *Kingdom and Colony at War: Sixteen Studies on the Anglo-Zulu War of 1879* (University of Natal Press and N & S Press, Pietermaritzburg and Constantia, 1990).

– with Henderson, S., *The Buffalo Border 1879: The Anglo-Zulu War in Northern Natal* (Department of History, University of Natal, Research Monograph No. 6, Durban, 1983).
Laband, J.P.C. and Wright, J., *King Cetshwayo kaMpande (c. 1832–1884)* (Shuter & Shooter and KwaZulu Monuments Council, Pietermaritzburg and Ulundi, 1983).
Lloyd, A., *The Zulu War* (1973).
Lugg, H.C., *Historic Natal and Zululand* (Shuter & Shooter, Pietermaritzburg, 1949).
MacKenzie, J.M. (ed.), *Popular Imperialism and the Military, 1850–1950* (Manchester, 1992).
Martineau, J., *The Life and Correspondence of the Right Hon. Sir Bartle Frere, Bart., G.C.B., F.R.S., Etc.* (1895), vol. II.
Maxwell, L., *The Ashanti Ring: Sir Garnet Wolseley's Campaigns 1870–1882* (1985).
McBride, A., *The Zulu War* (1976).
Morris, D.R., *The Washing of the Spears: A History of the Rise of the Zulu Nation under Shaka and its Fall in the Zulu War of 1879* (1966).
Regan, G., *Someone had Blundered . . . A Historical Survey of Military Incompetence* (1987).
Smail, J.L., *From the Land of the Zulu Kings: An Historical Guide for Those Restless Years in Natal and Zululand, 1497 to 1879* (Pope, Durban, 1979).
Spiers, E.M., *The Army and Society 1815–1914* (1980).
– *The Late Victorian Army 1868–1902* (Manchester, 1992).
Strachan, H., *European Armies and the Conduct of War* (1983).
Van Crefeld, *Command in War,* (Harvard University Press, Cambridge, Massachusetts, 1985).
Whitehouse, H., *Battle in Africa, 1879–1914* (Fieldbooks, Mansfield, 1987).
Wilkinson-Latham, C., *Uniforms and Weapons of the Zulu War* (1978).
Young, J., *They Fell Like Stones: Battles and Casualties of the Zulu War, 1879* (1991).

5 Articles

'Army', *Encyclopaedia Britannica* (Edinburgh, 9th edition, 1875), vol. II.
Bailes, H., 'Technology and Imperialism: A Case Study of the Victorian Army in Africa', *Victorian Studies*, 24, 1, Autumn 1980.
Burroughs, P., 'Imperial Defence and the Victorian Army', *Journal of Imperial and Commonwealth History*, XV, 1, October 1986.
'Cambridge, Earls and Dukes of', *Encyclopaedia Britannica* (Cambridge, 11th edition, 1910), vol. V.
Carlyle, J.E., 'The Zulu War', *British Quarterly Review*, 69, 1879.
'Chelmsford, 1st Baron', *Encyclopaedia Britannica* (Cambridge, 11th edition, 1910), vol. VI.

Dominy, G.A., 'Maps. Plans, Diagrams and Sketches of the Anglo-Zulu War', *S.A. Archives Journal*, 21, 1979.

Forbes, A., 'Lord Chelmsford and the Zulu War', *The Nineteenth Century*, February 1880.

Gallagher, T.F., 'Cardwellian Mysteries: The Fate of the British Army Regulation Bill', *Historical Journal*, XVIII, 2, 1975.

Guy, J.J., 'A Note on Firearms in the Zulu Kingdom with Special Reference to the Anglo-Zulu War, 1879', *Journal of African History*, XII, 4, 1971.

Hall, Major D.D., 'Artillery in the Zulu War, 1879', *Military History Journal*, 4, 4, January 1879.

Harness, Lieutenant-Colonel A., 'The Zulu Campaign from a Military Point of View', *Fraser's Magazine*, 101, April 1880.

Harries-Jenkins, G., 'The Development of Professionalism in the Victorian Army', *Armed Forces and Society*, 1, 4, August 1975.

Jackson, F.W.D., 'Isandhlwana, 1879: The Sources Re-examined', *Journal of the Society for Army Historical Research*, XLIX, 173, 175, 176, 1965.

Laband, J.P.C., 'Introduction', *Companion to Narrative of the Field Operations Connected with the Zulu War of 1879* (N & S Press, Constantia, 1879).

Smith, K.W., 'The Campaigns against the Bapedi of Sekhukhune, 1877–1879', *Archives Year Book for South African History, 1967 (II)* (Publications Branch of the Office of the Director of Archives, Johannesburg, 1967).

Strachan, H., 'The Early Victorian Army and the Nineteenth Century Revolution in Government', *English Historical Review*, XCV, 1980.

Tylden, Major G., 'The Frontier Light Horse, 1877–79', *Journal of the Society for Army Historical Research*, 18, 1939.

– 'The Waggon Laager', *Journal of the Society for Army Historical Research*, XLI, 168, 1963.

Verbeek, J.A. and Bresler, V., 'The Role of the Ammunition Boxes in the Disaster at Isandhlawana, 22nd January, 1879', *The Journal of the Historical Firearms Society of South Africa*, 7, 6, December 1977.

6 Theses and Reports

Laband, J.P.C and Thompson, P.S., 'The Colonial Defences of Natal 1879', Report to University of Natal Research Fund, January 1981.

Laband, J.P.C., 'Kingdom in Crisis: The Response of the Zulu Polity to the British Invasion of 1879', Ph.D. thesis, University of Natal, 1990.

Mathews, J., 'Lord Chelmsford and the Problems of Transport and Supply during the Anglo-Zulu War of 1879', unpublished M.A. thesis, University of Natal, 1979.

– 'Lord Chelmsford: British General in Southern Africa, 1878–1879', unpublished D. Litt. et Phil. thesis, University of South Africa, 1986.

Index

Individual military units have been entered under British campaign formations: British units; *amaButho*; Colonial units; Imperial units. Fortifications have been entered under Forts, laagers, camps and posts. In accordance with modern practice, Zulu words are entered under the stem and not under the prefix. Zulu names are all spelled in the current, standard fashion, and the Gazetteer should be consulted for correlation with the nineteenth century form.

ARMY RECORDS SOCIETY (FOUNDED 1984)

Members of the Society are entitled to purchase back volumes at reduced prices.
Orders should be sent to the Hon. Treasurer, Army Records Society,
c/o National Army Museum,
Royal Hospital Road,
London SW3 4HT

The Society has already issued:

Vol. I:
The Military Correspondence of
Field Marshal Sir Henry Wilson 1918–1922
Edited by Dr Keith Jeffery

Vol. II:
The Army and the
Curragh Incident, 1914
Edited by Dr Ian F.W. Beckett

Vol. III:
The Napoleonic War Journal of
Captain Thomas Henry Browne, 1807–1816
Edited by Roger Norman Buckley

Vol. IV:
An Eighteenth-Century Secretary at War
The Papers of William, Viscount Barrington
Edited by Dr Tony Hayter

Vol. V:
The Military Correspondence of
Field Marshal Sir William Robertson 1915–1918
Edited by David R. Woodward

Vol. VI:
Colonel Samuel Bagshawe and the
Army of George II, 1731–1762
Edited by Dr Alan J. Guy

Vol. VII:
Montgomery and the Eighth Army
Edited by Stephen Brooks

Vol. VIII:
The British Army and Signals Intelligence during the First World War
Edited by John Ferris

Vol. IX:
Roberts in India
The Military Papers of Field Marshal Lord Roberts 1876–1893
Edited by Brian Robson